Lecture Notes in Computer Science 16478

The series Lecture Notes in Computer Science (LNCS), including its subseries Lecture Notes in Artificial Intelligence (LNAI) and Lecture Notes in Bioinformatics (LNBI), has established itself as a medium for the publication of new developments in computer science and information technology research, teaching, and education.

LNCS enjoys close cooperation with the computer science R & D community, the series counts many renowned academics among its volume editors and paper authors, and collaborates with prestigious societies. Its mission is to serve this international community by providing an invaluable service, mainly focused on the publication of conference and workshop proceedings and postproceedings. LNCS commenced publication in 1973.

Cristiano Maciel · Davide Lucio Spano ·
Carmelo Ardito · André Freire · Raquel Prates
Editors

Blending Experiences in Interaction Design

INTERACT 2025 IFIP TC 13 Workshops
Belo Horizonte, Brazil, September 8–12, 2025
Revised Selected Papers, Part I

Springer

Editors
Cristiano Maciel
Universidade Federal de Mato Grosso
Cuiabá, Brazil

Davide Lucio Spano
University of Cagliari
Cagliari, Italy

Carmelo Ardito
Polytechnic University of Bari
Bari, Italy

André Freire
Universidade Federal de Lavras
Lavras, Brazil

Raquel Prates
Universidade Federal de Minas Gerais
Belo Horizonte, Brazil

ISSN 0302-9743 ISSN 1611-3349 (electronic)
Lecture Notes in Computer Science
ISBN 978-3-032-22933-5 ISBN 978-3-032-22934-2 (eBook)
https://doi.org/10.1007/978-3-032-22934-2

This Springer imprint is published by the registered company Springer Nature Switzerland AG
The registered company address is: Gewerbestrasse 11, 6330 Cham, Switzerland

Foreword

This volume presents a series of revised papers selected from workshops organized by IFIP TC 13 Working Groups (WGs) during the 20th IFIP TC13 International Conference on Human-Computer Interaction, INTERACT 2025, held in September 2025 at the Universidade Federal de Minas Gerais, in the city of Belo Horizonte, the capital city of the state of Minas Gerais in Brazil.

Eleven workshops were held across two days at the start of the INTERACT 2025 conference. Eight were organized by the IFIP TC13 Working Groups (WGs), as listed below:

- HCI Education and Education for HCI: Current Opportunities and Challenges, organized by *WG 13.1 - HCI Education;*
- HCSE Workshop on Balancing Interaction, Artificial Intelligence, and Human Value, organized by *WG 13.2 - Methodologies for User-Centered Systems Design;*
- Navigation for People with Disabilities and Older People: Current Challenges and Opportunities, organized by *WG 13.3 - HCI, Disability and Aging;*
- Technology Design for and with Neurodivergent Users: Considerations from Research Practices, organized by *WG 13.3 - HCI, Disability and Aging;*
- Engineering Methods for HCI and UX in AI-Driven Systems, organized by *WG 13.4/2.7 - User Interface Engineering;*
- Transparent Autonomy and Human Work Interaction Design Workshop, organized by *WG13.6 - Human-Work Interaction Design;*
- Addressing Global HCI Challenges at the Time of Geopolitical Tensions through Planetary Thinking and Indigenous Methodologies, organized by *WG 13.8 - Interaction Design and International Development;*
- Effective Map-Based Interfaces and Interactions, organized by *WG 13.10 - Human-Centred Technology for Sustainability.*

The chapters in this volume are the outcome of a thorough and competitive selection process that started with selecting workshops for INTERACT 2025. The IFIP TC13 WGs organizers were encouraged to propose workshops to extend the work of the working groups. The workshops could be in diverse formats, including paper and poster presentations followed by forum discussions or collaboration sessions with participants. The selection process of workshops was juried by the INTERACT 2025 workshop co-chairs.

The organizers selected participants to the workshops, and also picked which workshop papers were eligible to be extended to chapters in this volume. For the selected papers, participants were requested to revise their contributions to include the comments and remarks they received during the event. To ensure the quality of these post-proceedings we requested that the proposed chapters must be peer-reviewed by the workshop organizers. In addition, workshop organizers were invited to write a summary chapter for their workshop, reporting on the aims and outcomes of the workshops.

The selected chapters in this volume show the state of the art of research according to the aims of the workshops and demonstrate the maturity of the work performed by

IFIP TC13 WGs. In total 56 chapters are published in these two volumes organized into 8 sections corresponding to IFIP TC13 workshops held at INTERACT 2025.

Interested readers of this volume should note that IFIP TC13 WGs are open to new members. The full list of IFIP TC13 WGs is available at http://ifip-tc13.org/working-groups/. Please contact the officers of the WGs for further information on how to get enrolled in WG activities such as the workshops organized at the INTERACT conference.

January 2026

Cristiano Maciel
Davide Lucio Spano
Carmelo Ardito
André Freire
Raquel Prates

IFIP TC13 – The International Federation for Information Processing Technical Committee on Human–Computer Interaction

Established in 1989, the International Federation for Information Processing Technical Committee on Human–Computer Interaction (IFIP TC13) focuses on the field of human-computer interaction (HCI), an interdisciplinary area of study and research that focuses on the design, development, implementation and validation of human-centred interactive computational systems and devices. The field revolves around the interaction between living beings (users) and computational devices and the use thereof, or such devices as facilitators for social human-human interaction. Focusing primarily on knowing, understanding and comprehending how humans interact with computational systems and devices, the goal is societal improvements that serve people and communities by making computational systems and devices enabling, effective, inclusive, accessible, efficient, safe, secure, emotionally satisfying and enjoyable to use, while ensuring ethical use and promoting equal opportunities, diversity, digital equity and sustainable use of non-renewable resources.

The IFIP TC13 Committee currently consists of 55 Members from 39 IFIP Member National Societies and 11 Working Groups, representing specialists from various subdomains in HCI, and has members from across the world who seek to expand knowledge and find solutions to HCI issues and concerns within their domains. The TC13 WGs and their areas of interest are:

- WG 13.1 (HCI Education) aims to advance global HCI education by integrating emerging technologies, embedding HCI into diverse curricula, supporting pedagogical research and championing social responsibility in HCI teaching and learning.
- WG 13.2 (Methodologies for User-Centered Systems Design) aims to foster research, dissemination of information and good practice in the methodical application of HCI to software engineering. WG 13.2 encourages research into and development of HCI principles, methods and techniques applied to system design and integrated with principles, methods and tools, and the integration thereof into software engineering design methods.
- WG 13.3 (Human Computer Interaction, Disability and Aging) aims to make HCI designers aware of the needs of people with disabilities and older people and encourage the development of information and communication technologies and complementary tools which permit their adaptation to each specific user.
- WG 13.4/WG 2.7 (User Interface Engineering) aims at advancing the state of the art in all aspects of designing, building and evaluating interactive computing systems, with a particular focus on principled, methodological engineering approaches, including methods (human-, model- or AI-based approaches) and tools for modelling,

prototyping, developing and evaluating interactive computing systems, quality models for interactive systems, and new interface technologies suitable to improve user interaction.

- WG 13.5 (Resilience, Reliability, Safety and Human Error in System Development) seeks a framework for studying human factors relating to systems failure, develops leading-edge techniques in hazard analysis and safety engineering of computer-based systems, and guides international accreditation activities for safety-critical systems.
- WG 13.6 (Human-Work Interaction Design) aims at establishing relationships between extensive empirical work-domain studies and HCI design. It promotes the use of knowledge, concepts, methods and techniques that enable user studies to procure a better apprehension of the complex interplay between individual, social and organizational contexts and thereby a better understanding of how and why people work in the ways that they do.
- WG 13.7 (Human–Computer Interaction and Visualization) aims to establish a study and research program that will combine both scientific work and practical applications in the fields of HCI and visualization by integrating aspects such as scientific visualization, data mining, information design, computer graphics, cognition sciences, perception theory, or psychology.
- WG 13.8 (Interaction Design and International Development) aims to support and develop the research, practice and education capabilities of HCI in institutions and organizations based around the world considering their diverse local needs and cultural perspectives, to promote interaction design practice in cross-cultural settings, with a special focus to address the needs, desires and aspirations of people across the developing world and in emerging economies.
- WG 13.9 (Interaction Design and Children) aims to support practitioners, regulators and researchers to develop the study of interaction design and children across international contexts.
- WG 13.10 (Human-Centred Technology for Sustainability) aims to promote research, design, development, evaluation and deployment of human-centred technology to encourage sustainable use of resources in various domains.
- WG 13.11/12.1 (Human-Centred Intelligent Interactive Systems), established under the auspices of both TC13 (HCI) and TC12 (AI), aims to focus on how AI can empower humans and support their endeavours, as well as to find ways for humans to understand AI-based systems and the means to allow human control and oversight. By developing scientific foundations for human-centred intelligent interactive systems, it emphasises the human side of the interaction between people and AI.

The IFIP TC13 International Conference on Human-Computer Interaction, INTERACT, is the flagship conference of TC13, staged biennially in different countries around the world. The first INTERACT conference was held in 1984, at first running triennially and becoming a biennial event in 1993. INTERACT 2025 was the 20th Conference in the series. In 2015, IFIP TC13 setup a steering committee for the INTERACT conference series. The Steering Committee, currently chaired by Marco Winckler (France), is responsible for, among other things, promoting and maintaining the INTERACT conference as the premiere venue for researchers and practitioners interested in the topics of the conference and ensuring the highest quality for the contents of the event.

IFIP TC13 also stimulates working events and activities through its Working Groups, including, but not limited to, the Human-Centered Software Engineering Conference (HCSE) organised by WG 13.2, the Human Work Interaction Design Conference (HWID) organised by WG 13.6, and the Interaction Design and International Development Conference (IDID) organised by WG 13.8. A total of eight Workshops by the Working Groups were organised alongside INTERACT 2025.

Furthermore, IFIP TC13 recognises contributions to HCI through both its Pioneer in HCI Award and various paper awards associated with each INTERACT conference. Since the processes to decide the various awards take place after papers are sent to the publisher for publication, the recipients of the awards are not identified in the Proceedings.

- The IFIP TC13 Pioneer in Human-Computer Interaction Award recognises the contributions and achievements of pioneers in HCI. An IFIP TC13 Pioneer is one who, through active participation in IFIP Technical Committees or related IFIP groups, has made outstanding contributions to the educational, theoretical, technical, commercial or professional aspects of analysis, design, construction, evaluation and use of interactive systems. The IFIP TC13 Pioneer Awards are presented during an awards ceremony at each INTERACT conference.
- In 1999, TC13 initiated a special IFIP Award, the Brian Shackel Award, for the most outstanding contribution in the form of a refereed paper submitted to and delivered at each INTERACT Conference, which draws attention to the need for a comprehensive human-centred approach in the design and use of information technology in which the human and social implications have been considered.
- The IFIP TC13 Accessibility Award, launched in 2007 by IFIP WG 13.3, recognises the most outstanding contribution with international impact in the field of ageing, disability and inclusive design in the form of a refereed paper submitted to and delivered at the INTERACT Conference.
- The IFIP TC13 Interaction Design for International Development Award, launched in 2013 by IFIP WG 13.8, recognises the most outstanding contribution to the application of interactive systems for social and economic development of people around the world considering their diverse local needs and cultural perspectives.
- The IFIP TC13 Pioneers' Award for Best Doctoral Student Paper at INTERACT, first awarded in 2019, is selected by the past recipients of the IFIP TC13 Pioneer title. The award is made to the best research paper accepted to the INTERACT Conference, which is based on the doctoral research of the student and authored and presented by the student.

Further information on IFIP TC13 and its activities is available on the IFIP TC13 website: https://ifip-tc13.org/.

IFIP TC13 Members

Officers

Chair

Paula Kotzé, South Africa

Vice-chair for Conferences

Marco Winckler, France

Vice-chair for Media and Communications

Helen Petrie, UK

Vice-chair for Membership and Collaboration

Philippe Palanque, France

Vice-chair for Working Groups

Simone D. J. Barbosa, Brazil

Vice-chair for Finance (Treasurer)

Regina Bernhaupt, The Netherlands

Vice-chair for Awards

Barbara Rita Barricelli, Italy

Secretary

Janet Wesson, South Africa

Websites Manager

Antonio Piccinno, Italy

INTERACT Steering Committee Chair

Marco Winckler, France

Country Representatives

Australia
Aaron Quigley
Australian Computer Society
Austria
Paweł W. Woźniak
Österreichische Computer Gesellschaft (OCG)
Belgium
Bruno Dumas
IMEC – Interuniversity Micro-Electronics Centre
Brazil
André Freire
Simone D. J. Barbosa (Member Recommended by TC)
Sociedade Brasileira de Computação (SBC)
Bulgaria
Petia Koprinkova-Hristova
Bulgarian Academy of Sciences
Canada
Regan Mandryk
Canadian Computer Society
China
Yue Li
Zhengjie Liu (Member Recommended by TC)
Chinese Institute of Electronics – CIE
Croatia
Andrina Granić
Croatian Information Technology Association (CITA)
Cyprus
Panayiotis Zaphiris
Cyprus Computer Society
Czech Republic
Zdeněk Míkovec
Czech Society for Cybernetics and Informatics

Denmark
Jan Stage
Danish Federation for Information Processing (DANFIP)
Finland
Virpi Roto
Finnish Information Processing
Association (TIVIA)
France
Philippe Palanque
Marco Winckler (Member Recommended by TC)
Société Informatique de France (SIF)
Germany
Tom Gross
Gesellschaft fur Informatik e. V.
Ireland
Gavin Doherty (Member Recommended by TC)
Irish Computer Society
Italy
Fabio Paternò
Carmelo Ardito (Member Recommended by TC)
Barbara Rita Barricelli (Member Recommended by TC)
Associazione Italiana per l'Informatica ed il Calcolo Automatico (AICA)
Japan
Yoshifumi Kitamura
Information Processing Society of Japan
Netherlands
Regina Bernhaupt
Koninklijke Nederlandse Vereniging
van Informatieprofessionals (KNVI)
New Zealand
Mark Apperley
Judy Bowen (Member Recommended by TC)
Institute of IT Professionals New Zealand
Norway
Frode Eika Sandnes
Den Norske Dataforening (DND)
Poland
Marcin Sikorski
Komitetu Informatyki Polska Akademia Nauk (PAN)
Portugal
José Creissac Campos
Ordem dos Engenheiros Portugal
Serbia
Aleksandar Jevremovic

Informatics Association of Serbia (IAS)
Slovenia
Matjaž Kljun
Slovensko Društvo INFORMATIKA
South Africa
Janet L. Wesson
Paula Kotzé (Member Recommended by TC)
Institute of Information Technology Professionals South Africa (IITPSA)
Sri Lanka
Thilina Halloluwa
Computer Society of Sri Lanka (CSSL)
Sweden
Jan Gulliksen
Dataföreningen i Sverige
Swedish Computer Society
Switzerland
Denis Lalanne
Schweizer Informatik Gesellschaft (SI)
United Kingdom
José Luis Abdelnour Nocera
Helen Petrie (Member Recommended by TC)
British Computer Society (BCS), Chartered Institute for IT

International Members at Large Representatives

ACM

Gerrit van der Veer
Association for Computing Machinery

CLEI

César Collazos
Centro Latinoamericano de Estudios en Informatica

Expert Members

Ahmed Seffah, UAE
Anirudha Joshi, India
Antonio Piccinno, Italy
Constantinos Coursaris, Canada

Christos Fidas, Greece
Daniel Orwa Ochieng, Kenya
David Lamas, Estonia
Dorian Gorgan, Romania
Fernando Loizides, UK/Cyprus
Ivan Burmistrov, Russia
Kaveh Bazargan, Iran
Lourdes Moreno, Spain
Marta Kristin Lárusdóttir, Iceland
Nikolaos Avouris, Greece
Peter Forbrig, Germany
Torkil Clemmensen, Denmark

Working Group Chairpersons

WG 13.1 (HCI Education)

Lara Piccolo, Germany

WG 13.2 (Methodologies for User-Centered System Design)

Stefan Sauer, Germany

WG 13.3 (HCI, Disability and Aging)

Anna Bramwell-Dicks, UK

WG 13.4/2.7 (User Interface Engineering)

Davide Spano, Italy

WG 13.5 (Human Error, Resilience, Reliability, Safety and System Development)

Tilo Mentler, Germany

WG13.6 (Human-Work Interaction Design)

Élodie Bouzekri, France

WG13.7 (HCI and Visualization)

Gerrit van der Veer, Netherlands

WG 13.8 (Interaction Design and International Development)

José Adbelnour Nocera, UK

WG 13.9 (Interaction Design and Children)

Gavin Sim, UK

WG 13.10 (Human-Centred Technology for Sustainability)

Masood Masoodian, Finland

WG 13.11/12.14 (Human-Centered Intelligent Systems)

Albrecht Schmidt, Germany

Workshop Track Organization

André Freire	INTERACT 2025 General Chair
Raquel Prates	INTERACT 2025 General Chair
Carmelo Ardito	INTERACT 2025 Technical Program Chair
Cristiano Maciel	INTERACT 2025 Workshop Chair
Davide Lucio Spano	INTERACT 2025 Workshop Chair

Workshop Organization

HCI Education and Education for HCI: Current Opportunities and Challenges

WG 13.1 - HCI Education

Lara Piccolo	CODE University of Applied Sciences, Germany
Paloma Díaz	Universidad Carlos III de Madrid, Spain
Helen Petrie	University of York, UK
Shrikant Salve	Indian Institute of Information Technology Pune, India
Kaveh Bazargan	Allameh Tabataba'i University, Iran
Ahmed Seffah	Zayed University, UAE

HCSE Workshop on Balancing Interaction, Artificial Intelligence, and Human Value

WG 13.2 - Methodologies for User-Centered Systems Design

Stefan Sauer	Paderborn University, Germany
Carmelo Ardito	Polytechnic University of Bari, Italy
Regina Bernhaupt	Eindhoven University of Technology, The Netherlands

Navigation for People with Disabilities and Older People: Current Challenges and Opportunities

WG 13.3 - HCI, Disability and Aging

Helen Petrie	University of York, UK
Gerhard Weber	Technische Universität Dresden, Germany

Technology Design for and with Neurodivergent Users: Considerations from Research Practices

WG 13.3 - HCI, Disability and Aging

Vivian Genaro Motti	George Mason University, USA
David Gollasch	TU Dresden, Germany
Meinhardt Branig	TU Dresden, Germany
Bruna Cunha	University of São Paulo, Brazil

Engineering Methods for HCI and UX in AI-Driven Systems

WG 13.4/2.7 - User Interface Engineering

Lucio Davide Spano	University of Cagliari, Italy
Philippe Palanque	ICS-IRIT, France
Célia Martinie	ICS-IRIT, France
José Campos	University of Minho, Portugal
Albrecht Schmidt	Ludwig-Maximilians-Universität München, Germany
Barbara Rita Barricelli	University of Brescia, Italy
Passant El Agroudy	DFKI, Germany
Kris Luyten	Hasselt University, Belgium

Transparent Autonomy and Human Work Interaction Design Workshop

WG13.6 - Human-Work Interaction Design

Elodie Bouzekri	University of Brest, France
Torkil Clemmensen	Copenhagen Business School, Denmark
Antony William Joseph	Aalto University, Finland
Arminda Guerra Lopes	University of Castelo Branco, Portugal
Adriana Moreno Rangel	Federal University of Roraima, Brazil
Jose Abdelnour Nocera	University of West London, UK

Addressing Global HCI Challenges at the Time of Geopolitical Tensions through Planetary Thinking and Indigenous Methodologies

WG 13.8 - Interaction Design and International Development

Huatong Sun	University of Washington Tacoma, USA
Jose Abdelnour Nocera	University of West London, UK
Torkil Clemmensen	Copenhagen Business School, Denmark
Sheethal Liz Tom	IIE Varsity College, Cape Town, South Africa

Effective Map-Based Interfaces and Interactions

WG 13.10 - Human-Centred Technology for Sustainability

Masood Masoodian	Aalto University, Finland
Saturnino Luz	University of Edinburgh, UK

Reviewers

Anke Dittmar
Antonio Piccinno
Antony Joseph
Arminda Guerra
Artemis Skarlatidou
Åsa Cajander
Barbara Rita Barricelli
Bilal Naqvi
Carmelo Ardito
Cèlia Martinie
David Gollasch
Elodie Bouzekri
Fabio Paternò
Gerhard Weber
Helen Petrie
Jan Van Den Bergh
José Creissac Campos
Kris Luyten
Lucio Davide Spano
Marco Winckler
Maria Luigia De Bonis
Marta Kristín Lárusdóttir
Masood Masoodian
Philippe Palanque
Rebecca Cort
Regina Bernhaupt
Rosa Lanzilotti
Saturnino Luz
Stefan Sauer
Stefano Valtolina
Thomas Rist
Torkil Clemmensen
Vivian Motti

Organizers, Sponsors and Partners

Sponsors

In-Cooperation Partners

Contents

Human-Centered Software Engineering: Balancing Interaction, Artificial Intelligence, and Human Value

HCI Education and Education for HCI: Current Opportunities and Challenges

New Pedagogies, AI and Social Responsibility in HCI Education: Workshop Results

Lara S. G. Piccolo[1](✉), Paloma Díaz[2], Helen Petrie[3], Shrikant Salve[4], and Kaveh Bazargan[5]

[1] CODE University of Applied Sciences, Berlin, Germany
lara.piccolo@code.berlin
[2] Universidad Carlos III de Madrid, Madrid, Spain
pdp@inf.uc3m.es
[3] University of York, York, UK
helen.petrie@york.ac.uk
[4] Indian Institute of Information Technology, Pune, Pune, India
shrikant@iiitp.ac.in
[5] Allameh Tabataba'i University, Tehran, Iran
kbazargan@atu.ac.ir

Abstract. This paper presents the outcomes of the workshop *HCI Education and Education for HCI: Current Opportunities and Challenges*, held in a hybrid format at INTERACT 2025. Bringing together Human-Computer Interaction educators and researchers from across the globe, the workshop explored the evolving demands on curricula and pedagogies shaped by Artificial Intelligence (AI) and the urgent call to embed social responsibility in technology design. Eight research papers were presented across three themes: new pedagogical approaches, AI, and teaching social responsibility. The case studies demonstrated methodologies and tools that promote socially aware, active, and a more inclusive teaching and learning. AI was recognised as a valuable educational aid for personalisation, a challenge requiring careful integration to preserve students' agency, and an opportunity to co-create curricula aligned with current industry needs. Teaching and learning methods that foster empathy, inclusivity, and critical engagement with human values and accessibility were presented and discussed. The workshop outcomes emphasise rethinking HCI education as a socio-technical ecosystem that equips future designers, researchers, and technologists to use technology as a means for equitable and human-centred societal progress.

Keywords: Human-Computer Interaction · Education · Pedagogy · Curricula

Published by Springer Nature Switzerland AG 2026
C. Maciel et al. (Eds.): INTERACT 2025 Workshops, LNCS 16478, pp. 3–11, 2026.
https://doi.org/10.1007/978-3-032-22934-2_1

1 Introduction

Having up-to-date curricula and pedagogical approaches that respond to the technical and social transformations shaping the world today are critical in HumanComputer Interaction (HCI) Education.

The rapid and widespread adoption of Artificial Intelligence (AI) is one of these transformations. Its implications extend well beyond the technical domain, as it has reshaped how people and society perceive, interact with, and are influenced by digital systems. It also requires a rethinking of how technology design and development are taught and practised in industry. Furthermore, the Big Tech firms driving this transformation have accumulated growing influence over public policy and the governance structures that support it. Critical issues such as algorithmic bias, platform accountability, and equitable access to the benefits of technology should now be addressed both in classrooms and at the forefront of policy debates. This context underscores the need to move beyond a techno-centred model of computer science education [2] towards approaches that enable students to innovate responsibly, fairly, and with heightened awareness of societal impact.

Novel educational strategies are also essential to equip students with the capacity to leverage the potential of new technologies without eroding their critical thinking and problem-solving abilities [1]. In parallel with curriculum reviews, such as the publication of new ACM Computer Science Curricula 2023 [3], there is a growing need to support pedagogical innovations that foster adaptability and real-world engagement. Active learning approaches such as project-based learning [4] are particularly valuable for situating technical skills within societal contexts. However, their implementation should be approached thoughtfully to ensure academic rigour and inclusivity, maintaining equitable learning experiences for students with diverse needs and in various educational settings.

The challenges and opportunities arising from this socio-technical transition form the foundation of the discussions at the *Workshop on HCI Education and Education for HCI* at INTERACT 2025.

1.1 The Workshop

In line with the mission of the IFIP TC13 Workgroup 1[1] the workshop aimed to advance HCI education globally by fostering research and collaboration on pedagogy, emerging technologies, and social responsibility, while promoting equitable access to effective teaching and learning practices. Accordingly, the topics of interest included:

- New pedagogical practices (not necessarily thoroughly tested), including the use of innovative technologies in HCI education

[1] A working group of the International Federation for Information Processing (IFIP), Technical Committee 13 for Human Computer Interaction (HCI), devoted to HCI Education. https://wg1.ifip-tc13.org/,.

- Fostering interdisciplinarity in HCI
- Integrating ethics, social responsibility, and Diversity, Inclusion, and Equity (DEI) practices in HCI teaching
- Review of the updated ACM Curricula for Human-Computer Interaction, including new demands towards human-AI interaction
- (Multilingual) Open Educational Resources (OER) for HCI teaching and learning
- GenAI and the teaching and learning of HCI
- Reflecting on the interplay and avenues for cross-pollination between education for HCI and HAI
- Addressing interdisciplinarity with other computer science domains such as data science, blockchain, the metaverse, etc.

2 Activities and Participants

The full day workshop took place in Belo Horizonte, Brazil, in 9 of September of 2025 with a hybrid setup. Participants with affiliations in Brazil, Germany, Spain, United Kingdom, Iran, India, Uruguay, and Sweden had the opportunity to share and discuss their teaching and learning experiences across three main themes: **new pedagogical approaches**, **AI** and **teaching social responsibility**. Each theme had three accepted papers, although one paper on artificial intelligence was withdrawn.

To facilitate engagement, particularly for online participants, and to support the analysis of discussions, a Miró board, as illustrated in Fig. 1 was shared with all attendees. This allowed everyone to contribute with notes on challenges and opportunities, as well as provide suggestions and feedback to presenters beyond the Q&A following the paper presentations.

3 Papers

The papers presentation followed the thematic structure: New Pedagogical Approaches, AI and Teaching Social Responsibility.

3.1 New Pedagogical Approaches

New pedagogies were addressed in different ways, though having in common the active learning perspective. The first contribution proposed an educational approach that is systemic and experiential, moving from the traditional classroom setups to heritage temples as a space for socio-technical explorations. The other 2 contributions are grounded on the Project-Based Learning [4] approach. While one research focuses on potential new challenges of innovative and active learning environments for students with Attention-Deficit/Hyperactivity Disorder (ADHD), the other is addressing the need for organisational structures to best support projects execution and management.

Fig. 1. Screenshot of the Miró board used to facilitate engagement during and after the workshop, in which every paper have a dedicated space for questions and comments. The spaces were grouped according to the 3 sessions in the workshop.

Designing HCI Learning Experiences Through the Living Heritage of Temple Complexes: A Systems Thinking Approach. This research proposes an integrated framework using Systems Thinking to design HCI learning experiences within the living heritage of temple complexes in Secunderabad, India. By analysing the cultural, social, and spatial dynamics of eight temples, the study developed a hybrid pedagogical model that tailors learning aids, using non-digital tools (like storytelling and craft kits) for primary students and digital tools (like VR/AR simulations) for older students. This work defines temple complexes as authentic learning environments and socio-technical systems for teaching user-centred design and participatory methods, thereby promoting cultural empathy and interdisciplinary problem-solving across all educational levels.

Supporting Students with ADHD in Project-Based and Self-directed Learning. This case study situated in Germany sheds light on the tension within innovative learning models when it comes to balancing freedom and autonomy with structure, demonstrating that project-based and self-directed pedagogies alone do not ensure comprehensive inclusion for students with ADHD. The findings suggest that achieving inclusion requires structured support embedded within flexible pedagogical frameworks. Simple interventions are proposed, such as providing learning materials in advance, offering exemplars of completed work, and clearly signposting topic transitions. While these strategies primarily address the needs of students with ADHD, they have the potential to benefit all learners.

Usability Evaluation of Student Project Management System Implemented at IIIT Pune. This research reports the successful development and usability validation of a customised digital platform designed to manage the complex administrative workflows inherent in Project-Based Learning. This system innovation addresses significant administrative barriers, ensuring efficiency and clarity throughout the entire project lifecycle for students, faculty, and administrators, thereby strengthening the quality and scalability of the core PBL curriculum.

3.2 Artificial Intelligence

The impact of AI was addressed both in terms of curriculum and pedagogy. One study addressed the integration of AI into the curriculum, focusing on co-creating advanced courses with students and industry partners that specifically explore the convergence of Interaction Design (IxD) and AI, and ensure alignment between academic curricula and current market needs. Another study applied AI to generate personalised learning materials aimed at enhancing student motivation and analysing the impact of personalised learning.

Enhancing Classroom Learning Through Human-Computer Interaction (HCI) and AI-Driven Problem Generation. This research situated in Spain is establishing a model for enhancing student motivation and academic performance by integrating Generative AI with Human-Computer Interaction (HCI) principles to transform traditional problem-solving exercises into personalised learning experiences. The study details how Large Language Models (LLMs) can act as an interactive agent to create academic problems tailored to individual student interests and preferences, thereby addressing key motivational factors like autonomy and relevance, consistent with Self-Determination Theory (SDT). Experimental results validate this approach, showing that the personalised content significantly boosted student motivation.

Bridging Industry and Academia: Co-creating Interaction Design and Artificial Intelligence Courses. In case study situated in Sweden, the authors propose a validated methodology for collaborative curriculum design that ensures academic offerings remain highly relevant and reflective of evolving industry needs in rapidly changing technological domains. This co-creation process, involving workshops with industry representatives and surveys with students and alumni, successfully addressed the existing gap between theoretical knowledge and the market demands for professionals skilled at the intersection of Interaction Design and AI. The research yielded six concrete new course proposals, confirming strong consensus for three future-facing topics: Accessibility/Inclusive Design, Tools with AI, and Novel Interaction Methods using AI.

3.3 Teaching Social-Responsibility

The 2023 ACM Curriculum for Computer Science [3] defines "Responsibility in Design" as a key topic. The three contributions, collectively, address social responsibility by proposing active-learning based methodologies to embed ethical values, accessibility, and inclusion directly into the curriculum and design process. These approaches aim to move HCI beyond traditional usability concerns, providing students with practical experiences that foster empathy and a lasting sense of responsibility to guide their professional practice beyond their studies.

A 'Possibilistic' Approach to Teaching Accessibility in Higher Education. This work presents a pragmatic and motivational strategy for integrating essential accessibility and inclusive design competencies into higher education curricula despite constraints like limited instructional time and resources. This approach emphasises an active learning approach, requiring students to directly experience barriers using assistive technologies, practice technical production, and systematic evaluation of accessible content.

Integrating Value-Based Design Into HCI Education. This research suggests shifting the debate from general, controversial issues surrounding ethics in technology design to the specific impact of the "small decisions" of designers and programmers on human values. The case study demonstrates a low-resource method for embedding ethical responsibility into design process, in which students are confronted with the obligation to apply values into their designs throughout the development cycle. This approach encourages them to consider the multidimensional consequences their design choices have on values like justice, inclusion, and sustainability.

Integrating Accessibility and Inclusive Design in CS and HCI Education: Challenges and Opportunities for Educators. This research demonstrates low-cost simulation practical exercises as effective, memorable, and replicable methods for introducing computer science and HCI students to the critical importance of accessibility and inclusive design. This approach involves role-playing scenarios and low-cost kits (e.g., spectacles smeared with lip gloss, buttons taped to fingers) to simulate the difficulties people with disabilities and older people face when using familiar technologies like smartphones. By offering informative, fun, and inexpensive experiences, the exercises foster a lasting understanding of the needs and wishes of diverse users, ensuring they recall their responsibility in addressing these needs when designing interactive systems in the future.

4 Discussions on Challenges and Opportunities

4.1 Towards More Active Learning Approaches

A central challenge, discussed across all thematic sessions, was the need to strengthen pedagogical approaches that move beyond a purely technological focus. The discussions noted the risk of forming computer science and HCI graduates who struggle to situate their digital tools within complex, real-world contexts. When HCI pedagogy restricts contexts and examples to digital interfaces, it often overlooks the embodied, situated, and communal dimensions of human interaction.

In line with this perspective, the works presented suggested a movement towards more dynamic, student-centric models that emphasise active learning, real-world problem-solving, and personalisation. Central to these innovations is the adoption of pedagogical frameworks such as self-directed and project-based learning. However, participants stressed that adopting approaches like PBL is not merely a teaching style but a comprehensive pedagogical model that requires a supportive structure, including clear guidance, feedback loops, and scaffolding for diverse learners. Equally important is the need to balance guidance while boosting students' autonomy and independence.

4.2 Addressing AI Potentials and Dangers

The rapid emergence of generative AI presents both challenges and opportunities for HCI education. Participants discussed the need to create pedagogical frameworks and digital tools that integrate AI support in ways that strengthen, rather than replace, critical thinking and creativity. Educators need clear strategies to embed AI meaningfully into teaching and learning processes, not as a novelty, but as an enhancement to reflection, feedback, and personalised learning.

As a key opportunity, participants discussed how AI can support personalised teaching and learning. This is not only a chance to leverage motivation and engagement, but also a means to better include neurodivergent students. At a systemic level, it was demonstrated that the adoption of AI could motivate the co-creation of curricula between students, industry stakeholders, and educators, aligning learning outcomes with professional expectations while maintaining academic rigour. Moreover, teaching HCI methods that make AI features more explainable and accountable was seen as a key skill for future practitioners.

Nonetheless, participants cautioned that AI adoption must be accompanied by the creation of affordable and accessible tools, ensuring no learner or scenarios are excluded from this transformation due to limited resources.

4.3 Responsible Design Practices as Foundational Knowledge

Addressing the potentials and dangers of AI applications is not the only change required in the HCI curriculum. There is a strong mandate to properly embed principles of inclusivity, accessibility, and ethics. These principles, for example, are not yet comprehensively addressed in the most recent review of the ACM Curriculum for Computer Science [3], which serves as a global reference for HCI education.

Participants agreed that responsible design practices should be positioned as foundational, not peripheral, to the discipline. There was consensus on the need to connect HCI teaching content more closely with real-life social issues and to work with stakeholders, including accessibility experts, policy actors, and community representatives in curriculum development.

The studies presented highlight the value of teaching accessibility through hands-on practice and integrating value-based design to cultivate a sense of responsibility that accompanies students in their future as professionals. These initiatives address both legal requirements and a growing recognition that effective design must be inherently inclusive in practical ways. Particular emphasis was placed on teaching accessibility and inclusive design, including how and where these topics should be taught in low-resource environments or in departments where accessibility is undervalued. Involving experts in curriculum design and motivating young students, particularly male learners, to engage with inclusive design were identified as ongoing challenges.

4.4 Promising Directions and the Need for Future Research

Despite these obstacles, participants also identified promising directions. Viewing HCI learning environments as living socio-technical or pedagogical ecosystems offers a way to reconnect education with real-world contexts. Testing design solutions with neurodivergent learners, such as students with ADHD, was proposed as a potential route toward realising universal design principles in education. Similarly, low-cost and affordable tools can expand access to accessibility training globally, aligning with the ethical goal of democratising HCI education.

5 Final Remarks

This paper presented the results of the workshop *HCI Education and Education for HCI: Current Opportunities and Challenges*, held in a hybrid format at INTERACT 2025. A total of eight pieces of research were presented and discussed, highlighting priorities and emerging tendencies in the approaches adopted by HCI educators worldwide.

Taken together, these contributions reveal a field at a turning point. The confluence of transformative technologies such as generative AI, the maturation of new student-centred pedagogies, and a heightened sense of social responsibility marks a critical moment for the HCI education community to review both curricula and pedagogical approaches. This moment, therefore, demands a fundamental rethinking of how we prepare the next generation of designers, researchers, and technologists to build a more equitable and human-centred world, where technology serves as a tool to support positive societal change rather than one that dictates the directions society takes.

Acknowledgment. The organisers of this workshop are members of the IFIP Working Group 13.1 on HCI Education: https://wg1.ifip-tc13.org/. They thanks the participants for their valuable contributions and engagement in the discussions.

References

1. Denny, P., et al.: Computing education in the era of generative AI. Commun. ACM **67**(2), 56–67 (2024)
2. Khanal, S., Zhang, H., Taeihagh, A.: Why and how is the power of big tech increasing in the policy process? The case of generative AI. Policy So. **44**(1), 52–69 (2025). https://doi.org/10.1093/polsoc/puae012
3. Kumar, A.N., et al.: Computer Science Curricula 2023. ACM Press and IEEE Computer Society Press and AAAI Press (2024). https://doi.org/10.1145/3664191
4. Savery, J.R.: Overview of problem-based learning: definitions and distinctions. Essential readings in problem-based learning: exploring and extending the legacy of Howard S. Barrows **9**(2), 5–15 (2015)

Designing HCI Learning Experiences Through the Living Heritage of Temple Complexes: A Systems Thinking Approach

Nitin R. Sinha(✉) and Shiva Ji

Department of Design, Indian Institute of Technology Hyderabad, Sangareddy, India
md24resch04002@iith.ac.in, shivaji@des.iith.ac.in

Abstract. This paper investigates how systems thinking can be applied to design Human-Computer Interaction (HCI) learning experiences using the living heritage of temple complexes in Secunderabad. By exploring the cultural, social, and spatial dimensions of eight temple complexes, the research proposes both non-digital and digital aids tailored to learners at various educational stages. Non-digital tools such as storytelling, experiential learning, and tactile models foster engagement for primary students, while digital simulations, augmented reality, and interactive systems enhance learning at secondary, higher, technical, vocational, and professional education levels. Through qualitative case studies, stakeholder interviews, and participatory workshops, this research demonstrates how heritage-based HCI learning experiences promote systems thinking, cultural empathy, and interdisciplinary problem-solving. This study's primary contribution lies in showing how temple complexes can function as authentic learning environments for teaching HCI—specifically user-centred and participatory design principles—through a systems-thinking framework that fosters stakeholder reasoning, cultural sensitivity, and iterative design competence.

Keywords: Human-Computer Interaction (HCI) · Systems Thinking · Living Heritage · Temple Complexes · Community Co-Management · Experiential Learning · Digital and Non-Digital Aids

1 Introduction

In recent years, human-computer interaction (HCI) methodologies have been extensively integrated into cultural heritage education to enable various approaches to a historical context. By aggregating prior studies focusing on the application of HCI in the cultural heritage field, this literature review highlights systems thinking, design perspectives, and technology interventions, each contributing to the educational experience. HCI is central to re-contextualizing cultural heritage to promote democratization and diversification of history. Hirsch (2024) endorses multi-perspective and inclusive approaches enabled by HCI technologies, fostering sensemaking in a heterogeneous cultural background and considering participatory narratives moving away from expert-centered to people-centered narratives to achieve resonance.

Published by Springer Nature Switzerland AG 2026
C. Maciel et al. (Eds.): INTERACT 2025 Workshops, LNCS 16478, pp. 12–28, 2026.
https://doi.org/10.1007/978-3-032-22934-2_2

Cultural heritage management is complex and requires a systems thinking approach. In this context, such a thinking process has been singled out as a fruitful framework, as an interdisciplinary, user-centered perspective leads to out-of-the-box solutions to complex problems (Wang, 2024).

Technological innovations have transformed how cultural content is preserved and shared over time. In-depth learning environments are mainly generated closely with Virtual Reality (VR) systems. In a case study of students' experiences creating VR content about cultural heritage, Hu, Ng, and Lee (2019) reported that students gained better technological skills and motivation to learn more about cultural heritage from VR experiences. Serious games have shown great promise in increasing learner interest and knowledge retention in cultural heritage education. Marques, Pedro, and Araújo (2023) wrote a paper about gamification in cultural heritage. They presented results that indicate that it is an effective strategy for increasing the public's motivation and creating deeper understanding through interactivity. Evaluating visitor experiences with digital interpretation technologies is vital for successfully educating visitors about cultural heritage. Using visitor experiences study in Old Town, Zuoying, Liu (2020) found that digital displays also promoted the exploration and understanding of heritage sites, whilst areas for future design and implementation development were also noted. Although applying HCI methodologies in cultural heritage education is common, a measurable gap exists in systematically using systems thinking to design digital or non-digital educational tools in the temple heritage domain. Although several papers have discussed one or more technological interventions and design methods, this approach does not provide an integrated framework that considers systems thinking to effectively demonstrate the interrelatedness of stakeholders, resources, and processes in temple-based learning environments. To address these gaps, this research proposes a framework that integrates HCI and systems thinking concepts to make cultural heritage education more sustainable and scalable across various educational levels. Thus, the intersection of HCI methods and heritage education is a new engagement domain geared toward educating a broader audience. Employing systems thinking, design methods, and VR and serious games can help educators and practitioners preserve and promote cultural heritage through immersive and inclusive learning experiences.

1.1 Context and Background

Temple complexes in India serve as living heritage spaces, reflecting cultural practices, community management, and traditional knowledge. In cases studied at the city of Secunderabad, Telangana, India, these temples provide dynamic environments that can enrich HCI education through experiential and embodied learning. Applying systems thinking enables learners to explore the interconnectedness of temple activities, rituals, and spatial design.

The primary aim of this study is to utilize temple complexes as living laboratories to teach Human–Computer Interaction (HCI) principles—particularly user-centered design (UCD) and participatory design—across multiple educational levels. While students gain heritage literacy as a contextual benefit, the central learning outcomes focus on HCI competencies, including needs-finding, prototyping, iteration, and evaluation. Systems thinking provides the overarching framework to help learners reason about multi-stakeholder interactions, constraints, and trade-offs in culturally sensitive contexts. This study designs HCI learning experiences using both non-digital and digital aids to cater to learners across primary, secondary, higher, technical, vocational, and professional education. By incorporating traditional knowledge systems with interactive design methodologies, this approach fosters deeper learning and cultural sensitivity.

1.2 Problem Statement

HCI education often prioritizes digital applications without engaging learners in real-world environments. Additionally, primary learners may not benefit from digital tools, so alternative tactile and sensory learning experiences are required. This research addresses these gaps by proposing temple complexes as immersive educational sites that leverage systems thinking for both non-digital and digital learning.

1.3 Research Objectives and Questions

1. What HCI competencies can be effectively taught in temple contexts at different education stages?
2. How can temple complexes enhance HCI learning experiences at different educational stages?
3. What are the most effective non-digital aids for primary learners to engage with temple heritage?
4. How can digital tools complement systems thinking-based learning for older students?
5. What role does community co-management play in fostering heritage-based HCI education?

1.4 Scope and Significance

The study involves eight temple complexes in Secunderabad: Shri Ganesh Temple, Shri Shiva Temple, Shri Panchamukhi Anjaneya Swamy Temple, Shri Koneru Varaha Swamy Temple, Shri Laxmi Narayana Swamy Temple, Pot Market, Shri Laxmi Narayana Swamy Temple, General Bazaar, Shri Jagannath Swamy Temple, Shri Venugopal Swamy Temple. The insights will benefit educators, policymakers, heritage managers, and HCI designers by providing actionable strategies for integrating cultural heritage into educational curricula.

2 Methodology

A qualitative case study approach is used, incorporating three phases. Phase 1, Participant Observations, involves engaging with temple rituals, activities, and community practices. Phase 2, Stakeholder Interviews, focuses on collecting insights from priests, educators, community members, and students. Phase 3, Workshops and Co-Design Sessions, is dedicated to developing both non-digital and digital aids in collaboration with learners. This paper outlines the Phase 1 of the ongoing research. Ethical Considerations related to informed consent is obtained from all participants. Cultural sensitivity is maintained by respecting temple traditions and practices.

2.1 Principle-to-Practice Mapping

To directly align with User-Centred Design (UCD) principles, the study followed an iterative, participatory process that mapped theory to practical field implementation. Table 1 outlines this principle-to-practice translation.

Table 1. Principle-to-Practice Mapping of UCD in Heritage-Based HCI Learning Design

UCD Principle (ISO 9241-210)	Applied Practice in the Study
Understand and specify the context of use.	Conducted participant observations at eight temple complexes in Secunderabad to document rituals, spatial interactions, and stakeholder roles. Context profiles were created for each temple to inform design decisions.
Specify user requirements	Stakeholder interviews with priests, educators, artisans, students, and community members to capture functional and cultural requirements for both digital and non-digital learning aids.
Produce design solutions	Facilitated co-design workshops with learners at multiple educational levels to collaboratively develop prototypes of story cubes, AR guides, craft kits, and interactive maps.
Evaluate designs against requirements.	Implemented iterative testing of prototypes within temple spaces and in classroom settings, collecting feedback for refinement.
Iterate the design process.	Cycles of observation → prototype → test → feedback → refine repeated three times across different user groups.
Involve users throughout	Learners, priests, and educators were continuously engaged in decision-making, ensuring cultural authenticity and educational relevance.

This mapping ensures that the educational experiences are not only about learning HCI, but also learning through HCI, using the temple complex as a socio-cultural learning environment. The approach operationalizes UCD theory within a systems thinking framework, allowing for the iterative refinement of learning aids that remain contextually grounded.

3 Literature Review and Case Studies

3.1 Human-Centred Design and Educational Applications

Human-Centred Design (HCD), as formalised in ISO 9241-210, provides a structured framework for creating systems that are effective, efficient, and satisfying for the intended users (International Organization for Standardization [ISO], 2019). Core to this approach is understanding users' needs, involving them in the design process, and iterating based on feedback (Preece, Rogers, & Sharp, 2015). In educational contexts, HCD ensures that interventions—whether digital or non-digital—are tailored to learners' cognitive, social, and cultural contexts, thereby enhancing engagement and learning outcomes (Hornbæk & Hertzum, 2017).

Research in educational HCI highlights that participatory approaches increase learners' sense of ownership and can lead to more sustainable and culturally relevant solutions (Robertson & Simonsen, 2012). Such involvement is significant when designing for heritage-rich environments, where the authenticity of experience and respect for cultural practices are paramount (Ciolfi & Bannon, 2005).

3.2 HCI in Cultural Heritage Contexts

The application of HCI principles in cultural heritage has evolved from early digitisation and virtual reconstruction projects (Roussou, 2002) to more interactive, participatory experiences. Technologies such as augmented reality (AR), virtual reality (VR), and interactive storytelling have been shown to enhance visitors' understanding of heritage narratives (Petrelli, Marshall, & O'Brien, 2013; Bekele et al., 2018). However, studies have also noted the importance of embedding these tools within a broader sociocultural framework, to avoid technological determinism and ensure contextual fit (Ciolfi, Bannon, & Fernström, 2008).

In the Indian context, temple complexes present unique opportunities for applying HCI. They are not static historical artefacts but living ecosystems—spaces where rituals, festivals, craft traditions, and social exchanges converge. Designing HCI learning experiences in such environments requires striking a balance between technological innovation and cultural sensitivity, as well as community participation.

3.3 Educational Integration of Cultural Heritage

Integrating cultural heritage into formal and informal education has been shown to foster deep learning, intercultural understanding, and critical thinking (Hooper-Greenhill, 2007). Experiential learning theories, particularly Kolb's (1984) Experiential Learning Cycle, provide a strong pedagogical basis for such integration. In practice, this means engaging learners in authentic activities—such as observing rituals, interacting with artisans, and exploring architectural features—that allow for concrete experiences, reflective observation, abstract conceptualisation, and active experimentation.

Systems thinking offers an additional layer to this integration, enabling learners to perceive heritage sites as interconnected socio-technical systems (Meadows, 2008). By applying systems maps, causal loop diagrams, and stakeholder analysis, learners can gain a deeper understanding of the interdependencies between cultural, environmental, and technological factors in heritage management and design.

3.4 Research Gap

While there is a robust body of literature on HCI in cultural heritage and on heritage-based education separately, there is limited research that explicitly combines HCI's user-centered design principles, systems thinking methodologies, and multi-level educational integration in living heritage contexts. Most existing studies either focus on visitor engagement in heritage sites (Roussou, 2002; Petrelli et al., 2013) or on heritage-based pedagogy without embedding iterative, participatory HCI processes (Hooper-Greenhill, 2007).

This paper addresses this gap by presenting an educationally focused, principle-to-practice application of HCI design methods within the living heritage of Indian temple complexes. By incorporating both digital and non-digital aids, tailored to different educational stages from primary to professional studies, and by engaging directly with multiple stakeholders—including priests, artisans, educators, and learners—this work contributes a replicable model for heritage-integrated HCI learning experiences.

3.5 Learning Framework across Education Levels

Site Observations Across 8 Temple Complexes.
The site observations conducted across eight temple complexes in Secunderabad generated a multi-layered dataset that connects rituals, community practices, sensory-emotional engagement, and opportunities for technology integration into HCI learning frameworks.

For Primary Education, Shri Ganesh Temple and Shri Shiva Temple were selected to focus on cultural narratives, temple rituals, and sensory experiences. Non-digital aids included storytelling through illustrated scrolls and puppetry, clay model-making for temple sculptures, and mapping temples through collaborative drawings. Digital aids, although primarily used by educators for demonstration, included augmented reality (AR) storytelling through handheld devices and interactive digital puzzles with voice-guided mythological stories.

In Secondary Education, Shri Panchamukhi Anjaneya Swamy Temple and Shri Koneru Varaha Swamy Temple were utilized to explore symbolism, temple architecture, and community roles. Non-digital aids involved role-playing and scenario-based activities, temple walk-throughs with observation journals, and cultural board games centered on temple ecosystems. Digital aids included 360° virtual temple tours and interactive apps for understanding temple iconography.

For higher education, the Shri Laxmi Narayana Swamy Temple (Pot Market) and the Shri Laxmi Narayana Swamy Temple (General Bazaar) provided a platform for urban heritage conservation and participatory design, utilizing non-digital methods that included systems mapping on paper, physical models for spatial analysis, and scenario planning workshops. The digital approach incorporated GIS mapping tools for analyzing temple surroundings and design simulations using CAD software.

In Technical and Vocational Education, the Shri Jagannath Swamy Temple served as the focal point for learning about heritage craft skills, traditional temple construction, and conservation techniques. Non-digital aids included craft-based workshops using traditional materials and the documentation of temple restoration techniques. The digital aids employed 3D scanning and photogrammetry for digital heritage conservation, along with VR simulations demonstrating temple construction methods.

Lastly, Professional study-related data exploration at Shri Venugopal Swamy Temple emphasized community co-management, design ethics, and heritage technology. Non-digital learning experiences included stakeholder mapping exercises and debate sessions on heritage policies. The integration of digital tools involved AI-powered systems thinking analysis tools and data visualization dashboards for heritage management.

Ritual Observations.
Ritual practices (Table 2) varied in frequency, duration, and scale, providing unique contexts for experiential learning. Daily rituals, such as Ganesh Chaturthi Aarti at Shri Ganesh Temple and Hanuman Chalisa Recitation at Shri Panchamukhi Anjaneya Temple, fostered routine engagement. In contrast, annual festivals such as Ratha Yatra at Shri Jagannath Temple and Krishna Janmashtami at Shri Venugopal Temple attract large-scale community participation, with numbers exceeding 300–500 participants. The sensory richness of these rituals was notable, ranging from visual illumination and clay idols to olfactory cues of incense and flowers, auditory chanting and music, and tactile or kinesthetic engagement such as pulling temple chariots. These observations reveal the embodied, multi-sensory learning opportunities available in temple contexts.

Community Practices.
Community practices (Table 3) highlighted the diversity of knowledge transmission within temple ecosystems. Activities such as prasadam preparation (at Shri Shiva Temple) and flower garland making (at Shri Ganesh Temple) emphasized culinary and craft-based skills. Performative traditions, such as folk performances (Shri Venugopal Temple) and ritual documentation (Shri Laxmi Narayana Temple, General Bazaar), cultivated storytelling, archiving, and digitization skills. Structural practices, including traditional construction (e.g., the Shri Jagannath Temple), developed competencies in design and materials science. From a systems thinking perspective, these practices embody principles of supply chain management, co-management, conflict resolution, and sustainable design, thereby serving as live models for applied HCI pedagogy.

Sensory and Emotional Experience.
The sensory-emotional mapping revealed that learners engaged deeply through multiple modalities. Clay sculpting in Shri Ganesh Temple evoked joy and enhanced spatial awareness, while the olfactory experiences of incense and flowers in Shri Shiva Temple encouraged mindfulness. Chanting at Shri Panchamukhi Anjaneya Temple energized learners and improved cognitive retention, whereas tactile encounters with sacred objects at Shri Koneru Varaha Temple fostered cultural empathy. The Ratha Yatra at Shri Jagannath Temple scored the highest engagement (10/10), highlighting the potential of kinesthetic rituals to teach teamwork and collaboration. Overall, engagement ratings across temples ranged from 7–10, demonstrating that temple environments naturally facilitate high learning potential through emotional resonance (Table 4).

Technology Integration Opportunities.
The analysis identified pathways (Table 5) to complement non-digital learning with digital augmentation. For primary and secondary learners, story cubes, craft kits, and AR apps at Shri Ganesh Temple could scaffold interactive storytelling. For secondary

Table 2. Ritual Observation data

Temple Name	Primary Ritual Observed	Frequency	Time Duration	Community Participation	Key Sensory Elements
Shri Ganesh Temple	Ganesh Chaturthi Aarti	Daily	30 min	150+ Participants	Visual (Clay idols, lamps), Auditory (Mantras, Bells)
Shri Shiva Temple	Rudrabhishekam	Weekly	45 min	50 Participants	Olfactory (Sandalwood, Flowers), Tactile (Water, Milk)
Shri Panchamukhi Anjaneya Swamy Temple	Hanuman Chalisa Recitation	Daily	20 min	80 Participants	Auditory (Chanting), Visual (Murti Abhishekam)
Shri Koneru Varaha Swamy Temple	Varaha Jayanti Puja	Annual	90 min	200 Participants	Visual (Altar Decorations), Tactile (Sacred Offerings)
Shri Laxmi Narayana Swamy Temple (Pot Market)	Vaikunta Ekadasi Puja	Annual	60 min	300+ Participants	Visual (Temple Illumination), Auditory (Devotional Music)
Shri Laxmi Narayana Swamy Temple (General Bazaar)	Satyanarayana Vratam	Monthly	75 min	120 Participants	Visual (Floral Arrangements), Gustatory (Prasadam Tasting)
Shri Jagannath Swamy Temple	Ratha Yatra Festival	Annual	6 Hours	500+ Participants	Visual (Chariot Procession), Kinesthetic (Pulling of Chariot)
Shri Venugopal Swamy Temple	Krishna Janmashtami	Annual	2 Hours	350 Participants	Visual (Drama Enactments), Auditory (Flute Music)

and higher education students, scent simulation devices at the Shri Shiva Temple and chant recognition systems at the Shri Panchamukhi Temple would simulate ritual experiences. Higher and technical learners could benefit from VR environments (Shri Koneru

Table 3. Community Practices data

Community Practice	Temple Name	Stakeholders Involved	Skills Developed	Systems Thinking Insights
Prasadam Preparation	Shri Shiva Temple	Temple Priests, Devotees	Culinary, Time Management	Resource Utilization, Waste Management
Flower Garland Making	Shri Ganesh Temple	Local Artisans, Women Groups	Craftsmanship, Pattern Design	Supply Chain Management, Seasonal Variations
Folk Performance	Shri Venugopal Swamy Temple	Drama Artists, Musicians	Performance Arts, Storytelling	Cultural Narratives, Emotional Engagement
Ritual Documentation	Shri Laxmi Narayana Swamy Temple (General Bazaar)	Scholars, Photographers	Archiving, Digital Documentation	Knowledge Preservation, Heritage Digitization
Temple Management	Shri Koneru Varaha Swamy Temple	Trustees, Volunteers	Event Planning, Conflict Resolution	Community Co-Management, Decision-Making
Traditional Construction	Shri Jagannath Swamy Temple	Stone Masons, Architects	Structural Design, Material Science	Sustainable Design Practices

Varaha Temple) and multimedia archives (Shri Venugopal Temple). In contrast, vocational and professional learners could engage with AI-powered management dashboards (Shri Laxmi Narayana Temple, Pot Market), culinary heritage apps (General Bazaar), and digital collaboration platforms (Shri Jagannath Temple). Collectively, these interventions demonstrate a hybrid model of temple-based pedagogy, where non-digital traditions anchor authenticity and digital tools extend access and scalability.

Summary Insight.
The observations demonstrate that temple complexes function as multisensory, multi-sector ecosystems, ideally suited for HCI education. Rituals enable embodied learning, community practices support skills transfer, emotional experiences deepen engagement, and technology integration provides scalability. This layered dataset provides a robust empirical basis for designing human-centred, systems-oriented HCI learning experiences that span primary to professional education.

Table 4. Sensory and Emotional Experience data

Temple Name	Primary Sensory Experience	Emotional Response	Engagement Rating (1–10)	Learning Potential
Shri Ganesh Temple	Visual (Clay Sculpting)	Joyful, Engaged	9	Enhances Spatial Awareness
Shri Shiva Temple	Olfactory (Incense, Flowers)	Calm, Reflective	8	Encourages Mindfulness
Shri Panchamukhi Anjaneya Swamy Temple	Auditory (Chanting)	Energized, Focused	9	Improves Cognitive Retention
Shri Koneru Varaha Swamy Temple	Tactile (Sacred Objects)	Reverent, Curious	7	Develops Cultural Empathy
Shri Laxmi Narayana Swamy Temple (Pot Market)	Visual (Decorative Rituals)	Awe, Appreciation	10	Enhances Visual Storytelling Skills
Shri Laxmi Narayana Swamy Temple (General Bazaar)	Gustatory (Prasadam)	Satisfied, Connected	8	Promotes Culinary Heritage Learning
Shri Jagannath Swamy Temple	Kinesthetic (Ratha Yatra)	Excited, Empowered	10	Develops Collaborative Teamwork
Shri Venugopal Swamy Temple	Auditory (Music & Drama)	Inspired, Nostalgic	9	Enhances Performance Analysis Skills

Table 5. Technology Integration opportunities

Temple	Potential Digital / Non-digital Tool	Purpose	Target Audience
Shri Ganesh Temple	Story cubes, Craft kits AR Mobile App	Interactive storytelling	Primary & Secondary Students
Shri Shiva Temple	Scent Simulation Devices	Ritual Experience Emulation	Secondary & Higher Education
Shri Panchamukhi Anjaneya Swamy Temple	Sound Recognition System	Chant Analysis	Secondary & Vocational Learners
Shri Koneru Varaha Swamy Temple	VR Environment	Virtual Heritage Tour	Higher & Technical Education
Shri Laxmi Narayana Swamy Temple (Pot Market)	AI-powered Management Dashboard	Festival Planning Simulation	Vocational & Professional Learners
Shri Laxmi Narayana Swamy Temple (General Bazaar)	Prasadam Recipe App	Culinary Heritage Learning	Secondary & Vocational Learners
Shri Jagannath Swamy Temple	Digital Collaboration Platform	Event Management Training	Vocational & Professional Learners
Shri Venugopal Swamy Temple	Multimedia Archive	Cultural Performance Analysis	Higher Education & Researchers

4 Systems Thinking Analysis – Results and Discussions

Using a systems map (Fig. 1), the research visualized interconnected stakeholders, resources, and processes. Key components include stakeholders, such as students, educators, priests, artisans, and designers; resources, which encompass physical spaces, non-digital aids (story cubes, craft kits), and digital aids (AR, AI chatbots); and processes, including observations, workshops, iterative prototyping, and curriculum integration.

The Systems map for HCI Learning Experiences in Temple Complexes highlights stakeholders such as primary and secondary students, who engage in hands-on learning, storytelling, and physical interactions; higher education and vocational students, who focus on deep research, digital tools, and skill-based learning; technical learners, who explore AR/VR prototyping, AI chatbots, and simulation-based exploration; temple priests, who preserve oral history, rituals, and knowledge transfer; educators, who integrate temple knowledge into learning modules; and community members and artisans, who contribute to craft-based education and traditional learning techniques.

The resources identified include non-digital aids such as story cubes, fabric maps, temple puzzles, and craft kits; digital aids like AR guides, AI chatbots, and interactive learning portals; physical spaces such as temple courtyards, classrooms, and workshops; and human capital, including subject matter experts, priests, historians, and designers. The processes and activities consist of participant observations (engaging with temple

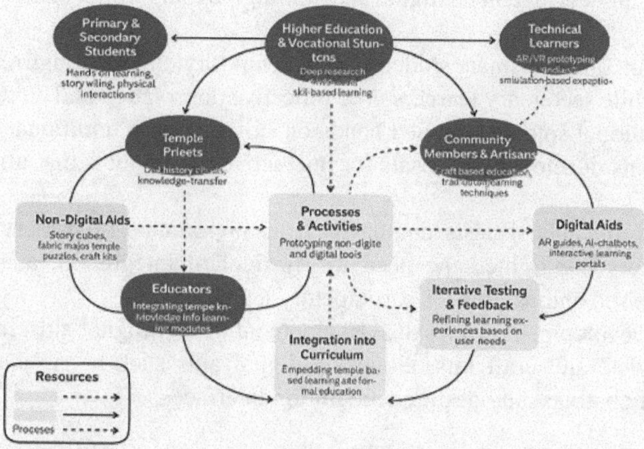

Fig. 1. Systems map with interconnections and relationships.

rituals and cultural mapping), workshops and co-design sessions (prototyping non-digital and digital tools), iterative testing and feedback (refining learning experiences based on user needs), and integration into the curriculum (embedding temple-based learning into formal education).

A Causal Loop Diagram (CLD) helps visualize the relationships between system components, identifying key loops such as the Learning Engagement Loop (R1), where more interactive non-digital aids lead to higher student engagement, increased cultural retention, and demand for more learning aids; the Technology Integration Loop (B1), where more digital aids lead to higher technical skill development but pose a risk of over-reliance on digital tools, necessitating hybrid learning models; the Community Involvement Loop (R2), where increased involvement of artisans and community members strengthens authenticity, boosting learner interest and participation; and the Temple Preservation Loop (B2), where technological interventions in temples pose risks of cultural dilution, requiring ethical design principles in HCI solutions.

A stock and flow diagram quantifies the movement of resources, identifying bottlenecks and areas for improvement. Key stocks include available non-digital aids (such as story cubes, puzzles, and maps), available digital aids (such as AR guides, VR models, and AI chatbots), engaged learners (students actively using the learning tools), and the cultural knowledge transfer rate (the extent to which temple knowledge is retained). Key flows include inflows such as new tool development, community participation, and technology integration, while outflows involve cultural dilution, over-reliance on digital tools, and inadequate educator support.

Emergent archetypes and policy solutions address challenges like Fixes that Fail, where digital interventions are introduced without cultural understanding; Shifting the Burden, where over-reliance on technology replaces hands-on learning; and Success to the Successful, wherein unequal digital access limits learning opportunities. Proposed solutions include community-led design workshops, low-cost non-digital toolkits, and hybrid learning models that blend digital and non-digital tools within contextual learning environments.

Learning Outcomes: Primary students engaged in storytelling through temple models and artifacts, while secondary learners used reflective observation and cultural mapping exercises. Vocational students applied hands-on skills to learn traditional crafts, while technical students developed proposals for interactive digital tools that utilized AI and AR.

Stakeholder Insights: Priests emphasized the importance of preserving oral traditions, educators highlighted the need for curriculum integration, and community members expressed enthusiasm for participatory learning.

Prototype Development proposals: Development of non-digital aids, including fabric maps, puzzles, and craft kits, alongside digital aids such as AR-based heritage exploration, AI chatbots, and gesture recognition interfaces.

Observational Insights for Systems Thinking

Feedback loops are evident in temples, wherein interconnected rituals and community participation influence temple management. For example, during Ganesh Chaturthi at Shri Ganesh Temple, feedback from devotees guides future festival planning. Leverage points emerge through community-driven waste management initiatives during festivals, offering opportunities to apply sustainable solutions. Emergence is observed in unique collaborative performances and participatory rituals, which often create spontaneous learning environments. Delays are evident in the flower supply chain at Shri Koneru Varaha Swamy Temple, where tracking these delays can teach learners about logistical constraints.

4.1 Cross-Stage Synthesis

Across all levels, the results indicate a coherent educational progression where complexity, autonomy, and technological integration increase gradually. Each stage reinforces systems thinking by translating lived experience into design knowledge:

Education Level	Focus	Key Competencies	Representative Evidence
Primary	Ritual observation, storytelling	Contextual inquiry, empathy	Story cubes, drawings
Secondary	Role-play, cultural mapping	Interaction analysis, systems thinking	Observation journals, VR tours
Higher	Participatory design	Stakeholder analysis, system modeling	GIS maps, CAD prototypes
Technical/Vocational	Craft-based engagement	Tangible interaction, digital preservation	3D scans, craft documentation
Professional	Co-management & ethics	Reflective design, governance modeling	Dashboards, debates

The iterative blend of non-digital and digital aids created a robust learning ecosystem rooted in experiential design and reflective practice (Kolb, 1984).

4.2 Summary of Findings

Overall, this research demonstrates that temple complexes, when approached as living socio-technical systems, can serve as transformative educational ecosystems for HCI learning. The education-first organization aligns with experiential and human-centered learning philosophies, ensuring that digital interventions are grounded in authentic cultural, sensory, and ethical foundations.

The findings highlight that embedding HCI learning in heritage contexts enhances empathy, systemic awareness, and design reflection across all education levels, thereby addressing a key pedagogical gap in contemporary HCI education (Rogers et al., 2015; Dourish, 2001).

5 Conclusion

The study identified the need to balance digital and non-digital learning, ensuring students do not become overly dependent on technology while reinforcing traditional knowledge transmission. Scalability and accessibility remain crucial for ensuring that the learning experience is adaptable across different educational levels without compromising cultural depth. Sustainability of learning aids necessitates the use of eco-friendly materials for physical tools and lightweight digital applications. Stakeholder engagement requires deeper collaboration with priests, artisans, and community members to enhance authenticity. Additionally, customization based on learner level is vital, tailoring tools for different education stages, such as story-based tools for primary students and AR models for higher education learners. Our approach is designed around living heritage as a pedagogical ecosystem, not temples alone. Temples are one example because they combine rituals, community participation, and multi-sensory environments. However, the same framework applies to other contexts where cultural, social, and technical systems intersect, such as:

•Craft villages (e.g., pottery, weaving clusters) where tacit skill transfer can be structured into HCI education.

•Urban heritage precincts (markets, community squares) where complex socio-technical interactions can be mapped.

•Performing arts traditions (theatre, dance, music) that naturally integrate embodiment, co-creation, and feedback.

•Ecological heritage systems (sacred groves, water bodies) where community-based sustainability practices can be connected to systems thinking in HCI.

This study demonstrates how HCI learning experiences can be enriched by engaging with temple heritage through systems thinking. The iterative design of both digital and non-digital aids fosters a deeper connection with cultural narratives, providing a sustainable model for interdisciplinary learning. For primary learners, non-digital storytelling and hands-on activities promote experiential learning, while secondary and higher education students benefit from digital simulations and interactive technologies. The research underscores the importance of community co-management in heritage-based education. By applying a systems thinking approach, educators and designers can create immersive and contextually relevant learning experiences. This interdisciplinary model serves as a blueprint for integrating cultural heritage into global HCI education.

Further research should explore the scalability of this approach in other heritage contexts, contributing to inclusive and sustainable educational practices. Future steps include redesigning the learning model by introducing a flexible, multi-modal learning framework integrating systems thinking insights, iterative prototyping and testing through co-design sessions across all eight temples to refine the learning aids, developing a hybrid learning strategy that blends non-digital and digital methodologies into temple-based curriculum modules, and addressing ethical and cultural considerations to ensure respectful technology integration in temple spaces while maximizing student engagement.

Appendices

Participant Observation Questionnaire

Section 1: General observation details

Date and Time of Observation:

Temple Name:

Location within Temple (e.g., sanctum, courtyard, mandapam, water tank):

Type of Event or Ritual Observed:

Weather and Environmental Conditions:

Section 2: Temple Rituals and Practices

1. What are the main rituals being performed? Describe the sequence of events.
2. What symbolic actions or gestures are involved in the rituals?
3. Who are the key participants (e.g., priests, devotees, musicians)?
4. Are there any specific chants, hymns, or prayers? Document their purpose.
5. How are ritual objects like lamps, flowers, or offerings used?
6. Is there gender-specifi or age-specific roles observed in rituals?
7. What emotional responses are visible among the participants?
8. How do participants engage with temple deities and sacred spaces?

Section 3: Community and Social Dynamics

9. How are temple visitors interacting with each other?
10. Are there any hierarchical structures (e.g., lead priests, senior devotees) evident?
11. What is the involvement of children, elders, and marginalized communities?
12. Are there visible forms of community service (e.g., free meals, assistance)?
13. How do the rituals influence a sense of belonging or spirituality?
14. Are there collaborative activities like singing, dancing, or storytelling?
15. How is knowledge of rituals transmitted within the community?

Section 4: Physical and Spatial Analysis

16. How is the temple space utilized during rituals and events?
17. Are there any dedicated spaces for specific activities (e.g., meditation, education, or social gatherings)?
18. How is sound, light, and incense used within the temple environment?
19. Are there any non-verbal communications observed (e.g., gestures, expressions)?
20. What materials and architectural elements are emphasized during rituals?
21. How does the spatial layout support or hinder the flow of activities?

Section 5: Educational and Learning Aspects

22. Are there any storytelling or teaching sessions observed?

23. How are traditional practices explained to younger generations or newcomers?

24. Are learners engaged through non-digital aids like temple murals, scriptures, or sculptures?

25. Are there digital displays, projectors, or augmented reality (AR) aids used?

26. What role do priests or elders play in knowledge transfer?

27. Are informal learning methods like observation and imitation evident?

28. How are visitors encouraged to participate in educational experiences?

Section 6: Perceptions and Reflections

29. How would you describe the overall atmosphere of the temple during the event?

30. Were there any moments of heightened emotional or spiritual engagement?

31. What values or beliefs were evident in the rituals and interactions?

32. Did the participants exhibit a sense of community ownership and co-management?

33. What aspects of the experience seemed particularly meaningful to participants?

34. Were there any visible conflicts or challenges? How were they resolved?

35. What insights did you gain about the temple's role in community learning and engagement?

Section 7: Recommendations and Suggestions

36. What opportunities exist to enhance community participation in temple activities?

37. How could non-digital aids be used more effectively for educational purposes?

38. Are there potential applications for digital tools like VR, AR, or interactive storytelling?

39. What further research or observations would you recommend for deeper insight?

References

Dourish, P.: Where the Action Is: the Foundations of Embodied Interaction. MIT Press (2001)

Hirsch, L. et al. & (2024). Human–Computer Interaction (HCI) Advances to Re-Contextualize Cultural Heritage toward Multiperspectivity, Inclusion, and Sensemaking. Appl. Sci., 14(17), 7652. doi:https://doi.org/10.3390/app14177652

Hornbæk, K., Hertzum, M.: Technology acceptance and user experience: a review of the experiential component in HCI. ACM Trans. Comput.-Hum. Interact. **24**(5), 1–30 (2017). https://doi.org/10.1145/3127358

Hu, X., Ng, J., Lee, J.H.: VR creation experience in cultural heritage education: a preliminary exploration. Proc. Assoc. Inf. Sci. Technol. **56**(1), 422–426 (2019). https://doi.org/10.1002/pra2.42

International Organization for Standardization. ISO 9241-210: Human-centred design for interactive systems. ISO (2019).

Kolb, D. (1984). Experiential Learning: Experience as the Source of Learning and Development.

Liu, Y.: Evaluating visitor experience of digital interpretation and presentation technologies at cultural heritage sites: a case study of the old town, Zuoying. Built. Heritage. **4**(14) (2020). https://doi.org/10.1186/s43238-020-00016-4

Marques, C.G., Pedro, J.P., Araújo, I.: A systematic literature review of gamification in/for cultural heritage: Leveling up, going beyond. Heritage. **6**(8), 5935–5951 (2023). https://doi.org/10.3390/heritage6080316

Meadows, D.: Thinking in Systems: a Primer.(2008).

Petrelli, D., Ciolfi, L., Dulake, N.: Digital Heritage Engagement through Interactive Installations (2016).
Preece, J., Rogers, Y., Sharp, H.: Interaction Design: beyond Human-Computer Interaction, 4th edn. Wiley (2015)
Robertson, T., Simonsen, J.: Participatory design: an introduction. In: Simonsen, J., Robertson, T. (eds.) Routledge International Handbook of Participatory Design, pp. 1–17. Routledge (2012)
Roussou, M.: Virtual heritage: From the research lab to the broad public. Virtual Reality, Archaeology and Cultural Heritage International Symposium, 93–100 (2002).
UNESCO: Managing Cultural World Heritage (2013).
Wang, B.: Applications of human-computer interaction in the field of cultural heritage preservation. Appl. Comput. Eng. **105**, 50–56 (2024)

Supporting Students with ADHD in Project-Based and Self-directed Learning

Maya Alroy, Prasanna Gunasekera, and Lara Piccolo(✉)

CODE University of Applied Sciences, 12043 Berlin, Germany
{maya.alroy,pras.gunasekera,lara.piccolo}@code.berlin
https://code.berlin/

Abstract. While innovative pedagogical approaches present unique challenges for inclusive teaching and learning, the impact of ADHD in higher education remains underexplored. This exploratory study examines the challenges faced by students with ADHD at a German university of applied sciences, where technology and digital design related programmes are grounded in interdisciplinary project-based and self-directed learning. A focus group with students diagnosed with ADHD revealed specific challenges related to focus and time management within this flexible learning context. The study also identified supportive strategies for designing learning materials, including making interactive material available in advance and repetition of key concepts. Findings show that flexibility alone does not ensure inclusive teaching and learning; students with ADHD require structured support embedded within flexible pedagogical frameworks. These strategies benefit all students, contributing to broader discussions on inclusive higher education practices.

Keywords: ADHD · Higher Education · Digital Design · Neurodiversity

1 Introduction

Attention Deficit/Hyperactivity Disorder (ADHD) is a prevalent neurodevelopmental condition, affecting executive function, attention, and emotional regulation. ADHD is classified into three types: hyperactive-impulsive, inattentive, and combined. The hyperactive-impulsive type often presents with fidgeting, excessive talking, and impulsive responses; the inattentive type (more common in girls and adults) impairs attention, the ability to follow instructions, and working memory, whilst increasing distractibility; and the combined type exhibits both symptom clusters [1]. Co-occuring conditions, such as anxiety or depression, further complicate many aspects educational pathways [8,19].

This case study is situated in Germany, where, as in most European countries, the prevalence of ADHD among higher education students remains poorly

Published by Springer Nature Switzerland AG 2026
C. Maciel et al. (Eds.): INTERACT 2025 Workshops, LNCS 16478, pp. 29–38, 2026.
https://doi.org/10.1007/978-3-032-22934-2_3

documented. Historical patterns of underdiagnosis, privacy regulations, and the absence of standardised tracking mechanisms have resulted in a fragmented understanding of prevalence [7]. As a benchmark, approximately 6% of the college student population in the United States is diagnosed with ADHD [11]. However, research suggests [17] that even where prevalence rates are documented, ADHD symptoms may be more common in student populations than available evidence indicates, due to underdiagnosis and limited awareness.

Although ADHD is not classified as a learning disability, it significantly impacts academic performance through challenges with focus, organisation, time management, and executive function [19]. Despite its relevance, academic experiences of students with ADHD in higher education remain underexplored [5].

This case study is motivated by lived experience with ADHD and a commitment to improving inclusion and accessibility in higher education. It is situated at CODE University of Applied Sciences, an institution that diverges from traditional German academic models through its self-directed pedagogical approach, emphasising students autonomy and adaptive learning pathways. Whilst this framework offers opportunities for personalised learning, it may also present distinct challenges for students whose executive functioning differences could interact in complex ways with such learning environments. By examining student experiences in digital design and technology related study programmes at CODE, this exploratory study explores how higher education institutions moving towards new pedagogical approaches, e.g. [20], can adapt teaching and learning practices to reduce barriers that prevent students with ADHD from thriving.

2 Background

2.1 ADHD Educational Impact

Recognised as a medical condition in the 20th century [12], ADHD is a developmental impairment of the brain's self-management system [19]. Though commonly perceived as a childhood disorder, symptoms often persist into adulthood. Despite research focusing largely on children's learning [18], ADHD is neither a learning disability nor does it affect intelligence [19].

ADHD impacts students through difficulty maintaining attention to detail, frequent careless errors, challenges sustaining focus during lectures or reading, struggles with task prioritisation, and avoidance of tasks requiring sustained mental effort [19]. Notably, attention patterns can be paradoxical: whilst individuals with ADHD struggle with routine or uninteresting tasks, they can exhibit hyperfocus, intense concentration on activities that capture their interest [2]. Higher education students with ADHD face significantly lower grades and higher dropout rates compared to peers without ADHD [10]. Challenges extend beyond academics to navigating support services, managing workloads, and coping with stigma [13], often contributing to lifelong underachievement and unrealised potential [16].

In Germany, federal and state laws mandate equal opportunities for students with disabilities, including ADHD. The Federal Participation Act and Higher

Education Framework Act require accommodations such as modified assessments and accessible learning environments [4]. Yet implementation varies across institutions, resulting in inconsistent support.

2.2 Innovative Pedagogy Context

The innovative educational structure adopted in this study context employs a flexible learning model based on multidisciplinary, project-based learning that addresses real-world challenges [15]. Curriculum delivery is organised around Learning Units (LUs), which are teaching and learning events associated with modules, typically held in person. LUs range from traditional lectures and hands-on workshops to self-directed projects that apply acquired knowledge.

Lecturers can be full-time professors or freelance practitioners with a notable expertise in their fields. They have autonomy in selecting tools and methods for content delivery. For example, some user interface design sessions are delivered on commercial tools, familiarising students with current industry-standard software. Other lecturers facilitate project activities on collaborative online whiteboard platforms, whilst others adopt a flipped classroom approach [3], wherein students access pre-recorded materials in advance and attend LUs to apply that knowledge. Students from three study programmes, Software Engineering, Business Management, and Digital Design and Innovation, may enrol in modules from any programme, resulting in frequent cross-programme attendance within LUs. Students have flexible access to one-to-one and project group sessions with lecturers.

This flexible and personalised educational approach tend to attract students with ADHD who have experienced frustration with traditional educational systems characterised by large lecture halls and impersonal educator-student relationships. However, currently accommodation policies for students with diverse needs focus primarily on examinations, allowing them to propose alternative assessment formats in consultation with module coordinators. Provisions for ongoing support within LUs remain limited.

3 Methodology

With the objectives to understand challenges and strategies by students with ADHD to navigate the flexible and self-directed learning at CODE, a focus group was organised with students who have an ADHD diagnose.

Participants were recruited through posts on the workplace communication tool, outlining the research objectives, participant requirements, session duration, and mentioning that refreshments and fidget items would be provided. Preliminary individual conversations were conducted with potentially interested participants to inform about the activity. All participants received and informed consent forms and information sheets prior to the session.

A focus group format was deemed appropriate as it leverages the tendency for individuals with ADHD to benefit from associative thinking, where hearing others' experiences can trigger additional memories and insights. In addition, a group setting creates a more comfortable environment for sharing experiences compared to individual interviews.

The session was facilitated by a student, under the guidance and supervision of two researchers. Participants were asked about how they prepare themselves for the LU sessions, helpful strategies adopted, reasons why they would stop joining LUs, how they feel about approaching the lecturers and how the ideal teaching/learning experience would look in their opinion. The discussions were recorded and transcribed for further qualitative analysis.

The session was conducted at the university campus in a room arranged with chairs in a circle formation. A central table provided refreshments and fidget items, whilst a television screen displayed current questions to support participants with short-term memory challenges.

4 Results

The focus group session lasted 2.5 h with a break. It comprised five participants (three females, two males; mean age = 27.8 years) representing three study programmes: Software Engineering (n = 2), Digital Design and Innovation (n = 2), and Business Management (n = 1). The reluctance to self-identify due to fear of stigma represents a known challenge in ADHD research [9] and likely influenced the limited participant pool in this study.

Anonymised transcriptions and consent forms were returned to participants individually, following review and scanning. To ensure anonymity, participants were designated as Participant 1–5 (P1–P5).

4.1 Data Analysis

The findings were structured temporally: 'Before LU', 'During LU', and 'After LU'. A colour-coding system was employed to categorise notes: white for titles, red for negative experiences, green for positive experiences, blue for thoughts, and purple for feelings. Notes containing direct quotes were tagged with the corresponding participant's number. Following the initial organisation, analytical comments were added incorporating participants' verbatim quotes and observed emotional responses. Responses to the final question envisioning an ideal LU environment were analysed through separate affinity mapping to identify alignment and divergence between actual and desired experiences.

The structured data was then represented as empathy maps [6], a method that encompasses thoughts, seeing, hearing, doing, pains, and gains of the target group, as illustrated in Fig. 1. Notes from the 'ideal experience' scenario were integrated to the diagram.

4.2 Main Findings

The data suggest that students with ADHD struggle to navigate the flexible educational system, often feeling overwhelmed by inconsistent resources across modules and study programmes. Most reported challenges occur during LUs.

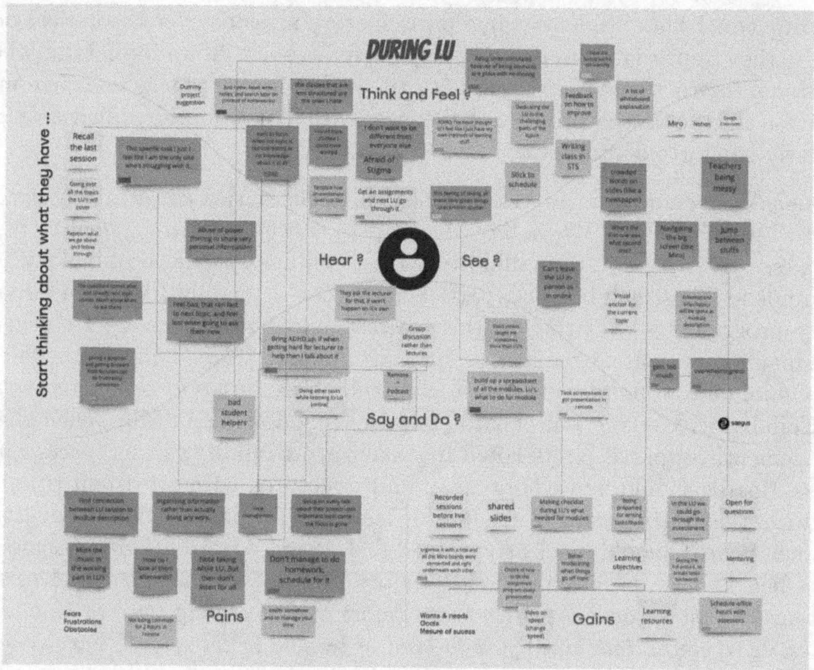

Fig. 1. Illustrative diagram used for data analysis. It represents an Empathy Map for the phase 'During the LU', adopting a colour code for notes for negative or positive experiences, thoughts and feelings.

A significant gap exists in structured, holistic support for students with ADHD. Many students must approach each lecturer individually to negotiate accommodations. Whilst some participants felt comfortable disclosing their condition, others hesitated due to fear of stigma: *"I do not want to be different from everyone else."* (P3).

Participants praised the flipped classroom format [3], which transforms LUs into workshops or discussions. However, this approach presents a challenge: as students gain access to pre-recorded materials, attendance tends to decline [14].

Before the LUs. LU registration at the beginning of each semester emerges as a significant source of anxiety. Students with ADHD employ various preparatory strategies, such as mapping the semester by first articulating their goals, then reviewing LU and module descriptions to identify connections and understand expectations. Several participants reported initially registering for 'everything' to alleviate anxiety, subsequently withdrawing from some modules. Faculty guidance through one-to-one sessions to select and prioritise modules is particularly valued at this stage.

During the LUs. Students value participatory sessions over theoretical ones. Whilst they appreciate discussions, they prefer smaller group formats to whole-classroom interactions. Consistent with the literature [19], focus and time management emerge as the primary challenges, with repetition identified as a particularly supportive strategy.

Focus: As documented in ADHD research, focus varies considerably according to interest level: *"When the LU itself is super interesting, then it is like the sweet time."* (P5). Unfamiliarity with discipline-specific terminology (P1) can impede focus maintenance, particularly when attending LUs from different study programmes. Relating to this interest-driven attention [2], P1 suggests that mandatory content requires additional support: *"Should have more help for something that is mandatory"*, such as providing examples of completed work.

Collaborative online whiteboard platforms (e.g. FigJam or Miro) can enhance engagement, yet participants noted that navigating infinite canvas spaces causes stress. Boards should be well organised and structured with consistent titles and headings that align with LU agendas or learning objectives, whilst connections between boards should be clearly defined and described. Additionally, some students benefit from previewing boards before LUs to familiarise themselves with content: *"I just go over the Miro board before the class, and tried to look at the topics we're gonna talk about just to kind of be able to follow."* (P1).

Following the self-directed learning model, lecturers make extensive resources available for reading and learning. However, participants indicated that resources across modules and study programmes require more consistent organisation.

Time Management: Although time management is a typical challenge for students with ADHD, participants also identified lecturers' time management as problematic. Lecturers must balance time between addressing questions about curriculum delivery and supporting students' knowledge application in projects. This balance is particularly important because assessments are based on individual submissions rather than group project outcomes.

A common issue reported was lecturers dedicating excessive time to specific project questions, deviating from the LU's original agenda. Additionally, participants expressed a desire to receive formative feedback on individual assessments within LUs, comparable to the feedback provided for group projects.

Consistent Structure and Repetition as Supportive Strategies: Participants praised the practice of recapping previous sessions content before introducing new material. They suggested consistently labelling the topics across learning objectives, teaching material and resources: *"This is our topic if you want to cover, and this is the learning resources that could help with this topic."* (P3). Repeating and maintaining consistent visual anchors for current topics in slides and boards-such as consistent slide titles-helps students orient themselves. Clear verbal signposting when transitioning to new topics was also identified as beneficial.

After the LUs. This phase involves transitioning from LUs to assessments. Some students reported difficulty connecting LU content with module descriptions, which are sometimes written at a more abstract level to accommodate ongoing developments in the field.

When initial responses from lecturers were unclear, students requested repeated one-to-one sessions. However, they avoid explicitly mentioning that questions have been previously answered, instead rephrasing queries to circumvent feelings of guilt or shame about their memory challenges. To address this, faculty members could compile frequently asked questions and distribute them to all students prior to assessments, normalising the need for clarification.

As coping strategies, students reported creating to-do lists or spreadsheets before assessments, marking tasks as completed to generate feelings of accomplishment and satisfaction.

The ideal teaching and learning experience provides students with a clear list of topics required to cover all learning objectives, with all related materials explicitly mapped to each topic. This includes pre-recorded teaching content that students can watch at their own pace. Participants suggested organising content in a serialised format, akin to a television series, with each episode representing one discrete topic.

Assessment preparation emerged as a critical concern. Students requested dedicated preparation time within the LU schedule and expressed preference for a backwards design strategy: first examining a complete exemplar, then deconstructing it into component tasks. Consequently, access to previous student assessments as examples and step-by-step templates guiding progression towards completed work was deemed highly desirable. Additionally, participants advocated for flexible submission formats, such as essays, presentations, or software demonstrations.

5 Discussion

5.1 Organisational Issues

In compliance with regulations, the university provides flexibility for assessments. Any student can propose alternative assessment formats and discuss these with module coordinators, provided the work can be evaluated against the learning objectives. However, this option is rarely utilised. According to [13] and reinforced by the data, students refrain from approaching lecturers to avoid potential stigma or humiliation. Therefore, two distinct measures are needed: a) implementing a proactive support system whereby all educators are informed of accommodation needs in advance; b) fostering an institutional culture that actively positions the university as an inclusive environment, where differences are not only welcomed but celebrated and leveraged as strengths.

5.2 Tackling Pedagogical Challenges

Whilst self-directed and project-based learning approaches can benefit students' engagement and sense of purpose, tapping into their ability to hyperfocus [2] on topics of genuine interest, students have varying needs for structured learning. Consistency throughout curriculum delivery and one-to-one support emerge as crucial aspects for students with ADHD. The project-based learning approach at CODE also requires lecturers to balance efforts between supporting knowledge application in projects and preparing students for individual assessments [15].

A lecturers' guideline would be beneficial for creating teaching and learning resources, ensuring consistency across media, platforms, and, where possible, modules and study programmes. Such guidance should support lecturers in designing structured interactive learning experiences that trigger reflections and discussions on fundamental knowledge, whilst maintaining focus on enabling students to tackle assessments with confidence. Strategies for reinforcing concepts, making connections, and transitioning between topics should be consistently applied.

The ideal teaching and learning experience described by participants featured templates and step-by-step guidance through design processes. As a pedagogical challenge, templates should not pose a constraint that limits students' creativity and ability to adapt acquired knowledge to their project's context. Although some modules and LUs already adopt the design process template strategy [15], this approach has not yet been formally validated with students nor implemented consistently across modules or study programmes.

These recommendations, however, reflect only the student perspective, without lecturers' input on what is feasible and appropriate. Therefore, more comprehensive research is needed to develop inclusive teaching and learning practices that balance student needs with pedagogical constraints.

6 Conclusion

Despite its exploratory nature and limited scope, this study demonstrates that self-directed, project-based pedagogy alone does not ensure comprehensive inclusion of students with ADHD, revealing the complex interplay between providing flexible learning environments and the need for structured support.

The findings reveal critical tensions in innovative pedagogical models: whilst flexibility enables hyperfocus on topics of genuine interest, students with ADHD require consistent resource organisation, clear structural anchors, and explicit guidance for individual assessments. Simple interventions, such as providing learning materials in advance, offering exemplars of completed work, and clearly signposting topic transitions, can significantly reduce anxiety and support focus. Equally important is fostering an inclusive institutional culture that reduces stigma and normalises accommodation requests.

Although situated within CODE's distinctive educational model, the challenges identified and strategies proposed extend beyond this single context. Universities adopting flexible or project-based learning approaches face similar imperatives to balance autonomy with structure. Despite limitations in scale and perspective, this case study offers insights for designing inclusive learning environments that primarily address the needs of neurodivergent students thereby potentially benefiting all learners.

References

1. American Psychiatric Association: Diagnostic and Statistical Manual of Mental Disorders, 5th edn. American Psychiatric Association Publishing, Washington, DC (2020)
2. Ayers-Glassey, S., Smilek, D.: The relations between hyperfocus and similar attentional states, adult ADHD symptoms, and affective dysfunction. Curr. Psychol. **43**, 11254–11266 (2024). https://doi.org/10.1007/s12144-023-05235-3
3. Bergmann, J., Sams, A.: Flip your classroom: reach every student in every class every day. Int. Soc. Technol. Educ. (2012)
4. BMAS: Extrat of federal law 2016 teil i nr. 66, VOM 29. dezember 2016 (in German) (2016). https://www.bfarm.de/SharedDocs/Downloads/DE/Kodiersysteme/BTHG.pdf?__blob=publicationFile. Accessed 28 May 2025
5. DuPaul, G.J., et al.: academic trajectories of college students with and without ADHD: predictors of four-year outcomes. J. Clin. Child Adolescent Psychol. 1 (2021). https://doi.org/10.1080/15374416.2020.1867990
6. Ferreira, B., Silva, W., Oliveira, E., Conte, T.: Designing personas with empathy map. In: Proceedings of the 27th International Conference on Software Engineering and Knowledge Engineering, pp. 501–505 (2015)
7. Ginsberg, Y., Quintero, J., Anand, E., Casillas, M., Upadhyaya, H.P.: Underdiagnosis of attention-deficit/hyperactivity disorder in adult patients: a review of the literature. primary Care Companion or CNS Disord. **16**(3), 23591 (2014)
8. Gormez, A., Kocer, E., Kurtulmus, A., Kirpinar, I.: Prevalence of ADHD and comorbid conditions among university students. Eur. Psychiatry **41**(S1), S475–S476 (2017)
9. Grimes, S., Southgate, E., Scevak, J., Buchanan, R.: University student perspectives on institutional non-disclosure of disability and learning challenges: reasons for staying invisible. Int. J. Incl. Educ. **23**(6), 639–655 (2019)
10. Henning, C., Summerfeldt, L.J., Parker, J.D.: ADHD and academic success in university students: the important role of impaired attention. J. Atten. Disord. **26**(6), 893–901 (2022)
11. Hotez, E., Rosenau, K.A., Fernandes, P., Eagan, K., Shea, L., Kuo, A.A.: A national cross-sectional study of the characteristics, strengths, and challenges of college students with attention deficit hyperactivity disorder. Cureus **14**(1), e21520 (2022). https://doi.org/10.7759/cureus.21520
12. Janice Rodden, W.D.: The History of ADHD and Its Treatments—additudemag.com (2019). https://www.additudemag.com/history-of-adhd/. Accessed 27 May 2025
13. Lefler, E.K., Sacchetti, G.M., Del Carlo, D.I.: ADHD in college: a qualitative analysis. ADHD Attent. Deficit Hyperact. Disord. **8**, 79–93 (2016)
14. MacKay, J.R.: Show and 'tool': how lecture recording transforms staff and student perspectives on lectures in higher education. Comput. Educ. **140**, 103593 (2019)
15. Piccolo, L., Buzzo, D., Knobel, M., Gunasekera, P., Papathoma, T.: Interaction design as project-based learning: perspectives for unsolved challenges. In: Proceedings of the 5th Annual Symposium on HCI Education, pp. 59–67 (2023)

16. Rivas-Vazquez, R.A., Diaz, S.G., Visser, M.M., Rivas-Vazquez, A.A.: Adult ADHD: underdiagnosis of a treatable condition. J. Health Serv. Psychol. **49**(1), 11–19 (2023)
17. Shanbhag, P., Nayak, R.: PMH74 - prevalence of self-reported adult ADHD symptoms among university students: a multidisciplinary comparison. Value Health **18**(3), A128 (2015). https://doi.org/10.1016/j.jval.2015.03.746, https://www.sciencedirect.com/science/article/pii/S1098301515008037
18. Spiel, K., Hornecker, E., Williams, R.M., Good, J.: ADHD and technology research–investigated by neurodivergent readers. In: Proceedings of the 2022 CHI Conference on Human Factors in Computing Systems, pp. 1–21 (2022)
19. Thomas, B.E.: The definition of ADHD: new insight into symptoms, causes—additudemag.com (2022). https://www.additudemag.com/adhd-definition/. Accessed 27 May 2025
20. Vorvoreanu, M., Gray, C.M., Parsons, P., Rasche, N.: Advancing UX education: a model for integrated studio pedagogy. In: Proceedings of the 2017 CHI Conference on Human Factors in Computing Systems, pp. 1441–1446 (2017)

Usability Evaluation of a Project-Based Learning Management System at IIIT Pune

Amrut Pathane, Anurag Kawade, Omkar Dhumal, Mohd Samar Bin Mahtab, Priya Jadhav, and Shrikant Salve(✉)

Department of Computer Science and Engineering, Indian Institute of Information Technology, Pune, Pune, India
shrikant@iiitp.ac.in

Abstract. Students undertake projects at various levels, from first year to final year, as an integral part of their academic curriculum. Many institutes use MS Excel and Google forms to manage these project activities which is a very tedious task. But there are many project management issues with these tools like limited data capacity, slow performance, manual validation, integrity (easy to break), poor support for multi-user support, limited automation and security, not scalable for growing datasets. To solve these problems, we have developed a project management system (website), especially for our institute- Indian Institute of Information Technology, Pune, India. This tool was designed and developed by applying the Nielsen's Ten Usability Heuristics. This research paper briefly discusses the proposed system and mainly focused on usability evaluation of it. Twenty four participants including BTech, MTech, PhD students and Faculty were involved in usability evaluation of this prototype using SUS scale. The mean SUS score of all participants is 86 out of 100, which is very good. This suggests that proposed system is a highly usable project management tool.

Keywords: Usability Evaluation · Project Management System · SUS

1 Introduction

1.1 Project-Based Learning at IIIT Pune

Project-based learning is a fundamental component of the curriculum at the Indian Institute of Information Technology, Pune (IIIT Pune), across both undergraduate (BTech) of duration four year (eight semesters) and postgraduate (MTech) of duration two years (four semesters) programs. Students engage in structured project work starting from the early semesters, continuing through to graduation. These academic projects are broadly classified as either minor or major projects. The BTech students project journey begins in the fourth semester with Minor Project I, followed by Minor Projects II and III in the fifth

Published by Springer Nature Switzerland AG 2026
C. Maciel et al. (Eds.): INTERACT 2025 Workshops, LNCS 16478, pp. 39–51, 2026.
https://doi.org/10.1007/978-3-032-22934-2_4

and sixth semesters, respectively. In the seventh semester, students undertake either a six-month industry internship or initiate Major Project I, which continues as Major Project II in the eighth semester. MTech students follow a similar progression, beginning with minor projects in the first and second semesters, and continuing with major projects or internships in the third and fourth semesters.

The structure and coordination of minor projects vary by semester. In the fourth semester, BTech students individually work on Minor Project I. Instead of forming groups or selecting faculty mentors, each student develops a project idea independently and prepares a detailed presentation. These presentations are evaluated by a panel assigned by the department. From the fifth semester onward, students undertake Minor Projects II and III in groups of 4–5 members. For these, students are required to submit project details, including domain, group members, and ranked faculty preferences via a Google Form. Faculty members manually review the incoming requests, typically using Excel sheets, and either accept or pass a group based on their specialization and availability. This manual coordination process becomes increasingly complex and lacks transparency, especially when faculty must process large volumes of preferences and coordinate across semesters and departments.

Students face many issues, such as the absence of a centralized tracking and communication platform, which leads to confusion about project status, mentor assignment, and coordination. For faculty, managing preference-based allocations manually is time-consuming and often results in uneven workloads. To streamline this workflow, we need to develop a web based solution for Student Project Management System at IIIT Pune to digitize every stage of the project life-cycle, from group formation and faculty allocation to administrative oversight. The system should aim to reduce manual effort, ensure fairness, and improve transparency by offering structured, role-specific features, including integrated communication tools.

1.2 Need for a Digital Solution

Managing academic projects has long been a core administrative activity in engineering institutions. As the number of students and projects increases, traditional methods of coordination based on spreadsheets and forms become inefficient, error-prone, and difficult to scale. Many institutions, including IIIT Pune, continue to rely on tools such as MS Excel and Google Forms, which offer limited automation, lack robust data validation, and are poorly suited for multi-user collaboration. The project management system may involve several critical tasks: forming student groups, submitting and reviewing faculty preferences, assigning mentors, and setting up evaluation panels. When performed manually or semi-digitally, these steps introduce delays, inconsistencies, and a lack of accountability, especially in larger cohorts. Common issues include students joining multiple groups, faculty being overloaded with requests, and administrators having to manually reconcile preferences or modify data. These challenges not only slow down operations but also compromise fairness and diminish the overall experience for all stakeholders. In response to these persistent issues there is need to develop centralized project management platform tailored for academic institutions. The system can be designed to support students, faculty, and administrators throughout the entire project lifecycle, offering automation, real-time communication, and structured workflows to ensure efficiency, transparency and usability. To further investigate this we are investigating what other have done in this area.

2 Related Work

We found some related work in the literature, which is discussed in this section. Akinyemi et al. [1] presented an early model of a Students Project Management and Allocation System aimed at reducing the inefficiencies in manual project allocation. Their work focused primarily on automating the selection process and proposed a rule-based algorithm to match students with supervisors, though it lacked integration with academic workflows and reporting tools. Soms et al. [2] proposed a web-based project management system tailored to undergraduate students, incorporating features such as document upload, supervisor comments, and progress tracking. While functional, their system was limited by the lack of a structured evaluation methodology and did not address administrative reporting or data analytics. Inegbedion et al. [3] designed a database system for cataloging students' projects to improve technical and retrieval. Although effective for project storage, the system did not extend into real-time interaction or supervision features critical for managing active project lifecycles. Fakoya et al. [4] implemented a final year project record management system. Their system included student registration and document management capabilities, but was restricted to local use and did not incorporate cloud-based or scalable infrastructure, which limits its adoption in larger institutions. Ram [5] conducted a broad survey on existing Student Project Management Systems, highlighting common challenges such as low system usability, poor documentation, and security issues. However, the study was limited to descriptive analysis and did not propose any architectural solutions or novel improvements.

Olayinka [6] recently developed a more advanced Student Project Management System that introduced multi-role user authentication and enhanced project tracking. This system marks a significant improvement by including supervisor feedback loops and dashboard visualizations, although it is still in development and lacks peer-reviewed validation. In a broader educational context, Gu et al. [7] explored interdisciplinary learning through a combination of Project-Based and Research-Based Learning approaches. While their work is not directly focused on system implementation, it provides a pedagogical foundation that supports the necessity of project management in fostering student-centered learning environments. Anugrah et al. [8] emphasized the importance of character education through project-based learning management. Their model outlines a framework for managing student projects in a values-driven curriculum, which complements the project management by highlighting the role of project management in holistic student development. Finally, Perez-Perez et al. [9] contributed a sustainability model in healthcare project contexts, offering insights into long-term project viability and stakeholder engagement. Though domain-specific, some of their principles such as modular system design and dynamic resource allocation are conceptually relevant to the scalability aspects of project management platforms.

However, most of the existing systems discussed in the literature either lack real-time collaboration, role-based access control, or are not tailored for academic project workflows. The current Excel-based system was found to be error-prone, difficult to manage, and not secure for handling student data. After interacting with students, faculty, and administrators, we observed common concerns such as lack of transparency in group allocation, manual errors during evaluations, and absence of centralized communication. These limitations showed the need for a structured and automated system.

2.1 Comparison with Existing Project Management Tools

Mainstream project management tools such as Trello [10], ClickUp [11], and Notion [12] offer robust capabilities for task tracking and collaboration. However, they are designed for general-purpose and professional environments and thus lack features specific to academic project workflows like IIIT Pune discussed in section above. Also, these platforms do not support education-specific roles (students, faculty, administrators) or institutionally aligned workflows such as faculty preference-based allocation, academic group constraints, or evaluation panel configuration. For example, commercial platforms do not provide built-in mechanisms for preference-based faculty assignment, structured validation of group formation rules, or faculty-to-group interaction histories.

Although AI-powered functionalities, such as intelligent suggestions or automated reminders, are available in some tools, they are typically focused on improving productivity rather than academic coordination. The student project management system should incorporates domain-specific rules, role-sensitive dashboards, and integrated communication channels to support project-based learning at scale. Therefore, while commercial platforms are flexible and widely adopted in industry, the proposed system should address the pedagogical and administrative gaps that are critical in academic contexts, offering a scalable, structured, and education-focused alternative. The next section provides the methodology used for development of the proposed student project management system especially designed for IIIT Pune.

3 Methodology

To address the issues identified during the literature study, we have proposed a website for student project management at IIIT Pune. We named it SPMS@IIITP, a Student Project Management System. In addition, we carried out a usability evaluation of SPMS@IIITP to test its usability. The methodology therefore includes both the design and development of the system and a usability evaluation phase using the System Usability Scale (SUS). Together, these steps allow us to assess how effectively SPMS@IIITP supports project-based learning workflows for students, faculty, and administrators. The following subsections describe the system design process and the usability evaluation procedure in detail.

3.1 Tools Used: Student Project Management System @ IIIT Pune (SPMS@IIITP)

The development process began with planning and designing the interface through wireframes and prototypes before building the final website. We first created low-fidelity wireframes to sketch out the basic layout of the system. These wireframes helped us decide where different features should be placed and how users would move through the system.

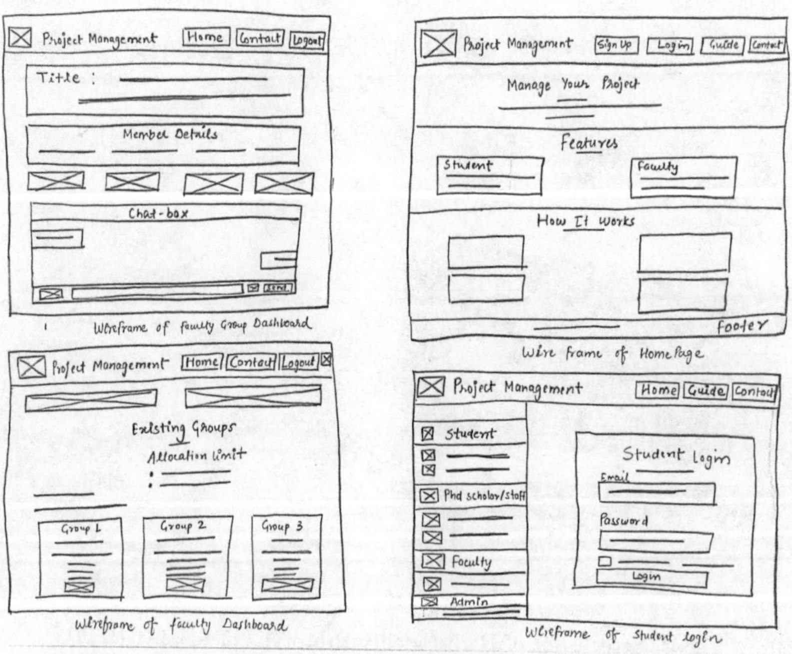

Fig. 1. Screenshot of Low-Fidelity Wireframe of the SPMS@IIITP.

Figure 1 shows low-fidelity wireframes, including (a) a faculty group dashboard with an integrated chat box, (b) the homepage, (c) a faculty dashboard listing existing groups, and (d) the student login page, used to plan the overall layout and user flow. After finalizing the wireframes, we designed a high-fidelity prototype. This included the actual look and feel of the website. The prototype gave stakeholders a better idea of how the final system would look and behave.

Fig. 2. Screenshot of High-Fidelity Prototype of SPMS@IIITP.

The prototype was designed using Figma [13], a collaborative interface design tool that enabled real-time feedback and iterative improvements.

Figure 2 shows the high-fidelity Figma prototype, including (a) the homepage, (b) the faculty login page, and (c) the faculty dashboard with existing groups, with arrows indicating the typical navigation flow between these screens. After the prototype was approved, we started building the actual SPMS@IIITP website.

3.1.1 Working of SPMS@IIITP The system was designed to support three major user roles: students, faculty, and administrators, each with a dedicated interface and features based on their responsibilities. Students can register, form project groups, and submit faculty preferences. Once the groups are allocated with a faculty, students can communicate with the group members and the faculty using the built-in chat feature. Faculty members can review student preferences, choose or pass project groups, monitor ongoing projects, and provide feedback. Administrators are provided with tools to manage the entire process. They can upload and update student data, oversee faculty and project group allocations, and ensure smooth coordination between all parties. They can also perform important actions like setting group allocation limits according to degree or semester for a faculty, creating panels for group evaluation and managing groups. The platform ensures that each user follows a guided workflow, which improves the clarity and consistency of project activities throughout the semester. By following a step-by-step design and development approach, starting from wireframes to final implementation, we were able to build a system that is intuitive, role-based, and addresses the shortcomings of the previous Excel-based manual process. The visual stages and feedback loops during design helped ensure that the final product meets the actual needs of users. Together, these stages helped us develop a structured and user-friendly system, ensuring the final product met the needs of all users.

3.2 System Usability Scale (SUS)

The System Usability Scale (SUS) is a standardized questionnaire developed by John Brooke [14] in 1986 to measure the perceived usability of interactive systems. Since its inception, SUS has gained widespread adoption across both academic and industrial settings due to its simplicity, reliability, and versatility. It provides a quick and effective means of evaluating a system's usability by capturing user impressions across multiple dimensions such as ease of use, functionality integration, and confidence during use. SUS was selected for this study due to its simplicity, reliability, and wide acceptance in both academic and industry usability research. It is particularly effective for evaluating early-stage prototypes involving diverse user groups, as it yields a single, quantifiable score reflecting users' overall perception of system usability [15]. Given SPMS@IIITP's multi-role interface and educational context, SUS provided an efficient yet comprehensive metric for capturing user satisfaction and interface quality across students, faculty, and administrators. SUS consists of a fixed set of ten items that alternate between positive and negative statements. Respondents rate their agreement with each statement using a 5-point Likert scale, ranging from Strongly Disagree (1) to Strongly Agree (5). The structure of the questionnaire is intentionally designed to reduce response bias and ensure comprehensive feedback across usability dimensions.

To evaluate the usability of the SPMS@IIITP, the SUS responses from twenty four participants were analyzed using the standard method developed by John Brooke. The SUS includes ten alternating positive and negative statements rated on a 5-point Likert scale. For each participant, scores were adjusted accordingly: 1 was subtracted from responses to positively worded items (items 1, 3, 5, 7, 9), while negatively worded items (2, 4, 6, 8, 10) were scored by subtracting the response from 5. These adjusted values were summed and multiplied by 2.5 to yield a final SUS score out of 100. It is important to note that this score does not represent a percentage but instead acts as a usability index, where higher scores correspond to better user satisfaction and ease of use.

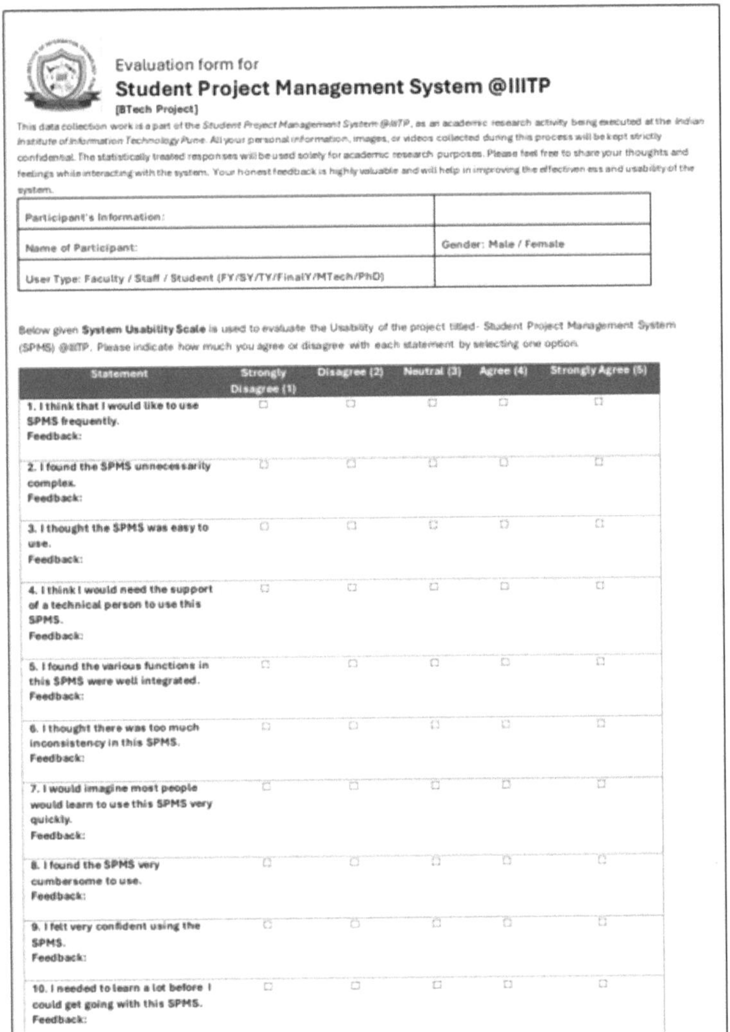

Evaluation form for

Student Project Management System @IIITP

[BTech Project]

This data collection work is a part of the *Student Project Management System @IIITP*, as an academic research activity being executed at the *Indian Institute of Information Technology Pune*. All your personal information, images, or videos collected during this process will be kept strictly confidential. The statistically treated responses will be used solely for academic research purposes. Please feel free to share your thoughts and feelings while interacting with the system. Your honest feedback is highly valuable and will help in improving the effectiven ess and usability of the system.

Participant's Information:	
Name of Participant:	Gender: Male / Female
User Type: Faculty / Staff / Student (FY/SY/TY/FinalY/MTech/PhD)	

Below given **System Usability Scale** is used to evaluate the Usability of the project titled- Student Project Management System (SPMS) @IIITP. Please indicate how much you agree or disagree with each statement by selecting one option.

Statement	Strongly Disagree (1)	Disagree (2)	Neutral (3)	Agree (4)	Strongly Agree (5)
1. I think that I would like to use SPMS frequently. **Feedback:**	☐	☐	☐	☐	☐
2. I found the SPMS unnecessarily complex. **Feedback:**	☐	☐	☐	☐	☐
3. I thought the SPMS was easy to use. **Feedback:**	☐	☐	☐	☐	☐
4. I think I would need the support of a technical person to use this SPMS. **Feedback:**	☐	☐	☐	☐	☐
5. I found the various functions in this SPMS were well integrated. **Feedback:**	☐	☐	☐	☐	☐
6. I thought there was too much inconsistency in this SPMS. **Feedback:**	☐	☐	☐	☐	☐
7. I would imagine most people would learn to use this SPMS very quickly. **Feedback:**	☐	☐	☐	☐	☐
8. I found the SPMS very cumbersome to use. **Feedback:**	☐	☐	☐	☐	☐
9. I felt very confident using the SPMS. **Feedback:**	☐	☐	☐	☐	☐
10. I needed to learn a lot before I could get going with this SPMS. **Feedback:**	☐	☐	☐	☐	☐

Fig. 3. SUS Questionnaire Used for SPMS@IIITP Usability Evaluation.

Figure 3 shows the printed SUS questionnaire that was administered to participants to quantitatively evaluate the perceived usability of SPMS@IIITP. One of the major advantages of SUS is its technology-agnostic nature, which allows it to be used across a wide range of platforms from desktop software and mobile applications to web-based systems. Its ability to generate a single usability score scaled between 0 and 100 also simplifies comparison across systems and user groups. As a result, SUS has become a de facto standard in usability testing, enabling practitioners and researchers to benchmark user experience efficiently and cost-effectively. Given its structured format and ease of administration, SUS is especially suited for academic evaluations where participants span multiple roles with differing technical backgrounds. Its concise questionnaire ensures consistent data collection without overwhelming respondents, making it ideal for environments like IIIT Pune where users include students, faculty, and administrative staff. By yielding a standardized usability score, SUS enables straightforward comparison with established benchmarks and provides clear insights into how effectively a system supports its intended user interactions. This makes it a valuable tool not just for product evaluation, but also for guiding iterative improvements in academic software systems like SPMS@IIITP.

3.3 Participants/Users

The main users of academic project management systems are students, faculty members, and administrative staff. Each user group has different needs: Students want an easy and transparent way to form groups, choose preferences, and track progress. Faculty members need efficient tools to view student preferences, manage group load, provide feedback, and conduct evaluations. Administrators require a centralized dashboard for scheduling, assigning faculty, tracking deadlines, and exporting reports, and an effective system should meet the needs of all these users in a smooth and user-friendly manner.

A total of twenty-four users participated in the usability evaluation of the SPMS@IIITP. These participants were selected from all key user groups to ensure a balanced perspective and meaningful feedback. They included six prefinal year BTech students, five second-year BTech students, five first-year BTech students, three MTech students, one Ph.D. scholar, four faculty members actively involved in supervising projects, and one administrative staff member. This combination of students, faculty members, and an administrator reflects the primary stakeholder groups that will use SPMS@IIITP in regular academic settings. Although the sample size is modest, it captures variation in academic level, role, and experience with project-based learning, enabling a balanced view of the system's usability. Participants were selected carefully based on interest and academic background. Students who showed genuine interest in using the system and had good academic standing were shortlisted to ensure meaningful insights from users who could engage deeply with the system.

3.4 Evaluation Process

Before filling out the SUS questionnaire, all participants were given a short walkthrough of the system's main features. They were then allowed 15–20 min of hands-on interaction to explore core functionalities such as login, group creation, preference selection, and dashboard views. This helped ensure that their feedback was based on actual usage rather than theoretical understanding and that they were comfortable navigating the main features of the system.

The evaluation process was conducted in a structured manner to respect academic schedules and roles. Users were invited to the lab group-wise based on their roles, with BTech first-year students called first, followed by second-year, third-year, MTech, and Ph.D. students. Afterwards, faculty members and the administrator participated so that each group could be addressed with role-specific explanations and demonstrations. Each group was first given a brief introduction about SPMS@IIITP, its purpose, and a demo specific to their user role. Following this, they were allowed a short practice time of around 10–15 min to explore the interface and become comfortable using the system before performing any tasks. This staged approach ensured that participants had sufficient familiarity with the interface, reducing confusion and allowing them to focus on the tasks rather than basic navigation. Following the practice session, each participant was given a set of predefined tasks aligned with their user role. For students, the tasks included creating a new account, logging into the system, forming a group of 4–5 members, checking group status, viewing the group dashboard, and using the chat feature to communicate with their teammates. Faculty members were provided with login credentials beforehand and were asked to access their dashboard, review the list of existing groups and new group requests, choose or pass a group based on given conditions, open a specific group dashboard, and test the chat feature to interact with students; the admin was asked to log in, add student details to the database, check the list of existing groups, manage group members by adding or removing students, allocate or deallocate faculty to specific groups, set group allocation limits for faculty, and create evaluation panels as required.

The entire evaluation session, including explanation, practice, and task completion, lasted approximately 30–45 min per group. Participants were encouraged to interact freely with the system and complete their tasks without external assistance unless they faced any technical issue, which helped simulate realistic usage conditions. This structure ensured that the collected feedback reflected genuine user interaction with SPMS@IIITP. After the hands-on session, participants filled out a printed copy of the SUS questionnaire. The questionnaire consisted of ten statements alternating between positive and negative phrasing, which participants rated on a five-point Likert scale ranging from "Strongly Disagree" to "Strongly Agree," and they were also given the option to write open-ended feedback to share specific praises, difficulties, or suggestions related to their experience. This procedure ensured that feedback was grounded in actual system interaction and that usability insights were drawn from a contextually relevant and demographically diverse sample, combining structured quantitative

Fig. 4. Team members explaining the SPMS@IIITP platform to students.

Fig. 5. Students interacting with the system.

responses with qualitative input to capture a holistic picture of SPMS@IIITP's usability performance. As a token of appreciation for their time and contribution, participants were given chocolates after completing the session. This small gesture helped acknowledge their effort and encouraged positive engagement with the evaluation process. It also reinforced a supportive environment where participants felt their input was valued.

Figure 4 shows the project team explaining the SPMS@IIITP platform and its key features to student participants as part of the usability evaluation session. Figure 5 shows students interacting with the SPMS@IIITP interface on laboratory computers, performing representative tasks such as login, group creation, preference selection, and dashboard exploration.

4 Results and Discussion

The average SUS score for SPMS@IIITP was 84.79, which is significantly above the commonly accepted threshold for excellent usability (80.3). According to established SUS benchmarks, this score is equivalent to an "A" grade, indicating that the system was not only perceived as highly usable but also enjoyed by the users. This high score implies that the interface was easy to navigate, the functionalities were logically arranged, and the system delivered a satisfying experience across diverse user groups. In practical terms, a score above 80 suggests that users are highly likely to use the system again and to recommend it to others, an important marker of user approval and trust in the platform. All responses were collected after hands-on interaction with the system, ensuring that participants' judgments were grounded in actual usage rather than hypothetical assumptions.

Beyond the numerical results, the open-ended feedback provided by participants offered richer context for interpreting the SUS scores. Students appreciated the clean design and the clarity it brought to project group formation and faculty communication. Many reported that the system made the process less stressful and more transparent. Faculty members responded positively to features that allowed for effective monitoring of student groups, project evaluations, and streamlined decision-making. The admin users highlighted the ease of using configuration tools, especially for managing group data and assigning faculty, which was previously a tedious task. These observations confirm that SPMS@IIITP succeeded in delivering a coherent and role-sensitive user experience.

At the same time, some valuable suggestions for improvement emerged from the feedback. A few faculty members recommended visual tweaks such as softer color tones for prolonged viewing comfort. Students mentioned the need for a better onboarding process, especially for first-time users, and additional collaborative features like integration with GitHub or Google Meet. While none of these points indicated critical flaws, they provide direction for enhancing the system's usability further. Overall, the high SUS score, combined with constructive feedback, not only validates the current design of SPMS@IIITP but also offers an informed roadmap for its continued refinement and user-centered evolution.

5 Conclusion

The findings from the System Usability Scale (SUS) evaluation clearly demonstrate that SPMS@IIITP offers a highly usable and effective solution for managing student project workflows. With an average SUS score of 84.79, the system ranks in the top 10% of all systems evaluated using this metric, indicating strong user satisfaction, intuitive design, and functional coherence across all user roles–students, faculty, and administrators. Such a score reflects more than just ease of use; it confirms that the proposed system succeeds in delivering a seamless, purpose-driven experience that aligns well with users' expectations and academic needs. Furthermore, the qualitative feedback gathered from participants complements the SUS results by highlighting the system's strengths in simplifying complex processes such as group formation, project supervision, and administrative oversight. The feedback also emphasized the clarity, responsiveness, and role-based navigation of the platform. While users suggested minor visual and functional enhancements, no major usability concerns were identified, reinforcing the robustness and readiness of proposed system for real-world deployment.

In light of these results, it can be concluded that SPMS@IIITP outperforms the existing system currently used for project management. Its superior usability, efficiency, and user-centered design make it a strong candidate for full-scale implementation. The platform not only addresses the limitations of the current process but also introduces scalable improvements that support better collaboration, transparency, and academic engagement. Therefore, it is well-suited to replace the existing system and can be formally adopted as the primary platform for managing student project workflows at IIIT Pune.

Acknowledgements. The authors extend their sincere gratitude to all the students, faculty members, and administrative staff of IIIT Pune who participated in the process of Usability Evaluation. Their valuable time, honest feedback, and insightful suggestions were instrumental in assessing the usability of the Student Project Management System at IIIT Pune (SPMS@IIITP). This study would not have been possible without their active engagement and support.

References

1. Akinyemi, S.O., Lawal, O.O., Adepoju, O., Adebayo, S.: Students Project Management and Allocation System. iSTEAMS Conf. Proc. **17**(1), 83–92 (2019)
2. Soms, N., Prashanth, S., Preethika, P., Kumar, D.D.: Student project management system. Int. J. Adv. Res. Eng. Sci. Manag. (IJARESM) **9**(3), 1293–1300 (2021)
3. Inegbedion, F., Dickson, O.C.: Development of a database management system for cataloguing students' projects. FUTO J. Ser. **6**(1), 78–89 (2020)
4. Fakoya, J.T., Ibiyomi, M.A., Akcem, A.A.: Students' final year projects record management system. Int. J. Sci. Eng. Technol. **13**(2) (2021)
5. Ram, C.S.: Survey on student project management system. Int. Res. J. Mech. Eng. Inf. Technol. (IRJMEIT) **5**(6) (2018.)
6. Olayinka, S.O.: Student Project Management System. University of Ibadan, Department of Computer Science (2024)
7. Gu, L., Othakanon, L., Jirojphan, W.: Development of primary interdisciplinary education course based on project-based learning combined with research-based learning. Int. J. Soc. Adm. Sci. Res. (IJSASR) **5**(1), 711–722 (2025)
8. Anugrah, F., Wasliman, I., Sauri, R.S., Rostini, D.: Building a characterized generation: project-based management of the pancasila student profile. J. Integr. Elementary Edu. **5**(1) (2025)
9. Pérez-Pérez, I.C., Aguirre-Arias, M., González-Gamez, L.: Proposal of a sustainability model for comprehensive medical centers in the south of the state of Tamaulipas. J.-Microeconomics **8**(14), 1–7 (2024)
10. Fog Creek Software. Trello: Project management software for boards, lists & cards (2011). https://trello.com. Accessed 25 Aug 2025
11. Mango Technologies, Inc. (ClickUp). ClickUp: The everything app for work - tasks, docs, goals & chat (2017). https://clickup.com. Accessed 25 Aug 2025
12. Notion Labs, Inc. Notion: All-in-one workspace for notes, tasks, wikis & databases (2016). https://www.notion.so. Accessed 25 Aug 2025
13. Figma, Inc. Figma: Collaborative interface design tool (2016). https://www.figma.com.0 Accessed 25 Aug 2025
14. Brooke, J.: SUS: A "Quick and Dirty" Usability Scale. In: Jordan, P.W., Thomas, B., Weerdmeester, B.A., McClelland, I.L. (eds.) Usability Evaluation in Industry, pp. 189–194. Taylor & Francis, London (1996)
15. Salve S.V., Bhutkar G.D.: Usability evaluation of mobile app to support road safety. In: Proceedings of the Pilot4HWID Workshop on Pilot Implementation for Testing Human-Work Interaction Designs, INTERACT'21, Bari, Italy (2021)

Enhancing Classroom Learning Through Human-Computer Interaction (HCI) and AI-Driven Problem Generation

Julio Rufo[1](✉), Gregorio Robles[2], Lola De-Acuña[3], and Nicolás Sánchez-Gómez[3]

[1] University of La Laguna, Santa Cruz de Tenerife, Spain
jrufotor@ull.edu.es
[2] University Rey Juan Carlos, Madrid, Spain
gregorio.robles@urjc.es
[3] University of Seville, Seville, Spain
macuna@us.es, nicolassg@us.es

Abstract. Improving student engagement and comprehension in STEM education remains a persistent challenge, particularly when traditional problem-solving exercises fail to resonate with learners' interests. This study explores how integrating Human-Computer Interaction (HCI) principles with AI-driven problem generation can enhance classroom learning outcomes by personalizing educational content. We address the problem of low student motivation by leveraging Large Language Models (LLMs) to create academic problems tailored to individual learners' preferences, hobbies, and motivational drivers. Our approach positions the AI as an interactive agent that dynamically adapts problem contexts using HCI frameworks, fostering a more engaging learning experience. In a controlled classroom experiment, one group received standard textbook problems while another engaged with AI-generated, personalized scenarios-such as engineering challenges embedded in science fiction narratives. Both groups were assessed through pre- and post-activity surveys, classroom participation, and targeted evaluations. Preliminary findings indicate that personalized problem generation significantly boosts student motivation, conceptual understanding, and enthusiasm for learning. Participants also expressed interest in applying this method across other academic subjects. These results suggest that combining generative AI with HCI can create more inclusive, adaptive, and effective learning environments, laying the groundwork for future personalized education systems.

Keywords: Human-Computer Interaction (HCI) · Generative AI · AI in Education · Personalized Learning · Student Engagement · STEM Pedagogy · Educational Technology

C. Maciel et al. (Eds.): INTERACT 2025 Workshops, LNCS 16478, pp. 52–61, 2026.
https://doi.org/10.1007/978-3-032-22934-2_5

1 Introduction

Human-Computer Interaction (HCI) is an interdisciplinary field bridging computer science, cognitive psychology, and design principles to create user-centric computing technologies. Teaching and learning HCI [1] requires an integrative approach that emphasizes theoretical knowledge, practical skills, and sensitivity to human behavior and capabilities. Effective instruction in HCI not only involves traditional educational methodologies, but also requires innovative approaches to foster creativity, empathy, and technical proficiency among learners.

Teaching HCI effectively begins with imparting foundational theories such as affordances, mental models, usability principles, and user-centered design [3]. Norman's theory of affordances and constraints [7], Shneiderman's Eight Golden Rules of Interface Design [10], and Nielsen's usability heuristics provide structured frameworks to understand interaction [6]. Educators should integrate these theories early, facilitating learners' abilities to critically analyze existing interfaces and predict user interactions.

Figure 1 illustrates the core components that influence student motivation within the classroom environment [2]. At the center of the model is Motivation, which is shaped by five key factors: Autonomy, Recognition, Teaching Method, School Environment, and Relevance and Meaning.

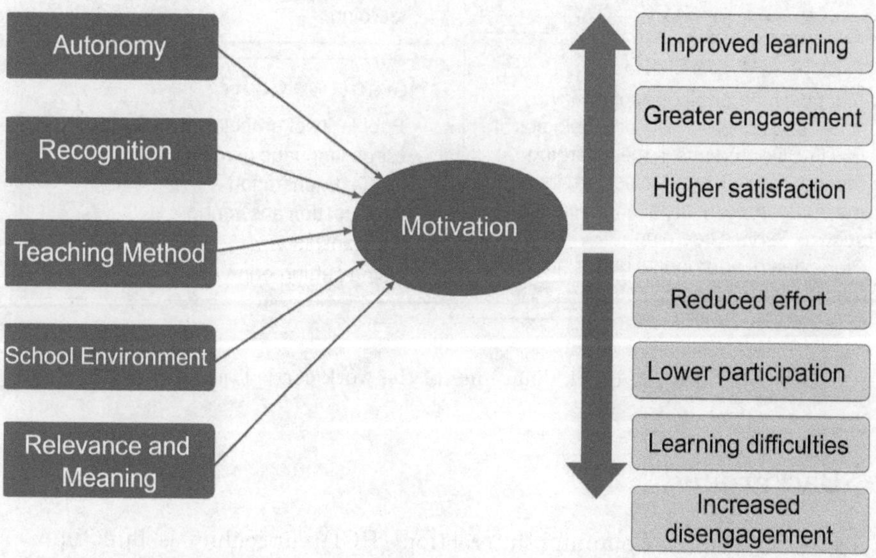

Fig. 1. Components of the students motivation.

When these elements are positively implemented, such as when students are given meaningful choices, receive constructive feedback, engage with interactive and inclusive teaching methods, learn in a supportive environment, and perceive the subject matter as personally relevant, they collectively act as catalysts for increased motivation. This is visually represented by the upward green arrow, linked to outcomes such as improved learning, deeper engagement, greater satisfaction, and enhanced academic achievement.

This paper addresses the challenge of making complex problems more accessible and understandable to students. Our primary objective is twofold: first, to enhance student motivation, and second, to analyze the impact of personalized learning approaches.

To achieve these goals, we explore the use of cutting-edge Artificial Intelligence (AI) technologies. By leveraging the latest advancements in AI, we aim to develop innovative methods that can tailor the presentation of problems to individual student needs, thereby fostering a more engaging and effective learning experience. Figure 2 represents the basic blocks of this research and aims to provide insights into how AI can be leveraged to create a more personalized and engaging educational environment.

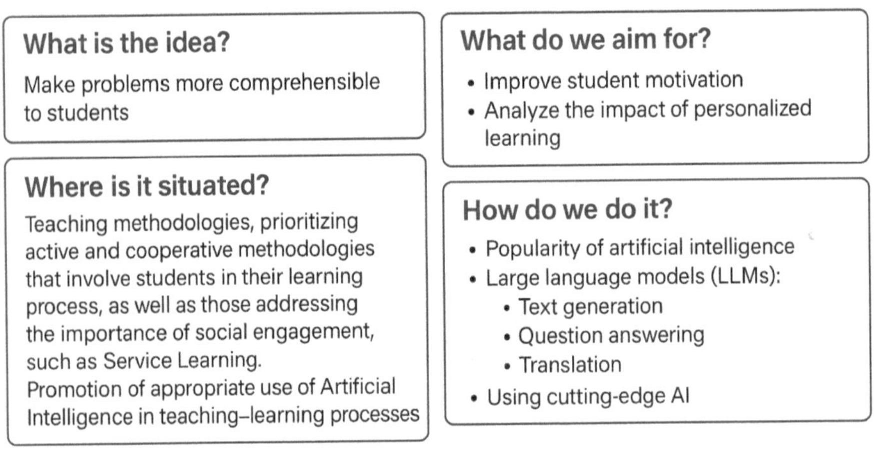

Fig. 2. Block diagramm of the work carried out.

2 Background

A successful Human-Computer Interaction (HCI) curriculum is built upon a diverse blend of instructional methodologies that collectively foster both theoretical understanding and practical competence [4]. To cultivate critical thinking and problem-solving abilities, Project-Based Learning [8,9] plays a central role. By engaging students in collaborative efforts to address real-world design challenges—such as redesigning existing application interfaces using real user feedback—students are encouraged to apply abstract concepts in concrete, meaningful ways.

Complementing this, Active Learning Strategies [5]-including classroom discussions, user observations, usability evaluations, and rapid prototyping-further enhance student engagement. These activities not only reinforce key HCI principles but also create an interactive and reflective learning environment.

Equally important is Experiential Learning [4], which exposes students to authentic professional contexts through internships, participatory user research, and interaction design projects in collaboration with industry partners. These opportunities ground student learning in real-world complexities and help bridge the gap between academic instruction and practical implementation.

To support these pedagogical strategies, leveraging contemporary tools is imperative. Students should gain hands-on experience with prototyping and evaluation platforms such as Figma, Adobe XD, Sketch, Axure, and usability testing software. Exposure to emerging technologies—including Virtual Reality (VR), Augmented Reality (AR), Artificial Intelligence (AI), and voice interfaces-broadens students' understanding of new interaction paradigms and positions them to address the rapidly evolving landscape of digital systems.

Nevertheless, educators face numerous challenges. The pace of technological change, varying student backgrounds, and the need to balance theoretical depth with practical application demand continuous curriculum refinement. Instructors must stay abreast of the latest research and industry practices while providing differentiated instruction that accommodates diverse learning needs. yyy support mechanisms are essential to ensure inclusivity and equity in learning outcomes.

3 Method

To evaluate the impact of generative AI in personalized learning, a comparative study was designed involving two groups: a control group and an experimental group. Both groups followed the same instructional structure, consisting of an initial survey, classroom problem-solving activities, an assessment exam, and a final reflective survey. However, the key distinction lay in how the experimental group leveraged AI to tailor the learning experience.

The process began with all students completing an initial survey designed to gather insights into their motivation toward the subject, personal interests, preferred learning styles, and group work preferences. Questions also explored how willing they were to relate their hobbies to academic content and whether they favored theoretical explanations, practical problem-solving, or hands-on construction activities.

In the control group, this survey served only as a diagnostic tool. Students then participated in standard classroom activities, tackling a predefined set of problems, followed by an exam assessing their grasp of the material. The final survey gathered feedback on their experience, perceived engagement, and learning outcomes.

The experimental group, by contrast, used the initial survey not just diagnostically but as a driver for customization. The responses were fed into a generative AI model designed to create personalized problems. These AI-generated exercises were crafted to align with individual interests and learning preferences. For instance, a student interested in sports might receive physics problems set within athletic contexts, while someone favoring collaborative work might be assigned group-based challenges. These customized exercises were then used in both classroom problem-solving sessions and the assessment exam.

To ensure relevance and coherence, the prompts used to generate these problems followed a structured approach. Each prompt defined the AI's role as a problem creator, described the educational context and learning goals, provided an example for consistency, and included both the student's personal data and the specific topic to be covered.

Following the instructional phase, students in the experimental group also completed a final survey. In addition to reflecting on engagement and comprehension, they were asked to assess the relevance and clarity of the AI-generated content and its impact on their learning motivation.

Throughout the study, data was collected on multiple fronts: exam performance, participation levels, qualitative feedback, and comparative engagement metrics. Educators also reviewed the AI-generated problems for quality, cognitive challenge, and pedagogical alignment. This holistic approach, shown in Fig. 3, allowed for a nuanced understanding of how personalized, AI-driven content could influence learning effectiveness and student satisfaction.

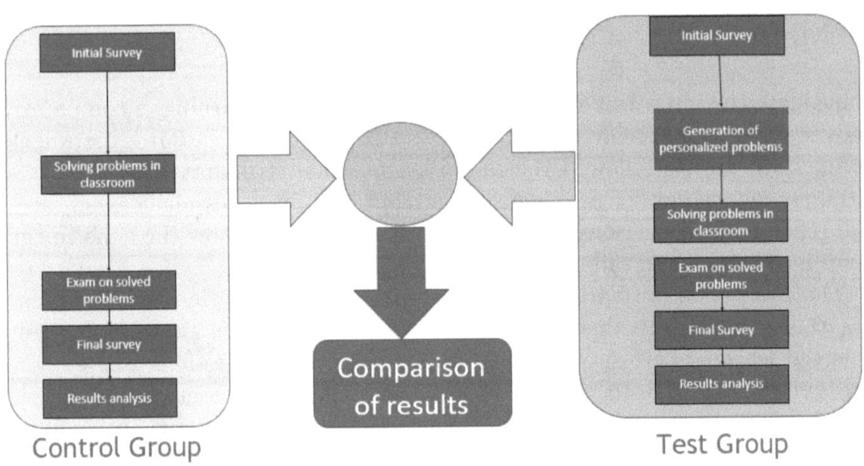

Fig. 3. Methodology diagram of the work carried out.

The design of the AI prompt was critical to the effectiveness of this approach. Each prompt followed a structured format to ensure consistency, relevance, and pedagogical quality. The prompt included a definition of the AI's role, clearly stating that it should act as a problem generator. A brief description of the information provided (i.e., the student's profile) and the expected result, which was a customized academic problem. An example problem, included to guide the tone, format, and cognitive level of the AI-generated content. The data extracted from the student's survey, such as their interests (e.g., sports or music), preferred learning method, and group work inclination. Finally, the academic topic or concept to be addressed, such as Ohm's Law or logical circuit design. By integrating this structured information into the prompt, the AI was able to generate exercises that were not only aligned with the course's learning objectives but also tailored in a way that increased relevance and engagement for each student.

4 Results

An experimental study was carried out with 60 undergraduate students enrolled in an introductory electronics course. Results are presented in Fig. 4 and suggest a positive impact of AI-personalized problem generation on student motivation and academic performance. Participants were randomly divided into two equal groups: a control group and an experimental group, each consisting of 30 students. Initial surveys confirmed that both groups exhibited comparable levels of motivation and interest, establishing a balanced starting point for comparison. The intervention involved the integration of AI-driven personalized problem generation in the experimental group. Following this implementation, student performance and motivation were systematically evaluated.

The findings highlight a clear positive trend among students exposed to personalized AI-generated problems. Engagement levels in the experimental group were significantly higher, with an average rating of 4.3 out of 5-approximately 25% greater than the control group's average of 3.4. In terms of academic performance, students in the experimental group achieved an average problem-solving accuracy of 81.7%, notably outperforming the control group, which averaged 73.2%. Qualitative feedback further reinforced these results, with students expressing appreciation for the contextual relevance and alignment of the problems with their personal interests. Collectively, these outcomes suggest that the use of AI to tailor problem sets to individual student profiles can enhance both motivation and academic success in technical education settings.

5 Discussion

The findings of this study lend compelling support to the hypothesis that personalization in educational content-particularly when enabled by generative AI and grounded in Human-Computer Interaction (HCI) principles-can significantly enhance student motivation and performance. The notable improvements in engagement levels and test scores observed in the experimental group underscore the potential of this approach to address long-standing challenges in STEM

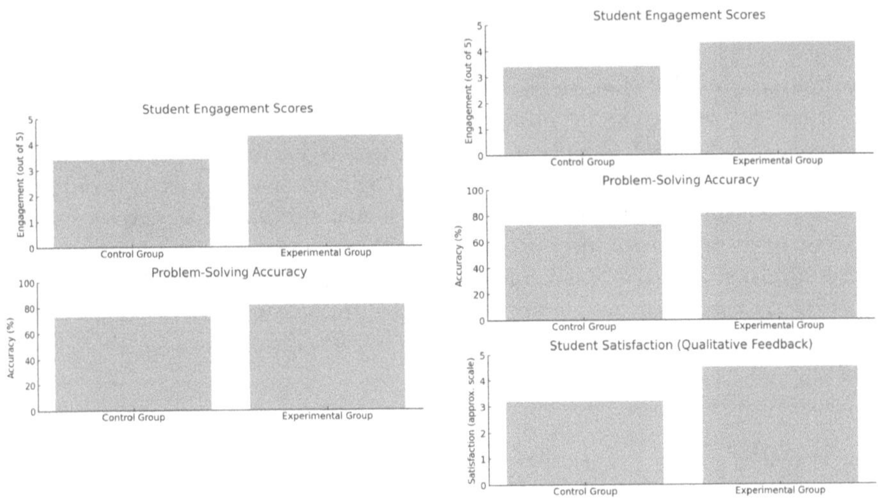

Fig. 4. Key metrics comparing the control and experimental groups.

education, where student disconnection and lack of contextual relevance often hinder learning outcomes.

One of the most salient observations emerging from the study is the way in which contextualization—by aligning problems with students' interests and hobbies—encourages deeper emotional and cognitive involvement. This outcome is consistent with Self-Determination Theory (SDT) [2], which emphasizes the importance of autonomy, competence, and relatedness in fostering intrinsic motivation. By enabling learners to see themselves and their personal context reflected in academic tasks, the AI-driven personalization functioned as a catalyst for greater ownership over the learning process.

Moreover, the success of this approach aligns well with constructivist learning paradigms, which advocate for educational experiences rooted in the learner's prior knowledge and individual meaning-making. Students from the experimental group not only performed better but also reported higher satisfaction, suggesting that personalized content can bridge the gap between abstract concepts and real-world applicability.

From an HCI perspective, the study exemplifies how designing interactions with educational systems—where AI acts as a dynamic partner—can redefine the role of the learner from passive recipient to active participant. The integration of generative AI effectively transformed the AI from a tool into an interactive agent, capable of adapting its outputs based on human input, thereby enhancing the sense of responsiveness and interactivity that is central to HCI.

Despite the encouraging outcomes, several limitations and challenges warrant discussion. The quality of the AI-generated problems is heavily dependent on the design of the prompts. While the current study employed a structured prompting framework, developing high-quality, pedagogically sound prompts at scale remains a non-trivial task, especially in multidisciplinary environments. Inaccurate or overly simplistic problem generation could undermine the benefits of personalization.

The study raises interesting questions about scalability and automation. The current model, while effective, assumes a controlled setting and a relatively small cohort. Implementing similar strategies across larger institutions or diverse educational systems will require robust AI governance frameworks, including quality control, ethical oversight, and transparency in content generation.

Finally, while the experimental group showed notable improvements, long-term retention and the transferability of these gains to other subjects or learning contexts remain areas for future inquiry. The novelty effect of using AI might contribute to short-term engagement, but sustained benefits will depend on integrating these systems into broader pedagogical strategies.

6 Conclusions and Future Research

This study demonstrates the significant potential of integrating Human-Computer Interaction (HCI) principles with generative Artificial Intelligence (AI) to enhance classroom learning experiences. By using survey-based student profiles to generate personalized academic problems, the approach fosters greater engagement, motivation, and academic performance among learners. The experimental results affirm that aligning educational content with students' interests and learning preferences can lead to more meaningful interactions and improved learning outcomes.

The intervention aligns with key theories in educational psychology, including self-determination theory and constructivism, highlighting the value of autonomy and contextual relevance in the learning process. Moreover, the study provides a practical illustration of how AI, when guided by HCI design principles, can act as an adaptive agent capable of transforming traditional instructional models into more personalized and student-centered experiences.

Collaborative learning models represent a rich area for exploration, specifically, how generative AI can facilitate group-based problem creation by accounting for group dynamics, shared interests, and cooperative strategies. In tandem, the development of teacher-AI co-design frameworks could empower educators to participate more actively in shaping prompts and curating AI-generated content, ensuring alignment with pedagogical goals and responsiveness to classroom needs. Additionally, issues of equity and accessibility warrant further investigation. Research should examine how AI-personalized learning tools serve students from diverse backgrounds, including those with learning disabilities or limited access to digital resources.

As AI continues to evolve, its integration with HCI frameworks provides a compelling foundation for designing more responsive, inclusive, and effective educational systems. By addressing current limitations and pursuing these research directions, future educational technologies can better support learners' journeys and contribute to the democratization of high-quality, personalized learning experiences.

Acknowledgments. This study was funded by Universidad de La Laguna with project PIE-INT 2024-31. “Mejora de la motivación del alumnado a través del uso de Inteligencia Artificial Generativa (MM-IA)”.

Disclosure of Interests. The authors state that they have no competing interests. Author Julio Rufo has received research grants from Universidad de La Laguna.

References

1. Churchill, E.F., Bowser, A., Preece, J.: Teaching and learning human-computer interaction: past, present, and future. Human-Comput. Inter. **29**(5–6), 349–378 (2014). https://doi.org/10.1080/07370024.2014.966939
2. Deci, E.L., Ryan, R.M.: Intrinsic motivation and self-determination in human behavior. Springer (1985). https://doi.org/10.1007/978-1-4899-2271-7
3. Wolf, M.: Lessons Learned from Designing Non-traditional Interfaces for Educational Applications in South Africa. In: Kotzé, P., Marsden, G., Lindgaard, G., Wesson, J., Winckler, M. (eds.) INTERACT 2013. LNCS, vol. 8120, pp. 755–763. Springer, Heidelberg (2013). https://doi.org/10.1007/978-3-642-40498-6_70
4. Kim, H., Lee, S.: Experiential learning to teach user experience in higher education: a scoping review. Front. Comput. Sci. **4**, 812907 (2022). https://doi.org/10.3389/fcomp.2022.812907
5. Nawahdah, M., Al-Samarraie, H.: Enhancing HCI education through active learning. In: Proceedings of the 17th International Conference on Education and New Learning Technologies (EDULEARN 2025). IATED (2025). https://library.iated.org/download/NAWAHDAH2025ENH
6. Nielsen, J.: 10 usability heuristics for user interface design (1995). https://www.nngroup.com/articles/ten-usability-heuristics/, nielsen Norman Group
7. Norman, D.A.: Affordance, conventions, and design. Interactions **6**(3), 38–43 (1999). https://doi.org/10.1145/301153.301168
8. Ribu, K., Patel, T.: Systematic integration of project-based learning in an undergraduate human-computer interaction course: a case study. In: Proceedings of the 20th International Conference on Engineering and Product Design Education (EPDE 2018), pp. 220–225. The Design Society (2018)
9. Roldan, W., Ju, W.: Pedagogical strategies for reflection in project-based HCI education with end users. In: Proceedings of the 2021 Designing Interactive Systems Conference (DIS '21), pp. 1134–1145. ACM (2021). https://doi.org/10.1145/3461778.3462113
10. Wong, E.: Shneiderman's eight golden rules will help you design better interfaces (2025). https://www.interaction-design.org/literature/article/shneiderman-s-eight-golden-rules-will-help-you-design-better-interfaces, interaction Design Foundation

Bridging Industry and Academia: Co-Creating Interaction Design and Artificial Intelligence Courses

Mexhid Ferati[1](✉), Rafael M. Martins[2], Juan P. Velásquez[1], Fisnik Dalipi[1], Timmy Öberg[1], and Arianit Kurti[1]

[1] Informatics Department, Linnaeus University, Växjö, Sweden
{mexhid.ferati,juan.velasquez,fisnik.dalipi,timmy.oberg,arianit.kurti}@lnu.se

[2] Computer Science and Media Technology Department, Linnaeus University, Växjö, Sweden
rafael.martins@lnu.se

Abstract. This paper explores the co-creation process between industry and academia in the development of courses within Interaction Design and Artificial Intelligence. Through a collaborative workshop with industry representatives and a survey targeting current students and alumni, we gathered insights into their needs, expectations, and priorities for future educational offerings in these fields. The co-creation process resulted in the development of several new course proposals, which were assessed by students and alumni coming from two bachelor programs. The findings present six courses with descriptions alongside their ratings. We also present qualitative feedback from students and alumni regarding their perceptions and anticipated value of these courses. The study highlights the importance of engaging industry stakeholders, students and researchers in curriculum development to ensure academic relevance and industry alignment. This work contributes to ongoing discussions on collaborative curriculum design in higher education, particularly in fields undergoing rapid change.

Keywords: Co-creation · workshop · survey · courses · Interaction Design · Artificial Intelligence

1 Introduction and Background

Educational practices and curricula development in Interaction Design (IxD) and Artificial Intelligence (AI) are individually well established, with each field benefiting from decades of experience and refinement. As AI becomes increasingly integrated into applications, its influence on IxD is growing (De Silva and Halloluwa, 2025), but there is still a gap in educational literature and curricula that address their intersection and the alignment with expectations and needs from students and the current market. Studies have discussed the value of interdisciplinary AI education, yet most initiatives remain either technically or design-oriented without clear directions of convergence (Kim et al., 2025; Kok et al., 2024). Reviews of curriculum development suggest limited examples

C. Maciel et al. (Eds.): INTERACT 2025 Workshops, LNCS 16478, pp. 62–70, 2026.
https://doi.org/10.1007/978-3-032-22934-2_6

where interaction-focused pedagogy is paired with AI learning outcomes (Ntunka & Maladzhi, 2024). Other works highlight the lack of integration between AI platforms and human-centred approaches in higher education (Azhar et al., 2024; Liu et al., 2024). Design students engaging with smart home technologies revealed that the existing design education does not adequately address current issues in automation and human-machine interdependence (Kuo & Xia, 2023).

As a further challenge, in the evolving landscape of IxD and AI education, academia and industry often find themselves at crossroads, each with different priorities and approaches (Windl, 2022; Wyatt & Piggott, 2019). Traditionally, academic institutions stress theoretical knowledge, encouraging students to investigate foundational ideas and participate in critical thinking, while the industry demands professionals who can apply knowledge to practical solutions that meet urgent market needs. IxD students, for example, may face difficulties articulating their professional roles and expected tasks in industry contexts (Sørum, 2017). A study further emphasizes the need to align AI curricula with evolving job market demands and suggests developing frameworks through closer collaboration between academia and industry (Li et al., 2019). Co-creation with industry can be one way to foster a more synergistic relationship between academia and industry, ensuring that course contents remain relevant and reflective of current industry practices (Laundon, 2023).

This paper reports on a co-creation effort related to the development of advanced courses for two new Master-level educational initiatives: a specialization in Human-Computer Interaction (HCI) and a Master program in Interactive AI Systems. The outcome of the study revealed a list of six courses that were proposed by industry representatives and assessed by student participants. The description of the courses along with their ratings from student surveys, provide a solid foundation for further development and accreditation of the proposed courses.

2 Methodology

The data collection for this study employed two methods: a workshop with companies and a survey with students and alumni. The two methods were applied in sequence, where the survey was used to assess the acceptance of the results from the workshop. By assessing the data from both perspectives, we intended to strengthen the trustworthiness of the research and allow for a richer interpretation of the results, promoting a more holistic and nuanced understanding of the findings through different lenses (Creswell and Creswell, 2022).

2.1 Workshop with Companies

Representatives from four different Swedish companies took part in the workshop, which lasted around three hours and took place within a Swedish university. The size of the companies ranged from small (few employees) to large (several hundreds), and they provide products and services within software design and development, education technologies, and forestry. Two of the participants had a strong background in IxD, which constituted their professional role within their respective companies, while the other two participants had leadership positions.

A visual presentation was created to introduce the central theme of the workshop and the five-step process to be followed, inspired by the Design Thinking approach (Lewrick, Link & Leifer, 2018): *problematisation, ideation, design, sharing* and *closing* (see Fig. 1). During the workshop introduction, participants were informed that the aim was to get their insights and opinions about potential courses on advanced level within the topics of IxD and Interactive AI, contributing to aligning educational offerings with industry needs.

In the *problematisation* phase we set out to understand the participants' needs and visions, using a set of interview cards designed with two categories of questions inspired by the SUE influence framework (2024): (1) current concerns in today's education (pains and comforts of actual professionals) and (2) tomorrow's education (gains and anxieties of new professionals). The *job-to-be-done* presented was to identify what skills and knowledge the industry needs from high-quality future professionals in AI and IxD.

Fig. 1. The five workshop phases conducted with representatives from the industry.

During the *ideation* phase participants were instructed to use post-it notes to express all their ideas for courses and to write down as many ideas as possible. For each idea, they were asked to think about a possible scenario, i.e., expand on what each course would be like, what the main activities would be, the technology to be used, how to use it, etc.

These initial ideas were further expanded during the *designing* phase, where participants were arranged in groups and instructed to propose at least two courses by following a provided template. For each course, participants were requested to indicate how they would help future professionals to be more attractive in the market. The course template had fields such as name of the course, focus (AI/IxD), main skills, and content.[1]

During the *sharing* phase, participants presented the courses they had brainstormed. Each group had 10 min to present their ideas to the audience. Finally, in the *closing* phase, all attendees reflected on the workshop, the main takeaways, and the potential future work.

2.2 Survey with Students and Alumni

A survey comprising 15 questions was designed and distributed to current students and alumni from two bachelor programs at a Swedish university: Interaction Design (IxD) and Web Programming (WP). The IxD program focuses on delivering courses covering the topics of user involvement and understanding their needs, interface requirements,

[1] The survey and workshop materials can be found here: https://osf.io/t6g3f/files

prototyping and evaluation. With strong focus on qualitative methods, the program utilizes approaches such as Participatory Design, User-Centred Design, Design Thinking and Inclusive Design to design usable and accessible interfaces. The WP program focuses on programming and the aim is to create web applications for different platforms using methods that are common in the industry. The education focuses on code quality, security, and testing. Both programs are carried out in close collaboration with the business community.

The first seven questions were demographic and inquired whether the participants were current or former students, which program they were enrolled in, which mode (campus or distance), and whether they are currently employed. Then participants were presented with the six courses that were proposed during the workshop with companies (which are presented in Sect. 3, Results and Discussion). For each course, participants could read a concise overview of its objectives and the knowledge they would acquire. Participants were asked to rate each course in a 5-item Likert scale (*Not Interested* to *Very Interested*) and answer optional open-ended questions about their motivation for the given rating, the content they would like to see in the course, and any other comments. Participants were also encouraged to indicate their preference for the course to be offered on campus, distance or both. Finally, participants could also provide suggestions for other courses within related topics that we had not covered in the survey.

It took approximately 10 min to complete the survey, which was open for 14 days. It was hosted within the university platform and the dissemination was done using emails and Slack. Before starting the survey, the participants were informed about the purpose of the survey, the voluntary nature of participation, and ethical and confidentiality aspects regarding data collection and storing. In total, 61 respondents shared their opinions; 40 from the IxD program and 21 from the WP program.

3 Results and Discussion

3.1 Workshop Outcomes

From the first phase, the discussions revolved around various topics that could be represented into courses, such as AI, accessibility, tools and platforms for learning and prototyping, research and practical skills, etc. As we progressed through the workshop phases, participants were encouraged to focus and propose concrete courses, specifically providing the following: title of the course, focus of the course, skills it develops, content, and anything else they wished to add. Among several course ideas that were proposed and discussed, the following were the main outcomes of this phase:

- **Novel Interaction Methods using AI.** This course proposes a blend of traditional Human-Computer Interaction methods with AI, moving beyond basic aspects like "prompting". Specifically, the course should focus on building interfaces with AI-driven applications to enhance their UX. Additionally, aspects of requirements, prototyping, testing and stakeholder involvement, were suggested as content for the course. Finally, the course should also include mentorship elements that can help strengthen ties with companies.

- **Accessibility/Inclusive Design.** Being aware of the existing accessibility regulations and their increased relevance, participants highlighted the importance of developing and offering a course within accessibility and inclusive design. They explained that the course should focus on a broad spectrum of disabilities, but also include temporary impairment cases (e.g., injury). The course should teach students how to test websites and apps for accessibility issues, fix them, and understand user needs from an accessibility standpoint.
- **Process-based Understanding of an Organisation.** This course was proposed to offer students an understanding of an organisation and their role in it. Specifically, the course should cover aspects of managing and steer processes, and how one becomes an enabler within an organisation. The course should start by offering an overview of the overall organisation process and then moving closer to specific roles and processes.
- **AI Non-functional Requirements.** This course should focus on AI from the non-functional aspects, such as business principles of AI, security aspects, and GDPR as a framework to discuss ethical concerns and regulations. Data integration and transparency should also be covered.
- **Business Agility and AI.** This course should initially cover the fundamentals of understanding business agility, which later should be explored and evaluated in relation to AI and how it will affect it. Students should learn to work under simulated constraints that companies face. Additionally, they should comprehend how companies evaluate progress and outcomes.
- **Tools with AI.** Much of the discussion in the workshop was around AI and how we should teach about the fundamentals of AI. In relation to this, the focus of this course was to improve tools that are currently used by students in the education environment by leveraging recent advances in AI. Specifically, students would practice using tools to generate prototypes. (e.g., Figma, Adobe XD), analyse data (e.g., Microsoft Excel), and presenting (e.g., Microsoft PowerPoint) coupled with recent AI enhancements.

3.2 Survey Outcomes

The aim of the survey with current students and alumni was to gather feedback on the six courses that we identified as most relevant during the workshop, which we described in the previous section. The course that received the overall highest score was Accessibility/Inclusive Design with a mean value of 4.23 (out of 5), followed by Tools with AI (M: 4.07) and Novel Interaction Methods Using AI (3.80). Interestingly, these three courses received the highest rating in the same order by both, Interaction Design) and Web Programming (WP), respondents. This demonstrates strong consensus for these three courses regardless of the program. The means and 95% confidence intervals (CIs) for the ratings of the six courses are shown in Table 1, where the courses are ordered from highest to lowest in terms of perceived importance. The three highest-rated courses are further developed for integration into different study programs.

The open comments provided by some respondents offer further insights into their opinions regarding these courses. Their comments mainly discuss practical AI and IxD aspects, emphasizing the educational needs and desires of students. Students recognize the increasing importance of AI skills in the IxD field, as suggested by one respondent:

"I want to get benefits from AI tools in interaction design as much as possible to save time and effort. It is really important to have the ability to adapt AI tools in our courses."

Table 1. The list of courses with ratings offered by participants.

Course	Mean and 95% CI
Accessibility/Inclusive Design	4.23 ± 0.276
Tools with AI	4.07 ± 0.303
Novel Interaction Methods Using AI	3.80 ± 0.326
Process-based Understanding of an Organization	3.36 ± 0.346
AI Non-functional Requirements	3.33 ± 0.292
Business Agility and AI	3.15 ± 0.329

Students expressed desires to integrate these technologies into practical applications within design, with similar results found in other studies (Cavallin, 2024; Lively and Hutson, 2024). Specifically, they emphasize the need for courses that focus on hands-on projects and case studies, ensuring students can apply theoretical knowledge effectively. These courses should ideally bridge the gap between theory and real-world applications, as one respondent stated:

"I would also like to learn practical methods for integrating AI into business processes to better adapt to evolving customer needs, market trends, and operational challenges."

and another stating:

"Preferably a lot of focus on the practical use of AI."

Considering these expressed needs, students suggest courses focused on AI usage in pitching ideas portfolio development and professional presentation skills. Interestingly, such needs point to a pedagogical shift that prioritizes practical AI fluency and iterative skill development within curricular design. To this end, partnerships with industry could provide valuable resources for further course development.

Reflecting on the difference between IxD and WP respondents, the comments show that IxD students showed a deeper preference for AI integration into design processes, such as user experience enhancement, prototype development, and creative process documentation. Additionally, they emphasized the needs for learning about tools and methodologies within design. WP students, on the other hand, concentrated more on the practical applications like efficiency gains, using AI to streamline workflows for time-saving purposes, portfolio development, and enhancing presentation skills. These comments were in relation to courses: Novel interaction methods using AI, AI-nonfunctional requirements, and Tools with AI. One WP student, however, commented:

"Since generative AI for public use is relatively new, it feels uncertain and risky to develop a course about this, as our use of the tool will probably develop drastically in the coming years."

This insight raises concerns that it could require significant time to keep the course updated, and the skills learned might quickly become irrelevant.

IxD and WP respondents, showed similar inclinations towards acknowledging the importance of accessibility principles, with IxD respondents expressing the need to integrate these into curricula for inclusivity, whereas WP respondents focused on understanding and meeting legal accessibility aspects in their solutions with emphasis on technical aspects, as one respondent stated:

"...teach accessibility in web development and not just UX (e.g., ARIA, navigation with keyboard/without mouse, etc.)".

Similar findings are reported in studies by Lazar et al. (2019) and Keith and Whitney (2011). Both cohorts recommended the accessibility course should cover POUR[2] (Perceivable, Operable, Understandable, and Robust) principles and WCAG[3] (Web Content Accessibility Guidelines) guidelines, as one respondent stated:

"Being able to understand the meaning of POUR in a deeper way would have been good to get a better understanding of why WCAG has developed its guidelines."

and another stating that:

"Many companies are now forced to follow WCAG laws so it sounds like a very good course."

Respondents' feedback—especially their desire to understand POUR and WCAG not just in theory but through implementation—suggests that curriculum development should not only acknowledge accessibility as a principle but also as a practical, legislatively grounded, skill set. Furthermore, Burgstahler and Cauce (2020) highlight that hands-on learning and engagement with legal frameworks like WCAG foster deeper understanding and long-term competency among students.

Respondents from two programs also shared a common sentiment regarding business-oriented courses, finding them too broad and not directly relevant to their roles. In summary, IxD students appeared more focused on AI integration into design processes and methodologies, whereas WP students emphasized practical applications in efficiency and professional skills.

4 Conclusion

This study reports on the co-creation process of advanced courses within Interaction Design and AI. The results from a workshop with industry representatives and a survey with current students and alumni proposed six courses that represent a blend of IxD and AI. These findings echo broader trends in design and computing education, where there is a growing emphasis on equipping students with adaptive, future-facing skills in AI integration.

Three courses, *Novel Interaction Methods*, *Inclusive Design*, and *Tools with AI*, are being further developed. The proposed content of the first two courses aligns well with the HCI field and are planned to be offered as part of an HCI specialization track within the Master's program in Informatics.[4] The decision to include these two courses within the HCI specialization, is pedagogically grounded in the need to address emerging domains such as inclusive design and AI-enhanced interaction that extend beyond traditional UX or HCI content. These courses provide focused depth and research-oriented competencies aligned with evolving professional and academic demands. The delivery of these courses supports industry collaboration and a balanced integration between foundational HCI principles and novel application areas.

[2] https://ialabs.ie/understanding-the-pour-principles-of-accessibility/

[3] https://www.w3.org/TR/WCAG22/

[4] https://lnu.se/en/programme/informatics-master-programme/vaxjo-international-autumn/

The first course (*Novel Interaction Methods*) will also be offered as an elective within the Master's program in Interactive AI Systems.[5] The third course (*Tools with AI*) is being considered to be offered in one of the existing bachelor programs.

The study is rather limited in terms of the number of companies involved and geographical scope with participants from two programs mainly coming from the region of south Sweden. With such limitations in mind, the study can be replicated to reach a wider scope and diversity of participants. In addition, the concrete near future plan is the three highest rated courses to be further developed, accredited, and offered within the respective advanced programs.

Acknowledgments. Authors would like to thank KK-Stiftelsen in Sweden for supporting this research. We also thank company representatives, students, and alumni for their participation and their opinions.

Disclosure of Interests. The authors have no competing interests to declare that are relevant to the content of this article.

References

Aghajani, K., Zohrevandi, M.: Enhancing speech emotion recognition: a deep learning approach with self-attention and acoustic features. J. Supercomput. **81**, 704 (2025)

Azhar, M., Hin, H.S., Kian, N.T.: SPARC: a framework for enhancing early childhood reading through augmented reality, conversational AI, and IDC theory. In: Proceedings 2024 International Conference Emerging Technologies in Education (2024)

Burgstahler, S., Cauce, A.M.: Creating Inclusive Learning Opportunities in Higher Education: a Universal Design Toolkit. Harvard Education Press (2020)

Cavallin, E.: Exploring the use of GenAI in the design process: a workshop with design students. AHFE Int. **122**, 89–95 (2024)

Creswell, J.W., Creswell, J.D.: Research Design: Qualitative, Quantitative, and Mixed Methods Approaches, 6th edn. SAGE Publications, Thousand Oaks (2022)

De Bruyne, T.: The SUE Influence Framework© explained. SUE | Behavioural Design Academy (2024), https://suebehaviouraldesign.com/influence-framework-explained/

De Silva, C., Halloluwa, T.: Augmenting human potential: the role of LLMS in shaping the future of HCI. Interactions. **32**(2), 42 (2025)

Domínguez, J.C.E., Munar, L.S., Beltrán, P.A.C.: Inclusive interactive multimedia experiences in school contexts with learning analytics integration. IEEE Rev. Iberoam. Tecnol. Aprendiz. **20**, 96 (2025)

Keith, S., Whitney, G.: Mainstreaming accessibility? Multidisciplinary problems or technical solutions. Int. J. Knowl. Web Intell. **2**(1), 53–63 (2011)

Kim, Y.J., Kim, G., Stoiber, A.: Playful design for AI literacy: creating inclusive learning and assessment opportunities. Int. J. Hum.-Comput. Stud. **199**, 103508 (2025)

Kok, C.L., Ho, C.K., Koh, Y.Y., Thanh, N.T.C.: Preparing future engineers: strategies for integrating AI platforms in higher education. In: IEEE TENCON 2024 Conference Proceedings (2024)

Kuo, J.Y., Xia, Z.: Exploring intelligent user interfaces from design students' perspectives on smart home products through peer assessment, focus group and ChatGPT. In: Storga, M., et al. (eds.) Leveraging Transdisciplinary Engineering in a Changing and Connected World, pp. 161–170. IOS Press, Amsterdam (2023)

[5] https://lnu.se/en/programme/interactive-ai-systems-master-programme/vaxjo-international-autumn/

Laundon, M., Williams, P., Williams, J.: Benefits of co-creating higher education learning resources: an industry participant perspective. Aust. Educ. Res. **51**(4), 1627–1646 (2024)
Lazar, A., Lazar, J., Pradhan, A.: Using modules to teach accessibility in a user-centered design course. In: Proceedings 21st International ACM SIGACCESS Conference Computers and Accessibility, pp. 554–556. ACM, New York (2019)
Lee, S.Y., Law, M., Hoffman, G.: When and how to use AI in the design process? Implications for human-AI design collaboration. Int. J. Hum.–Comput. Interact. **41**(2), 1569–1584 (2025)
Lewrick, M., Link, P., Leifer, L.: The Design Thinking Playbook: Mindful Digital Transformation of Teams, Products, Services, Businesses and Ecosystems. Wiley, Hoboken (2018)
Li, Y., Wang, X., Xin, D.: An inquiry into AI university curriculum and market demand: facts, fits, and future trends. In: Proc. SIGMIS-CPR 2019. ACM, New York (2019)
Liu, Y., Xie, J., Liang, S., Wang, Y.: Design and implementation of online interactive activities for deep learning in the era of generative AI. In: Proceedings ACM International Conference Educational Technology (2024)
Lively, J., Hutson, J.: The role of student motivation in integrating AI into web design education: a longitudinal study. Forum Educ. Stud. **2**(2), 1242–1242 (2024)
Ntunka, M.G., Maladzhi, R.W.: Enhancing project-based learning in engineering disciplines through emerging technologies: a systematic literature review. In: IEEE International Education Forum (2024)
Sørum, H.: Design of digital products in the future: a study of interaction design students and their perceptions on design issues. In: Marcus, A. (ed.) Design, User Experience, and Usability: Theory, Methodology, and Management, DUXU 2017, LNCS, vol. 10288, pp. 740–754. Springer, Cham (2017)
Weinstein, N., Itzchakov, G., Maniaci, M.: Exploring the connecting potential of AI: integrating human interpersonal listening and parasocial support into human-computer interactions. Comput. Hum. Behav.: Artif. Intell. **4**, 100149 (2025)
Wei, W., Zhao, A., Ma, H.: Understanding how AI chatbots influence EFL learners' oral English learning motivation and outcomes: evidence from Chinese learners. IEEE Access. **13**, 56699 (2025)
Windl, M., Feger, S.S., Zijlstra, L., Schmidt, A., Wozniak, P.W.: 'It is not always discovery time': Four pragmatic approaches in designing AI systems. In: Proceedings 2022 CHI Conference Human Factors in Computing Systems, pp. 1–12. ACM, New York (2022)
Wyatt, J., Piggott, A.: The design of not-so-everyday things: designing for emerging experiences. AIS Trans. Hum.-Comput. Interact. **11**(4), 244–252 (2019)

A Possibilistic Approach to Teaching Accessibility in Higher Education

Mireia Ribera[1(✉)] and Silvia Andrea Cristian Ladaga[2]

[1] Departament de Matemàtiques i Informàtica, Universitat de Barcelona, Barcelona 08007, Spain
ribera@ub.edu

[2] Departament Didàctica i Organització Educativa, Universitat de Barcelona, Barcelona 08007, Spain
cladaga@ub.edu

Abstract. This position paper presents a strategy for integrating accessibility teaching into higher education, illustrated by the course "*Usability and User Experience for People with Disabilities*", offered within the Digital Contents master's program. Due to constraints in existing curricula and the limited instructional time allocated to these topics, the proposed approach adopts an active, learning-by-doing methodology that focuses on motivation, hands-on involvement, and both individual and group reflection. The course, which is elective and has received excellent student feedback, follows a pedagogical model aligned with constructivist principles, fostering meaningful learning, autonomy and responsibility in technical design, consistent with existing studies in the fields of HCI and accessibility. The paper also seeks to raise awareness of the need to dedicate greater time and attention to accessibility teaching in higher education. Future work includes gathering similar case studies and experiential tasks on accessibility, conducting a realistic evaluation of their implementation, and developing a shared repository of teaching materials.

Keywords: Accessibility Education · Accessibility - Learning by Doing · Accessibility - Case Study

1 Introduction

The growing relevance of accessibility and in general, inclusive design—both in physical and digital environments—along with increasing reliance on the latter for everyday tasks, population aging, budgetary constraints in pension systems, and legal requirements, make accessibility a necessary competency for professionals across various disciplines

Within this context, there is an urgent need to incorporate accessibility education into university curricula. Amid slow-paced reforms, pre-established curricula, and limited teaching resources in many universities, this position paper highlights the importance of creating space within existing courses or offering compact elective formats to foster positive reception of accessibility-related content. The possibilistic approach described

Published by Springer Nature Switzerland AG 2026
C. Maciel et al. (Eds.): INTERACT 2025 Workshops, LNCS 16478, pp. 71–78, 2026.
https://doi.org/10.1007/978-3-032-22934-2_7

in this paper implies a focus on feasibility—that is, it prioritizes feasible, measurable, and concrete actions toward real improvements in accessibility within the usual constraints of the university (time, credits, resources). We consider that this positioning does not diminish the standard but rather sequences and scales it, as described in the case study.

In the context described, it is proposed that accessibility courses adopt a learning-by-doing strategy, emphasize student engagement, and mitigate frequent time constraints by:

- **Motivation and practice**, as key elements to encourage an active learning attitude;
- **Scaffolding**, by providing support that enables students to progressively reach higher levels of competence;
- **Collaborative work**, to strengthen social, reflective, and critical thinking skills;
- **Formative assessment and self-reflection strategies**, designed to enhance metacognitive skills and learner ownership.

The proposal, outlined below, presents a pedagogical strategy that prioritizes direct experience, student motivation, and a methodology grounded in learning by doing. These constructivist practices—based on experiential learning and problem-solving—are aligned with contemporary approaches to meaningful and reflective learning, promoting student autonomy and motivation [1]. They also help counterbalance the limited time often allocated to elective courses. Furthermore, existing studies support that learning by doing in fields such as HCI and accessibility fosters a deeper, more practical, and ethically grounded understanding of technological design [2, 3]. By shifting from abstract instruction to meaningful action, students develop not only technical skills but also commitment, empathy, and a sense of responsibility as future professionals.

We find it necessary to clarify that, while the course proposal is grounded in Accessibility (as a demonstrable threshold to remove specific barriers in response to legal obligations and standards, and as a first approach to the field), the perspective of Inclusive Design (as a strategy that integrates from the outset the diversity of people, contexts, and abilities to enhance the overall experience) [4] is the general objective we pursue in our students' learning process. We recognize that accessible compliance helps prevent critical exclusions, while inclusive design enhances overall usability. In this same sense, and within the context of this presentation, HCI as a framing discipline and inclusive design as one of its strategies incorporate human diversity (contexts, cultures, ages, languages, abilities, etc.) from the beginning in order to reduce exclusion. The aspects of accessibility provide the verifiable conditions that allow people with disabilities to operate the system on equal terms.

We therefore understand that a learning-by-doing methodology, along with the evidence gathered through its implementation, will encourage students and academic planners to progressively acknowledge the value of giving greater prominence to this type of content.

2 The Case Study

The course Usability and User Experience for People with Disabilities is an elective worth 2.5 ECTS credits, equivalent to approximately 20 h of in-class instruction and a total workload of 62.5 h (see Schedule in Table 1). It is offered as part of the previously mentioned Master's program in Digital Content Management. This program is aimed at professionals seeking to redirect their careers toward the digital sector and covers topics such as marketing, user experience, SEO, among others. Enrolled students typically have backgrounds in journalism, audiovisual communication, and occasionally more technical profiles, and the program consistently leads to high employability outcomes. The course has been offered since the program's inception — initially under the title Accessibility—and was renamed in 2023 to better reflect its content. It is one of the highest-rated courses in the program, consistently receiving scores of 9 out of 10 across all editions.

Table 1. Course Schedule Overview.

Day	Content	Practical activities
Day 1	User profiles and needs (I)	Hands-on exploration of assistive technologies (I)
Day 2	User profiles and needs (II)	Hands-on exploration of assistive technologies (II)
Day 3	Plain language and easy-to-read principles	Web simulation tools.
Day 4	WAI and WCAG guidelines	Text rewriting exercises
Day 5	Legal frameworks and web accessibility evaluation	Web evaluation practice (I)
Day 6	Accessible documents: text	Web evaluation practice (II)
Day 7	Accessible documents: charts and slides	Practice with textual documents (I)
Day 8	Multimedia content: barriers and solutions	Practice with textual documents (I)
Day 9	Multimedia content: video players, subtitles, audio descriptions	Practice with multimedia content (I)
Day 10	Accessibility as a process: steps, roles, and responsibilities	Practice with multimedia content (II)

The course addresses motivation from a dual perspective: on the one hand, it offers a brief introduction to different user profiles; on the other, it presents the legal and regulatory requirements of accessibility. In addition to highlighting the direct benefits for users, the course also discusses broader societal advantages, including studies on social and economic impact [5], and the limitations of government systems in meeting the needs of people with dependencies. The legislative framework, WCAG guidelines, and web evaluation practices are introduced and contextualized within broader government policies. The WCAG are presented with a critical lens, referencing their origins [6] to discuss inherent biases. Principles of plain language and easy-to-read formats are introduced to emphasize the critical role of text in both usability and accessibility. This approach aligns with the two most common arguments used to motivate accessibility:

the 'stick' (fear of legal consequences) and the 'carrot' (serving more users and adhering to ethical principles).

Scaffolding and learning-by-doing strategies come into play when addressing documents and multimedia content from the perspective of accessibility requirements in content creation. Students receive detailed, step-by-step guides —for example, on accessible MS Word documents, accessible graphics, subtitling, and audio description—along with guidance on tools and procedures. See, for instance, [7], where an open educational resource is shared with the students, featuring a step-by-step guide to creating accessible Word documents developed by the course instructor. They also receive starting materials that contain accessibility errors, which they must redesign and improve. In several editions those materials came from real organizations collaborating with the master's degree to reinforce the experiential learning. At this stage, the classes become theory-practice sessions lasting two hours: the first hour is dedicated to demonstrating the necessary techniques and answering questions, while the second focuses on task execution. Web accessibility evaluation is also introduced, based on WCAG 2.2, but using a simplified version, pairing each success criterion with recommended tools and evaluation methods.

The following section briefly describes the activities and assignments of the course:

Activity 1 (A1): Exercise with NVDA or VoiceOver, and MS Word Immersive Reader — Graded activity, 10%. Students are asked to work with assistive technologies to experience barriers and access strategies. First, they complete a hands-on exercise with a screen reader (NVDA on Windows or VoiceOver on macOS) following the WebAIM guide "Using NVDA/VoiceOver to Evaluate Web Accessibility." As evidence, they must record an audio file of the full interaction (minimum 5 min) and write a brief, objective description of the experience. Then, they explore the Immersive Reader in MS Word: open the task document, activate Immersive Reader, and read the document using different settings. Students must include screenshots of the various Immersive Reader settings and a short recording (30 s to 1 min) of the reading aloud option.

Activity 2 (A2): Exercise to create an accessible document — Graded activity, 20%. Students are required to create an accessible MS Word document from a provided document that contains accessibility issues. They must preserve the original style while ensuring compliance with accessibility requirements (e.g., contrast, heading structure, use of styles); when the initial style conflicts with accessibility, this must be documented. Tools such as Colour Contrast Analyser (TPGi) or WebAIM Contrast Checker should be used. Plain language should be applied, detailing the changes introduced compared to the original. Accessibility should be completed by applying alternative text, semantic columns and page breaks, metadata, and by validating the document with Word's Accessibility Checker, including a short summary of the guidelines followed. The document should then be converted into an accessible PDF. A comparison between the student's accessible document and the original must be included in a short report addressed to the professors. Deliverables also include a technical report describing the decisions and processes followed, and a client report outlining the accessibility problems found in the original document. *(Provided materials: original PDF, plain text file (.txt), and bitmap images.)*

Activity 3 (A3): Website Evaluation — Graded activity, 20%. Students are asked to conduct an accessibility evaluation of a provided website with known issues, using an ad hoc protocol developed by the instructors based on the main points of WCAG 2.2, Levels A and AA. The results will be presented in a brief report for the client, including for each issue: the affected WCAG criterion, its priority, a concrete example, a description of the problem, a recommended solution, and, when relevant, references to accessible techniques or design patterns. The report will conclude with an executive summary highlighting key findings and recommended actions.

Activity 4 (A4): Video Accessibility — Graded activity, 20%. Students are asked to practice captioning and audio description on videos proposed by the instructor, or, upon approval, on a video of their own choice. The work includes generating and synchronizing captions, as well as preparing a script and an audio description track when applicable, documenting the applied criteria and decisions (segmentation, timing, speaker identification, description of relevant visual information). A short client report must be produced, outlining the accessibility requirements applicable to the video and justifying the adopted choices. All files used and generated during the process (e.g., subtitles, AD script) must be submitted, along with an explanation of the process and decisions made.

In all activities, students are required to submit a brief reflection at the end, highlighting difficulties encountered, surprises, and key learnings.

As emerges from the text, the four proposed activities articulate an experiential and sequential pathway that enables students to engage in a direct experience of accessibility barriers (A1: screen readers and Immersive Reader) through production and validation of accessible resources (A2: office document; A4: subtitles and audio description), passing through systematic evaluation based on WCAG 2.2 (A3). This progression combines learning by doing, integrates verifiable standards (A/AA criteria, validators, simulators), and promotes inclusive practices (plain language, alternative access methods, consideration of disabilities and contexts).

In terms of competencies, the activities develop: literacy in assistive technologies and accessibility criteria; technical judgment to diagnose non-compliance and propose justified solutions; design and production skills for accessible materials with decision traceability; and critical reflection on impact, limitations, and professional transferability.

Regarding assessment, the course includes an individual multiple-choice test covering key terminology and concepts, which accounts for 30% of the final grade. The test is not intentionally designed as not particularly difficult and serves as a checkpoint, being the only individual assessment. Passing this test is required to complete the course. In addition, students complete four group assignments (described above), weighed at 10%, 20%, 20%, and 20%, respectively. The average grade for these assignments must also meet the passing threshold.

Group formation (two to three members) is self-managed by students, who organize themselves according to their interests and affinities. In this way, we aim to foster relationships, motivation, and co-responsibility in collaborative work, which helps reduce individual workload (ensuring coherence with the course credits), promotes peer dialogue (through the metacognitive reflection proposed for each activity), and enriches both the experience and the learning process.

Assignments are submitted throughout the course and receive prompt feedback, allowing time to address questions and propose solutions. Past iterations of the course have shown that students engage more effectively with understanding and applying accessibility guidelines after having ‘struggled’ with them firsthand during task completion.

In response to the tasks, students often make **their own need**s visible (e.g., “in my case, I suffer from depression, which makes short-term learning difficult for me, and I have some attention deficit”), become aware of **real limitations** (“to experience other ways of accessing content that, without the tools, are difficult to imagine”), and show **empathy** toward other experiences (“I liked the activity because it puts me in the shoes of a person with visual impairment, something that doesn’t happen very often”). At the same time, during the **practical exercises**, immediate and transferable learning becomes evident, and the course content is valued as **relevant and useful** for professional development: “while doing the exercises, you immediately realize how important it is for the created elements to be **properly implemented**. [...] I did the exercise of closing my eyes and could never visualize the data properly. It confirms that taking this elective course within the master’s was a good decision, as it has motivated me to care about these issues.”

Other student comments bring out complementary nuances: **the effectiveness of minimal changes** —“I find it amazing that with so few actions we can contribute so much; with just a couple of clicks, someone else gains access to quality content, and that’s something I won’t forget”—; the **mediation of assistive tools** —“I was surprised by how differently we perceive everything when these tools mediate the interaction; that’s why knowing how they work is vital when creating any piece of content”—; a **vision of accessibility as an inclusive experience** —“it’s not just about creating easy-to-use environments, but about ensuring a dignified and inclusive experience”—; and the **shift from compliance to ethical conviction** —“it’s not only about meeting regulations and standards; it’s a real necessity”; “applying good practices is not just another technical requirement, but a commitment to equity and inclusion.”. **Professional self-criticism** also appears —“in marketing and content management projects, accessibility was almost never a real priority”— and **awareness of shortcomings in major brands** —“it’s surprising that the website of such a well-known brand has deficiencies that affect users with cognitive, visual, or auditory disabilities.” Finally, several contributions highlight **a change in perspective and future projection** —“from now on, I’ll pay more attention when evaluating and developing websites”; “the WCAG 2.2 provide a clear structure to improve accessibility; I feel better prepared to incorporate them and contribute to a more inclusive web”— as well as the systematic consideration of diverse audiences —“I understood the complexity of usability and the importance of thinking about different audiences when producing content.”

We understand that the principles of this proposal, together with the examples of tasks and the students’ observations, support the pedagogical validity of the approach and justify its transferability beyond this course. Moreover, they can be adapted to other contexts, student levels, and institutional environments.

3 Potential Criticisms of the Proposal

Although efforts have been made to justify the proposal within the current context, several counterarguments could be raised.

One fundamental concern for the HCI and accessibility learning community is the legitimacy of offering a course under limited-resource conditions, as this could potentially influence students' perceptions of the discipline. While it is clear that the ideal scenario would involve courses with more time, resources, and compulsory status, the accumulated experience with this course demonstrates that even under these constraints, it has succeeded in sparking student interest in the subject. Many former students have adopted accessibility as a guiding principle in their professional paths, incorporating it into their personal ethos, even if they do not pursue it as a central focus in their careers.

A second potential criticism concerns the generalizability of the proposal to other disciplines and contexts. In this regard, the intention of the current proposal is not to serve as a universal model, but rather as an illustrative example and a didactic framework. It is ultimately up to each instructor to adapt the tasks, resources, and assessment strategies to their specific academic context. We believe that the academic community can benefit from high-quality, university-level teaching materials in this area, as such resources are still relatively scarce.

A final criticism might question the need to include accessibility training at the university level, given the existence of professional certifications and continuing education courses that already address these learning needs. In response to this argument, it is relevant to revisit the debate on the fundamental role of the university, as articulated by Collini [8]. In an increasingly technology-mediated society, we argue that the university has a responsibility to provide a person-centric perspective—one that can guide technological development toward socially just and sustainable goals. This vision is reflected in key documents shaping university curricula [9, 10].

4 Closing Reflections

This position paper presents a possibilistic approach to integrating accessibility into university education under limited resources, illustrated through the course Usability and User Experience for People with Disabilities. This approach implies that the pedagogical intervention has been conceived pragmatically, incorporating sequential tasks of increasing complexity that are concrete and attainable, contextualized within available resources and acknowledging the limitations of the context. It also implies that it is evidence-based, ensuring that progress is documented and transferability is facilitated, as students complete the course with reusable processes (checklists, review pathways, and tools). The course design and sample assignments are provided as a contribution toward building a knowledge base for teaching accessibility in higher education. The proposal addresses the rigidity of existing curricula and the limited attention typically given to accessibility by offering a motivational, practice-oriented strategy. Students engage in learning through doing, while personal and group reflection is actively encouraged. Key challenges included curricular rigidity, limited contact hours, and uneven prior exposure to accessibility, which required differentiated scaffolding. To intentionally raise awareness, we coupled hands-on labs with assistive technologies with brief reflective prompts and before/after self-assessments, making the human impact of technical fixes explicit. Resistance in the structure is lowered through a very good evaluation by the students. The inclusion of the subject also permeated other subjects which were more sensitive to creating accessible materials.

This initiative aims to raise awareness of the need to allocate more space and weight to accessibility-related content within academic programs. Avenues for further development include the collection of similar integration strategies across various disciplines, a reality check on their implementation in current study programs, and the development of a shared repository of instructional materials and exemplary practices.

Acknowledgments.. This work was partially funded by the Spanish projects PID2022-141566NB-I00 (AEI-MICINN) and PID2022-136436NB-I00 (AEI-MICINN). Part of the English translation of this manuscript was assisted by ChatGPT (OpenAI), under the supervision of the authors, who reviewed and edited all output for accuracy, clarity, and academic tone.

Disclosure of Interests The authors have no competing interests to declare that are relevant to the content of this article.

References

1. Saldaña, J., Omasta, M.: Qualitative Research: Analyzing Life. Sage Publications, New York (2016)
2. Christiansen, E.: Educated by design: learning by doing in the didactics of interaction design. ITcon – J. Inf. Technol. Constr. **9**, 121–134 (2004)
3. Shi, W., Khan, S., El-Glaly, Y., Malachowsky, S., Yu, Q., Krutz, D.E.: Experiential learning in computing accessibility education. In: Proceedings of the ACM/IEEE 42nd International Conference on Software Engineering: Companion Proceedings, pp. 250–251. ACM, New York (2020)
4. Dickinson, C., Hernandez Trillo, A.H., Crossland, M.D.: Inclusive and universal design. In: Dickinson, C., Hernandez Trillo, A.H., Crossland, M.D. (eds.) Low Vision: Principles and Management. Elsevier, Amsterdam (2024). https://doi.org/10.1016/b978-0-323-87634-6.00016-7
5. Centre for Inclusive Design, The benefit of designing for everyone, https://centreforinclusivedesign.org.au/the-benefits-of-designing-for-everyone-report/, last accessed 2025/05/26
6. Térmens, M., Ribera, M., Porras, M., Boldú, M., Sulé, A., Paris, P.: Web content accessibility guidelines: from 1.0 to 2.0. In: In: 18TH International Conference on World Wide Web, pp. 1171–1172. ACM, New York (2009)
7. Mireia Ribera Guia Word 365, https://www.ub.edu/adaptabit/guies-contingut-accessible/guia-word-365/, last accessed 2025/05/26
8. Collini, S.: What Are Universities for? Penguin, London (2012)
9. Kumar, A., Raj, R.: Computer science curricula 2023 (CS2023): the final report. In: 55th ACM Technical Symposium on Computer Science Education, vol. 2, pp. 1867–1868. ACM, New York (2024)
10. Ladner, R., Ludi, S., Domanski, R.: Teaching about Accessibility in Computer Science Education, in submission (2023). https://csed.acm.org/wp-content/uploads/2023/12/Accessibility-Final-1.pdf

Integrating Value-Based Design into HCI Education

Paloma Díaz(✉), Teresa Onorati, and Ignacio Aedo

Computer Science and Engineering Department, Universidad Carlos III de Madrid, Madrid, Spain
{pdp,tonorati}@inf.uc3m.es, aedo@ia.uc3m.es

Abstract. As technology becomes pervasive and impacts our daily activities and relationships, deploying responsible technologies turns into a key learning outcome for computer science and engineering. As many of the issues are related to how humans interact with technology, Human Computer Interaction courses need to integrate responsibility in design, as suggested in the new ACM Computer Science Curricula. In this paper, we describe two experiences of applying values-based design in courses on Human-Computer Interaction (HCI). Instead of receiving lectures on values and ethics, students are confronted with the obligation to apply them into their designs. Through this active learning approach, we realised that the projects students developed were better conceptualised, and included more functionalities compared with the outcomes of previous cohorts.

Keywords: HCI education · Values-based Design · Responsibility in Design · Active learning

1 Introduction

As digital technologies become increasingly pervasive in our daily lives, the HCI community has been focusing on developing design methodologies that consider not only usability but also the ethical and social implications of the envisioned technologies [8,10]. Indeed, the 2023 ACM Curriculum for Computer Science [14] recognises responsibility in design as a key knowledge unit focused on *"understanding and evaluating the impacts and implications of a computational system on its users, including issues in ethics, fairness, trust, and explainability"*. Developing students' skills in responsibility and ethics in design involves making them aware of their responsibility in anticipating and addressing the multidimensional consequences their design choices may have on individuals, societies, and the environment [7]. Responsibility in design entails considering how technological designs impact core human values and principles, including well-being, justice, equality, diversity, peace, and sustainability, among others.

Another reason to focus on values in HCI courses is to align course assignments with students' preferences. Computer Science and Engineering (CSE) students have often been reported struggling with engaging in HCI courses, which

Published by Springer Nature Switzerland AG 2026
C. Maciel et al. (Eds.): INTERACT 2025 Workshops, LNCS 16478, pp. 79–87, 2026.
https://doi.org/10.1007/978-3-032-22934-2_8

they frequently consider trivial or unnecessary [1,15]. Compared to other areas where programming and hardcore abilities are all that are required, HCI necessitates a different perspective and a set of skills more closely aligned with design sensibilities. Students have to deal with wicked problems that do not have a single, definitive solution. Not all CSE students feel comfortable in this open and undefined problem space, which requires interdisciplinary and human-centric approaches. However, recent studies show that GenZ is more inclined towards activities that promote personal growth, fit their values, and where they could have some social impact [9] and, therefore, making HCI more value-based could help in raising their interest in the discipline.

In this paper, we describe two experiences of integrating a value-based design approach in HCI-related courses, in particular, a course on User Interfaces for a Bachelor in CSE, and a course on Human Computer Interaction in a research Master in Computational Science and Technology. In both cases, an active learning approach was applied. Active learning is an educational approach that emphasises the student's engagement in the learning process. Rather than being passive receptors of information, they take action and reflect on the impact of their design decisions [4]. The courses didn't receive any additional resources nor teachers have a multidisciplinary background since both are assigned to the Computer Science and Engineering Department. Hence, the design of the assignments was adapted to the teaching conditions of the courses, and ended up in an approach that can fit many teaching scenarios were resources are scarce.

2 Related Works

"Accountability and Responsibility in Design" is one of the six knowledge units of HCI defined in the new ACM Computing Curricula [14]. This knowledge unit aims to raise students' awareness of the impact of computational technologies beyond their potential utility or profitability, focusing on issues such as ethics, fairness, trust, and explainability. However, as it implies developing and applying non-technical, attitudinal skills, teaching responsibility might be a complex challenge. Responsibility is typically taught in the CS curriculum through two approaches: stand-alone ethics courses or embedding responsibility into all courses and activities where values can be compromised, such as when programming AI tools or devising a new interactive system for healthcare or any other use that might imply compromising or promoting values. The new ACM curriculum advocates an embedded ethics approach, which was originally applied at Harvard University [11].

Within our teaching group, given resource limitations and the lack of multidisciplinary support, we initiated a project three years ago to integrate microethics [3] into HCI-related courses using active learning assignments [5]. Microethics shifts the debate from general, controversial issues surrounding technology to the impact that the specific, small decisions of designers and programmers have on human values. For instance, instead of focusing on a broad question like the impact of AI in society, it focuses on providing information about the carbon footprint of a specific algorithm implemented by students. In this way, responsibility moves from prominent actors (i.e., companies and governments) to the students. This approach involves applying an active learning method to help students develop technological responsibility as they create technology.

Values-based design is a convenient approach to integrating an ethical perspective in the whole development cycle of interactive systems, so that students can learn specific strategies they can apply in their professional work, as claimed in [16]. Values-based design methods aim to design technologies that embed moral, cultural, and political values throughout the software development lifecycle [2,13]. These methods place values at the centre of the development process, influencing how systems are conceptualised, developed, and implemented. The process identifies values compromised and related to the problem at hand at three different levels of abstraction, namely abstract, concrete, and implementation, which are faced throughout the development cycle from three perspectives, namely **WHY** (Value view), **HOW** (Modelling view), and **WHAT** (Business view). This holistic and practical approach aligns with an active-learning approach to teaching responsibility in design. As stated by [8], it is crucial to integrate a values-based approach as part of the HCI curricula in all learning activities that cover the entire design process.

3 Two Experiences on Integrating Value-Based Design in HCI Education

In this paper, we report on two experiences of integrating values-based design into HCI courses that we conducted during the 2024 academic year. Both experiences are entirely different in terms of the number of students, but, what is more important, in their maturity. Both aspects suggested using a different approach in each course to make the experience both helpful and manageable, as no additional human resources were provided despite the project being officially approved as a Teaching Innovation Project at the University.

The first experience is an undergraduate course on User Interfaces, taught in the 5th semester of a Computer Science and Engineering program to a total of 240 students enrolled in two different campuses. According to the University teaching model, each course is divided into two types of groups: master groups dedicated to theoretical lessons, and small groups focused on practical work. Students attend two sessions each of the 14 weeks of the semester, one in the master group and one in the small group, both lasting 100 min. During the 2024 academic year, the course was organized into three master groups and six small groups. The values-based approach is integrated into both the theoretical lectures and the practical work. In the master group, one of the lectures is dedicated to an active learning workshop where students are introduced to the basic principles of values-based design and then asked to apply them to a real-world scenario. In the small group, students spend the last month of classes working on a final project, designing a website based on a set of predefined requirements. Part of these requirements is to select and describe the ethical values considered while designing the proposed solution.

The second experience is a graduate course on Human-Computer Interaction taught as part of a research Master program in Computational Science and Technology. In this case, students have a more mature profile and a multidisciplinary and international background. The number of enrolled students is 13, and they attend a 2-hour session per week. Sessions are devoted to exploring basic concepts of HCI, including novel interaction paradigms such as immersive systems, data visualisation, ubiquitous computing, and embodied interaction, as well as development methods. In this later module, students learn about the application of software engineering practices to the design of interactive systems, including agile methodologies that put users and stakeholders at the centre of the process. As part of this module, one lecture focuses on creativity and ethics, two aspects that are particularly relevant to envisioning innovative and responsible interactive systems. This year, an active learning workshop on responsibility in design was incorporated.

The following subsections describe each of the experiences.

3.1 Responsibility in Design for Undergraduate Students of Computer Science

The undergraduate students in the User Interfaces course are asked to participate in a workshop that introduces them to values-based design through an active learning approach. The workshop is carried out in groups of two or three people during a theoretical lecture for each master group and is organised into three steps: Contextualization, Ideation, and Prototyping.

1. **Contextualization**, where they define the context, identifying the problem or combination of problems they are interested in, and the concerned ethical values.
2. **Ideation**, where they ideate a technological solution for the problem and the ethical values selected in the first step.
3. **Prototyping**, where they design a prototype of the solution.

During the **Contextualization**, the students can get inspiration from a set of cards describing examples of real-world problems and ethical values (e.g., equity, inclusion, wellness, and sustainability). After selecting some of the cards, they have to describe and justify the context in detail. In the **Ideation** step, they have complete freedom in deciding the technology to use (e.g., websites, mobile applications, or physical devices) and in the **Prototyping** step, they can build the solution using a variety of DIY materials, like cardboard, markers, post-its, pipe cleaners, and modeling clay.

The students particularly enjoyed this last step of the workshop because they had the opportunity to interact physically with different materials and stimulate their creativity. At the end of the workshop, we have collected and analyzed 26 projects, finding some interesting patterns. There are several shared problems, including recycling, access to technology for seniors, image gallery navigation, promoting a healthy lifestyle, and reducing food waste. Among the values, we found sustainability, accessibility, personal autonomy, and inclusion. For example, one of the groups of participants proposed a Digital Inclusion Assistant to simplify digital procedures, such as scheduling a medical appointment or requesting technical support, for older users, and help them achieve an autonomous and equitable lifestyle. These results offer valuable insights into the concerns that most worry our students.

After participating in the workshop, students are asked to integrate the values-based approach into their final project, which is a part of the course's practical work. In particular, they had to design a website based on a list of requirements provided by the assignment, while keeping in mind a set of ethical values they selected.

Upon reviewing the delivered projects, we noted a particular emphasis on ethical values similar to those identified during the workshop, including accessibility, inclusion, and privacy. The students have also proposed ad hoc design solutions for each of the considered ethical values. For example, to design an accessible and inclusive form for collecting data and registering users on the website, the students adopted an inclusive approach to writing labels, texts, and error messages, as well as selecting images and icons, with a focus on accessibility in the interaction with the input and output elements (e.g., buttons, text areas, and drop-downs).

3.2 Responsibility in Design for Graduate Students of a Master in Computer Science Research

The active learning workshop for graduate students enrolled in the HCI course of the research Master was organised in two sessions and embedded the values-based design approach [2,13] within the agile Design Sprint method [12]. Students are proposed a generic topic, the Smart Digital City, for which they have to work in groups to propose an innovative idea following the five steps of the method:

1. **Understand**, where they chose a specific problem or combination of problems to work on, and they frame it properly.
2. **Diverge**, where they develop as many ideas as possible.
3. **Converge**, where they decide which are the winning ideas that are worth being implemented in this first iteration.
4. **Prototype**, where they build a quick-and-dirty apparatus that can be shown to real users and stakeholders.
5. **Test**, where they validate the proposed idea.

In the first step, **Understand**, they are asked to study and frame the problem they chose using some card problems we already developed for workshops aimed at attracting young students to computer science and engineering degrees [6]. They can pick a card problem, combine several cards into a bigger problem or identify a new problem. Cards are only used as inspirational material. Once chosen, they describe the problem using the 5W (Who, What, Where, When, Why) matrix and select the values that are related to the problem. In this case, values are analysed from the WHY and WHAT perspectives of the values-based design method. To facilitate value identification, students were provided with a set of cards featuring values such as justice, equity, wellness, inclusion, sustainability, transparency, accessibility, privacy, security, solidarity, and personal autonomy. They were also encouraged to include other values they considered could be promoted by their idea or compromised if the solution to the problem was not properly designed.

In the second step, **Diverge**, students are asked to list potential ideas using any of the methods seen in the lectures. Students are reminded that they cannot judge ideas yet, but are encouraged to put them on the table, even if they seem crazy or unfeasible. At the end of the process, they must describe the process they followed and the list of ideas they generated. In this step, values are not embedded as the goal is to promote free thinking and individual and group creativity. Since ideas are not assessed in any way, values do not come into play at this stage.

During the third step, **Converge**, values take a key role as they will help to discriminate ideas or to adapt them to comply with the selected values. Students face the inclusion of values from the HOW perspective of the values-based design method. To choose the winning ideas, students can employ traditional methods, such as SWOT matrices. They are also engaged in an embodied 6 Thinking Hats activity where they analyse ideas wearing six physical hats that represent six different personalities: rational (white hat), negative (black hat), creative (green hat), emotional (red hat), optimistic (yellow hat), and leader (blue hat). At the end of this step, they must create a scenario and at least two personas that describe the final idea, justifying how the selected values are met.

In the fourth step, **Prototype**, and given the time limitations and students' different backgrounds, they create a short video that simulates the functionality of their idea in a real scenario. In this way, the focus is on the three perspectives of the values-based design framework showing what values are included in the solution, why and how.

Finally, in the **Test** phase, they have to propose an evaluation procedure, focusing on the features of the idea but also on the values it respects and promotes.

At the end of the course, we collected two projects that presented innovative ideas centred on human values. During the workshops, two of the authors, who also served as course instructors, assisted students with their questions, most of which concerned values. For instance, initially, they attempted to identify only one value. After discussing other perspectives with them, both groups identified several values they wanted to work with, either because their idea would promote those values or because the implementation could compromise them if they were not considered critical requirements.

Although we couldn't conduct a formal evaluation of students' satisfaction, the subjective impression was that they engaged more with the problems than in previous courses, where we had focused only on creativity. Integrating values also inspired exploration of functionalities that would have otherwise been dismissed. For instance, a group proposed an intelligent nutritional agent that considered values such as personal autonomy, wellness, accessibility, transparency, security, and privacy. While wellness may seem the most obvious choice for such a technology, including the other five values forced them to consider how to implement it in a more responsible and inclusive way, making the idea more credible and innovative.

4 Conclusions: Challenges and Opportunities in Embedding Ethics in HCI Assignments

In the experiences we described in this paper, students expressed particular interest in ethical values such as accessibility, sustainability, inclusion, and privacy. They also applied a values-based approach to make more ethical design choices, such as adopting, for the first time after many years of teaching the same course, inclusive language in the forms. The values-based approach influences each step of the design process, including contextualization, where students are more willing to work on sensitive issues that affect society, such as recycling, making technologies accessible to seniors, reducing food waste, and promoting a healthy lifestyle. After these experiences, that are now replicated in other courses involving industrial designers, we can identify some opportunities and challenges in embedding values into HCI education.

Firstly, integrating responsibility in design into HCI education is both a necessity and an opportunity to increase interest in this discipline. Often regarded as a non-core, irrelevant topic, many students are reluctant to choose it or to devote time to the assignments, since they perceive it as more of a designer's task than a computer engineer's. However, students should be aware that values must be considered throughout the software development life cycle, as decisions made during analysis will affect how the system is implemented and whether technology will eventually be adopted. This approach also offers an opportunity for self-expression since the course assignments can be aligned with the students' concerns in terms of the values they cherish.

Another benefit of this approach is that it helps students realise that the software they develop often affects people, society, or the environment and, hence, they must assume responsibility for their actions. The sooner they get used to strategies to integrate ethics into the software development process, the better software developers they will be. A values-based approach engages designers more responsibly and earlier with questions related to equity, justice, sustainability, and other values, and to anchor their design decisions in these values. These decisions will lead to the development of more ethical products that inspire stakeholders and their behaviours, and consequently create a positive impact on society.

Embedding ethics in active learning activities also prepares students to participate in multidisciplinary teams by developing key interdisciplinary skills in modern engineering and technology development, such as ethical awareness and, in our specific case, creativity, critical thinking, teamwork, and communication. In the experiences reported in this paper, we observed that teamwork was crucial for introducing ethics into the design process and encouraging a more active and critical approach to communication to be able to compare different perspectives and select values to integrate. We also found that adding values during problem framing boosted creativity, as students were pushed not only to think about the obvious functionalities but also to align with the values they had selected, which in some cases required incorporating new functionalities.

However, embedding ethics in HCI education also comes with some challenges that are mainly related to the pedagogical approach followed. In the first place, students need to develop specific strategies to integrate ethics into their professional practice, rather than merely learning about theoretical challenges or ethical risk analysis [16]. In our case, this challenge was faced by integrating values from the very beginning of the assignment, forcing them to define why, how and what values are related to the problem and then carry out the different phases of the development cycle focusing on how the selected values had any impact on the artifacts created, be they scenarios, personas, user journeys or prototypes. Instead of implementing the solution right away without considering the implications of their decisions in terms of design, the value-based approach teaches students to shift their focus to the problem framing phase, gaining a deeper and more responsible understanding of the requirements and, consequently, being aware of their impact on society.

In addition, teachers need to maintain neutrality and avoid dictating values or specific positions, since the goal is not to proselytise but to encourage students to take stances and think critically about values and the impact their actions have on promoting or compromising them. Students have to engage in exploring and understanding the impact of their design decisions, rather than learning theories by listening to moral lessons. In this way, they will develop the required awareness and skills in applied ethics that could make a difference when joining the job market.

Ideally, ethical challenges should be posed by companies or communities in an experiential learning process, so that students can interact with real problems and real people. However, this kind of external stakeholders' engagement is difficult to achieve in many higher education institutions. An alternative to trying to cope with everything within the scope of formal education would be to complement the approach presented here with the multiple activities organised by students and companies in the form of hackathons and experiential learning bootcamps. Even though no external stakeholders were involved in the experiences reported in this paper, students still had an opportunity to engage with ethical values and real problems, thereby realising how adding the design ethics perspective enlarged the potential utility and impact of their ideas.

Acknowledgments. This project is part of the activities of the Women and Technology Chair of Telefonica-UC3M.

Disclosure of Interests. Authors have no competing interests.

References

1. Aberg, J.: Challenges with teaching HCI early to computer students. In: Proceedings of the Fifteenth Annual Conference on Innovation and Technology in Computer Science Education, pp. 3–7 (2010)
2. Aldewereld, H., Dignum, V., Tan, Y.H.: Design for values in software development. In: Handbook of Ethics, Values, and Technological Design: Sources, Theory, Values and Application Domains, pp. 831–845 (2015)
3. Bezuidenhout, L., Ratti, E.: What does it mean to embed ethics in data science? an integrative approach based on microethics and virtues. AI Soc. **36**(3), 939–953 (2021)
4. Bonwell, C.C., Eison, J.A.: Active learning: creating excitement in the classroom. 1991 ASHE-ERIC higher education reports. ERIC (1991)
5. Díaz, P., Onorati, T., Aedo, I.: Using active learning and critical thinking to identify and apply ethical values in engineering education. In: 2024 IEEE Global Engineering Education Conference (EDUCON), pp. 1–10. IEEE (2024)
6. Díaz, P., Onorati, T., Montero, Á.: Using an HCI perspective to encourage young students to pursue computer science and engineering careers: the "envisioning the digital city" workshop. In: IFIP Conference on Human-Computer Interaction, pp. 239–252. Springer (2023)
7. Dignum, V.: Responsible Artificial Intelligence: How to Develop and Use AI in a Responsible Way, vol. 2156. Springer (2019)
8. Eriksson, E., Nilsson, E.M., Hansen, A.M., Bekker, T.: Teaching for values in human-computer interaction. Front. Comput. Sci. **4**, 830736 (2022)
9. Fodor, M., Jaeckel, K.: What does it take to have a successful career through the eyes of generation z-based on the results of a primary qualitative research. Int. J. Lifelong Educ. Leadersh. **4**(1), 1–7 (2018)
10. Pillai, A.G., et al.: Co-designing resources for ethics education in HCI. In: Extended Abstracts of the 2021 CHI Conference on Human Factors in Computing Systems, pp. 1–5 (2021)
11. Grosz, B.J., et al.: Embedded ethics: integrating ethics across cs education. Commun. ACM **62**(8), 54–61 (2019)
12. Knapp, J., Zeratsky, J.: The design sprint (2012). Accessed 28 Sept 2018
13. Kroes, P., van de Poel, I.: Design for values and the definition, specification, and operationalization of values. In: Handbook of Ethics, Values, and Technological Design: Sources, Theory, Values and Application Domains, pp. 151–178 (2015)
14. Kumar, A.N., et al.: Computer science curricula 2023 (2024)
15. Oleson, A., Solomon, M., Ko, A.J.: Computing students' learning difficulties in HCI education. In: Proceedings of the 2020 CHI Conference on Human Factors in Computing Systems, pp. 1–14 (2020)
16. Tejo, L.C., Silva, P.A.: Engaging with ethics in the HCI design process: a study of ethical design practice in different work contexts. Int. J. Hum.-Comput. Stud. 103634 (2025)

Integrating Accessibility and Inclusive Design in CS and HCI Education: Challenges and Opportunities for Educators

Helen Petrie[1(✉)] and Jenny Darzentas[2]

[1] Department of Computer Science, University of York, York YO10 5DD, UK
helen.petrie@york.ac.uk

[2] Department of Product and Systems Design Engineering, University of the Aegean, Ermoupoli, Syros 84100, Greece
jenny@aegean.gr

Abstract. The ACM has recently revised its recommendations for curricula for first degree level computer science (CS) education, including a very comprehensive guide with a framework for organizing CS education at this level. HCI features strongly and there is emphasis on accessibility and inclusive design in both the recommendations for CS core teaching and HCI knowledge area content. But the accessibility and inclusive design content could be very challenging for HCI teachers without expertise in the area. This paper will discuss the ACM curricula recommendations in this area and stimulate discussion about them. It will also present initiatives to support HCI teachers responsible for this material and a set of practical exercises we have successfully used in teaching first year CS students about accessibility and inclusive design.

Keywords: Accessibility · Inclusive Design · Computer Science Curriculum · Practical Exercises

1 Introduction and Background

The ACM and IEEE have recently revised the recommendations for curricula for computer science (CS) education, presenting a very comprehensive guide for CS educators [2]. It has produced a very complex and detailed curricula framework document, running to nearly 500 pages of text. The attention to accessibility and inclusive design is very welcome, with considerable emphasis being placed on these topics. The curricula recommendations are divided into two areas, the CS Core, which covers topics "every graduate must know" (p. 21) and the Knowledge Areas (KAs) which are "topics for in-depth study". It is accepted that any qualification in CS can cover only some of those KAs. Human Computer Interaction (HCI) consists of six KAs (out of 17 KAs in total), in addition to the CS Core, so plays a prominent part in the recommended curricula.

In the overall framework, the CS Core comprises 270 h of teaching with 18 h devoted to the KA on "Society, Ethics and the Profession" (SEP). One component of SEP is two

Published by Springer Nature Switzerland AG 2026
C. Maciel et al. (Eds.): INTERACT 2025 Workshops, LNCS 16478, pp. 88–94, 2026.
https://doi.org/10.1007/978-3-032-22934-2_9

hours of teaching on "Diversity, Equity, Inclusion and Accessibility" (DEIA). Of course, that is not a great deal of time in a core of 270 h. However, for students specializing in HCI there is a whole KA on "Accessibility and Inclusive Design". This includes recommendations for four specific topics, each with a number of subtopics:

Background:
Demographics and populations (permanent, temporary, and situational disability)
International perspectives on disability
Attitudes towards people with disabilities
Techniques:
UX (user experience) design and research
Software engineering practices that enable inclusion and accessibility.
Technologies:
Examples of accessibility-enabling features, such as conformance to screen readers
Inclusive Design Frameworks:
Creating inclusive processes such as participatory design
Designing for larger impact

For researchers knowledgeable about accessibility and inclusive design, this is an interesting list of topics, which requires some analysis and interpretation. But many HCI teaching groups will not have someone who is particularly knowledgeable about this area, and this list might seem very daunting.

2 Providing Material for the ACM Curricula

Work has also been undertaken to provide more detailed and concrete information about what might be included about accessibility within the ACM curricula for computer science, particularly for those who do not have prior knowledge of the topic. Ladner, Ludi & Domanski [3] are developing a document elaborating on the basic content which might be included in introductory courses, and highlighting resources which can be useful. They also provide useful examples of how accessibility can be included in a number of courses on other topics such as HCI, but also introductory CS courses, courses on web development and design, software engineering, AI and machine learning and project work.

The outline of the content is a very helpful guide for anyone new to teaching accessibility, whether they have prior knowledge about it or not. They suggest covering:

- A discussion of the different types of disabilities, both permanent and temporary and their impacts; approaches to conceptualizing disability, including the medical and social models; difficulties of defining and measuring disability
- A discussion of a range of assistive technologies used by individuals with disabilities in accessing computers and the internet such as screen readers, keyboard-only input, switch control, eye gaze, and speech control
- Presentation of accessibility standards and legislation such as the Web Content Accessibility Guidelines (WCAG) [7], the European Accessibility Act [1] and Section 508 of the US Rehabilitation Act [6], all of which are relevant to accessibility
- Presentation and discussion of accessibility research and other research which has had an impact on technology for people with disabilities, such as speech synthesis and spoken speech recognition.

3 Initiatives to Support those Teaching Accessibility

There are several initiatives which support the teaching of accessibility. For example, TeachAccess [5] is an organization in the USA founded in 2015 with the broad aim of "bringing together industry, education, and disability advocacy organizations to address the digital accessibility skills gap by equipping learners to build toward an inclusive world." TeachAccess provides many courses on accessibility and many resources for teaching and learning about accessibility through its website. It has recently started a TeachAccess Europe initiative.

An international initiative has also been started to try to support specifically HCI teachers who want or need to teach students about accessibility and inclusive design but who lack background knowledge or expertise on the topics, the Global Research and Education Alliance for Assistive Technology (GREAAT). This is a network of academics who research and teach in the areas of accessibility and inclusive design, currently from the Universities of Guelph and McGill in Canada, the Universities of Cardiff, Dundee, Glasgow, King's College, Reading, Swansea and York in the UK and the University of Maryland in the USA. The aim of the initiative is to provide support and resources for HCI teachers on both accessibility and inclusive design, as well as support for research activities. The initiative conducted scoping workshops in London in 2024 and Cardiff in 2025. The network is now planning a framework of support, further activities and funding for particular activities.

4 Low-Cost Simulation Practical Exercises for Teaching Inclusive Design and Accessibility

Even experienced researchers and teachers with expertise in accessibility and inclusive design can find teaching on these topics is a challenge. Students find it difficult to relate to the material and to understand how the needs and wishes of disabled and older people might be very different to their own. At the University of York some years ago it was decided that all students in their first year of their CS degree, regardless of their specialization (which might be AI, cybersecurity, data science or pure CS) would take a course on HCI and it would include an introduction to accessibility and inclusive design. Motivating over 300 students, mainly 18-year-olds and 80% young men, on these topics has been particularly difficult. Before the COVID-19 pandemic it was possible to have a lecture and demonstration of assistive technology by a blind professional, which was very successful. But such a possibility is not an option for many HCI teachers and became impossible with the pandemic. However, we have also developed a set of exercises to introduce students to the needs and problems of users with a number of disabilities which are informative, fun for both students and teachers and inexpensive. These can be deployed by most HCI teachers without great difficulty or background knowledge. We have described them in some detail in a previous paper [3] and are happy to support teachers in deploying them, but we describe them briefly in the next section.

The first year CS students at the University of York receive three hours of teaching about accessibility and inclusive design. This comprises a one hour lecture and a two hour practical session which also starts with a short lecture setting the context for the practical work and explaining the procedures for the day. In a one hour lecture it is only possible to give the briefest of introductions to some concepts about accessibility and inclusive design. The aim of the practical session is to give the students insights into why it is so important to consider the needs and wishes of disabled and older people throughout the design and development of technologies and to do this in a memorable yet amusing way. They get to experience using familiar technologies (one of their colleague's mobile phones) as disabled and older users by means of simple simulations and role-playing scenarios.

One issue which needs to be addressed immediately and is emphasized throughout the practical session is that a simulation of the effects of disability or aging is not the same as the lived experience of people in these situations, and some people find the idea of such simulations disrespectful. It is very important to us as researchers and teachers who want to respect the lived experience of people with disabilities and older people and we communicate this to the students. However, we have found that the students can gain interesting insights from the practical and hopefully have a interesting experience that they may remember later when they are professionals designing or developing interactive systems. The details of what we teach them may no longer be relevant, but if they remember that it is important to consider the needs and wishes of disabled and older people, we would consider the practical exercises to have been a success. We have also not witnessed any incidents at all in which the students trivialized or mocked the exercises.

To create the low-cost simulation kit, we sourced easy to obtain and the most inexpensive materials we could find, mainly from a local supermarket. To simulate various visual disabilities, four sets of spectacles were created, using very inexpensive low magnification reading spectacles. These were then prepared in the following ways to simulate different visual impairments:

- Cataracts: spectacle lenses were smeared with a greasy substance (clear lip gloss worked well)
- Diabetic retinopathy: Spots of white corrector fluid/white paint were dotted across the lenses.
- Glaucoma: White correction fluid/white paint was applied around the edge of the lenses.
- Age-related macular degeneration: Black shoe polish was smeared in the middle of the lenses, and a little greasy substance (clear lip gloss) was smeared around the edge of the lenses.

To simulate the lack of dexterity associated with ageing (e.g. due to arthritis), students were asked to tape small buttons to the joints of their fingers (particularly those fingers or thumb that they use on a mobile phone) and then put on two or three thin latex-free protective gloves, to create several layers glove between fingers and objects (see Fig. 1).

Students worked in groups of four or five. Each group was provided with all the kit required for the simulations plus a large full bottle of mineral water with a baby's nappy on the base to simulate a baby required for the exercises. Each group was given two different personas and scenarios and four tasks to undertake. Here are several examples:

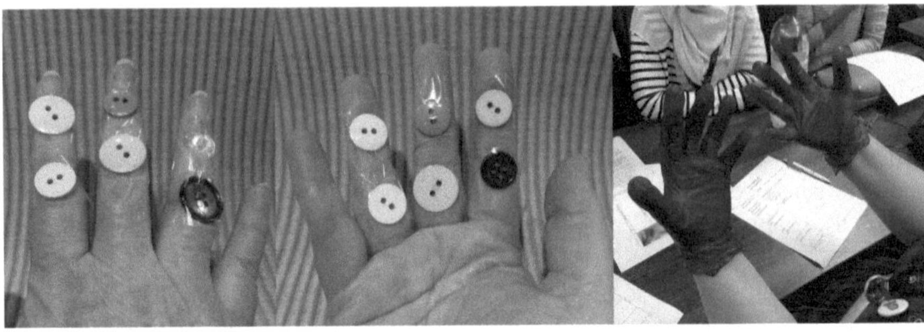

Fig. 1. Buttons and gloves to simulate dexterity issues (Copyright: Helen Petrie).

Persona 1 and Scenario 1.
Chris is 25 years old and has been partially sighted since birth. They want to meet up with a friend, Helen, to have a coffee.

Task: Text your friend Helen on XXX (lecturer provided her number to make the task as realistic as possible, the students could hear her phone receiving messages during the exercise) asking when she is free.

Instructions for Task 1:

Wear one pair of the glasses provided (your choice) to simulate visual impairment.

Be careful if you wear glasses already not to strain your eyes. (If you wear glasses and the simulation glasses cause strain, just do the task without your own glasses on).

Swap phones with someone else in your group, preferably someone who has a phone you are not familiar with, so you are doing the task with an unfamiliar phone.

Persona 2 and Scenario 2.
Sam is a 69-year-old grandparent who is babysitting their six-month-old grandchild. The baby is crying and after having had a look under the nappy, Sam realises that the baby has a bad case of nappy rash.

Task 2: Send a text message to the child's parent's mobile (XXX), asking whether you should call the doctor.

Instructions for Task 2:

Wear a pair of the provided glasses AND the buttons on your joints AND two gloves on the hand (three if you can manage it) you use to operate a phone in order to simulate an older person with visual disability and some dexterity problems in their fingers.

Do the task standing up, holding the baby (rocking it to try to stop it crying). Don't put the phone on the table (too easy!), tuck it under your chin.

At the end of the practical we asked students to participate in an evaluation of the exercise, this was optional, but 63 students in all completed a short questionnaire. Table 1 summarizes some of the questions on which students rated their experiences. It shows that students found the practice helped them understand the difficulties that people with disabilities and older people might encounter with smartphones, that the practice as fun and that they would recommend trying the simulation to colleagues. We also asked open-ended questions which showed that some of the students had interesting insights from the experience, including rather unexpectedly things that being at university might be more difficult for students with disabilities (there were several students with disabilities in the class).

Table 1. Ratings of overall experience of the practical exercise (N = 63).

Question	Median rating (SIQR)	Wilcoxon one sample test
To what extent did this practical help you understand more about the difficulties people with disabilities and older people might encounter with smartphones? Rated: Not at all (1) – A great deal (7)	4.00 (1.00)	F = 5.74, $p < 0.001$
To what extent was the practical fun? Rated: Not at all (1) – Very much (7)	5.00 (1.00)	F = 6.43, $p < 0.001$
Would you recommend trying these simulation techniques to a colleague who was developing an app? Rated: Never (1) – Definitely (7)	5.00 (1.00)	F = 5.79, $p < 0.001$

In all this practical was enjoyable for both teachers and students. We found it was an interesting but respectful way of giving students some insight into the problems that people with disabilities and older people face with technology that hopefully they may remember in years to come when they are developing technologies.

5 Conclusions

There is growing realization that it is very important for the designers and developers of digital technologies to have some awareness and knowledge of the needs of users with disabilities and older users. One opportunity to instill such knowledge is during higher education. Many designers and developers start their careers with a CS degree, possibly later specializing in HCI or an aspect of design. Finding space in the CS curriculum for teaching on accessibility and inclusive design is difficult, but organizations such as the ACM and IEEE are championing the inclusion of such material, albeit in a small way. However, teachers on CS courses may lack the appropriate knowledge and skills to undertake such teaching. A number of initiatives are now providing such support, both in terms of courses, resources and ideas for how to engage students in this important topic.

References

1. European Union: European Accessibility Act (2025). https://eur-lex.europa.eu/legal-content/EN/TXT/?uri=CELEX%3A32019L0882
2. Kumar, A.N., Raj, R.K., Aly, S.G., et al.: Computer Science Curricula 2023. ACM Press, IEEE Computer Society Press and AAAI Press (2024). https://doi.org/10.1145/3664191

3. Ladner, R.E., Ludi, S., Domanski, R.J.: Teaching about accessibility in computer science education. ACM Inroads. **16**(2), 28 (2025)
4. Petrie, H., Darzentas, J.: Introducing computer science students to inclusive design and accessibility: evaluation of practical exercises with a low-cost simulation kit. In: International Conference on Computers Helping People with Special Needs (ICCHP). Springer Nature, Cham Switzerland (2024)
5. TeachAccess: Who we are. https://www.teachaccess.org/
6. U.S. Department of Justice: Section 508 Home Page (2023). https://www.justice.gov/crt/section-508-home-page-0
7. World Wide Web Consortium (W3): Web Content Accessibility Guidelines Version 2.2. (2024). https://www.w3.org/TR/WCAG22/

Human-Centered Software Engineering: Balancing Interaction, Artificial Intelligence, and Human Value

HCSE Workshop on Balancing Interaction, Artificial Intelligence, and Human Value: Insights and Takeaways
IFIP WG 13.2 Workshop at INTERACT 2025

Stefan Sauer[1], Carmelo Ardito[2](✉), and Regina Bernhaupt[3]

[1] Paderborn University, Paderborn, Germany
sauer@uni-paderborn.de
[2] Polytechnic University of Bari, Bari, Italy
carmelo.ardito@poliba.it
[3] Eindhoven University of Technology, Eindhoven, The Netherlands
r.bernhaupt@tue.nl

Abstract. This edition of the Human-Centered Software Engineering (HCSE) workshop focused on the intersection of interaction, artificial intelligence, and human value. The workshop had three main topics: (1) Human–AI Interaction and Cognitive Models for Future Systems, (2) Methods and Framework for Usability and User Experience, and (3) Smart and Secure Digital Futures. In the series of HCSE workshops and conferences, we see the need to explore and understand how software engineering and human–computer interaction can accommodate AI-driven decision-making, adaptive interfaces, and autonomous systems that become ubiquitous. The submissions focused on how to design this future interaction with AI. Interestingly, there is a need to re-interpret and revisit existing frameworks and understanding on how to support usability and user experience on the one hand and allow for smart and secure systems on the other. A key challenge for the future will be the balancing of these properties in human-centered design and development processes.

Keywords: Human Value · Artificial Intelligence · Automation · Human-Centered AI · Ethics and Transparency in AI · Digital Transformation · Sustainability · Agile Development · Low-Code Development · Cybersecurity · Usability · User Experience

1 Introduction

Digital transformation is advancing towards almost all aspects of life, work, and business. It reshapes how we live, it changes the way people work and how we shape societies. Many of the changes we saw the past two to three years were

Published by Springer Nature Switzerland AG 2026
C. Maciel et al. (Eds.): INTERACT 2025 Workshops, LNCS 16478, pp. 97–103, 2026.
https://doi.org/10.1007/978-3-032-22934-2_10

driven by Artificial Intelligence (AI), but beyond this trend there is an increasing spread of digitalization in general that affects the research domains of human-computer interaction (HCI) and software engineering. Although these innovations create unprecedented opportunities, they also pose significant challenges in ensuring that technology remains transparent, ethical, and aligned with user needs [3]. The workshop and conference on Human-Centered Software Engineering (HCSE) is thus more relevant than ever. Traditional software engineering methodologies, which have long focused on correctness, efficiency, scalability, and automation, must now evolve to incorporate human-centric principles that prioritize explainability, trust, and responsible AI development [4].

Building on the well-established themes of IFIP WG 13.2 workshops, the workshop during INTERACT 2025 in Belo Horizonte, Brazil brought together researchers from several disciplines to address the challenges on how to design, develop, and evaluate with a focus on the human, preserving human values and providing excellent experience when interacting with partly autonomous, AI-driven systems.

The workshop at INTERACT 2025 is a follow-up of the successful workshops organized at INTERACT 2015 in Bamberg, Germany [6], INTERACT 2017 in Mumbai, India [7], INTERACT 2019 in Paphos, Cyprus [1], INTERACT 2021 in Bari, Italy [5], and INTERACT 2023 in York, UK [2].

These workshop proceedings are based on ten papers that came out of the workshop submissions, the peer-reviewed selection and reviewing process of contributions that were presented at the workshop, and the final research papers for the proceedings.

In the following we summarize and describe the themes, topics, and contributions of these papers and provide some insight about open research questions and topics that need addressing in the near future.

2 Research Topics and Contributions

The workshop had three main research topics that are discussed in the following.

2.1 Design of Human–AI Interaction and Cognitive Models for Future Systems

The first session on "(Design of) Human–AI Interaction and Cognitive Models for Future Systems" reflects the need to understand how humans engage with increasingly intelligent and autonomous technologies. As AI-based systems and Digital Twins become parts of everyday life, we need to understand the design of these interactions.

The paper *"A Conceptual Framework for Designing Temporal Interactions with Digital Twin-enabled Systems"* introduces a systematic approach to designing interactions with Digital Twins (DTs), emphasizing the integration of past, present, and future as temporal dimensions for which we need to design. By proposing seven temporal interaction patterns based on the analysis of four autonomy levels of systems and the different engagement styles users have, this work provides designers with a rich conceptual toolkit for crafting temporal experiences that balance user agency and system intelligence.

In *"Conversational Agent Integration into Diagnostic Application for Primary Ciliary Dyskinesia"*, the authors explore the design and integration of LLM-powered conversational agents into medical image annotation tools. Through a user-centered approach and qualitative evaluation, the study highlights design challenges such as defining assistant scope, dialogue structuring, and UI integration, offering practical insights for deploying conversational agents in high-stakes domains such as healthcare.

The paper *"Enhancing LLM-Based Information Seeking with Search Trails: A Case Study"* addresses the limitations of traditional text-based interfaces in supporting complex information-seeking tasks. By introducing an interactive mind-map-based interface through the ChatInVis tool, the authors demonstrate how visualizing search trails can foster reflection, improve navigation, and enhance learning during exploratory searches, as validated by a user study with 20 participants.

Finally, *"User Mental Models as a Lens for Evaluating Explainable-AI System Outputs"* proposes a cognitive-science-informed framework for assessing Explainable-AI (XAI) systems. Moving beyond surface-level clarity metrics, this work emphasizes how expert users construct and refine mental models when interacting with explanations. Illustrated through the Brain Age Predictor case study, the framework offers a nuanced perspective for designing XAI interfaces that support informed and reflective decision-making.

Together, these contributions underscore the importance of designing for cognition, transparency, and adaptability in Human–AI interaction. They invite researchers and practitioners to consider not only what AI systems can do, but how they communicate, collaborate, and co-evolve with human users in future socio-technical ecosystems.

2.2 Methods and Frameworks for Usability and User Experience

The second cluster, "Methods and Frameworks for Usability and User Experience", addresses the methodological foundations that underpin effective user-centered design (UCD) and evaluation practices in specialized and safety-critical domains. These contributions collectively emphasize the importance of rigorous, context-sensitive approaches to usability and user experience, highlighting how frameworks and tailored methods can bridge disciplinary gaps and ensure meaningful outcomes.

The paper *"Suitability of Selected User Research Methods in Medical Applications"* foregrounds the critical role of user research strategies in applied UCD within medical contexts. Drawing on long-term case studies, the authors argue for adaptive research methods—such as exploratory discussions, contextual inquiries, and observation—that respect domain-specific constraints while fostering trust and knowledge transfer. This work provides an empirical guide for tailoring research approaches to the needs of medical experts, ensuring validity and efficiency in collaborative design processes.

In *"From Data to Dialogue: Rethinking Feedback Delivery Styles of Digital Twin in Preventive Healthcare Context"*, the authors challenge conventional feedback paradigms by conceptualizing Human Digital Twins (HDTs) as relational entities capable of engaging in bidirectional dialogue. Through design explorations including physicalization workshops and speculative role-based studies, the paper identifies principles such as customization, adaptivity, and temporal responsiveness as essential for evolving HDTs beyond static feedback toward dynamic, user-centered interaction models.

Finally, *"Simulator-Based Distraction Analysis Procedure for User Testing of In-Vehicle Interfaces"* addresses the persistent challenge of evaluating driver distraction in usability studies without access to high-end laboratory setups. The authors propose a lightweight, simulator-based procedure incorporating eye-tracking, distraction metrics (TA-PT and TO-ST), and visualization techniques (heatmaps and scanpath overlays). Validated through a proof-of-concept study, this approach demonstrates how resource-efficient methods can yield actionable insights into attentional demand and interface design trade-offs.

Collectively, these papers underscore the necessity of methodological innovation in advancing usability and user experience research. They advocate for approaches that are not only scientifically robust but also practically adaptable, enabling researchers and practitioners to navigate the complexities of interdisciplinary collaboration and real-world constraints.

2.3 Smart and Secure Digital Futures

The third cluster, "Smart and Secure Digital Futures", explores emerging approaches for embedding intelligence and security into everyday environments and collaborative technologies. Taken together, these contributions address three critical dimensions of future socio-technical systems: unobtrusive sensing of human states, the safeguarding of privacy in immersive contexts, and the advancement of cybersecurity education through AI-driven simulation frameworks.

The paper *"SensingChair: Capturing Group Mood Dynamics through Sensing with Objects in Physical Spaces"* introduces the concept of sensing-through-objects as a privacy-preserving alternative to traditional affective sensing. By leveraging pressure sensors embedded in chairs, the authors demonstrate how posture-based indicators can infer group mood without resorting to intrusive visual or physiological data. A preliminary study validates the feasibility of this approach and opens pathways for designing mood-aware workspaces that prioritize well-being while respecting user privacy.

In *"Perspectives on Privacy and Security in Collaborative AR – Insights From a Scoping Review and an Expert Interview Study"*, the authors investigate the complex interplay between technological innovation and user protection in collaborative augmented reality (AR). Through expert interviews, the study reveals systemic gaps in privacy and security practices, highlighting the dependency of end-users on developers and the lack of prioritization by organizations.

The paper *"Enabling Cyber Security Education through Digital Twins and Generative AI"* explores how Digital Twins (DTs) and Large Language Models (LLMs) can advance cybersecurity education by enabling realistic, AI-driven simulation environments. The proposed Cyber Red Team Knife (CRTK) framework combines DTs and LLMs to strengthen both defensive and offensive training strategies. The paper advocates for more robust software support, greater awareness of privacy and security implications, and the adoption of AI-driven tools to strengthen resilience across digital ecosystems, particularly as these technologies permeate sensitive and professional contexts.

Together, these contributions underscore the dual imperative of designing smart environments that are adaptive, trustworthy, and secure, inviting researchers and practitioners to envision socio-technical futures where innovation is grounded in ethical responsibility and human-centered values.

3 Synopsis

This proceedings volume brings together cutting-edge research on human–AI interaction, usability frameworks, and smart digital futures, reflecting the interdisciplinary challenges and opportunities that define next-generation socio-technical systems. Across three thematic clusters, the contributions explore how design, cognition, and ethics intersect in shaping technologies that are not only intelligent but also human-centered, trustworthy, and adaptive.

The first cluster, "Design of Human–AI Interaction and Cognitive Models for Future Systems," addresses the growing complexity of interactions with AI-driven systems. "A Conceptual Framework for Designing Temporal Interactions with Digital Twin-enabled Systems" introduces a systematic approach for managing temporal dimensions—past, present, and future—in Digital Twin interactions, offering designers a rich conceptual toolkit for balancing user agency and system autonomy. "Conversational Agent Integration into Diagnostic Application for Primary Ciliary Dyskinesia" examines the integration of LLM-powered agents into medical workflows, highlighting design challenges and lessons learned from a user-centered case study. "Enhancing LLM-Based Information Seeking with Search Trails: A Case Study" rethinks information-seeking by visualizing search trails through an interactive mind-map interface, enabling reflection and deeper learning. Finally, "User Mental Models as a Lens for Evaluating Explainable-AI System Outputs" reframes XAI evaluation around cognitive processes, proposing a mental-model-based framework that supports trust and informed decision-making.

The second cluster, "Methods and Frameworks for Usability and User Experience," focuses on methodological innovation for designing and evaluating systems in specialized domains. "Suitability of Selected User Research Methods in Medical Applications" emphasizes tailoring user research strategies to the constraints and needs of medical experts, ensuring validity and efficiency in collaborative design. "From Data to Dialogue: Rethinking Feedback Delivery Styles of Digital Twin in Preventive Healthcare Context" proposes design principles for creating adaptive, bidirectional feedback between Human Digital Twins (HDTs) and users, moving beyond static information toward dynamic dialogue. "Simulator-Based Distraction Analysis Procedure for User Testing of In-Vehicle Interfaces" introduces a lightweight, simulator-based approach for analyzing driver distraction, providing practical metrics and visualization techniques for usability testing in resource-limited settings.

The third cluster, "Smart and Secure Digital Futures," explores the integration of intelligence and security into everyday environments and collaborative technologies. "SensingChair: Capturing Group Mood Dynamics through Sensing with Objects in Physical Spaces" presents a privacy-preserving approach to affective sensing by embedding unobtrusive sensors in furniture, enabling mood-aware workspaces without intrusive data collection. "Perspectives on Privacy and Security in Collaborative AR – Insights From a Scoping Review and an Expert Interview Study" investigates systemic gaps in privacy and security practices in collaborative AR, advocating for improved developer support and heightened awareness as these technologies enter sensitive contexts. "Enabling Cyber Security Education through Digital Twins and Generative AI" explores how Digital Twins (DTs) and Large Language Models (LLMs) can advance cybersecurity education by enabling realistic, AI-driven simulation environments.

4 Looking Ahead: Future Research and Societal Impact

The research presented in this volume underscores a critical trajectory: as AI systems become pervasive, their success will hinge not only on technical sophistication but on their ability to align with human values, cognitive processes, and ethical principles. Future work must deepen our understanding of adaptive interaction models, trust calibration in AI systems, and privacy-preserving sensing—especially as technologies migrate into domains such as healthcare, mobility, and collaborative workspaces. Societally, these innovations carry profound implications. They promise to enhance well-being, democratize access to intelligent tools, and foster inclusive participation in digital ecosystems. At the same time, they demand vigilance against risks related to autonomy, bias, and surveillance. The challenge for researchers and practitioners is to design futures where intelligence and responsibility co-evolve, ensuring that smart systems serve as partners in human flourishing rather than being sources of inequity or harm. We hope this collection inspires continued dialogue and interdisciplinary collaboration toward building secure, transparent, and human-centered digital futures.

5 Conclusion

To summarize, this workshop was a success. It encouraged active participation and meaningful exchange. By combining research presentations with focused feedback sessions and moments dedicated to community building, we fostered an environment where ideas could be both shared and constructively challenged. The diversity of topics and approaches highlighted the richness of the field and opened new avenues for collaboration.

References

1. Ardito, C., Bernhaupt, R., Palanque, P., Sauer, S.: Handling security, usability, user experience and reliability in user-centered development processes. In: Lamas, D., Loizides, F., Nacke, L., Petrie, H., Winckler, M., Zaphiris, P. (eds.) INTERACT 2019. LNCS, vol. 11749, pp. 759–762. Springer, Cham (2019). https://doi.org/10.1007/978-3-030-29390-1_76
2. Ardito, C., Bernhaupt, R., Sauer, S.: Human-centered software engineering: rethinking the interplay of human–computer interaction and software engineering in the age of digital transformation. In: Abdelnour Nocera, J., Kristín Lárusdóttir, M., Petrie, H., Piccinno, A., Winckler, M. (eds.) Human-Computer Interaction – INTERACT 2023, pp. 638–643. Springer, Cham (2023)
3. European Parliament and Council of the European Union: The EU artificial intelligence act (2024). https://artificialintelligenceact.eu/
4. Sauer, S., Ardito, C., Bernhaupt, R.: Human-centered software engineering: balancing interaction, artificial intelligence, and human value. In: Ardito, C., et al. (eds.) Human-Computer Interaction – INTERACT 2025, pp. 377–381. Springer, Cham (2025)
5. Sauer, S., Bernhaupt, R., Ardito, C.: Human-centered software engineering for changing contexts of use. In: Ardito, C., et al. (eds.) INTERACT 2021. LNCS, vol. 12936, pp. 548–552. Springer, Cham (2021). https://doi.org/10.1007/978-3-030-85607-6_75
6. Winckler, M., Bernhaupt, R., Forbrig, P., Sauer, S.: User experience and user-centered development processes. In: Abascal, J., Barbosa, S., Fetter, M., Gross, T., Palanque, P., Winckler, M. (eds.) Human-Computer Interaction – INTERACT 2015, pp. 661–662. Springer, Cham (2015)
7. Winckler, M., Larusdottir, M., Kuusinen, K., Bogdan, C., Palanque, P.: Dealing with conflicting user interface properties in user-centered development processes. In: Bernhaupt, R., Dalvi, G., Joshi, A., Balkrishan, D., O'Neill, J., Winckler, M. (eds.) Human-Computer Interaction – INTERACT 2017, pp. 521–523. Springer, Cham (2017)

A Conceptual Framework for Designing Temporal Interactions with Digital Twin-Enabled Systems

Yaxin Zheng[1,2(✉)], Harm van Essen[1], Scott Mitchell[2], Liam Fennessy[2], Laurene Vaughan[2], and Regina Bernhaupt[1]

[1] Eindhoven University of Technology, Eindhoven, The Netherlands
{y.zheng,h.a.v.essen,r.bernhaupt}@tue.nl

[2] RMIT University, Melbourne, Australia
{scott.mitchell,liam.fennessy,laurene.vaughan}@rmit.edu.au

Abstract. Designing effective interactions with Digital Twins (DTs) is challenging because temporal information integrates past data, present monitoring, and future predictions. Designers lack systematic guidance for determining how users and DT-enabled systems communicate and interact with each other. This paper introduces a conceptual framework for designers engaged in DT interaction design. The framework integrates three aspects as follows: 1) We use the "Time Machine" analogy to develop seven temporal interaction patterns of DTs across three temporal dimensions: past (Retrospective Reflection, User Action Based on Past Data), present (Immediate Action, Ongoing Adaptation), and future (Predictive Prompting, User Reflection Based on Prediction, User Action Based on Prediction). 2) We synthesize four autonomy levels of DT, from user-driven to shared agency to system-guided to system-autonomous. 3) We introduce Digital Twin Engagement Style (visible vs. invisible, proactive vs. reactive) and User Engagement Style (intentional vs. unintentional, active vs. passive) to fully characterize the interaction space. The design framework provides designers with systematic perspectives for exploring and designing temporal interactions of DT-enabled systems. Future work will validate the framework.

Keywords: Digital Twin · Temporal Interaction · Temporal Interface · Design Analogy

1 Introduction

Digital Twins (DTs) are not only a virtual replica of a physical entity [3], but also adaptable models that can respond to real-time environmental and operational changes [9]. The temporal dimension of DTs is a fundamental aspect that distinguishes DTs from static digital models. Unlike traditional representations, DTs continuously evolve over time by mirroring real-world changes, capturing historical data, and predicting future states [5,9,14]. They can also be

Published by Springer Nature Switzerland AG 2026
C. Maciel et al. (Eds.): INTERACT 2025 Workshops, LNCS 16478, pp. 104–118, 2026.
https://doi.org/10.1007/978-3-032-22934-2_11

used to analyze and forecast product performance during production, as well as to enhance the product's functionality and efficiency throughout the product's entire life cycle [16].

DT's temporal nature enables DT systems to analyze past behaviors, monitor real-time interactions, and simulate potential future scenarios, offering a dynamic and adaptive design solution to end-users, see Fig. 1. Temporal Interfaces for DTs are user interfaces where time-based changes are central to interaction [22]. They provide an integrated view across three temporal dimensions: past (historical data), present (live monitoring), and future (predicted outcomes). While temporal interfaces determine what temporal information is presented and how it is structured, temporal interactions capture the diverse ways users engage with this information, from reflecting on past patterns to responding to present alerts to planning based on future predictions. We define **Temporal Interaction** as the interactions in which users engage with temporal information through digital twin interfaces, enabling users to access, interpret, and act upon data across different time horizons.

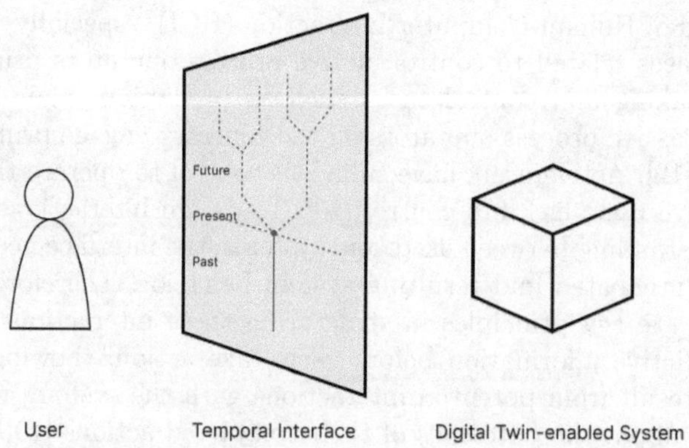

Fig. 1. A temporal interface captures the temporality of digital twins for interactions between user and system.

Our research question is: *How might we support designers to design temporal interactions with digital twin-enabled systems?* First, building upon and refining the "Time Machine" analogy proposed in our prior work [22], in this paper, we conceptualize seven temporal interaction patterns that characterize how users move among past, present, and future states when engaging with DTs. These temporal interaction patterns provide a lens for understanding how DTs can support reflection, real-time action, and future-oriented decision-making. Second, we introduce DT autonomy levels to characterize the degree of system initiative and user initiative. Third, we synthesize DT engagement styles and user engagement styles to characterize the full spectrum of DT-User relationships. These contributions together provide a theoretical foundation and initial design framework for creating temporal interfaces that enable more meaningful interactions between end-users and DT-enabled systems.

2 Theoretical Background

2.1 Interaction Design in HCI

Perception and interpretation are key to understanding situational contexts [15]. A user can interact with a system in different ways. For explicit interaction, a user initiates actions and expects a response from the system [21]. For implicit interaction, the system often passively monitors users over time to adaptively adjust interaction aspects [21]. Implicit interaction occurs without the user's explicit request, conscious awareness, notice, or initiative [7]. In implicit interaction, systems interpret user actions as input even when users perform those actions without the primary intention of interacting with the system [7]. Ju et al. [7] proposed to describe system-initiated interaction as proactive interaction while user-initiated interaction as reactive interaction.

In the field of Human-Computer Interaction (HCI), especially when it comes to user interfaces related to control, active process operators primarily engage in decision-making and control tasks such as prediction, planning, and control [10,12]. Passive process operators on the contrary engage primarily in monitoring tasks [12]. Active users have sufficient control to operate the technology, whereas passive users lack full control [10]. To design interactions that support mutual understanding between users and systems, the interface needs to communicate both anticipated and resulting system behavior. Therefore, feedforward and feedback are key principles in structuring these interactions. Feedforward provides predictive information before users take action, showing what consequences will result from potential interactions with the system, while feedback informs users about the outcomes of their completed actions [19]. In DT's context, both mechanisms could enable users to navigate temporal information: feedforward supports prospective scenario exploration and prediction, while feedback facilitates retrospective analysis of how past states evolved into present conditions.

2.2 Temporality in HCI and Digital Twin

The concept of time combines two different but familiar ideas: succession, the perception of events occurring in a sequential flow as the present becomes the past, and duration, the interval between those events, understood not as a separate entity, but as an intrinsic quality of what persists over time [8]. Time and temporality exist in physical objects, interfaces, experiences, and interactions: physical objects age and evolve; interfaces display temporal information; and the temporal nature of user experience is intrinsic to the duration of each interaction [4].

Tan et al. identify three levels of human understanding of temporal reasoning: 1) time-time relation; 2) time-event relation; and 3) event-event relation [18]. These three levels of understanding could guide designers to shape how people perceive time. While HCI researchers have long focused on time-centered interfaces to enhance work-related activities [13], DTs offer a different opportunity: rather than simply optimizing how users interact with time, they create dynamic temporal replicas that allow users to move between or compare past, present, and future states of systems [22]. The "happening" of the change of time unfolds in two temporal dimensions: the pace of the change itself and the pace at which people become aware of it [13]. People may suddenly notice a slow-building change and feel confused, or gradually realize that a rapid change has occurred, missing the window to respond effectively [13]. DTs help bridge this perception gap by tracking changes in real-time and alerting users to both changing trends and abrupt shifts, enabling more timely awareness and intervention [5].

Temporal concepts are necessary to everyday experience and are deeply embedded in language, manifested through expressions such as waiting, pausing, catching up, next, today, tomorrow, and now [2]. Given this fundamental role of temporality in human experience, understanding users' conceptual models of any system or process requires recognizing how they experience time in their daily lives. This means not only the temporal framework users adopt when viewing information (short-term, long-term, present, retrospective, or prospective), but also how these perspectives should shape the temporal framing of systems and interactions, as well as the presentation of temporal data [2].

3 Construction of Framework

3.1 Method

To support designers in temporal interaction design, we aim to construct a conceptual framework. Conceptual frameworks emphasize understanding and interpretation, distinguishing them from quantitative models that focus on theoretical explanation [6]. Drawing on Jabareen's (2009) [6] eight-phase methodology for conceptual framework analysis, we synthesized our design research approach into four main phases: (1) literature review to map key concepts; (2) systematic categorization and integration to identify relationships among concepts; (3) iterative synthesis to develop a coherent conceptual framework; and (4) validation of the conceptual framework. In this paper, we focus on the first three steps, and we will conduct validation in future work.

3.2 Temporality of Digital Twin

"Time Machine" Analogy for Conception of Temporal Dimension of Digital Twins. Figure 2 is an updated version of the one presented in our previous work [22]. It illustrates the concept of a DT and its relationship with

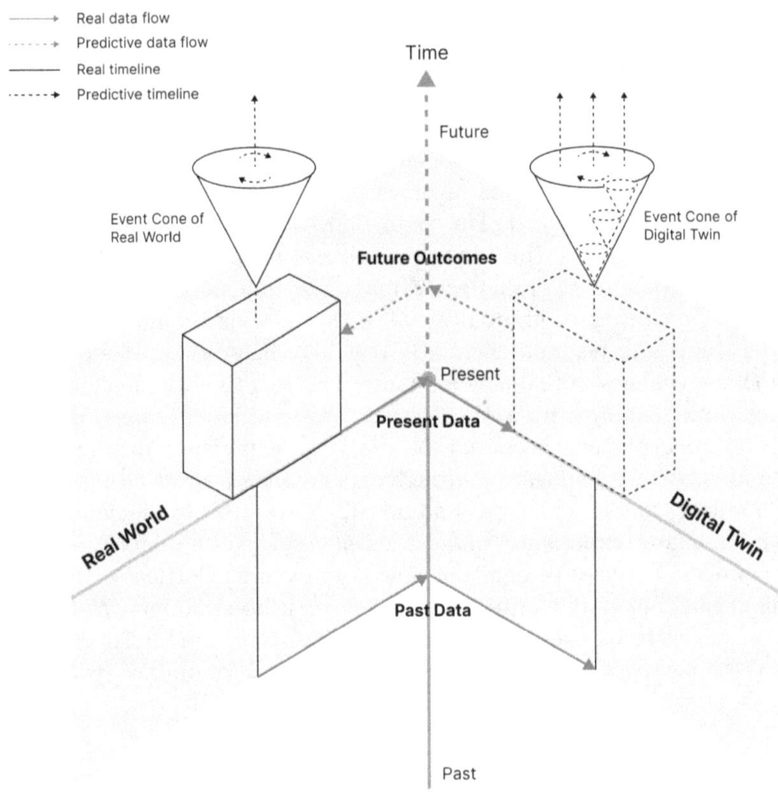

Fig. 2. "Time Machine" Analogy for Conception of Digital Twins.

the real world over time, specifically focusing on future predictions based on past and present data. From Fig. 2, a DT collects and stores past data, enabling it to forecast future events. This dual capability to revisit past data and predict future outcomes allows the DT to function much like a "Time Machine" that traverses both the past and the future. Here is a detailed explanation of Fig. 2:

- **Real World and Digital Twin**: These are represented by two cubes, one solid (Real World) and one dashed (Digital Twin). These cubes represent the physical entity and its digital counterpart.
- **Time Axis**: This is a vertical line indicating the flow of time from the past towards the future. It suggests that the diagram considers different time states, past, present, and future. The origin represents the present. Anything greater than the origin represents the future and anything less than the origin represents the past. This is similar to navigating through different times in a time machine, observing or changing events at different points.

- **Past Data**: This is shown at the bottom of the time axis, indicating that historical data is used to inform the DT and, by extension, to predict future events in the real world.
- **Present Data**: The present data is real-time monitoring and actions by the DT and the real world, which decides the path forward.
- **Future Outcomes**: This aspect is shown as a one-way arrow from the DT to the real world. This implies that future events in the real world can be predicted and optimized by the DT.
- **Feedback Loop**: The red arrows symbolizing future outcomes, present data, and past data between the real world and the DT can be likened to the concept of a time loop in time travel narratives, where actions taken in one time frame affect outcomes in another.
- **Event Cone of Real World and Digital Twin**: These cones represent the potential future outcomes or events that can occur in real world and DT contexts. The cones are oriented upwards, suggesting the future possibilities based on current data. Drawing inspiration from Voros [20], the vertical axis of the event cone represents the passage of time in a linear progression, from the past to the future. Within the cone, smaller cyclical patterns emerge, representing recurring activities or repetitive events. These cycles, such as daily routines or seasonal trends, are embedded in the overall linear timeline, adding a dynamic layer of contextual understanding. The DT's event cone is imagined as a series of interconnected cones at key predictive points, representing how different futures could emerge and interact based on changing data and conditions. These cones mimic how a time machine might allow one to explore multiple future scenarios before they happen. This diagram illustrates how future possibilities can influence current decisions, creating a dynamic interaction between past, present, and future.

Overall, the "Time Machine" analogy and associated diagram act as a conceptual tool that could be used to support designers in understanding how DTs can predict, optimize, and potentially influence future outcomes based on a systematic analysis of past and present data.

Temporal Interaction of Digital Twin. Building on the Time Machine analogy, we developed seven temporal interaction patterns organized across three temporal dimensions: past, present, and future (see Table 1). These seven interaction patterns emerged from analyzing the distinct ways users engage with temporal information in DT-enabled systems. Each pattern addresses a unique combination of temporal dimension (past/present/future), user intent (reflect/react/adapt/plan), and system role (prompt/react/co-adapt), providing designers with a comprehensive vocabulary for temporal interaction design.

Past-oriented interactions enable learning from historical data:

- **Retrospective Reflection** refers to situations in which users look back and reflect after a missed opportunity for action. For example, the system may present: "If you had acted yesterday, you could have saved 9% of electricity."

Table 1. Temporal Interaction Patterns of Digital Twin

Time Dimension	Past		Present		Future		
Type of Temporal Interaction	Retrospective Reflection	User Action Based on Past Data	Immediate Action	Ongoing Adaptation	Predictive Prompting	User Reflection Based on Prediction	User Action Based on Prediction

- **User Action Based on Past Data** describes cases where the system presents past data and the user intentionally modifies their action based on this information.

Present-oriented interactions address immediate needs and ongoing adaptation:

- **Immediate Action** occurs when the system provides real-time cues or alerts that prompt users to act in the present moment.
- **Ongoing Adaptation** represents users and the DT continuously co-adapt through iterative feedback loops, creating a dynamic partnership where both parties adjust based on evolving conditions.

Future-oriented interactions leverage predictive capabilities for proactive decision-making:

- **Predictive Prompting** represents system-initiated cues that anticipate future states, providing suggestions across different temporal ranges (e.g., next hour or next day).
- **User Reflection Based on Prediction** refers to situations where users reflect on possible future outcomes before deciding what action to take.
- **User Action Based on Prediction** describes users directly adjust their behavior based on DT forecasts.

3.3 Autonomy Levels of Digital Twin

Table 2. Autonomy Levels of Digital Twin

Autonomy Level	Description
1 Low (User-driven)	Digital Twin only responds when the user acts.
2 Moderate (Shared / Interactive)	Digital Twin responds proactively and provides feedback; user and Digital Twin co-act.
3 High (System-guided)	Digital Twin predicts, prompts, or supports user decisions before user's active action.
4 Very High (System-autonomous)	Digital Twin autonomously adapts and acts independently while keeping humans in the loop, often operating without explicit user intention or intervention.

While temporal interaction patterns above describe what users and systems do across time dimensions, they do not specify who initiates or controls these interactions. We introduce DT autonomy levels to address this gap by characterizing the degree of system initiative and autonomy. We propose four levels of digital twin autonomy (see Table 2), which range from purely user-driven operation to fully system-autonomous. This classification provides a vocabulary for discussing how DTs vary in initiative, decision-making capacity, and the degree of control shared with users, and serves as a foundation for analyzing and designing temporal interactions across different contexts.

Parasuraman et al. [11] proposed a widely adopted framework describing ten levels of automation, ranging from situations in which the human performs all tasks to those in which the system decides and acts everything automamously. More recently, Agrawal et al. [1] outlined three levels of automation specific to DT, including (1) a baseline with no DT involvement, (2) partial automation where the DT assists in decision-making or analyze, and (3) full automation, in which the DT autonomously manages the system.

Building on these prior classifications and focusing specifically on how users interact with DTs in everyday contexts, we propose a refined four-level spectrum of autonomy of DTs. This spectrum captures the shifting distribution of initiative, decision-making responsibility, and control across user–system relationships:

1. Low (User-driven): DT is reactive and operates only when the user initiates interaction. The user is the primary decision-maker.
2. Moderate (Shared/Interactive): DT responds proactively and provides feedback in coordination with the user. Interaction is cooperative, with action and awareness shared between human and system.
3. High (System-guided): DT anticipates needs and may prompt, recommend, or frame decisions before the user takes explicit action. The system guides user behavior while the user retains agency.
4. Very High (System-autonomous): DT adapts and acts independently, adjusting parameters or performing operations without requiring user initiation. The user remains "in the loop" but may be unaware of system adjustments unless they seek to intervene.

This four-level autonomy model provides a conceptual foundation for analyzing how different forms of temporal interaction with DTs shape user experience, decision-making, and perceived control.

3.4 Digital Twin Engagement Style and User Engagement Style

Digital Twin Engagement Style. DT autonomy levels describe the degree of system initiative. However, DT-enabled systems with the same autonomy level can interact very differently depending on how they communicate and how users engage. We therefore introduce Digital Twin Engagement Style (visible vs. invisible, proactive vs. reactive) (see Fig. 3) and User Engagement Style (intentional

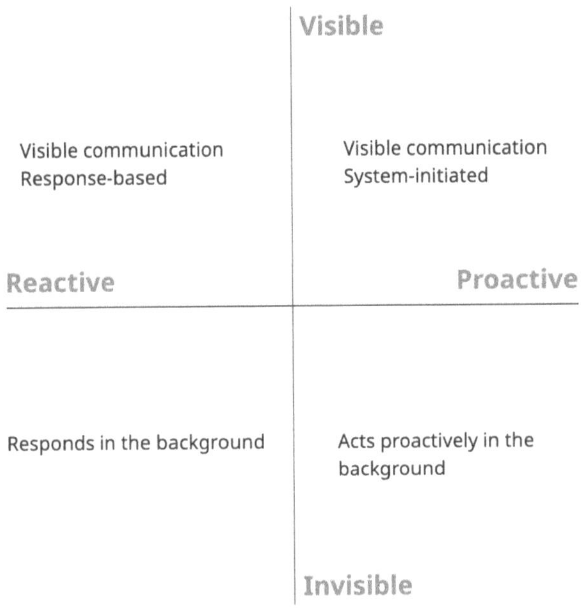

Fig. 3. Digital Twin Engagement Style.

vs. unintentional, active vs. passive) (see Fig. 4) to fully characterize the interaction space.

A set of interaction definitions was selected to describe DT's engagement style. First, according to Ju et al. [7], interactions can be characterized as proactive when initiated by the system or reactive when initiated by the user. Second, a key challenge in DT interface design is determining the appropriate visibility of interactions, which should be foregrounded and which should operate quietly in the background. To address this, we propose **Proactive-Reactive** and **Visible-Invisible** as two axes for characterizing DT engagement style, see Fig. 3. **Visible-Proactive** interactions are characterized by system-initiated communication that is clearly displayed in the interface, proactively informing users of changes or opportunities. **Visible-Reactive** interactions provide visible real-time feedback in response to user actions, making the system's responses apparent. **Invisible-Proactive** interactions involve the system acting autonomously and silently in the background, making decisions without explicit user awareness. **Invisible–Reactive** interactions occur when the DT responds directly to user commands, but its internal state, reasoning, and model remain hidden. The DT executes what the user requests, without displaying feedback, explanations, or predictions.

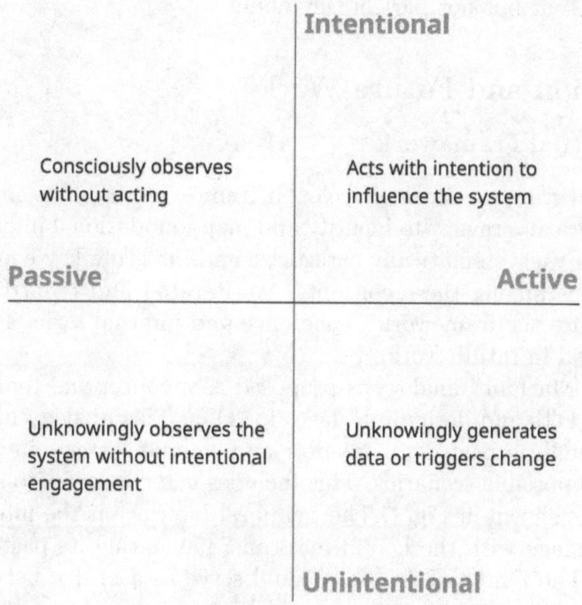

Fig. 4. User Engagement Style.

User Engagement Style. Active process operators in HCI are characterized by engagement in decision-making and control tasks such as prediction, planning, and control [10,12]. Building upon this foundation, we introduce two dimensions (**Active–Passive**, **Intentional-Unintentional**) to characterize user engagement, see Fig. 4. First, **Active–Passive** describes whether the user's behavior is represented in DTs' model. A user is active when their actions are sensed and incorporated into the system, and passive when their presence or behavior does not affect the model, even if they may still be mentally or physically engaged. Second, **Intentional-Unintentional** distinguishes user intentions to influence the system during interaction. In intentional interactions, users consciously and purposefully perform actions to achieve specific system responses, contrasting with unintentional interaction (as part of implicit interactions) when user performs input actions without specific intention [17]. In **Intentional-Active** interactions, users purposefully perform actions with the explicit goal of influencing system. In **Intentional-Passive** interactions, the user consciously engages in reflection, observation, or monitoring, but their actions do not directly affect DTs' model. **Unintentional-Active** interactions occur when users inadvertently generate data or trigger system changes through their actions, without intending these effects. **Unintentional-Passive** interactions represent the user neither intends to influence the system nor produces data into the DT model. The user is present but not part of the model.

4 Discussion and Future Work

4.1 Conceptual Framework

The conceptual framework was developed from exploration to integration. We began with literature review to identify and map foundational interaction design concepts. Then we systematically categorize and integrate key concepts, exploring relationships among these concepts. We iterated and refined the synthesis process to ensure the framework's coherence and internal logic. The framework will be validated in future work.

The "Time Machine" analogy is proposed as a conceptual tool for designers to understand DTs and design interfaces for DTs. This analogy highlights DTs' capability to analyze past data, monitor and control systems in real-time, and forecast future possible scenarios. This includes what we refer to as the *Temporal Interface*, as shown in Fig. 1. The temporal interface is the interaction space where users engage with the DT in real time, navigating its past, present, and future states. The temporal interface could serve as a bridge between information, decision-making, and actions, providing a visual and interactive representation of time-based changes. The temporal interface enables temporal interactions, the dynamic exchange between users and the DT-enabled system across past, present, and future time horizons. Users could not only view information, but also explore, test, and make informed decisions, making DTs not just static digital replicas but dynamic decision-supporting tools.

Next to the temporal perspective, we consider how DTs distribute agency and initiative across temporal interactions. We synthesized four autonomy levels of DT (see Table 2) based on Parasuraman et al. [11] and Agrawal et al. [1] research. At lower levels of automation, the DT-enabled system functions primarily as a reactive, user-driven system, which means the user remains active in shaping the system's state through intentional or unintentional actions. As autonomy increases, the DT begins to take more initiative: anticipating needs, prompting decisions, and influencing user behavior. This results in shared agency between user and system. At the highest level of automation, the DT becomes system-autonomous, continuously adapting and acting based on sensed patterns. In this case, the user's role naturally shifts toward a more passive or supervisory mode, as the system assumes responsibility for ongoing decision-making and control. This progression shows that automation is not just a technical feature; it's a relational property that shapes how responsibility, awareness, control, and value are distributed between users and DT-enabled systems. Designers need to consider how to balance transparency, trust, and user-perceived control to prevent over-automation and preserve meaningful human engagement.

Building on the temporal perspective and autonomy of DTs, we also consider the relationship between user and DT-enabled system to characterize the interaction space. The **Digital Twin Engagement Style** (visible-invisible

× proactive-reactive) adjusts Ju et al.'s [7] work and explicitly addresses interface visibility, an important design decision in DT systems where not all interactions should be equally visible. **User Engagement Style** (active-passive × intentional-unintentional) builds on HCI's active/passive operator concepts [10,12] while incorporating intentionality [17], recognizing that users may generate valuable and actionable data through both deliberate actions and unconscious behaviors. These relationships may not be static but shift in response to system parameters, user settings, context, time, etc. The intersection of these frameworks with our temporal interaction patterns creates a rich design space for DT interactions, enabling designers to systematically consider when and how temporal information should be presented, who initiates the interaction, and whether user engagement is active or passive, intentional or unintentional.

The framework above could be valuable to designers from three perspectives. **First, for inspiration and exploration**, the framework provides a structured inspiration guide: What temporal horizons can the interface address? What autonomy level should it employ? Should the interface or information be visible or invisible? Do DT-enabled systems initiate interactions proactively, or do users initiate them? How do users engage? When designers consider such scenarios for interacting with DTs, the seven temporal interaction patterns of DTs (Table 1) provide them a new perspective on how to include temporal dimensions for DT interaction design. Combining this temporal perspective with the 16 permutations of DT Engagement Style and User Engagement Style (visible/invisible × proactive/reactive × intentional/unintentional × active/passive) maps a rich design space, offering fundamentally different interaction relationships rather than defaulting to familiar approaches. For instance, DT visible-proactive engagement with user unintentional-active engagement could help users reflect on their past behavior and what can be improved for the future. **Second, for systematic analysis**, with this framework, designers could analyze existing or envisioned interfaces, recognize temporal interaction patterns, autonomy levels of DT, and DT engagement style and user engagement style. As a result, they could identify missed opportunities and understand why certain temporal interfaces succeed or fail. **Third, for synthesis of new interfaces**, the framework supports designers to synthesize concrete new interfaces by formulating design requirements and evaluation criteria. For instance, if the interface should support retrospective reflection, then requirements could be formulated specifying what information should be displayed, and how people are stimulated to reflect actively or passively.

4.2 Future Work

The framework provides a systematic conceptual contribution for temporal interaction design with DT-enabled systems. We will validate this framework in future work as follows:

- We will systematically analyze existing DT implementations to determine whether our proposed perspectives capture the full range of temporal inter-

actions observed from literature and practice and whether any critical dimensions are missing.
- We will examine whether the framework's dimensions are well-defined and accurately characterize temporal interactions through expert review sessions with HCI researchers and DT practitioners
- We will determine whether designers can effectively use the framework in real design processes. We will apply the design framework to design home energy scenarios and interfaces for DT-enabled smart homes, exploring opportunities such as retrospective reflection on consumption patterns, real-time adaptation to dynamic pricing, and action based on predicted future needs. This real-world design process will validate the framework's practical value and demonstrate refinement opportunities.

5 Conclusion

This paper developed an initial conceptual framework for temporal interactions of DTs, exploring the relationships between users and DT-enabled systems. A key contribution of this paper is the operationalization of temporal interactions with DT-enabled systems through multiple analytical lenses. 1) Building on the "Time Machine" analogy, we established seven temporal interaction patterns across past (Retrospective Reflection, User Action Based on Past Data), present (Immediate Action, Ongoing Adaptation), and future (Predictive Prompting, User Reflection Based on Prediction, User Action Based on Prediction). These patterns address how users perceive and respond to temporal information across different time horizons. 2) We synthesized four autonomy levels of DT to specify who initiates or controls these interactions. 3) We introduced Digital Twin Engagement Style (visible vs. invisible, proactive vs. reactive) and User Engagement Style (intentional vs. unintentional, active vs. passive) to fully characterize the relationships between users and DT-enabled systems. The design framework provides designers with systematic perspectives for three key activities: exploring temporal interaction possibilities, analyzing existing or envisioned DT interfaces, and generating new temporal interaction designs. Future work will validate the framework.

References

1. Agrawal, A., Thiel, R., Jain, P., Singh, V., Fischer, M.: Digital Twin: Where do humans fit in? **148**, 104749. https://doi.org/10.1016/j.autcon.2023.104749, https://www.sciencedirect.com/science/article/pii/S0926580523000092
2. Daniel Buzzo: Temporal Representations in Human Computer Interaction : Designing for the Lived Experience of Time. Ph.D. thesis, University of the West of England, Bristol (United Kingdom) (2017)
3. Grieves, M., Vickers, J.: Digital Twin: Mitigating Unpredictable, Undesirable Emergent Behavior in Complex Systems. In: Kahlen, F.-J., Flumerfelt, S., Alves, A. (eds.) Transdisciplinary Perspectives on Complex Systems, pp. 85–113. Springer, Cham (2017). https://doi.org/10.1007/978-3-319-38756-7_4

4. Halperin, B.A., McElroy, E.: Temporal tensions in digital story mapping for housing justice: Rethinking time and technology in community-based design. In: Proceedings of the 2023 ACM Designing Interactive Systems Conference, pp. 2469–2488. DIS '23, Association for Computing Machinery, New York, NY, USA (2023). https://doi.org/10.1145/3563657.3596088, https://dl.acm.org/doi/10.1145/3563657.3596088
5. Hribernik, K., Cabri, G., Mandreoli, F., Mentzas, G.: Autonomous, context-aware, adaptive digital twins-state of the art and roadmap. Comput. Ind. **133**, 103508 (2021). https://doi.org/10.1016/j.compind.2021.103508
6. Jabareen, Y.: Building a Conceptual Framework: Philosophy, Definitions, and Procedure **8**(4), 49–62. https://doi.org/10.1177/160940690900800406
7. Ju, W., Leifer, L.: The Design of Implicit Interactions: Making Interactive Systems Less Obnoxious **24**(3), 72–84. https://www.jstor.org/stable/25224184
8. Ho Lee, S., Beom Kim, S., Hern Kim, B., Sung Lee, H.: LUNE: Representing Lunar Day by Displayed Lighting Object. In: Extended Abstracts of the 2019 CHI Conference on Human Factors in Computing Systems, pp. 1–4. CHI EA '19, Association for Computing Machinery, New York, NY, USA (2019). https://doi.org/10.1145/3290607.3313240
9. Liu, Z., Meyendorf, N., Mrad, N.: The role of data fusion in predictive maintenance using digital twin. AIP Conf. Proc. **1949**(1), 020023 (2018). https://doi.org/10.1063/1.5031520
10. Montague, E., Xu, J.: Understanding active and passive users: The effects of an active user using normal, hard and unreliable technologies on user assessment of trust in technology and co-user **43**(4), 702–712. https://doi.org/10.1016/j.apergo.2011.11.002, https://www.sciencedirect.com/science/article/pii/S0003687011001670
11. Parasuraman, R., Sheridan, T., Wickens, C.: A model for types and levels of human interaction with automation **30**(3), 286–297. https://doi.org/10.1109/3468.844354, https://ieeexplore.ieee.org/document/844354
12. Persson, A., Wanek, B., Johansson, A.: Passive versus active operator work in automated process control—a job design case study in a control centre **32**(5), 441–451. https://doi.org/10.1016/S0003-6870(01)00022-9, https://www.sciencedirect.com/science/article/pii/S0003687001000229
13. Rapp, A.: How do people experience the temporality of everyday life changes? Towards the exploration of existential time in HCI **167**, 102899. https://doi.org/10.1016/j.ijhcs.2022.102899, https://www.sciencedirect.com/science/article/pii/S1071581922001227
14. Rosen, R., von Wichert, G., Lo, G., Bettenhausen, K.D.: About the importance of autonomy and digital twins for the future of manufacturing. IFAC-PapersOnLine **48**(3), 567–572 (2015). https://doi.org/10.1016/j.ifacol.2015.06.141
15. Schmidt, A.: Implicit human computer interaction through context **4**(2), 191–199. https://doi.org/10.1007/BF01324126
16. Semeraro, C., Lezoche, M., Panetto, H., Dassisti, M.: Digital twin paradigm: a systematic literature review. Comput. Ind. **130**, 103469 (2021). https://doi.org/10.1016/j.compind.2021.103469
17. Serim, B., Jacucci, G.: Explicating "Implicit Interaction": An Examination of the Concept and Challenges for Research. In: Proceedings of the 2019 CHI Conference on Human Factors in Computing Systems, pp. 1–16. CHI '19, Association for Computing Machinery. https://doi.org/10.1145/3290605.3300647

18. Tan, Q., Ng, H.T., Bing, L.: Towards benchmarking and improving the temporal reasoning capability of large language models. In: Rogers, A., Boyd-Graber, J., Okazaki, N. (eds.) Proceedings of the 61st Annual Meeting of the Association for Computational Linguistics (Vol. 1: Long Papers), pp. 14820–14835. Association for Computational Linguistics. https://doi.org/10.18653/v1/2023.acl-long.828, https://aclanthology.org/2023.acl-long.828/
19. Vermeulen, J., Luyten, K., Hoven, E., Coninx, K.: Crossing the bridge over Norman's Gulf of Execution: Revealing feedforward's true identity. In: Proceedings of the SIGCHI Conference on Human Factors in Computing Systems, pp. 1931–1940. CHI '13, Association for Computing Machinery. https://doi.org/10.1145/2470654.2466255, https://dl.acm.org/doi/10.1145/2470654.2466255
20. Voros, J.: A generic foresight process framework. Foresight **5**(3), 10–21 (2003). https://doi.org/10.1108/14636680310698379
21. Wilson, A.D., Oliver, N.: Multimodal Sensing for Explicit and Implicit Interaction. https://www.microsoft.com/en-us/research/publication/multimodal-sensing-explicit-implicit-interaction/
22. Zheng, Y., van Essen, H., Mitchell, S., Fennessy, L., Vaughan, L., Bernhaupt, R.: Design of temporal interfaces of digital twins in domestic energy consumption. In: Ardito, C., et al. Human-Computer Interaction – INTERACT 2025. INTERACT 2025, Belo Horizonte, Brazil, September 8–12, 2025, Proceedings, Part II, pp. 477–498. Springer, Cham (2025). https://doi.org/10.1007/978-3-032-05002-1_25

Conversational Agent Integration into Diagnostic Application for Primary Ciliary Dyskinesia

Adriana Pikartová[1], Martin Dubovský[1](✉), Miroslav Laco[1], and Wanda Benesova[2]

[1] Faculty of Informatics and Information Technologies, Slovak University of Technology in Bratislava, Ilkovicova 2, 841 04 Bratislava, Slovakia
dubovsky.martin@gmail.com

[2] Faculty of Information Technology, Czech Technical University in Prague (CTU in Prague), Thakurova 9, 160 00 Prague 6, Czech Republic

Abstract. With recent advance in development of large language models (LLM), a new topic for research in the area of Human-AI interaction (HAI) has emerged - interaction with conversational agents. Design and development of conversational agents present both design challenges regarding Human-Computer Interaction (HCI) and HAI experiences which have to match current tech challenges and limitations. One domain that could greatly benefit from such agents is medicine, where the focus is currently on creating digital imagery datasets for future applications and this process brings tedious and repetitive tasks to be performed by medical experts. In this paper, we focus on the case study of design and integration of a conversational agent (CA) into a medical image annotation tool. We propose an innovative design approach for integration of a conversational agent into existing user interface (UI) of an annotation tool using user-centered approach. We explored challenges of interaction with the conversational agents including definition of assistant's scope, designing user-oriented dialogues, user interface design and interaction. According to the proposed approach, we integrated the CA into a medical imaging annotation tool for Primary Ciliary Dyskinesia (PCD) diagnostics and evaluated it through user testing with five participants for qualitative evaluation of the designed approach. Our work explores the potential of LLM-powered conversational agents, emphasizes the discussion about the importance of conformity with the existing HAI principles, according to the case study with PCD diagnostic application. In conclusion, we derive insights into the design process and integration of conversational agents, for future development of CA in medical applications from our case study.

Keywords: Conversational Agents · Human-AI Interaction · Large Language Models · User Experience

Published by Springer Nature Switzerland AG 2026
C. Maciel et al. (Eds.): INTERACT 2025 Workshops, LNCS 16478, pp. 119–134, 2026.
https://doi.org/10.1007/978-3-032-22934-2_12

1 Introduction

In certain domains, such as medical imaging, the user interfaces (UI) supporting domain experts' workflows are complex, apart from the vast effort put into the UI and user experience (UX) design. Moreover, working with such interfaces requires higher level of expertise, thus increasing the cognitive load while using the UI. New or infrequent users may struggle to understand the interface layout, discover available tools or the correct usage of the application. This can negatively affect the usability and error proneness of the application, which is a significant concern especially in the medical domain. Integration of conversational agents into UI can potentially tackle this issue. [6,12] Conversational agents could help the domain experts to navigate in the application or to perform certain tasks and accelerate their workflows. In the past, conversational agents on websites were often very limited, provided very poor user experience and caused frustrations with scripted responses that failed to effectively understand the user intent. However, since the introduction of LLMs as a technology, the situation is rapidly changing, providing more robust and complex solutions to use in domain-oriented application design. [8]

This paper aims to provide an insight into our case study on a CA integrated into an UI for domain experts in the field of medicine. Users can interact with the CA via natural language to ask questions, give commands, or request guidance. To explore and validate this concept in a real-life scenario, we integrated the CA into a prototype of medical imaging annotation tool for Primary Ciliary Dyskinesia (PCD) diagnostics, based on existing tools for PCD diagnostics. [1,7]. PCD is a rare genetic condition caused by structural and functional defects in motile cilia - cells responsible for airway clearance. This disorder can result in chronic respiratory disease, hearing loss and infertility. Diagnostics involve the use of transmission electron microscopy to examine the ciliary ultrastructure, following international classification criteria based on microtubular arrangement and dynein arm defects. [1,2] Ciliary defect identification process is time-consuming and requires domain experts to annotate large amounts of defective cilia to be able to consider a diagnosis. The annotation process is based on assigning category and sub-category labels to cilia using click-based interaction.

We proposed an approach to integrate CA into the complex domain of PCD diagnostics and medical imaging. Based on this proposal, we integrated the approach into a prototype of a PCD diagnostics app. We evaluated usability using moderated user testing sessions. Through this evaluation, we identified usability issues with improvement suggestions that could serve as a basis and recommendations for future integration of CAs into similar medical applications.

2 Related Work

A notable research gap exists in the study of CAs incorporated into medical diagnostics and annotation applications, both from a technological point of view and UX design, because there is limited research published nowadays. In this chapter, we provide adetailedd analysis on CA toolsfrom them the medical domain [3,4] as well as outof thede of the medical domain [5,14] and studies focusing on prototyping of conversational agents [6,12].

The study by Abbasian et al. [3] introduced the openCHA framework for integrating LLM-based agents into conversational agents in the medical domain, from a technical point of view. OpenCHA includes two major components, *Interface*, which consist of agents responsible for planning, retrieving, and processing information, executing actions, and generating responses, and *Orchestrator*, which can access external sources, search engines, or translators via API calls. However, the framework is missing support for direct interaction with the UI of the application, which is a crucial feature in medical imaging. An Orchestrator component is also present in the study of LLM-based multimodal multi-agent framework by Gebreab et al. [4], which adopts a similar CA structure design for automation of administrative tasks in the medical domain. Neszlényi et al. [5] propose CAGPT, a CA that integrates natural language processing and intuitive user interfaces. The disadvantage of CAGPT is the integration of only one LLM, the OpenAI ChatGPT. Another example from different domains is Flute X GPT, proposed by Chin et al. [14], a music tutoring application with an LLM-based agent that offers real-time support and feedback to users learning to play the flute, integrating an LLM with a multimodal setup which includes both software and hardware. User data is collected through motorized gloves with sensors, a sensor-equipped flute, and audio input, which is then processed by the agent giving feedback to the user or performing a series of actions within the UI. This architecture proposes two major components, *Parser* and *Manager*, *Parser* being responsible for dividing the output of LLM into thoughts, speech, and actions, while *Manager* handles interaction between LLM and the rest of the system. The aforementioned studies share similar design patterns and structures for CA system design and development, which seem to be slowly becoming a standard within the problem.

Other relevant studies focus on CA prototyping. Feng et al. propose Canvil [6], a tool for designing chatbot personas. The authors developed a template in the form of a Figma plugin to help UX designers shape the behavior and responses of a chatbot. Using this template, designers can define the persona of the model, the audience setting, the core instructions, the guardrails, and the limitations, and provide examples of the input and desired output, and validate the user scenarios designed in the early stages of design. Another research initiative for the effective prototyping of intelligent assistant interfaces powered by LLM is PromptInfuser [12], proposed by Petridis et al. PromptInfuser is a Figma plugin that aims to improve the prompting for LLM with the context of the user interface. This plugin allows designers to assign specific elements in the interface as context information for the LLM. The results of the study suggest that designing AI and UI simultaneously has proven to be more efficient than traditional methods of separate development. [12].

The analyzed studies focus on technical solutions and lack the user's point of view, missing direct UI interaction [3,4] and motivation to take full control of the application at any time. Based on this, we decided to adopt the technical solutions of openCHA with a clear distinction between Interface and Orchestrator, in combination with the structure proposed in Flute X GTP. We propose an approach for CA integration with our user at the center of the CA design.

3 Case Study

The main goal of the paper is to propose an approach to design and implement a conversational agent. To verify the proposed approach, we adopted it in a case study on an extension to the PCD diagnostic tool. The access to domain experts in the field of PCD diagnostics to ensure the success of our user-centered approach is secured by our long-term collaboration, as mentioned in work performed by Fedosenya et al. [7], and Felšöová et al. [1].

To introduce the reader into the existing UI of the tool for PCD diagnostics as part of the ongoing research [1,7], we briefly describe the UI components. In our case study, we introduced UI for CA, consisting of the user interface of a medical imaging annotation tool and a conversational agent (CA) as a side element, as can be seen in Fig. 1. The design process methodology of both components follows the traditional Human-Centered design process (HCD), with some adjustments addressing the unique nature of the research topic.

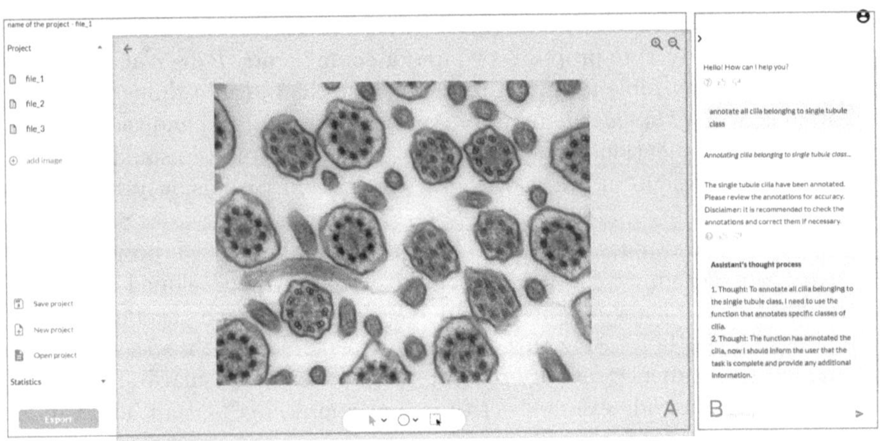

Fig. 1. Complete UI proposal of image annotation tool prototype with our CA during performing of *Annotating cilia* scenario, A - existing UI of the PCD diagnostic tool [1,7], B - our UI proposal for CA as a contribution of this paper.

During the *Observation* phase, we analyzed the performed user research and interviews in the aforementioned studies [1,7] and collected insights on the diagnostic process in the PCD domain and potential challenges for human-AI interaction that would benefit from CA integration. In accordance with the findings, we formulated the following requirements for the PCD annotation application UI:

- Project consists of several images
- Cilia have a main class and a subclass (dynein arms)
- Statistics of annotated cilia for all images are displayed at all times
- Statistics can be exported to a csv file using a predefined template
- Notes/comments about the project or individual images can be written and exported
- Option to adjust user preferences
- Selecting a region within the image
- Changing visibility of annotations

In the *Idea generation* phase, we also designed a persona representing the domain expert, an experienced medical specialist in the PCD domain who is often frustrated due to the complexity of their work routine and the difficulty of navigating various software tools. Their main goal is to boost their workflows and be able to focus more on their patients. We proposed corresponding user scenarios for the PCD annotation application UI, including *project management*, *annotating cilia* (class and subclass selection), *editing and deleting annotations*, *viewing basic statistics*, *customizing the annotation color scheme and mapping*, *adjusting the opacity of the annotation overlay on the medical image*, *undo and redo*, and basic viewing tools regarding medical image data.

During the *Prototyping* phase, we developed the first iteration of a high-fidelity prototype in Figma, where the Canvil widget was used to plausibly simulate the cilia annotation functionality. To validate the first iteration, we conducted a moderated interview accompanied by a thinking-aloud user testing session with the domain expert. The second iteration of the high-fidelity prototype was developed in the form of an interactive prototype, a single-page application, as commonly used prototyping tools did not sufficiently support the extent of the proposed interaction scenarios to be tested effectively. The cilia classification system aligns with Southampton PCD guidelines for PCD diagnostics [2].

3.1 Proposed Approach to Conversational Agent Integration

Based on user scenarios distilled from existing tools and existing user research by Fedosenya et al. [7] and Felšöová et al. [1] and current LLM-based conversational agent capabilities during the *Observation* phase, we identified a set of requirements for the CA:

- Visually highlight tools or elements within the interface
- Annotating cilia (all or a specific class)
- Disclose the level of confidence or accuracy for automated annotation
- Provide a step-by-step explanation of how to perform an action
- Answer domain-specific questions
- Control the interface
- Users can access the CA from anywhere
- Users can disable the CA and perform actions manually

According to the gathered requirements, in *idea generation* phase, we identified a persona and six user scenarios for the conversational agent:

In the *Guidance (step-by-step instructions)* user scenario, the domain expert (DE) is motivated to complete a task, although unsure how to do so. The user wants to receive guidance or a specific set of steps required to successfully perform the task. The domain expert asks CA a question, and the CA provides the steps to complete the task. DE then reads the instructions and asks further questions if necessary. The scenario resolves in DE successfully completing the task.

For the *Activating tools* scenario is the motivation of DE is to use a certain tool in order to complete a task, but is not sure where the tool is or how does it work, and intends to activate and use the tool. User asks the CA a question, and the CA activates the desired tool and provides a brief explanation about its functionality. Scenario resolves in successfully completing the task using the activated tool.

The *Locating UI components* user scenario focuses on visual hints within the user interface. The motivation of the user is to use a certain component, but they cannot find it in the UI. DE asks the CA about the location of a specific component, and CA highlights the component to provide visual guidance and a text description of its location.

The motivation of DE in *Performing tasks in the user interface* scenario is to perform a task quickly, without having to directly utilize the UI, and wants the CA to perform the task. DE gives the CA the order to perform the desired task, and CA asks whether the user is satisfied with the result. If the user is not satisfied, CA performs "undo" if possible.

In *Answering domain-specific questions*, the user wants to search for more domain-related information or is not sure about a particular domain problem. In this case, the DE asks the CA a domain-specific question, while the CA provides the desired information, along with resources, with the source of information to critically evaluate the quality of the presented information.

The *Annotating cilia* user scenario makes CA display an output of automated cilia detection using black-box methods resembling future AI integration. During this scenario, it is necessary to ensure the CA-provided output of automated detection is reviewed by DE, to avoid wrong decisions made by DE caused by faulty cilia detection output provided by CA. The user should have the possibility to review and modify any annotation performed automatically by the system.

We designed user-flows for every proposed user scenario, representing the conversation and interaction flow with emphasis on approval and full control from the domain expert over proposed CA results, to prevent potentially erroneous situations. During the design process, we created a list of potential user queries for every scenario, further specifying CA's scope, such as "annotate all cilia with secondary defects" (*Annotating cilia* scenario) or "where can I change color scheme?" (*Locating UI components*), which later served as a valuable resource for prototyping and evaluation of proposed user scenarios.

3.2 Prototyping Using Rapid Coding Approach

After the *Idea generation* phase, we proceeded to create a Canvil template for every CA user scenario to further support the CA design and to validate proposed user scenarios. The fields *model profile*, *audience setting*, and *guardrails* remained similar for all user scenarios, as we designed only a single chatbot persona. [6] The *core instructions* were custom per scenario. *Core instructions* field describes a series of logical steps the model should take to complete the task. In some cases, we also specified the desired *output format*. We tested the created Canvil templates with OpenAI's ChatGPT-4o[1]. At the end of each prompt for ChatGPT, we included *final instructions*, directing the model to follow closely all instructions defined in the template. ChatGPT generated an answer based on our specifications and followed the intended flow of conversation. To simulate negative outcomes, we explicitly specified that the assistant cannot complete the task or recognise the tool. This dialogue design process, combined with interaction with a real AI chatbot, allowed us to efficiently test our dialogue design and collect valuable feedback to shape CA's behavior and responses and uncover potential issues.

To ensure alignment of our design process with common practices in designing CA agents, we mapped used techniques and outcomes to 4 aspects identified in a study by Sadek et al. [8] contemplating conversational agents design. Conforming with the standards, Table 1 illustrates the mapping of CA aspects of the proposed CA with the design process phases, methods, and techniques for each phase.

During the dialogue design process, we experimented with different prompts and descriptions of the model. In addition to contributing to the overall design of the CA, we discovered that the generated responses can be leveraged in prototype testing without the need for real-time AI integration, thus enabling rapid prototyping and iterative design of user interfaces with CA integration.

4 Conversational Agent Framework Proposal

For translation of our conceptual design into a functional implementation we proposed the CA framework (see overview diagram in Fig. 2), consisting of four agent components (Interpreter agent, Planner agent, Vision agent and Response agent) which handle processing of queries and forming responses, a component for executing actions (Executor) and Tools (necessary artifacts for user scenario resolution), along with their description. Functional implementation was essential for user testing purposes to obtain user feedback on the proposed approach to CA integration.

InterpreterAgent is the first component in the pipeline, receiving raw user queries. It is tasked with interpreting the query for other agents, determining the optimal path for execution, formulating an instruction for the PlannerAgent, and creating a temporary response - a short information message displayed for the user during query processing.

[1] https://platform.openai.com/docs/models/gpt-4o.

Table 1. CA aspects mapped onto the design process of our proposed CA tool for PCD annotation

Aspect	Description	Techniques used	Design phase
Appearance	The visual embodiment of the CA.	sketching, prototyping	prototyping
Evaluation	CA's personality and responses were evaluated via ChatGPT.	interacting with existing CAs	idea generation
Goals	Defined as requirements and CA scenarios.	brainstorming, conversation flow design	idea generation
Dialogue	Includes flowcharts of conversations and generated responses/scripts.	conversation flow design, interacting with existing CAs	idea generation
Interactions: Behaviors & Use-Cases	Defined as CA scenarios, flowcharts, and using the Canvil template - core instructions, example inputs/outputs.	conversation flow design, scenario-based thinking	idea generation
Interactions: Relationships & Roles	Designed using the Canvil template - model profile, audience setting.	conversation flow design, interacting with existing CAs	idea generation
Interactions: Problems & Solutions	Flowcharts include negative scenarios/potential problems. Solutions were proposed with the Canvil template - core instructions, guardrails. Additional problems were identified during testing with Canvil (hallucinations), and solutions were proposed and evaluated.	brainstorming, interacting with existing CAs	idea generation
Interactions: Persona / Personality	Persona of the CA was designed using the Canvil template - model profile, example outputs fields.	interacting with existing CAs	idea generation
Interactions: Modalities	The CA uses text as a means of communication.	brainstorming	observation

PlannerAgent is the central component of this framework, responsible for solving the problem by creating a plan on how to approach it. This agent uses ReAct prompting, proposed by Yao et al. [9]. The plannerPrompt derived from this study and adapted to fit our needs instructs the PlannerAgent to think about the user question, determine the action to take, and what its input needs to be. Based on the result, PlannerAgent decides the next steps - whether the user's question can be answered or if additional actions need to be taken.

Executor is responsible for performing the actions determined by the PlannerAgent. The entire response from the PlannerAgent is sent to the Executor, where it is parsed to extract the function name and input parameters. The identified function is then executed, and the result is sent back to the PlannerAgent.

Executor also contains the complete set of available functions that the PlannerAgent may consider using. While the Executor contains the actual implementations of available functions, the PlannerAgent handles structured representations (in our case, JSON format) of *Tools* within the plannerPrompt. The description follows the schema in OpenAI's API documentation [11], allowing it to be used with LLMs that support custom function execution. The schema contains the function name, a description, and details on its parameters.

We also experimented with **VisionAgent**, that would serve as a supporting component for understanding the application UI the CA is dedicated to operate over, however, we found VisionAgent to be counterproductive due to frequent potential misinterpretations and hallucinations [19] that would be caused by using a general-purpose LLM, and ultimately decided to remove it from the framework.

ResponseAgent is the final component of the framework. It receives the original user question and the final thought of the PlannerAgent and decides on the final response that will be displayed to the user. The response prompt, used to instruct the agent, is also used to shape the responses, communication style, and language used.

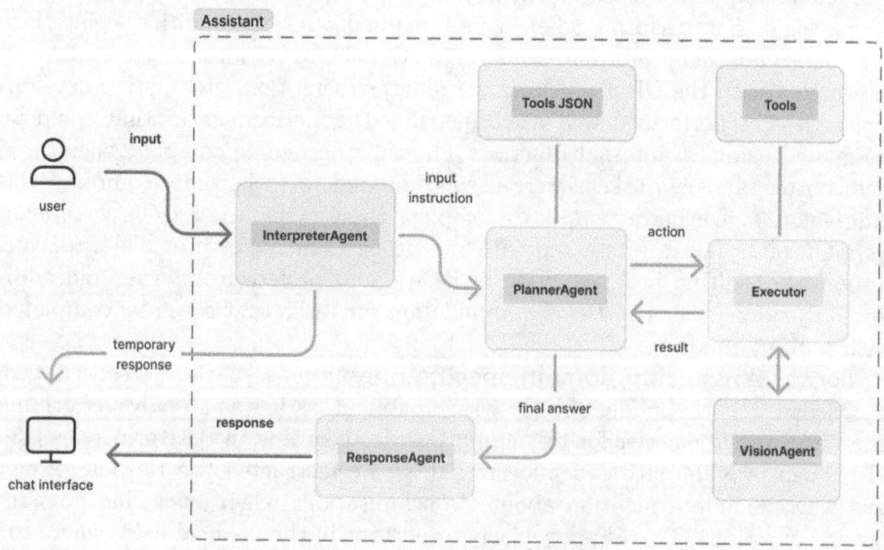

Fig. 2. CA framework components.

4.1 Implementation of CA Scenarios

Based on identified user scenarios, we identified attributes and capabilities the CA needed to support:

Guidance (Step-by-Step Instructions) and Locating UI Components. Scenarios require CA to understand the content and layout of the user interface. We considered various approaches to this issue, providing a list of Document Object Model (DOM) elements, UI documentation and image caption of the user interface processed by an additional multimodal LLM to extract its description representation.

We provided CA with a hierarchical list of all UI elements and their properties using a custom *getElements()* function implemented for this purpose. The success of this approach heavily depends on the clarity and accuracy of element property naming. Performance of the *Locating UI components* scenario improved further when we provided hints about the interface incorporated into the tool's description. Despite these improvements, the CA was not able to fully comprehend the UI to provide accurate guidance for the user in *Guidance (step by step instructions)* scenario. Based on these findings, we decided to provide the CA with a structured representation of DOM elements and integrate details about the interface into descriptions, describing how CA should use the tool and how the user can perform the same task within the interface, such as "Use this function to add notes. Notes are located in the statistics drawer."

For **Performing tasks and Activating tools** scenarios, we proposed two options for implementation, *internal functions*, representing the existing application logic that performs when a user manually interacts with the interface and *DOM manipulation*, that would allow the CA to perform tasks by directly interacting with the UI via clicking, scrolling, writing text, etc. During development, the CA performed well when instructed to perform tasks that could be completed using an internal function. The time needed to complete such tasks was shorter, and less tokens were used compared to tasks that required *DOM manipulation*. During attempts to complete these tasks using *DOM manipulation*, CA often failed, interacted with the wrong elements or provided erroneous responses, resulting in a reduction of its use and preferring internal and additional functions over the *DOM manipulation* for tasks that could be completed with both methods.

For the **Answering domain-specific questions** scenario, we settled with knowledge that the model already was capable of, as it was already performing in an acceptable manner for testing purposes. According to HAI principles [13], LLMs can provide outdated information, so we instructed the ResponseAgent to always include a mention about CA's limitations when answering domain-specific questions. This is particularly important in the medical field, where the use of accurate and up-to-date data is crucial.

The scenario **Annotating cilia** was designed to provide a future possibility to integrate an annotation AI model when it is available. For testing purposes, we simulated AI outputs, using a closed Wizard of OZ approach [16,17]. This method lets users interact with what they believe is a fully functional system, but the system's responses are actually pre-defined and delivered to the user based on user interactions. The CA performs the annotation and suggests a review of annotated cilia from the domain expert, informing the domain expert about its limited capabilities when performing this task.

4.2 Technical Overview

The CA was implemented as a JavaScript module for integration purposes with the PCD diagnostic tool. Each agent component communicates with an LLM via API requests that contain an agent-specific prompt (a set of structured instructions for the LLM), context (all previous responses the LLM generated within one cycle - the processing of one user query), and current user query. API requests are routed through a Node.js backend, which forwards them to LLM via OpenRouter API - a proxy service offering access to several free and paid LLMs. [11] We opted to showcase our solution with the integration of Llama 3.3 70B Instruct [18], as the model is both free and robust compared to other free models OpenRouter provides. No data was stored by third-party providers, since OpenRouter allows users to disable logging of data and training on inputs. For real-life deployment, however, we recommend anonymizing any personal data to ensure maximum privacy.

5 User Testing

We propose validation of the CA by performing a scenario-based thinking-aloud user testing with five participants. The number of respondents should be sufficient to discover major usability issues of our proposed design, according to existing literature (Nielsen et al. [15]). Since the topic of our research is oriented on medicine and histopathology, our respondents should also come from the medical domain, although PCD expertise is not necessary, as the validation should focus on the CA functionality and usability rather than the PCD annotation interface itself. However, participants should receive a brief introduction to the PCD diagnostic problem.

We propose to gather demographic information about the participants, in addition to standard data such as age, education, and occupation, we should analyse their proficiency in the English language. This is important because all system prompts and tool descriptions for the CA were prototyped in the English language, and this skill is necessary to interact with the CA during validation sessions.

We propose to include a set of preliminary questions before a user testing session to assess participants' background and experience with medical image annotation, their knowledge of PCD, and their prior experience and habits related to the use of AI tools and conversational agents. The goal of this questionnaire is to identify any past exposure to AI technologies and uncover potential opinions or biases that could influence their interaction with the system.

We designed 13 test tasks for the testing sessions. The first task (T1) is an introductory task to ensure participants are able to open a medical image to start with the digital analysis. Nine tasks require the participants to try to use CA at least once (T2-T10) to complete the task. This approach was applied, as our primary goal is to evaluate the usability of the CA. These tasks include *creating annotations*, *modifying their class labels*, *modifying the dynein arm attributes*, *creating another annotation with various primary and secondary classes*, *changing primary and secondary classes on existing annotations*, *modifying the class colors and application settings*, *deleting all annotations*, and *applying batch changes to multiple annotations.* In the free-choice tasks (T11-T13), participants are free to decide whether to use CA to accomplish the task or not. They would be asked to *write a note summarizing the number of annotations along with their classes and dynein arm types*, *verify this information using the statistics feature*, and then *modify the dynein arms annotation according to statistics.* This combination of structured and exploratory tasks was designed to capture both usability aspects and user behavior in interacting with the CA.

During the testing sessions, we propose to record the task completion rate (TCR), and time to complete task (TCT) metrics, along with metrics regarding the CA: number of user questions during a task performing and number of Assistant's errors in a task. Interview questions after testing should focus on users' experience with the CA, their opinions on its responses and behavior, as well as their references regarding the usability of the CA. We also propose questions about participants' experience with using the application UI. We propose to collect Feedback questionnaire results after the testing, including statements about CA behavior, responses, and users' opinions about using the CA, to collect Net Promoter Score (NPS).

5.1 User Testing Results

We recruited five participants aged between 20 and 53 years, with basic to advanced English proficiency levels. All participants possessed a medical background and included medical students, medical assistants, and one histopathologist with 1–5 years of experience. Some participants talked during pre-testing interviews about their negative experiences with chatbots on websites, which indicates a potential bias towards CA assistants (Fig. 3).

	T1	T2	T3	T4	T5	T6	T7	T8	T9	T10	T11	T12	T13	%
P1	1	1	0,5	1	1	1	1	1	1	1	1	1	1	96,15
P2	1	1	0,5	1	1	1	1	1	0	1	0	1	1	80,77
P3	1	1	1	1	1	1	1	1	1	1	1	1	1	100
P4	1	1	1	1	1	1	0	1	1	1	0	0,5	1	80,77
P5	1	1	0	1	1	1	1	1	1	1	1	1	1	92,31
%	100	100	60	100	100	100	80	100	80	100	60	90	100	

tasks where users were required to use the CA at least once

CA used | CA not used | combination

Fig. 3. User testing results for the TCR metric with method used to complete the task.

Participants exhibited various interaction strategies when completing tasks with the CA. Two participants (P2 and P5) preferred to understand the process before acting, using the CA mainly for guidance rather than automation. P1 and P4 relied heavily on the CA, with P1 showing complete trust and achieving a high task success rate, possibly due to prior experience with AI tools. P3 adopted a balanced strategy—allowing the Assistant to act while verifying its output—which resulted in the best overall performance. Participants generally perceived any errors of the CA as their own, rarely used the "explain this response" feature, and showed little interest in viewing the CA's reasoning. Overall, the CA was viewed positively; users found it engaging, easy to understand, and particularly valued its task-performing and guidance capabilities. However, they criticized its slow response time and often preferred to complete tasks manually. Interviews revealed that most users would initially try to understand the interface independently and only use the CA in case of difficulties, with some preferring to delegate complex or repetitive medical tasks to it (Fig. 4).

	T1	T2	T3	T4	T5	T6	T7	T8	T9	T10	T11	T12	T13
P1	6	144	137	42	84	53	33	26	22	29	118	59	110
P2	9	400	266	125	283	69	189	113	301	90	145	116	166
P3	10	51	319	7	38	99	31	53	22	48	103	96	48
P4	4	147	52	115	170	187	91	58	18	44	61	126	49
P5	14	89	545	5	24	38	41	96	24	72	596	67	14
Avg	8,6	166,2	263,8	58,8	119,8	89,2	77	69,2	77,4	56,6	204,6	92,8	77,4

tasks where users were required to use the CA at least once
CA used | CA not used | combination

Fig. 4. User testing results for the TCT metric with method used to complete the task.

Based on the collected metrics, the testing participants positively evaluated the CA, but each of them approached it differently, indicating diverse patterns of interaction with AI-powered assistants in general. Two participants relied almost entirely on the CA to complete the tasks, while two preferred manual control, using the CA primarily to ask questions about capabilities or the purpose of the application. The fifth participant allowed the CA to perform tasks but verified its actions. Testing revealed limitations in CA's usability, particularly in *Guidance (step by step instructions)* scenario and performance-based issues. The CA often performed the task itself instead of giving instructions. The instructions written by the CA were also sometimes incorrect or incomplete. Testing revealed a few lower-severity issues, mostly related to the visual design of the CA response and functionality of certain elements of the user interface.

Top issues found included the CA incorporating functions and their descriptions into its responses (use function x to do y, retrieve IDs to do y...), which confused the users. Also, CA did not write the guide correctly in multiple tasks. In some cases, CA performed the task instead of writing a guide a few times. Another two major issues were connected with the annotation functionality, where participants could not find notes; when they had the statistics drawer opened, they overlooked them or mistook statistics for the note CA created. The second issue was recorded in the case when participants wanted to use the select area tool to select a single annotation, which was not possible. Collected NPS results suggest that the CA responses were clear and easy to understand, and a preference to use the CA instead of manual control.

Within this study, we acknowledge that the current findings reflect only a single case evaluated under a constrained experimental setup with limited testing. However, within these boundaries, the concept demonstrates initial validity as a meaningful direction for future CA adaptation and further complex evaluation in various medical applications. An important aspect is to ensure that the CA outputs can be meaningfully understood and critically evaluated by medical professionals, for example, by adopting the explainability and interpretability measures, so medical experts can clearly understand how the system makes its decisions. Trust calibration can also support more effective interaction between medical experts and CA and help smoother integration in the future. By helping users recognize when the system is reliable and when additional judgment is required, it can strengthen collaboration and ensure safety in clinical practice.

6 Conclusion

Conversational agents have the capability to help users perform tasks and assist them in navigating applications they are not familiar with. In this paper, we propose an approach in the form of a case study to integrate a CA into an existing user interface. We designed an interactive prototype of a medical image annotation interface within the domain of Primary Ciliary Dyskinesia, with integrated CA powered by an LLM network. Based on designed user scenarios and dialogues, validated using the Canvil template, we designed and developed a functional prototype of the CA, consisting of four agent components, an execution component, and a set of tools. Our proposed framework was developed for web interfaces and was designed to be adaptable for potential future use and validation across various domains with modifications to suit specific applications. The proposed CA framework discusses the benefits of LLM model integration in a highly-specific domain environment.

We validated the proposed framework within our developed PCD annotation application interactive prototype. We performed a user testing session with 5 respondents, which uncovered various strengths and limitations towards the use of CA in the application; however, to draw solid conclusions, the proposed approach should be validated with a broader number of participants and in various domain application interfaces. The user testing results indicate an enhanced user experience for domain experts while performing domain tasks. The decision to put emphasis on retaining full control over AI-generated results for the domain experts have resulted in higher confidence when using the designed application, and lower rejection rates. We believe that the CA integration could, under certain conditions, potentially speed up the diagnostic process and increase effectivity of domain experts.

Since data safety is an important issue, especially in the medical domain, the medical data in our application prototype was anonymized and could not be traced back to the patient. Another potential security threat is sharing sensitive medical data through a publicly accessible LLM agent. This threat can be mitigated, however, by utilizing a privately served LLM agent instance in the internal network.

Proposal validation demonstrated that the CA was generally perceived positively by participants; they found it engaging, comprehensible, and useful for both task execution and guidance. However, participants displayed diverse interaction strategies, ranging from high reliance to cautious use, reflecting individual preferences and various levels of trust in AI-powered systems. Several usability issues were identified during testing sessions, particularly in step-by-step guidance. The CA sometimes performed slowly or gave incomplete instructions, which made the work less efficient and slightly frustrated the users. These findings highlight the importance of balancing automation with user control and ensuring transparency in system behavior, along with the performance of the system.

In future work, improvements should focus on refining the CA's guidance capabilities, optimizing performance, and response time. Further studies with a larger and more diverse participant group are required to validate the findings and explore long-term adoption patterns. Integrating adaptive interaction strategies, where the CA adjusts its level of autonomy based on user expertise and task context, could further calibrate user trust and improve usability for CA integration in medical applications.

Acknowledgments. The authors would like to acknowledge the funding for the financial support of the grant APVV SK-IL-RD-23-0004. Moreover, we would like to thank for the support from the Recovery and Resilience Plan of the Slovak Republic under the call 'Transformation and Innovation Consortia' (project code: 09I02-03-V01-00012). The author contributes to this research as part of a consortium coordinated by InterWay, a. s.

References

1. Felšöová, A., et al.: Quantitative assessment of ciliary ultrastructure with the use of automatic analysis: PCD quant. Diagnostics **11**(8) (2021). https://doi.org/10.3390/diagnostics11081363. ISSN: 2075-4418
2. Shoemark, A., et al.: International consensus guideline for reporting transmission electron microscopy results in the diagnosis of primary ciliary dyskinesia (BEAT PCD TEM Criteria). Eur. Respir. J. **55**(4) (2020). https://doi.org/10.1183/13993003.00725-2019

3. Abbasian, M., et al.: Conversational Health Agents: A Personalized LLMPowered Agent Framework (2024). https://doi.org/10.48550/arXiv.2310.02374
4. Gebreab, S.A., et al.: LLM-based framework for administrative task automation in healthcare. In: 2024 12th International Symposium on Digital Forensics and Security (ISDFS) (2024). https://doi.org/10.1109/ISDFS60797.2024.10527275
5. Balazs Neszlenyi, K., Milos, A., Kiss, A.: CAGPT: enhancing user interaction with LLM integration. In: 2024 IEEE 22nd Jubilee International Symposium on Intelligent Systems and Informatics (SISY), Pula, Croatia, pp. 000619–000624 (2024). https://doi.org/10.1109/SISY62279.2024.10737548
6. Kevin Feng, K.J., et al.: Canvil: Designerly Adaptation for LLM-Powered User Experiences (2024). https://doi.org/10.48550/arXiv.2401.09051
7. Fedosenya, M., Dubovský, M., Laco, M.: Prototyping AI-infused annotation tool for primary ciliary dyskinesia diagnostics. In: Proceedings of the Future Technologies Conference (FTC) 2024 (2024). https://doi.org/10.1007/978-3-031-73110-5
8. Sadek, M., Calvo, R.A., Mougenot, C.: Co-designing conversational agents: a comprehensive review and recommendations for best practices. Des. Stud. **89**, 101230 (2023). https://doi.org//10.1016/j.destud.2023.101230. ISSN 0142-694X
9. Shunyu, Y., et al.: React: synergizing reasoning and acting in language models. In: International Conference on Learning Representations (ICLR) (2023). https://doi.org/10.48550/arXiv.2210.03629
10. OpenAI API. https://platform.openai.com/docs/api-reference/chat/create. Accessed 10 Mar 2025
11. OpenRouter. https://openrouter.ai/privacy. Accessed 19 Apr 2025
12. Petridis, S., Terry, M., Cai, C.J.: Promptinfuser: how tightly coupling AI and UI design impacts designers' workflows. In: Proceedings of the 2024 ACM Designing Interactive Systems Conference, pp. 743–756 (2024). https://doi.org/10.1145/3643834.3661613
13. Amershi, S., et al.: . Guidelines for human-AI interaction. In: Proceedings of the 2019 Chi Conference on Human Factors in Computing Systems, pp. 1–13 (2019)
14. Chin, D., Wang, Y., Xia, G.: Human-centered LLM-agent user interface: A position paper. arXiv preprint arXiv:2405.13050 (2024)
15. Nielsen, J., Landauer, T.K.: A mathematical model of the finding of usability problems. In: Proceedings of the INTERACT 1993 and CHI 1993 Conference on Human Factors in Computing Systems, pp. 206–213 (1993)
16. Browne, J.T.: Wizard of Oz prototyping for machine learning experiences. In: Extended Abstracts of the 2019 CHI Conference on Human Factors in Computing Systems (CHI EA '19). Association for Computing Machinery, New York, NY, USA, Paper LBW2621, pp. 1–6 (2019). https://doi.org/10.1145/3290607.3312877
17. Astrid, W., et al.: User experience evaluation with a wizard of oz approach: technical and methodological considerations. In: 2009 9th IEEE-RAS International Conference on Humanoid Robots, pp. 303–308 IEEE (2009)
18. Llama 3.3 70B Instruct. https://www.llama.com/docs/model-cards-and-prompt-formats/llama3
19. Zhengyi, H., Siyuan, L., Dacheng, T.: Review of Hallucination Understanding in Large Language and Vision Models. arXiv preprint arXiv:2510.00034 (2025)

Enhancing LLM-Based Information Seeking with Search Trails: A Case Study

Xabier Garmendia Diaz[1], Oscar Diaz[1], and Marco Winckler[2](✉)

[1] University of the Basque Country, Donostia, Basque Country, Spain
{xabier.garmendiad,oscar.diaz}@ehu.eus

[2] Université Côte d'Azur, I3S| INRIA wimmics/SPARKSteam, Nice, France
marco.winckler@univ-cotedazur.fr,
https://www.ehu.eus/, https://univ-cotedazur.fr/

Abstract. Information seeking refers to the process of searching for information to satisfy specific needs or answer particular questions. As users navigate this journey, they leave behind search trails: the sequences of steps, decisions, and interactions that document their exploration. These trails capture how users navigate through various sources and ideas, revealing the progression of their reasoning and discovery. Preserving and organizing these search trails contributes to improved learning, supports decision-making, and provides a head start for future information retrieval. Although large language models (LLMs) have significantly advanced information-seeking processes by providing rapid access to vast amounts of knowledge, their traditional text-based interfaces pose challenges such as difficulties for revisiting previous information and lack of structural organization, which hinders users from efficiently maintaining and reviewing their search trails. To address these challenges, we investigate the use of an interactive user interface based on mind maps to support LLM-based information seeking interactions. More specifically, we present the results of a user study with 20 participants using the ChatInVis tool (a browser extension that aims to replace user prompts with LLMs by structured visualization of user interaction). The study focused on usability aspects of the ChatInVis tool to facilitate exploration and retracing search paths. Moreover, the study also collected information on the insights that participants could get while using the tool to explore unknown topics. The results indicate that our approach allows users to revisit their search trails, fostering reflection on discoveries and identification of connections. Additionally, it enables users to navigate complex information, deepen their understanding, and perform searches more efficiently.

Keywords: LLM interactions · Search trails · Information seeking · Mind-map visualization · Analytic provenance

C. Maciel et al. (Eds.): INTERACT 2025 Workshops, LNCS 16478, pp. 135–154, 2026.
https://doi.org/10.1007/978-3-032-22934-2_13

1 Introduction

Information seeking is the process by which individuals or systems search for and retrieve information to fulfill a specific need or answer a question. This process typically involves recognizing an information gap, formulating a query, and utilizing various methods or tools, such as search engines, libraries, or databases, to locate relevant information [11]. Information-seeking tends to be explorative rather than linear. Information seeking is not just about finding answers, but about asking the right questions that lead to discovery. When the destination is unclear, the journey becomes exploratory. Without predetermined paths, the process involves navigating a complex terrain, often requiring one to backtrack, revisit, and refine their approach.

In academic, business, and everyday contexts such as health, information seeking is a fundamental activity for decision-making, problem-solving, and learning [15,21]. In this process, users identify possible information sources, differentiate between them, and select the most relevant sources to gather the data [6]. This involves locating, interacting with, and processing information in a structured manner. The steps, decisions, and sources consulted during information seeking are often referred to as a "search trail", which begins with a question and ends with a new question, inactivity, or timeout [9,19]. The search trail has shown to enhance transparency, improve search strategies [9], support collaboration [7], and foster learning [20]. When users find something intriguing, it becomes even more important to be able to retrace their 'search trail' to explain how results were obtained to exploit its benefits [7,9].

Large Language Models (LLMs), such as *GPT*, have significantly transformed the landscape of information seeking. These models provide an intuitive and flexible approach for users to search for and interact with information across various domains [17,18]. Unlike traditional methods that rely on search engines, libraries, or databases, LLMs facilitate a conversational method, enabling users to obtain detailed explanations, compose essays, and summarize content through natural language queries [22]. The primary intents driving the use of LLMs include text assistance, information retrieval, and problem-solving, reflecting the growing reliance on these models for a diverse range of information-related tasks [5]. This shift towards a more dynamic and user-friendly mode of information access marks a significant evolution in the process of information seeking. Yet, despite their impressive capabilities, current text-based interfaces, such as *ChatGPT*, face limitations when it comes to supporting information-seeking [16].

Traditional chatbots and search engines provide determinist behaviors and static responses. In contrast, LLMs (and generative AI in general) are non-deterministic and it is hard to see where we are going to in the conversation between two unknowns: the user and the LLM [4]. Indeed, when users engage in conversational exchanges with LLMs, they are asking follow-up questions or refining their questions based on previous responses. However, the steps in this process are rarely documented, making it difficult to trace the reasoning behind interactions or revisit previous points of inquiry. Two critical issues emerge as key to preserving and retracing these search trails:

- Difficulty in Revisiting Information: This problem has been documented by Suh et ali. [16] who argue that LLMs tend to deliver information in a sequential manner, making it difficult for users to revisit earlier discussions. This linear flow of information complicates efforts to return to previous points of interest or reference, which makes information retrieval more cumbersome.
- Lack of Structural Organization: this problem arrives because LLMs struggle to group related content and highlight connections between different pieces of information as illustrated by [10,16,21]. This lack of structural coherence can make it harder for users to interpret relationships and build a comprehensive understanding from the model's often fragmented outputs presented in disconnected pieces.

It has been suggested [12] that graphical representations, such as diagrams, maps, or charts, would overcome the limitations of LLMs by offering a non-linear and structured way to display information. In order to investigate the full potential of a graphical user interface to guide and retrace the interaction with LLMs, we present in this article a user study with the *ChatInVis* tool [1] which was specifically designed to support information seeking tasks with the help of LLM. *ChatInVis* is able to retrace search trails as a mind map. Our tool goes beyond documenting the user's questions and results: it also provides an interactive representation of the decisions made, the sequence of interactions, and the sources consulted. In addition to this, the *ChatInVis* tool supports the search trail formation providing exploration guidance through LLM-driven questions, incorporating external knowledge from PDFs or summarizing pieces of information.

This paper presents the results of a study involving 20 participants. The study evaluates the effectiveness of *ChatInVis* in supporting exploratory information-seeking tasks and retracing the search trail. The participants interacted with the tool across two distinct use case scenarios: one involving the creation of a mind map for an IT topic and another where they explored a pre-existing mind map. We found that participants considered *ChatinVis* highly engaging for exploring unknown topics. The study demonstrates that the tool enhances participants' ability to retrace their exploratory paths and offered structured guidance during complex information-seeking tasks. Hereafter, the Sect. 2 presents the related work in the domains of information seeking and user interfaces for interacting with LLMs. Section 3 briefly presents the user interface of *ChatinVis*. The Sect. 4 presents the user study, followed by Sect. 5 presenting the discussion, conclusions, and future work.

2 Related Work

2.1 The Role of Search Trails in Search Systems

Search trails help to record users' steps, decisions, and interactions during search activities. Various studies have examined the impact of search trails and their role in enhancing the information-seeking process.

Al-Sammarraie et al. found that novices could improve their query success rates and learn strategies by examining search histories of experts [2]. Findings of Franken et al. [7] confirm that users can improve the efficiency of collaborative search results by looking at trails left by others [8]. Xu et al. [20] showed that when search trails are visualized as graphs, they outperform traditional written reports in promoting collaborative search.

Hendahewa et al. demonstrated that recommending search trails based on previous users' behaviors can significantly improve both information coverage and overall search effectiveness [9]. This process facilitates knowledge acquisition (in both breadth and depth) by users in complex information spaces. Pedersen et al. [14] explored how research trails can be automatically generated (based on users' Web history) to allow easier information revisiting.

While previous research has primarily focused on search trails within traditional search engines and collaborative systems, the potential of search trails in the context of LLM-based information seeking remains largely unexplored.

2.2 Interactive Interfaces for LLM-Based Information Seeking

Table 1 provides an overview of various interaction systems designed to improve the usability of LLMs for information-seeking.

Table 1. Comparison of LLM-based information seeking interfaces with our approach.

System	Scope	Aim	Problem	Features
Graphologue [10]	general	comprehension in information-seeking	linear, unstructured LLM responses	graphical visualization of responses
Sensecape [16]	general	exploration & sensemaking	manage complex information & switch between foraging and sensemaking	hierarchical layers, multi-level navigation, exploration guidance
Knownet [21]	health	health information seeking	inaccurate and overwhelming health information	integration with knowledge graphs (KGs) to validate information, next step recommendations from KGs
CoQuest [13]	research	identifying research questions, research literature discovery	lack of context-aware questioning	Q&A mind-map interface with breadth and depth exploration, and LLM-enabled literature discovery; feedback to AI
ChatInVis	general	exploratory information-seeking	retracing and understanding exploration	mind-map visualization, provenance data, external knowledge integration, exploration guidance

Graphologue [10] converts textual LLM responses into interactive graphical charts, addressing the linear nature of LLM outputs. By visualizing complex data relationships, it enhances interpretability and helps users comprehend overwhelming information by parsing text from *ChatGPT-4* into new entities and relationships within a diagram. It reduces information overload through features like node collapsing and by dividing responses into separate diagrams. Similarly, *Sensecape* [16] introduces hierarchical abstractions in graphical outputs, mitigating information overload through multi-level navigation. It allows users to explore topics by moving information between different canvases and hierarchies while supporting topic recommendations for deeper exploration. Both tools improve content organization compared to traditional interface-based approaches by utilizing graphical charts and hierarchical abstractions. However, they lack mechanisms to retrace search trails or provide insights into the reasoning behind decisions made during the information-seeking process. Additionally, they do not support the inclusion of external knowledge, which is useful for comparing information from different sources in information seeking [6].
KNOWNET [21] and *CoQuest* [13] provide interactive interfaces for information seeking, each tailored to specific domains. The former focuses on health information seeking by integrating LLMs with external knowledge graphs (KGs). This integration ensures the validation of LLM responses, thereby enhancing the accuracy and reliability of the information. It also supports the exploration by suggesting next steps from the KG. In contrast, the latter targets the research domain, aiding in identifying research questions. It offers a question-and-answer mind-map interface that supports both breadth and depth in exploration and provides mechanisms such as typing feedback to the LLM. Despite its strengths in context-aware questioning, it does not include information overload mitigation mechanisms and does not support integrating different sources; although it provides the opportunity to suggest related literature through a paper retrieval pipeline from an existing pool of HCI papers. Therefore, while both systems contribute significantly to information-seeking tasks, they lack flexibility in domain and search trail exploration.

Previously presented tools provide useful interfaces for interacting with the LLMs, but lack mechanisms to retrace the explored search trail. *ChatInVis* [1] aims to bridge this gap by investigating how LLMs can enhance various aspects of the information-seeking process, including facilitating revisitation and supporting exploratory searches. The *ChatInVis* tool implements a search trail using a graphical visualization built upon the metaphor of mind-maps to organize information. This enables users to retrace their steps, revisit previous insights, and better understand the reasoning behind their inquiries. *ChatinVis* includes features like setting feedback and logging, enabling users to retrace and reconstruct their search trails. To provide exploration guidance, *ChatInVis* offers LLM-driven follow-up questions, integrates external knowledge sources (e.g., PDFs) to support comprehensive exploration, and provides functions for summarizing options and thus mitigating information overload. Further details about the tool are given in the next section.

3 Informed Search Trail Using *ChatInVis*

ChatInVis is a browser extension that works on top of *MindMeister*[1] which is a collaborative online tool for creating, editing, and sharing mind maps. *ChatInVis* is available for public download at the *Chrome Web Store*[2]. Note that an API key for the selected LLM is required. The source code is available in GitHub[3]. To promptly grasp *ChatInVis*, we highly recommend watching this 7' video[4]. Hereafter, we start by a brief description of the core concepts behind the tool and then illustrate its use.

3.1 Conceptual Model of the LLM Interaction Search Trail

The *ChatInVis* tool is based on conceptual elements describing search trails as shown by Fig. 1. As we shall see, the user interaction with LLMs is derived from these core concepts.

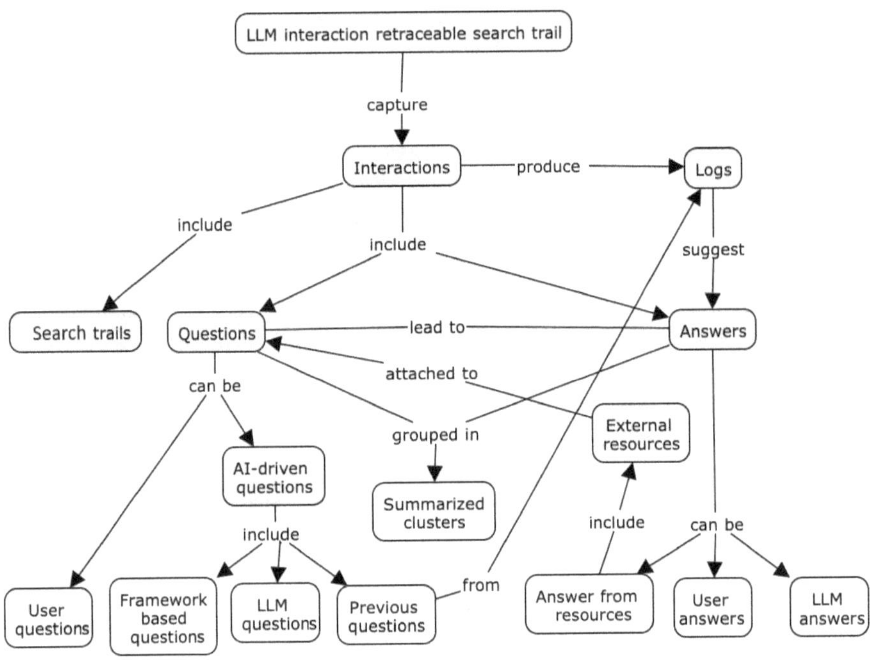

Fig. 1. Conceptual model of the search trail with *ChatInVis*.

[1] https://www.mindmeister.com/.
[2] https://rebrand.ly/chatinvis.
[3] https://github.com/onekin/Chatinvis.
[4] https://rebrand.ly/chatInVis_VideoAnonymous.

Interactions are the central hub of all activities done with the system. That includes **Questions**, **Answers**, and **Search Trails**. **Questions** originate from two primary sources: they may be either **User Questions** or **AI-driven Questions** (generated by the system). The question generation can be made without any particular constraint (the so-called **LLMs questions**) or by constraining the generation process to comply with **Framework-based questions** (like the 5W1H questioning approach) or by reusing **Previous questions** recorded in the **Logs**. **Questions** might lead to a set of possible **Answers** as follows: **LLM answers** are derived from the default LLM's knowledge base, **Answers from resources** employ specific **External resources** as knowledge base, or **User answers** when the user provides answers that can enrich the knowledge base. When **Questions** and/or **Answers** are too numerous and/or complex, the users can turn them into **Summarized clusters**. As users interact with the system, the sequence of questions and answers are combined to create **Search Trails**.

The analytic provenance incorporates the concept of **Feedback**, where users can rate and annotate answers capturing the user's insights and reasoning. To manage the complexity of multiple interactions, the search trail can contain related questions and answers grouped into clusters. Specifically, the **Question Clusters** and **Answer Clusters** represent nodes that group similar nodes together.

Whilst some concepts are visible to the users at the system's interface, others like the logging are not, such as for example those implemented as internal storage that ultimately affects the use of the tool. The visual concept of search trials follows the visual mapping as illustrated by Fig. 2. It shows how the **concrete** concepts of the conceptual model from Fig. 1, are represented in *ChatInVis*. User interactions are depicted with square shapes, LLM-generated elements with circles, and system log elements with cloud shapes. Questions, answers, and clusters are further distinguished using different icons and background colors. Resource-based answers are indicated by an attachment icon on the right, while feedback annotations appear as text within the answer itself. Additionally, the rating, from 0 to 4, is visually represented through the border color, from red to dark green, in a traffic light color scale. Although rating is not part of the conceptual model, this feature allows users to weight responses considered valuable.

3.2 A View at Glance of *ChatInVis*

Hereafter we present some of the key features of *ChatInVis* tool.

Question-answer interaction with LLM-Driven follow up questions. Figure 3 provides a view at glance of the mind map like user interface. Initially, it contains a single node (see Fig. 3.A) where the user can write a question. To see the LLMs' answer, the user must click on *question mark icon* (Fig. 3.B). Answers are presented as gray nodes featuring a summarized label. On the right side, there is a circle button allowing to open a box with further details about the answer. At the left, a *magnifier icon* allows continuing the exploration opening other exploration branches (Fig. 3.C, D, E...). The tool provides different alternatives for follow-up questions such as: an empty square box to allow user to insert a

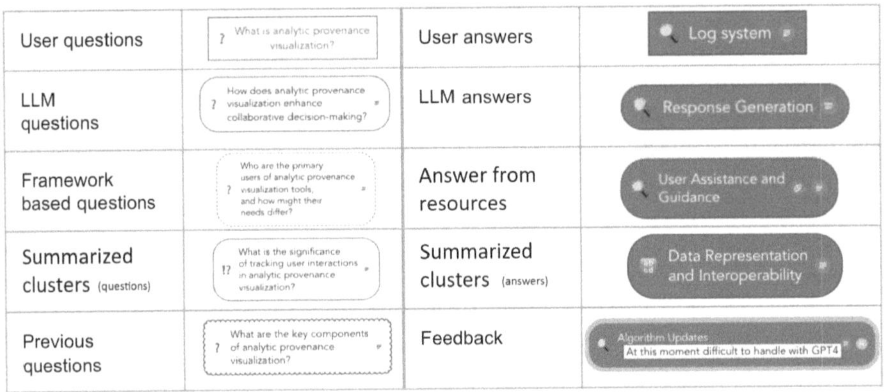

Fig. 2. Visual mapping of search trail concepts in *ChatInVis*.

new question (Fig. 3.C), similar questions found in the logs (Fig. 3.D), questions generated by the LLMs based on the current context (Fig. 3.E), and framework-based questions (like the "5W1H" framework) (Fig. 3.F) which can be predefined as templates in the systems settings. Also, in the setting, users can define the type and the numbers of generated answers and questions.

Users can provide **feedback** by annotating and rating the questions and answers generated by the tool, as shown in Fig. 4. Colors coding are used to identify key insights or areas of interest in the exploration.

As shown in Fig. 5, it is possible to attach **external information resources** (such as PDF documents) as source of the answers provided by the LLMs. The LLM then generates responses based on the content of the PDF, offering relevant text excerpts to support its answers.

To address information overload, *ChatInVis* offers a few **summarizing information** features to condense lengthy responses and grouping nodes into smaller clusters, as shown in Fig. 6. Users set the size of cluster nodes by selecting the parent node and choose the option "Summarize". This input is passed to the LLM, which generates new cluster nodes that group semantically similar nodes. This feature is available for both answers and questions nodes.

Logs. *ChatInVis* encodes user interactions through logs. It records various actions such as '*askQuestion*', '*selectAnswer*', '*setFeedback*', '*summarize*', and '*consultNote*' as the user interacts with the interface. For each record, the system stores the timestamp, the source of the map node, its value, and its predecessor value. Internally, each log also records the ID of the current map, the affected nodes' ID, and the user ID who created the log of the search trail.

Logs of search trail are stored in the local storage. The tool can retrieve and search through these logs when the system generates LLM-driven suggestions for previous questions. The logging can be activated or deactivated in the settings. Logs can be exported/imported enabling sharing of log data. The tool can also generate a report for the current mind map to review the analysis process.

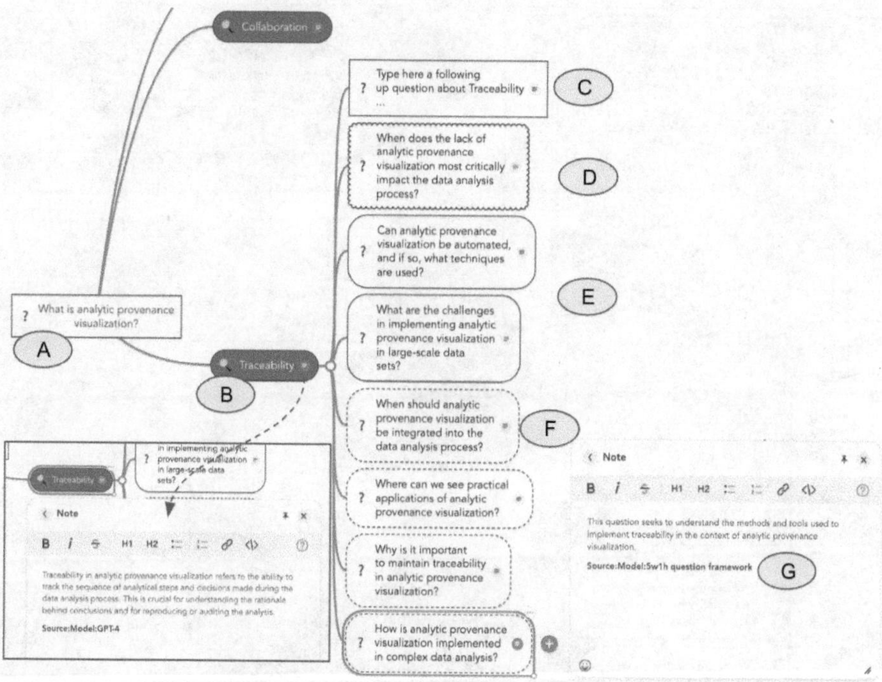

Fig. 3. Question-answer interaction in *ChatInVis*: A) (initial) user question B) answers for the first question; the right button inside each node allows users to view the complete answer. C) user question. D) previous question. E) LLM question. F) framework-based question. G) resources can be viewed in the note attached to each node, together with a description.

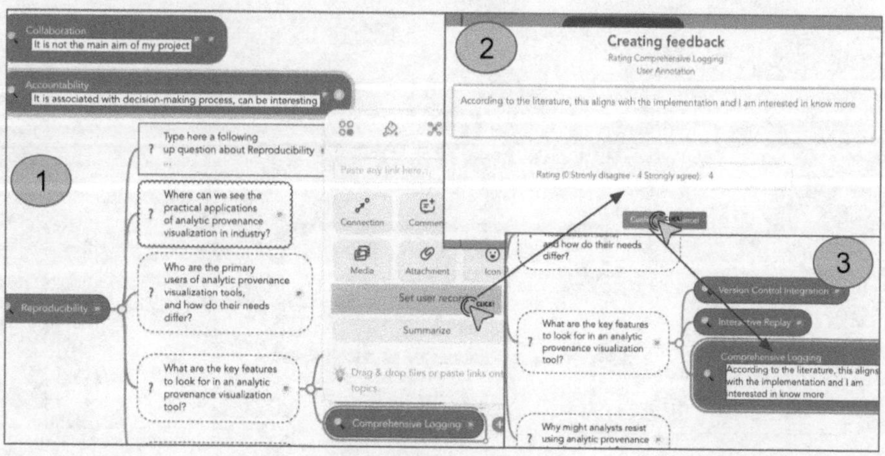

Fig. 4. Providing feedback to *ChatInVis*: (1) click right in node and selects 'Set user record'; (2) provide annotation and rating; (3) the node appearance is updated.

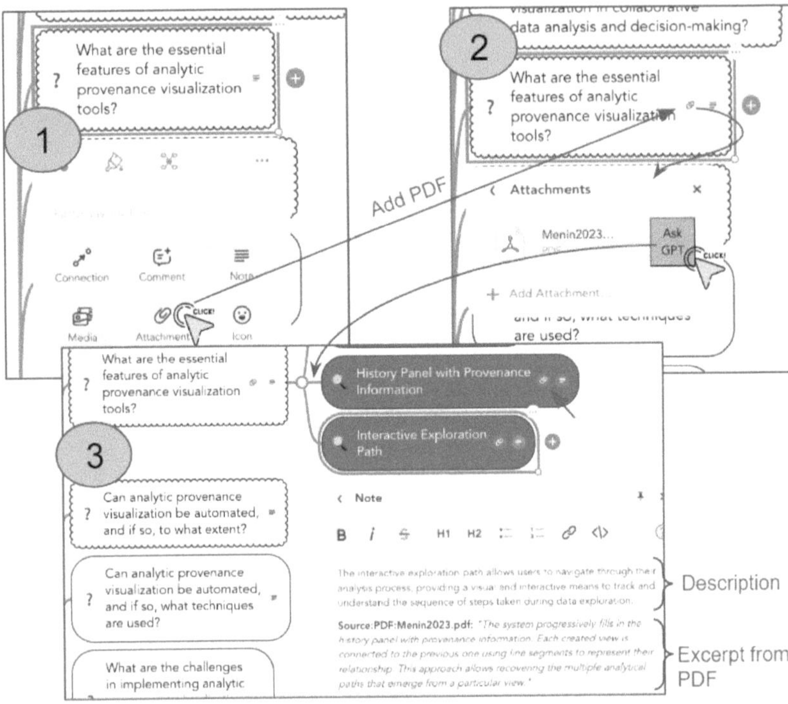

Fig. 5. An excerpt showing how to add information: (1) select attachment and upload a PDF to a node question; (2) select 'Ask GPT'; (3) answers point to source document and a excerpt.

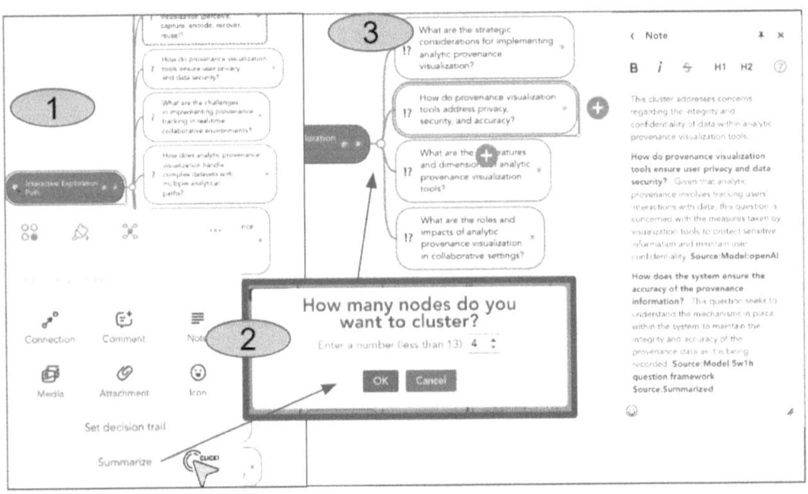

Fig. 6. Summarizing questions: (1) select 'Summarize'; (2) set the number of clusters; (3) questions are grouped maintaining previous data in the node to retrace the transformation. It is the same for summarizing answers.

4 User Study

We conducted a user study where participants were asked to use *ChatInVis* in individual sessions, completing tasks designed to assess both their interaction with the tool and its impact on their information-seeking processes. To achieve this, we collected user feedback and data addressing several research questions, each linked to our design objectives:

- *Q1. How effectively can users retrace their search trails using ChatInVis?*
- *Q2. How does ChatInVis support the formation of the search trail?*
- *Q3. What is ChatInVis usability?*

4.1 Participants

For this study we recruited 20 participants (8 female and 12 male), aged from 20 to 59 years (majority between 20-30 N=13), from different nationalities, including France, Italy, Spain, Argentina, Brazil, Costa Rica and United States. Participants were recruited from a convenience sample. They were all familiars with LLMs, at least having used *ChatGPT* once. Five participants had limited exposure to LLMs, using *ChatGPT* occasionally for tasks like writing support or generating ideas. Three others used LLMs more regularly but for quick, simple tasks several times a week. Five participants indicated frequent, almost daily use of LLMs, integrating them into both their professional and personal routines. Another group of seven participants used LLMs extensively for research and information-seeking tasks. The majority of the participants were Ph.D. students (n=7) and researchers (n=5). The rest included individuals with a master's degree (n=2), bachelor's degree (n=1), a professor (n=1), and 4 undergraduate students (n=4). Six participants reported being experts in knowledge graphs (topic for the use case scenario), and ten had at least moderate experience using mind maps. Semantic Web, graph-knowledge representation and artificial intelligence were the main research field of participants.

4.2 Protocol

The study began with a presentation of its goals, followed by a tutorial using the question *"What is analytic provenance visualization?"* Participants were informed about the study and provided written consent to participate.

During the tasks, we collected qualitative data, including user feedback, comments, and verbalized thoughts through a "think-aloud" protocol. Audio and screen recordings were made for qualitative analysis. Each task was followed by questions regarding its difficulty and the participants' opinions on the features used. All collected data was anonymized. Each session lasted approximately 90 min, with all participants using the same computer.

We run tasks in two distinct use case scenarios. After completing all scenarios, participants were prompted to provide demographic data, rate the usability of the tool using the *System Usability Scale (SUS)*, and tell things they liked and disliked in the tool. The study concluded with a debriefing session.

4.3 Use Case Scenarios

Use Case Scenario I asked participants to explore the question *"What are knowledge graphs?"* using *ChatInVis* with the *"gpt-4-1106-preview"* model. Considering the sample of participants, it was a topic that included people knowledgeable about the topic and others not familiar, what gave us different perspectives. Moreover, it is a question that contains complex relationships among concepts. For example, understanding knowledge graphs at a basic level involves recognizing their components (e.g., nodes and edges), data sources (e.g., structured databases, unstructured text), and their applications.

In this scenario, participants had to perform eight tasks. Task 1 prompted participants to create a mind-map and engage in a question-and-answer sequence to explore the topic freely. Task 2 requested to trace the origins of the information gathered in Task 1, testing the ability to source-check and verify the information. In Task 3, participants were asked to provide feedback on one of the answers generated by the LLM. Task 4 encouraged participants ask for additional questions for one of the answers, summarizing them, and reflect on the summarized content. Task 5 asked them to attach a research paper about knowledge graphs into a question node and use it to answer a question, while Task 6 asked participants to repeat the question without the document, testing the influence of external resources on their understanding. Task 7 focused on summarizing current answers retrieved by the PDF and without the PDF. Finally, Task 8 required participants to generate and analyze a report of their activity, providing an overview of their exploration process.

Use Case Scenario II addresses some aspects of asynchronous collaboration between users. More specifically, this scenario is aimed at assessing how participants interpret a search trail left by another user and how they engage with pre-existing information. For this case scenario, we presented a mind map previously created with *ChatInVis* that addresses the question *"What is Queen?"* This broad question can lead to various interpretations, encompassing topics such as the British monarchy, the rock band Queen, or chess pieces. This diversity allows participants to explore various aspects of the topic through the lens of another user's thought process, annotations are only displayed using *ChatInVis*. Participants were asked to perform a single task: to explore a mind map and think aloud as they do so. After exploring, they were asked to share their opinion on what they think the original participant was trying to achieve through their exploration of the topic.

Regarding the research questions, **Q1** was addressed in both scenarios. In the first scenario, participants revisited their own exploration (checking sources, consulting answers, etc.), while in the second, they interpreted another user's search trail. **Q2** was explored through the first scenario, where participants engaged with the tool to navigate and deepen their understanding of a given topic. Lastly, **Q3** was investigated through participant feedback on task difficulty, tool usability, and responses from the SUS questionnaire.

4.4 Results

From the 20 studies, we could extract a total of 245 comments from the transcription and the questionnaire, 104 classified as positive (what they value and appreciate), 75 as negative (e.g., bugs of the tool or negative aspects) and 66 as suggestions (e.g., improvements)[5]. Table 2 provides a summary of the main findings; Tasks 1-8 refer to the Scenario I and the Tasks 9 refers to the Scenario II. The comments were retrieved by the recording of the sessions. We observed that the content of comments grouped for each task can embrace more than one aspects of the tool. Therefore, we decided to discuss the most notable and recurring comments based on the features of *ChatInVis*.

Table 2. Task analysis informing user and tool times, positive and negative aspects, suggestions, and difficulties.

Task	User Time (Average)	Tool Time (Average)	Positive	Negative	Suggestions	Difficulty (1-5)
1	4 m 39 s	2 m 19 s	19	17	17	1.1
2	1 m 7 s	-	14	3	5	1.2
3	1 m 11 s	-	20	8	8	1.3
4	1 m 22 s	52 s	13	10	5	1.05
5	1 m 46 s	35 s	10	9	5	1.25
6	1 m 5 s	21 s	3	3	3	1.8
7	1 m 6 s	29 s	7	7	7	1.15
8	1 m 50 s	-	6	10	10	1.44
9	5 m 50 s	-	12	8	6	1.3

Question-Answer Interaction with LLM-Driven Follow up Questions. Overall, participants appreciated the system's flexibility in exploring different inquiry branches (as reported by U01, U06, U10, U19)[6], as said by U10: *"I'm exploring one path and it is easy to change the branch..."*. The system-generated questions were described as thought-provoking and engaging (by U05, U10, U15, U17, U18, U19), sparking curiosity and guiding deeper exploration. Additionally, the system also provided interesting connections between different user inquiries, enhancing exploration by showing how various topics intersect (U14). The quality and relevance of the answers were well-received, with users noting that they often met expectations (U01, U10, U14, U15, U19). For those unfamiliar with certain topics, the system introduced new vocabulary and concepts, aiding knowledge building (U14). The presentation of multiple options from different sources was seen as a key advantage, offering diverse perspectives that enriched the exploration experience (U04). The interface's clarity was praised (U03, U11), with colored questions and answers making navigation intuitive and

[5] Comments, task difficulty and time spent data: http://rebrand.ly/chatinvisDataset.
[6] Participants are identified as U01 to U20.

reducing user overwhelm while depicting the provenance of data (U13, U15). The system's adaptability was also valued, allowing users to modify questions and configure the number of questions to suit their needs (U13,U20).

Three participants noted repetition of questions (U04, U10, U17) and two reported an overwhelming number of questions generated (U01, U09), prompting frequent use of the summary function. As one participant noted: *"The number of questions was overwhelming... I'm going to do a summary because there are too many."* Participants also suggested introducing global questions that leverage the context of multiple answers to refine or expand information, helping users explore how different pieces of information interrelate (U15).

Feedback and Reuse of Feedback Logs. The annotating and rating feature was praised for its utility and ease of use. Participants found adding feedback straightforward (U01, U11), allowing them to *"...document thoughts and explore alternative paths effortlessly"*. The feedback feature was especially useful for documentation when revisiting maps after a while (U06, U19, U20), as one participant noted: *"It can be useful in terms of documentation... you come back one month later to this map, and you have some feedback points."* The intuitive color-coding for ratings was also appreciated (U01, U18), enabling users to quickly assess the importance of different sections as uttered by one participant: *"Color-coded feedback would help me quickly see what's useful or not."*.

Nonetheless, opinions were mixed with respect to the use of logs as input for suggesting answers. Some participants found this feature useful, as said by U19: *"It's very useful, especially when the user is not familiar with the topic they would like to explore."*. It was also seen (U12, U15) as a valuable feature for sharing similar interests with others. The potential for collaborative work was also highlighted (U06, U09, U11, U13). However, some participants expressed concerns about suggesting answers based on annotation ratings (U02, U10), fearing that inaccurate annotations could mislead other users, especially in fields requiring expertise. As one participant noted: *"Annotations from others... it's interesting, but it could become problematic easily... I will need a trustworthy annotation system"*, emphasizing the need for a controlled environment for sharing feedback logs. To address these concerns, participants suggested implementing a controlled system for using feedback logs to suggest questions and answers (U10, U19). They recommended regulating feedback log sharing through a moderation system to ensure accuracy and relevance. Another suggestion was to use feedback annotations and ratings to improve the system by training the LLM over time (U10, U19).

Use of External Knowledge. The integration of PDFs was highly valued by participants for enriching the system's information. A key benefit was the direct linking of source paragraphs to answers (U01, U02, U08, U12, U14, U20), which added credibility and context, helping users find relevant information quickly. Participants appreciated that the system not only provided responses but also directed them to specific sections of the attached paper. As one noted: *"I like that it does these two things: first, it gives you a response from the model, and second, it tells you, 'Okay, you can go check that part, and I don't have to read the* *entire article'."*. This feature was seen as a significant time-saver. Additionally, the ability to view the attached PDF directly on the mind map was considered convenient (U07).

By incorporating content from both the LLM and attached documents, the system provided a wider range of perspectives and details, which participants found useful for tasks like literature reviews. Some participants noted that responses generated from PDFs were more surprising and insightful, offering new angles that might not have been considered otherwise (U17). Suggestions for improvement included differentiating more clearly between nodes created from PDFs and those generated by the LLM (U17, U18).

Summarizing Information. This feature was highly praised by the participants, especially when dealing with a large number of questions (U01, U08, U11). As one participant noted, *"It is a very good concept because when the system provides you with many questions, you are overwhelming your field of view."* By condensing questions into summaries, the feature helped reduce cognitive overload. During the experiment, at least eight users (U03, U05, U07, U09, U10, U11, U12, U20) chose to summarize questions during the first task of Scenario I, which shows the need for the feature.

Some participants reported that summarized questions were more generalized, providing a broad overview before delving into specifics (U06, U14). This approach helped in setting context and focusing on key points (U15). When summarizing answers, users valued the integration of information from multiple sources, including PDFs and the LLM's responses (U03, U04, U10, U12, U13). This integration was particularly useful when the summary retained source references (U09, U11, U19), allowing users to track the origin of information. One participant (U15) pointed to the tool's ability to create a top-level taxonomy, integrating different concepts into a cohesive whole.

A notable issue raised was the loss of explored branches during summarization if a summarized node's branch is developed (U07). Participants suggested preserving original content alongside the summary or offering options to avoid overwriting details. Another suggestion was to let users choose the number of clusters for summarization, allowing more control over the process (U14, U20).

Log Report. This feature was valued for documenting and analyzing the research process, though it raised some concerns. Participants appreciated its ability to help them reflect on past activities. The feature also highlighted moments when users encountered obstacles (U08, U14, U20) by providing a timestamped log, aiding in pinpointing challenges. Additionally, it was seen as useful for conducting statistical studies and reproducing interactions for analysis (U04). However, some found the reports hard to understand, especially those without a computer science background (U07, U09, U11, U17), as the technical language made it less accessible.

Participants suggested improvements, such as a more structured format with indentation or color-coding (U13, U06, U18) to simplify navigation. They also proposed adding paths for each question or answer to clarify the research process (U07, U17) and exporting the report in more accessible formats like HTML or

JSON (U16, U19). Including a summary generated by the LLM (U17) and adding filters to sort actions by time, type, or source could further enhance usability.

4.5 Response to the Research Questions

Q1: How effectively can users retrace their search trails using *ChatInVis*? Our findings confirm that *ChatInVis* helps users in retracing their search trails, capturing exploration paths and enabling reflection on the search process and the provenance of information.

A benefit derived from the study of retracing the search trail is the ability to **reflect on discoveries**. As one participant noted: *"You have your history of exploration, and you can directly see the research branch. Not like in other tools, where we have only one back and forward."*. This reflection extends to interacting with others' exploration paths. A comment is revealing the potential of the potential *"seeing all the questions and the reasoning of the person makes it really easy to understand where they went... it's easy to retrace the steps based on what was explored, what was not opened, what questions were typed, and the annotations, which are clearly displayed"* (U02). Color-coded feedback seems effective as *"the color of the feedback marks helps to see what me or my potential co-worker found useful or not during the exploration..."*.

Retracing the search trail helps users **uncover connections** between pieces of information that may not be immediately obvious. Users often start with one concept and branch out to related ideas and then revisit their paths to reveal connecting ideas. Participants pointed that provenance of data through the visualization helped them identify how different sources connect.

Q2: How does *ChatInVis* support the formation of the search trail? The user study shows that *ChatInVis* supports search trail helping users to navigate complex information, to expand knowledge, and to streamline the search process.

Firstly, the tool reduces **navigating complexity** by visually depicting exploration process, allowing users to see different branches of the inquiry. A participant said it feels like *"a GitHub tree"* (U04), offering more structure than traditional chat interfaces. Another said: *"I enjoyed using mind maps; they allow exploration and interaction with answers and keep track of the exploration path."* A third participant described it as an *"interactive Wikipedia"* (U10).

The tool helps at **expanding knowledge** by suggesting related questions. Participants appreciated having multiple options from different sources, allowing for diverse perspectives. A participant commented: *"I really like that you have several options coming from different sources."* Compared to traditional chat interfaces like *ChatGPT*, a participant said that: *"it helps you make the questions, which can be difficult when starting from scratch"*. However, some found the abundance of suggestions overwhelming, describing it as a *"wall of text."*

In terms of **efficient search**, the tool provides structured pathways and minimizes time spent on irrelevant or redundant information. It offers search suggestions and a clear exploration path, helping users focus their efforts more effectively. A participant explained that: *"for topics where I know nothing, it* *seems super helpful because you do not even know where to start.".* Users appreciated the clear representation of their exploration paths, making it easy to revisit and explore alternate directions within a topic.

Q3: Is *ChatInVis* easy to use? The SUS score [3] for *ChatInVis* ranged from 70 to 100 (average 88.87) and suggests that the tool is usable. The score is coherent with the qualitative feedback from users. Fourteen participants explicitly described *ChatInVis* as easy to use, highlighting its clear interface and intuitive manipulation. These remarks highlight a positive user experience, emphasizing the straightforward interface interaction mechanisms. Users did not encounter difficulties in completing the study's tasks, with most tasks being rated as very easy. The highest average difficulty rating, on a scale from 1 (very easy) to 5 (very difficult), was 1.8 for Task 6 where some users found it counterintuitive to repeat a question using only the LLM with having a PDF attached.

5 Discussion

In the user study, when participants were asked who they would recommend the tool to, most said, *"anyone who wants to learn about a specific topic"*. Participants found *ChatInVis* especially valuable for those exploring new topics, describing it as a *"good start to begin to explore a new subject"* and noting that *"it gives you access to vocabulary and* ***associated*** *taxonomy, which can be useful when you do not have much knowledge on the topic."* While the ability to provide extensive new information can be attributed to the strengths of LLMs, the key contribution of *ChatInVis* lies in the bold word of the last comment: associated. Search trails as provided by *ChatInVis* contribute to build and preserve the associations between concepts during the exploration process, capturing the relationships that are often lost in more linear, traditional interfaces. By emphasizing the importance of documenting and retracing these associations, the tool enables users to reflect on their reasoning during exploration and revisit their discoveries.

Therefore, the solution is particularly effective for exploring open-ended questions where relationships among concepts are complex and multifaceted. For example, when exploring what knowledge graphs are, the tool enables users to understand not only the definition but the components (e.g., nodes and edges), sources (like structured databases and unstructured text), and their applications in various fields. This makes it highly suitable for tasks that benefit from deeper exploration, where users need to reflect, make decisions, and explore different dimensions of a concept while establishing connections between them. The integration of analytic provenance provides users with the ability to retrace their exploration steps, helping them review their reasoning, revisit key points, and understand the logical flow of their search trail. This enhances understanding, particularly when users need to explain their search process. It is worthy of notice that, for when looking for definitions and/or factual checking, search engines might outperform LLMs so that tool *ChatInVis* are more suitable to support exploratory search tasks. For users seeking quick answers to specific questions (e.g., definitions), the mind-map approach can be cumbersome and inefficient. In such cases, where a direct answer is sufficient, the additional steps and structure may introduce unnecessary complexity.

The importance of search trails goes beyond traditional information-seeking with LLMs. *ChatInVis* offers a solution that is applicable not only to information seeking but also to other exploration contexts like problem analysis, requirements gathering, research question scoping or strategic planning. Future work should address the idea of generating framework-based questions that allows users to adapt the style of inquiries to different contexts.

While participants were generally satisfied with the tool, opinions on paying for an *OpenAI* API key were divided (9 would refuse to pay). The requirement to register with *MindMeister* for using *ChatInVis* emerged as a potential barrier to adoption.

Participants noted that the volume of generated questions might become excessive, making frequent use of the summarization. Although summarization is intended to address this issue, it appears insufficient in fully alleviating the problem. Future work should focus on developing improved mechanisms to manage scalability and minimize information overload.

The tool relies on the user to interpret logs and search trails, lacking the ability to derive deeper insights on its own. A few users suggested leveraging the LLM's capabilities to assist in this area, proposing that the LLM could automatically identify and highlight relationships between different elements of the analysis. Future work will focus on enhancing how the logs generated during the search process are utilized.

Participants had mixed opinions on making logs openly accessible to others in a shared storage. Concerns about privacy and control over shared logs were significant, despite the fact they acknowledge the potential benefits.

6 Conclusions

This paper presented a user study of an innovative study on search trails implemented as part of the user interaction with LLMs. The tool, named *ChatInVis*, is an interactive system designed to enhance search trail exploration in information-seeking with Large Language Models (LLMs) by integrating mind-map visualizations and analytic provenance. *ChatInVis* contributes to addressing key limitations of current LLM interfaces, such as the lack of structural organization and difficulties in revisiting information, enabling users to effectively retrace their search paths. The user study shows that the tool is usable and it has potential to assist users in retracing their search trails and effectively navigating complex information spaces, particularly when searching for information on unfamiliar topics. Many participants in the study recognized the collaborative potential of *ChatInVis*, which opens avenues for further investigation into its contributions to collaborative decision-making through its analytical provenance features. Overall, this study contributes to addresses the challenges faced in LLM-based interfaces for complex information-seeking tasks by documenting and organizing search trails.

Acknowledgments. We thank the 20 study participants for their valuable feedback and insights.

Disclosure of Interests. The authors have no competing interests to declare that are relevant to the content of this article.

References

1. onekin/ChatInVis (Oct 2025). https://github.com/onekin/ChatInVis, original-date: 2024-06-12T13:50:29Z
2. Al-Sammarraie, M., Umapathy, K.: A research plan to study impact of a collaborative web search tool on novice's query behavior. In: 2016 International Conference on Collaboration Technologies and Systems (CTS), pp. 539–544. IEEE (2016)
3. Bangor, A., Kortum, P.T., Miller, J.T.: An empirical evaluation of the system usability scale. Intl. J. Human-Comput. Interact. **24**(6), 574–594 (2008)
4. Bejot, J.: Designing LLM interfaces: a new paradigm (Nov 2024). https://medium.com/@jasonbejot/designing-llm-interfaces-a-new-paradigm-11dd40e2c4a1
5. Burmester, M., Mast, M., Tille, R., Weber, W.: How users perceive and use interactive information graphics: An exploratory study. In: 2010 14th International Conference Information Visualisation, pp. 361–368. IEEE (2010)
6. Choo, C.W., Detlor, B., Turnbull, D., Choo, C.W., Detlor, B., Turnbull, D.: Information seeking. Web Work: Information Seeking and Knowledge Work on the World Wide Web, pp. 3–27 (2000)
7. Franken, S., Norbisrath, U., Prinz, W.: Search trails as collaboration artifacts–evaluating the ux. In: Mensch und Computer 2015–Proceedings, pp. 23–32. De Gruyter Oldenbourg (2015)
8. Franken, S., Norbisrath, U., Prinz, W.: The impact of searchtrails on the quality of collaborative search: A novel trail-based visualization facilitating the search process. i-com **16**(1), 3–14 (2017)
9. Hendahewa, C., Shah, C.: Evaluating user search trails in exploratory search tasks. Inform. Process. Manage. **53**(4), 905–922 (2017)
10. Jiang, P., Rayan, J., Dow, S.P., Xia, H.: Graphologue: exploring large language model responses with interactive diagrams. In: Proceedings of the 36th Annual ACM Symposium on User Interface Software and Technology, pp. 1–20 (2023)
11. Kingrey, K.P.: Concepts of information seeking and their presence in the practical library literature. Libr. Philos. Pract. **4**(2), 1–14 (2002)
12. Larkin, J.H., Simon, H.A.: Why a diagram is (sometimes) worth ten thousand words. Cogn. Sci. **11**(1), 65–100 (1987)
13. Liu, Y., et al.: How ai processing delays foster creativity: Exploring research question co-creation with an LLM-based agent. In: Proceedings of the CHI Conference on Human Factors in Computing Systems, pp. 1–25 (2024)
14. Pedersen, E.R., Gyllstrom, K., Gu, S., Hong, P.J.: Automatic generation of research trails in web history. In: Proceedings of the 15th International Conference On Intelligent User Interfaces, pp. 369–372 (2010)
15. Savolainen, R.: Everyday life information seeking: approaching information seeking in the context of "way of life." Library & information science research **17**(3), 259–294 (1995)
16. Suh, S., Min, B., Palani, S., Xia, H.: Sensecape: Enabling multilevel exploration and sensemaking with large language models. In: Proceedings of the 36th Annual ACM Symposium on User Interface Software and Technology, pp. 1–18 (2023)

17. Teubner, T., Flath, C.M., Weinhardt, C., van der Aalst, W., Hinz, O.: Welcome to the era of Chatgpt et al. the prospects of large language models. Business Inform. Syst. Eng. **65**(2), 95–101 (2023)
18. Thirunavukarasu, A.J., Ting, D.S.J., Elangovan, K., Gutierrez, L., Tan, T.F., Ting, D.S.W.: Large language models in medicine. Nat. Med. **29**(8), 1930–1940 (2023)
19. White, R.W., Huang, J.: Assessing the scenic route: measuring the value of search trails in web logs. In: Proceedings of the 33rd International ACM SIGIR Conference on Research and Development in Information Retrieval, pp. 587–594. SIGIR '10, Association for Computing Machinery, New York, NY, USA (2010). https://doi.org/10.1145/1835449.1835548
20. Xu, L., Zhou, X., Gadiraju, U.: How does team composition affect knowledge gain of users in collaborative web search? In: Proceedings of the 31st ACM Conference on Hypertext and Social Media, pp. 91–100 (2020)
21. Yan, Y., Hou, Y., Xiao, Y., Zhang, R., Wang, Q.: Knownet: guided health information seeking from LLMs via knowledge graph integration. IEEE Trans. Visual. Comput. Graph. (2024)
22. Zhang, T., Ladhak, F., Durmus, E., Liang, P., McKeown, K., Hashimoto, T.B.: Benchmarking large language models for news summarization. Trans. Assoc. Comput. Linguist. **12**, 39–57 (2024)

User Mental Models as a Lens for Evaluating Explainable-AI System Outputs

Carmelo Ardito(✉), Maria Luigia Natalia De Bonis, Tommaso Di Noia, Eugenio Di Sciascio, Giuseppe Fasano, and Angela Lombardi

Department of Electrical and Information Engineering, Polytechnic University of Bari, Bari, Italy
{carmelo.ardito,maria.debonis,tommaso.dinoia,eugenio.disciascio, giuseppe.fasano,angela.lombardi}@poliba.it

Abstract. Traditional evaluation methods for Explainable AI (XAI) often emphasize perceived clarity or task performance, overlooking the cognitive processes by which domain experts construct and refine their understanding. In this work, we propose a mental model-based evaluation framework that, grounded in cognitive science and Human-Computer Interaction (HCI), defines five analytical dimensions to assess how end users engage with XAI systems. Our goal is to support the design and evaluation of XAI interfaces that enable informed, trustworthy, and reflective decision-making in professional practice. We illustrate this perspective outlining how the mental model-based framework could be used to assess explanation effectiveness of Brain Age Predictor, an interactive interface for brain age prediction based on structural Magnetic Resonance Imaging (MRI) data.

Keywords: Explainable AI · Mental models · Human-centered AI · Evaluation framework

1 Introduction

In recent years, the integration of Artificial Intelligence (AI) into software systems has reshaped the way humans interact with digital tools. In sensitive domains like healthcare, for example AI offers powerful support for diagnosis and prognosis. However, these opportunities are paralleled by critical concerns: end users may be expected to rely on models whose inner logic remains opaque, limiting their ability to engage in reflective and responsible decision-making.

In high-stakes scenarios such as clinical practice, while such technologies promise efficiency and precision, they also challenge foundational values such as professional autonomy, transparency, and accountability. It is not sufficient for an AI system to perform well; users must be able to scrutinize its behavior

Published by Springer Nature Switzerland AG 2026
C. Maciel et al. (Eds.): INTERACT 2025 Workshops, LNCS 16478, pp. 155–166, 2026.
https://doi.org/10.1007/978-3-032-22934-2_14

and interpret its outputs in light of their domain knowledge and responsibilities [16].

Explainable AI (XAI) emerged in response to these concerns, aiming to enhance the interpretability of machine learning systems [18]. However, numerous studies indicate that current methods frequently fail to provide truly meaningful insights [13]. Instead of supporting users in reasoning about the system, many XAI techniques focus on superficial clarity or seek to increase user trust, factors that do not necessarily reflect actual comprehension.

This gap calls for a more human-centered perspective. From the point of view of Human-Computer Interaction (HCI) [23], interaction is not merely about usability or trust, but about how users build and refine mental representations, mental models, of a system's inner logic [9,11]. These models are essential for anticipating behavior, questioning outputs, and making informed decisions. However, most XAI evaluation practices remain detached from such cognitive foundations, instead relying on generic metrics such as perceived clarity or task performance [8].

In this work, we introduce a framework for evaluating XAI systems through the lens of mental model formation. Rather than focusing solely on the explanation content, our approach considers the broader interactional and cognitive processes through which users make sense of AI behavior. The framework is intended to assess whether the system design, including explanations, interface structure, and feedback mechanisms, supports the emergence of coherent and actionable understanding.

This work builds on our previous experience in neuroimaging, particularly in developing tools and methods for analyzing and interpreting complex brain data. Thus, we illustrate this perspective by outlining how the mental model-based framework could be used to assess explanation effectiveness of *Brain Age Predictor*, an interactive interface for brain age prediction based on structural Magnetic Resonance Imaging (MRI) data [4,15]. This scenario exemplifies both the promises and the challenges of integrating XAI into real-world healthcare contexts, where interpretability must go hand-in-hand with clinical validity and professional judgment.

Although the framework is still in its early stages, we are currently designing user studies to evaluate its effectiveness and practical relevance in real-world XAI scenarios.

2 Related Works

2.1 Explainability and Human Understanding in AI

Despite the growing attention to explainability in AI, many approaches remain anchored in assumptions that are not systematically validated from a human-centered perspective. According to Buçinca et al. [1], evaluations of XAI systems often rely on *proxy tasks*, indirect indicators such as perceived trust, user satisfaction, or task success, which are taken as signals of user understanding without measuring cognitive processes directly. Buçinca et al. critically examine this issue, arguing that such proxies may mask users' actual misconceptions about system behavior. They show how high levels of trust can coexist with poor mental models, leading to overreliance or misuse. Similarly, Coroamă et al. [2] highlight the epistemic risks of these evaluations, warning that success in a task may reflect strategy or guesswork rather than genuine comprehension.

Reliance on proxies reflects a broader issue: the field has prioritized the production of explanations over the study of how users engage with them cognitively. A comprehensive review by Nauta et al. [20] underscores this gap, showing that most XAI evaluations are clustered around a limited set of dimensions, such as explanation format or presentation clarity, while neglecting deeper user-centered aspects like conceptual coherence, contextual relevance, or controllability. As a result, the cognitive effects of explanation remain largely unexamined in practice.

2.2 Mental Models and XAI Evaluation

The tendencies described in the previous section highlight a core limitation in current XAI practices: the assumption that trust, clarity, or task success equate to genuine understanding. Such assumptions overlook the cognitive mechanisms through which users form and refine internal representations of a system's logic.

To address this gap, a growing body of research has turned to the concept of mental models, intended as users' internal, often partial and evolving representations of how a system operates [11]. Rooted in cognitive science, mental models are not seen as static knowledge structures, but as dynamic constructs shaped through interaction, feedback, and goal-driven exploration [10]. From this perspective, understanding is a process that unfolds over time, supported by system responses, interface cues, and explanatory strategies.

Kulesza et al. [12] exemplify this process-oriented view through the notion of *explanatory debugging*, a cycle in which users iteratively query the system, update their assumptions, and reassess predictions. This approach has been shown to enhance not only task accuracy, but also alignment between user expectations and model behavior. Likewise, Tullio et al. [24] demonstrate how misaligned mental models, regardless of system performance, can lead to both overuse and underuse, with potentially critical consequences in domains like healthcare.

These findings point to a crucial insight: the effectiveness of explanations cannot be separated from user's capacity to integrate them into a coherent mental framework. Gentile et al. [8] argue that correct decisions are not always indicative of correct reasoning, especially when background knowledge or contextual inference plays a role. Consequently, they call for evaluation approaches that reveal how users generalize from explanations and apply them to novel scenarios.

Recent methodological advances reflect this need. Zhang et al. [25] assess conceptual change by comparing users' understanding of the system output before and after exposure to explanations. Scarpato et al. [21] propose the *Forward Simulatability Score*, a metric that captures whether users can anticipate the system output given a new input, offering a more direct view of the internalization of the model logic.

Taken together, these contributions suggest that mental model-centered evaluation provides a more cognitively valid and domain-relevant understanding of explainability. However, in much of the existing literature, mental models remain implicit or are used post hoc to interpret results rather than serving as central design and evaluation targets.

In this work, we argue that the design and assessment of XAI systems should be grounded in accurate and adaptable mental models. The framework we propose is intended to address this need by embedding mental model formation within the evaluation process, enabling richer alignment between human reasoning and algorithmic behavior.

2.3 XAI Limitations in the Neuroimaging Domain

XAI methods are increasingly being applied in clinical settings, where system output interpretability [14] is essential to support diagnostic reasoning and informed decision-making. In particular *Brain Age Predictor*, i.e. the clinical use case in neuroimaging we have been working on, refers to the estimation of biological brain age from structural MRI and is gaining interest as a clinically meaningful biomarker. The discrepancy between predicted and chronological age, known in the literature as the Brain Age Gap (BAG), has been associated with various conditions, including cognitive decline and neurodegenerative diseases [7].

Several studies have explored the interpretability of brain age models using post hoc techniques such as SHAP [17] and saliency maps [19] to highlight the neuroanatomical features that drive predictions. Some of these investigations have relied on large-scale, multi-site datasets such as OpenBHB [6], which offer a valuable testbed while also revealing challenges related to scanner variability and acquisition heterogeneity [3].

However, many of these efforts focus on producing plausible explanations without evaluating whether such outputs truly support clinical reasoning or align with expert understanding [20]. As a result, there remains a gap between what current XAI techniques provide and what clinicians need to meaningfully interpret and act upon model outputs in real-world contexts.

The Brain Age Predictor system we have designed addresses that gap by embedding explanations within an interactive, human-centered interface for brain age prediction. Instead of treating explanations as isolated components, the overall interaction with the system is considered, including how explanation content, visual representations, and interface behavior support clinicians in developing accurate and usable mental models.

3 Mental Model-Centric Evaluation Framework

The proposed framework consists of five distinct yet complementary phases, designed to systematically assess the quality of XAI explanations in terms of their ability to support the construction of a functional mental model by the user. Each phase explores a specific component of the user's understanding and interaction with the system. Applying the framework requires the involvement of a pool of end users and at least one expert in both the application domain and artificial intelligence.

An overview of the five phases and their logical progression is illustrated in Fig. 1.

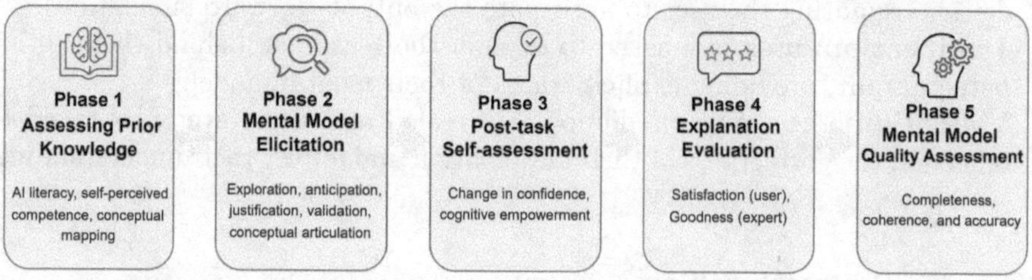

Fig. 1. Overview of the proposed mental model-centric evaluation framework.

Phase 1 - Assessing prior knowledge

This initial phase focuses on capturing individual differences in familiarity with AI concepts, users' self-perceived competence in interpreting AI-based explanations, and their preliminary conceptual understanding of how an explainable AI system functions.

- **AI knowledge:** assessed using the *AI Literacy Scale (AILS)*, a self-report questionnaire developed in English to measure general AI literacy in human–AI interaction contexts. It includes items rated on a 7-point Likert scale (1 = strongly disagree, 7 = strongly agree) and evaluates four dimensions: awareness, usage, evaluation, and ethics. An example item is: *"It is usually hard for me to learn to use a new AI application or product."*
- **Self-perceived competence:** measured through Likert-scale items (1 = strongly disagree, 7 = strongly agree) aimed at capturing how confident users feel when interpreting AI-based explanations. An example item is: *"I feel capable of understanding the explanations provided by AI systems."*
- **Conceptual mapping:** prior to system interaction, users are asked to externalize their initial understanding of how an explainable AI system operates. This is done through a conceptual mapping task, structured as a bipartite representation, in which users link concepts related to the functioning of the AI/XAI system with concepts from the application domain. The resulting map provides an early representation of how users organize and relate system mechanisms to domain knowledge, forming an initial trace of their mental model.

These factors can significantly influence how users build their mental model of the system.

Phase 2 - Mental model stimulation

This phase aims to stimulate and make explicit the user's internal representation of how the system works through a sequence of tasks that encourage exploration, anticipation, and reflective reasoning.

- **Exploration:** presentation of a prediction accompanied by its explanation to promote initial familiarization.
- **Anticipation:** presentation of an explanation without the corresponding prediction, requiring the user to anticipate the output (forward simulation).
- **Justification:** users are asked to explain the reasoning behind their anticipated output, providing explicit traces of their mental model.
- **Validation:** the actual prediction is revealed and users are encouraged to reflect on the correctness of their anticipation and adjust their understanding.

Phase 3 - Post-task self-assessment

This phase investigates whether and how users' self-perception of their interpretive competence changes after interacting with the system. This measure serves as an indirect indicator of *cognitive empowerment*, in line with the principles of Human-Centered AI (HCAI) [22], which promotes systems that not only explain but also strengthen users' ability to understand and critically engage with intelligent technologies.

Phase 4 - Explanation evaluation

This phase integrates both user and expert perspectives to evaluate the quality of the explanation, considering both perceived qualities and structural characteristics.

- **Perceived clarity and usefulness:** assessed using the *Explanation Satisfaction Scale* [10], focusing on users' subjective understanding and perceived utility.
- **Completeness and transparency:** evaluated by domain experts using the *Explanation Goodness Checklist* to assess the structural quality of the explanations.

Phase 5 - Mental model quality assessment

In the final phase, the quality of the resulting mental models is evaluated in terms of **completeness**, **correctness**, and **coherence**. This stage focuses on how well users' conceptual representations capture the logic of the system and whether their reasoning is accurate and internally consistent. A pre-processing step enables quantitative analysis by segmenting diagrams into two elements: concepts, and relations.

- **Completeness:** extent to which the user's mental model includes the key concepts identified in the expert reference model, regardless of how they are connected. This measure reflects the overall breadth of the user's understanding.
- **Correctness:** accuracy of the relations established among the included concepts, assessed by comparing them with the expert model to detect possible misinterpretations or direction errors.
- **Coherence:** internal logical consistency of the user's reasoning, including the identification of contradictory or negatively correlated relations (*negative coherence*) that may reveal conceptual conflict or instability within the model.

This frame of reference emphasizes that the goal is not only to make the explanation understandable, but also to support clinicians in developing a critical and reflective use of the model's output during decision-making (Table 1).

Table 1. Summary of the Mental Model-Centric Evaluation Framework.

Phase	When?	Action	Measures
1 – Assessing prior knowledge	Pre-task	(i) Assess AI literacy (ii) Assess self-perceived competence (iii) Elicit conceptual mapping	(i) AI Literacy Scale (AILS) (ii) Self-perceived competence (iii) Concept map
2 – Mental model stimulation	During task	(i) Exploration (ii) Anticipation (iii) Justification (iv) Validation	(i) Prediction and explanation tasks
3 – Post-task self-assessment	Post-task	(i) Reassess self-perceived competence after interaction	(i) AI Literacy Scale (AILS) (ii) Self-perceived competence (iii) Concept map
4 – Explanation evaluation	End of session	(i) Evaluate clarity and usefulness (user) (ii) Evaluate completeness and transparency (expert)	(i) Explanation Satisfaction Scale (ii) Explanation Goodness Checklist
5 – Mental model quality assessment	Post-collection	(i) Compare user and expert models (ii) Assess conceptual and relational quality of users' mental models	(i) Completeness (ii) Correctness (iii) Coherence

4 Example of Application

4.1 Brain Age Predictor

In a previous work on this research [4], we have proposed Brain Age Predictor, an interactive dashboard to support neurologists in studying brain aging. The system is a web application that leverages both a deep neural network trained in the brain age prediction task and the SHAP method [17] to explain the reasoning of the model.

The clinician uploads to the web system a set of morphological features extracted from the T1-weighted MRI of the brain of a patient. The regions considered in the extraction process are defined according to the Desikan-Killiany atlas [5]. A pre-trained deep neural network (DNN) [3] predicts the age of the patient and the BAG, defined as the difference between the patient's chronological age and the predicted brain age. In the example of Fig. 2, the patient "Carmelo Verdi", male, is 23-years old. The brain age predicted by the system is 26.64, therefore the BAG is +3.64.

Brain Age Predictor implements SHapley Additive exPlanations (SHAP) as XAI method. SHAP is used to estimate the contribution of each feature in determining the output of a model for a specific sample. A high absolute value of a SHAP value means a strong influence of the feature on the inference process. The system computes the explanations, which are delivered to the neurologist through two different visualization techniques: a tornado plot and a glass brain. The latter is visible in the example in Fig. 2.

The tornado plot visible in Fig. 2 shows the top nine features that influenced the most the final prediction, with the intrinsic curvature index of the left paracentral lobule being the most relevant feature. The sign of the SHAP value indicates the orientation of the influence: in the brain age prediction task, a positive SHAP value is associated with a feature that pushes the prediction to an "older" age, promoting a positive BAG. On the other hand, a negative SHAP value indicates that the feature contributed to a "younger" prediction and a negative BAG.

4.2 Mental Model-Based Evaluation of Brain Age Predictor

This section presents how the explanations of the Brain Age Predictor can be assessed through the lens of the mental model-centric evaluation framework.

First, a group of at least 15 neurologists and an expert also rooted in AI is gathered. The framework is administered individually to each neurologist: each clinician completes all phases independently.

Phase 1 Assessing Prior Knowledge. The starting point of the framework is the assessment of neurologist's prior knowledge about artificial intelligence through the *AI Literacy Scale (AILS)* administered as a pre-task questionnaire. The scale investigates the neurologist's familiarity with AI concepts, previous

Fig. 2. Screenshot of the interactive Brain Age Predictor dashboard.

exposure to AI-based tools, and perceived understanding of how AI systems operate. Subsequently, a self-perceived competency form assesses how confident the neurologist feels in using and interpreting artificial intelligence models and XAI outputs. Finally, users are asked to externalize their preliminary understanding of how the explainable AI system operates through a conceptual mapping task. In this exercise, neurologists connect AI-related concepts (e.g., model, features, explanation) with clinical concepts (e.g., cortical regions, brain age gap), producing an initial representation of their mental model.

Phase 2 Mental Model Stimulation. The second phase of the framework allows the mental model stimulation process through a sequence of proxy tasks and retrospective analyses. The neurologist is supported in the process by two figures: a facilitator, who guides and manages the session, and an observer, who documents user behaviors during task execution. The process flows as follows:

1. In the **exploration** step, the facilitator guides the neurologist through the web application by showing multiple predictions from different patients. This stage aims to familiarize the user with the system's interface and output format, without requiring direct interaction or modification of the parameters. The neurologist is invited to observe the variations in the predicted brain age and the corresponding explanations across patients.
2. The **anticipation** stage involves a proxy task in the form of a forward simulation. In this task, the neurologist is asked to qualitatively predict the output of the system.

3. The **justification** step is carried out as a retrospective process, in which the neurologist explains the reasoning behind the response to the previous anticipation task.
4. The **validation** step consists of asking the neurologist to compare her prediction with the system output. The neurologist is then asked to reflect on what led to the correctness or incorrectness of her prediction.

Phase 3 Post-Task Self-assessment. After completion of the interaction with the system, two questionnaires, the AILS and the self-assessment of perceived competence, are administered again together with the conceptual mapping task introduced in Phase 1. The repeated administration of these instruments makes it possible to measure changes in AI-related knowledge and self-perceived interpretive ability, while the bipartite concept map allows users to externalize how their understanding of the functioning of the system has evolved after interacting with the interface and explanations. Comparing pre- and post-task results across the three instruments serves as an indirect indicator of the cognitive empowerment experienced by neurologists, highlighting shifts in both confidence and conceptual organization related to the Brain Age Predictor.

Phase 4 Explanation Evaluation. The quality of the explanation as perceived by the neurologist is assessed through the administration of the Explanation Satisfaction Scale to the neurologists and the Explanation Goodness Checklist to the domain expert. The cited questionnaires are structured as suggested by Hoffman et al. [10].

Phase 5 Mental Model Quality Assessment. Quality assessment is structured as a shadow box task, where data collected in Phases 1 and 2 is compared to the understanding and outputs provided by the domain expert. The neurologists are not directly involved in this stage of the study. The assessment focuses on three complementary dimensions of mental model quality:

- **Completeness:** verify whether the neurologist's model includes the key concepts identified in the expert reference model, regardless of how they are connected. This dimension reflects the overall breadth of understanding.
- **Correctness:** assess the accuracy of the relations established among the identified concepts by comparing them with the expert model, in order to detect possible misconceptions or direction errors.
- **Coherence:** evaluate the internal logical consistency of the neurologist's reasoning, including the presence of contradictory or negatively correlated relations (*negative coherence*) that may indicate conceptual conflict or instability within the model.

5 Conclusion

XAI interfaces are often evaluated based on perceived clarity or user satisfaction. However, these dimensions do not necessarily ensure that users truly understand how the system works, nor that they are able to use it in an informed and conscious manner.

The framework proposed here invites us to rethink the explanation experience as an interactive and cognitive process, in which the construction of a mental model also serves as an indicator of the overall effectiveness of the system. This perspective has important implications for both evaluation and design: on the one hand, it encourages the development of new metrics centered on the quality of the user's mental model; on the other hand, it promotes interfaces designed not only to "display" explanations but to actively support their progressive and adaptive understanding.

User studies are being carried out to assess its effectiveness and practical relevance in real-world XAI scenarios.

Acknowledgements. This work was supported by LIFE: the itaLian system wIde Frailty nEtwork; by EPANSA (FAIR) - Enhancing Personal Assistants with Neuro-Symbolic AI and Knowledge Graphs, funded by the European Union Next-GenerationEU (NRRP – M4C2, Investment 1.3, D. R. No. 123 of 16/01/2024, PE00000013, CUP H97G22000210007); and by DEMETRA: "Development of an ensemble learning-based, multidimensional sensory impairment score to predict cognitive impairment in an elderly cohort of Southern Italy" (CUP D99J22001970006), Missione 6, Componente 2, Investimento 2.1 "Rafforzamento e potenziamento della ricerca biomedica del SSN", funded by the European Commission – NextGenerationEU.

References

1. Buçinca, Z., Lin, P., Gajos, K.Z., Glassman, E.L.: Proxy tasks and subjective measures can be misleading in evaluating explainable ai systems. In: Proceedings of the 25th International Conference on Intelligent User Interfaces, pp. 454–464 (2020)
2. Coroama, L., Groza, A.: Evaluation metrics in explainable artificial intelligence (xai). In: International Conference on Advanced Research in Technologies, Information, Innovation and Sustainability, pp. 401–413. Springer (2022)
3. De Bonis, M.L.N., et al.: Explainable brain age prediction: a comparative evaluation of morphometric and deep learning pipelines. Brain Inform. **11**(1), 33 (2024)
4. De Bonis, M.L.N., et al.: Explainable ai for brain age prediction: design, implementation, and formative evaluation of an interactive tool. In: HHAI 2025: Hybrid Human AI Systems for the Social Good, pp. 248–261. IOS Press (2025)
5. Desikan, R.S., et al.: An automated labeling system for subdividing the human cerebral cortex on MRI scans into GYRAL based regions of interest. Neuroimage **31**(3), 968–980 (2006)
6. Dufumier, B., Grigis, A., Victor, J., Ambroise, C., Frouin, V., Duchesnay, E.: Openbhb: a large-scale multi-site brain MRI data-set for age prediction and debiasing. Neuroimage **263**, 119637 (2022)

7. Franke, K., Ziegler, G., Klöppel, S., Gaser, C., Initiative, A.D.N., et al.: Estimating the age of healthy subjects from t1-weighted mri scans using kernel methods: exploring the influence of various parameters. Neuroimage **50**(3), 883–892 (2010)
8. Gentile, D., Jamieson, G., Donmez, B.: Evaluating human understanding in XAI systems. In: ACM CHI XCXAI Workshop (2021)
9. Greca, I.M., Moreira, M.A.: Mental models, conceptual models, and modelling. Int. J. Sci. Educ. **22**(1), 1–11 (2000)
10. Hoffman, R.R., Mueller, S.T., Klein, G., Litman, J.: Measures for explainable ai: explanation goodness, user satisfaction, mental models, curiosity, trust, and human-ai performance. Front. Comput. Sci. **5**, 1096257 (2023)
11. Johnson-Laird, P.N.: Mental models: Towards a cognitive science of language, inference, and consciousness. No. 6, Harvard University Press (1983)
12. Kulesza, T., Burnett, M., Wong, W.K., Stumpf, S.: Principles of explanatory debugging to personalize interactive machine learning. In: Proceedings of the 20th International Conference on Intelligent User Interfaces, pp. 126–137 (2015)
13. Liao, Q.V., Gruen, D., Miller, S.: Questioning the AI: informing design practices for explainable ai user experiences. In: Proceedings of the 2020 CHI Conference on Human Factors in Computing Systems, pp. 1–15 (2020)
14. Lipton, Z.C.: The mythos of model interpretability: In machine learning, the concept of interpretability is both important and slippery. Queue **16**(3), 31–57 (2018)
15. Lombardi, A., Monaco, A., Donvito, G., Amoroso, N., Bellotti, R., Tangaro, S.: Brain age prediction with morphological features using deep neural networks: results from predictive analytic competition 2019. Front. Psych. **11**, 619629 (2021)
16. Lu, S.C., Swisher, C.L., Chung, C., Jaffray, D., Sidey-Gibbons, C.: On the importance of interpretable machine learning predictions to inform clinical decision making in oncology. Front. Oncol. **13**, 1129380 (2023)
17. Lundberg, S.M., Lee, S.I.: A unified approach to interpreting model predictions. Adv. Neural. Inf. Process. Syst. **30**, 4765–4774 (2017)
18. Miller, T.: Explanation in artificial intelligence: insights from the social sciences. Artif. Intell. **267**, 1–38 (2019)
19. Müller, R.: How explainable ai affects human performance: a systematic review of the behavioural consequences of saliency maps. Int. J. Human-Comput. Interact. **41**(4), 2020–2051 (2025)
20. Nauta, M., et al.: From anecdotal evidence to quantitative evaluation methods: a systematic review on evaluating explainable ai. ACM Comput. Surv. **55**(13s), 1–42 (2023)
21. Scarpato, N., et al.: Evaluating explainable machine learning models for clinicians. Cogn. Comput. **16**(4), 1436–1446 (2024)
22. Shneiderman, B.: Human-centered artificial intelligence: reliable, safe & trustworthy. Int. J. Human-Comput. Interact. **36**(6), 495–504 (2020)
23. Staggers, N., Norcio, A.F.: Mental models: concepts for human-computer interaction research. Int. J. Man Mach. Stud. **38**(4), 587–605 (1993)
24. Tullio, J., Dey, A.K., Chalecki, J., Fogarty, J.: How it works: a field study of non-technical users interacting with an intelligent system. In: Proceedings of the SIGCHI Conference on Human Factors in Computing Systems, pp. 31–40 (2007)
25. Zhang, Y., Liao, Q.V., Bellamy, R.K.: Effect of confidence and explanation on accuracy and trust calibration in ai-assisted decision making. In: Proceedings of the 2020 Conference on Fairness, Accountability, and Transparency, pp. 295–305 (2020)

Suitability of Selected User Research Methods in Medical Applications

Erika Vaczlavova(✉), Miroslav Laco, and Wanda Benesova

Faculty of Informatics and Information Technologies, Slovak University of Technology, Ilkovičova 2, 842 16 Karlova Ves, Bratislava, Slovakia
erika.vaczlavova@gmail.com
https://vgg.fiit.stuba.sk

Abstract. In every phase of the user-centred design (UCD) process, the focus is on the essential methods of bringing users to the centre - the user research. An appropriate user research strategy and appropriately chosen research methods can make the design process more efficient and enhance the communication between domains. The approach to user research strategies and methods is even more critical for applied UCD, in collaboration within specialised domains, such as medicine. The domain experts from the field of medicine must obtain trust in the collaboration within the design process and in the designed system itself. Moreover, their resources and involvement must be considered wisely. This can be achieved by effective knowledge transfer methods and tailoring research methods, such as exploratory discussions, contextual inquiries, and observation, according to the specific needs within the specialised medical domain. Our contribution to the user research topic of appropriate tailoring and exploring of the suitability of user research methods is based on long-term case studies on various projects and hands-on experience. Based on domain experts' needs and limitations, especially in the medical education and research field, research methods must be tailored to their specific needs to ensure the methods yield meaningful and valid results. This paper provides an overview of relevant user research methods and their adaptation in the medical field, which can serve as an empirical guide for future UCD applications in this domain.

Keywords: Suitable User Research Methods · Digital Histopathology · User-Centered Design · User Experience · User Research

1 Introduction

Several aspects must be carefully considered in the design process of a digital system using a UCD methodology, particularly within medical education and research. Identifying the system's primary users is as important as understanding their core needs. An extensive user research process and its application in

Published by Springer Nature Switzerland AG 2026
C. Maciel et al. (Eds.): INTERACT 2025 Workshops, LNCS 16478, pp. 167–182, 2026.
https://doi.org/10.1007/978-3-032-22934-2_15

various forms are crucial. We explored these insights into suitable selection and tailoring user research methods in the medicinal domain during a long-term case study in a multidisciplinary team consisting of artificial intelligence (AI) experts, a user experience (UX) team, and pathology specialists who are not only engaged in clinical practice but also have insight into medical education as faculty members at a medical faculty in Slovakia. Digitising clinical workflows and integrating new technologies into medical education prepare students for the tools they'll encounter in future practice. It is a well-known gap in medical education worldwide where medical students have almost no experience with digitisation in medicine during their studies [19]. We designed an educational tool for the histopathology education at medical faculties, incorporating AI-powered functionalities to enhance the learning process and critical thinking of medical students. This tool modernises education, making it more efficient, as the current approach is outdated and ineffective. The tool was preceded by detailed user research and created according to a UCD framework we proposed. The communication framework is described in our previous work [21], where we described how the domain experts in a multidisciplinary team cooperate. To create a suitable user environment for such a tool, it is necessary to design it based on the information obtained from user research methods. While working on the annotation tool's design, we also created a medically focused dataset consisting of images scanned using Whole Slide Imaging (WSI) technology with specialised scanners [26]. These digitised histopathological samples are supplemented with annotations created by our experts. The annotations were developed based on research to ensure that the outputs are valuable for training AI models, but the annotation process does not differ significantly from routine diagnostics in the practice of specialists. The adopted annotation process was applied to the Nottingham grading scale for breast cancer diagnosis. We explore the most suitable user research methods, the way of tailoring them in the intentions of specialised medical contexts, drawing on insights from a long-term multidisciplinary case study in histopathology education. Through the systematic examination of ten commonly used UX research methods, we identify which techniques yield meaningful and valid results under real-world constraints of medical practice, resulting in practical guidelines derived directly from collaboration with medical educators and clinicians.

2 Related Work in User Research in Medical Applications

Wolcott and McLaughlin [23] discussed research methods in health professions education by outcome and offered literature-based recommendations. Research teams should explore methods suited to the question and time limits, considering a mix of qualitative and quantitative methods, such as interviews, usability tests, surveys, and experience maps, to strengthen the validity and reliability of the findings, as Shah et al. did [18]. The research is irreplaceable and also valuable for creating designs for real applications. Researchers investigated how domain experts from the field of pathology interact with an AI system named NaviPath in diagnosing breast biopsy cases. The goal of the research was to collect information about the decision-making process in AI-assisted pathology. The study was a mixed-methods approach, combining quantitative performance data and qualitative user feedback by using methods such as screen recordings to capture the interaction flow, semi-structured interviews, and thinking aloud sessions [6]. The research methods must be adapted to healthcare environments with high variability, sensitivity, and regulation [7]. Automated image analysis in digital pathology can also progress only based on a new understanding of how to design automated tools for such environments and how these tools influence the everyday practice of domain experts. The real needs of domain experts were collected by meeting minutes, design briefs, interviews, personal notes, and other artefacts to conduct a thematic analysis [14] similarly to Martin and Barnett, who were using interviews and contextual inquiries to get a context for medical imaging devices [13]. An advanced testing environment and tools such as eye-trackers can support the usability testing. In pathology, the testing can be the examination of slides, which is recorded by eye-tracking cameras, and the magnification data and zooming behaviours were extracted in an objective fashion by an automated algorithm. Based on the collected information in research summaries, the team can analyse the relationship between experience and metrics, such as time, zooming, and fixations [20]. As research in the field of medicine is demanding because of a shortage of domain experts and their time, the research can also be conducted based on previous research results. Chen et al. conducted a systematic review of 68 studies from 2012 to 2021 focused on explainable machine learning results presentation in medical image analysis. Also, this kind of research exposed critical gaps in how explainable AI is designed for medical imaging [3].

3 Contribution

We emphasise the need for appropriate selection and tailoring of the user research methods in designing various tools in medical education and research. We explored the suitability of methods throughout a long-term case study in the specialised histopathology domain. Our study outlines how UCD methodologies can be used effectively by keeping in close contact with domain experts. By appropriately tailored and suitable research methods, every stage of UCD is emphasised and builds on a strong information base. By adequately designing specialised applications and tools, we are enabling the integration of AI into medical education and research processes. We provide an overview of appropriate user research methods for the UCD design process in medicine, alongside empirical recommendations and guidelines for methodology modifications for future applications in UX design processes in medicine. The described exploration od the suitability of research methods shows the methods which are suitable after being tailored to be effective in collecting valuable information to design tools for a specific target user group. All the methods have an explorative character, and their usage and effectiveness are verified and substantiated by case study-driven use cases reflecting practical experience.

4 Empirical Evaluation of User Research Methods

Various domains have different specifics to be reflected in adjustments to the effective design process. This paper focuses on the specific domains of medical education and research. This work focuses on a specific group of users - domain experts in medicine with varying levels of expertise, reflecting the diversity of their needs and expectations. This case study involves domain experts in UX and the medical faculty. We are connected to medical students and professors with university education, research, and clinical practice backgrounds. During the ongoing long-term case study lasting 3 years, we cooperated in the design process of educational tools with supporting functions for medical students, improving practical experience, and collecting digitised histopathology tissues for various utilisation not only in the educational process but also in research and diagnostics. The collected and analysed data by domain experts in medicine, stored in designed solutions, serves as educational material and the basis for medical dataset creation. User research for dataset creation is connected to the Nottingham grading scale for breast cancer diagnosis [16]. During the collaboration, we concluded that user research results are crucial to every phase of the design thinking process [17]. Only based on information gained through user research can we effectively innovate and refine design candidates in either methodological or user interface prototype form. We use various user research techniques in this long-term case study and have described the ten most frequently used ones with the most relevant results. The selected user research methods were adapted based on empirical insights from case studies, ensuring their applicability to the specific needs of domain experts in specialised fields.

4.1 Applied User Research Methods in Medical Field

Case studies delivering products require responsible management. Effective communication requires understanding the other party, enabling the adaptation of the collaboration process and applied methods based on insights and findings. In multidisciplinary teams, it is crucial to distinguish areas of expertise and establish precise communication needs between the parties. The needs can be identified based on each stakeholder's field and requirements.

In Table 1, we summarised ten user research methods we explored during the long-term case study. We defined which of them are relevant for communicating the needs of medical domain experts and for understanding their workflows, decision-making, limitations, and mental models. As we can see, the three methods applied in the case study were in an unmodified methodological form; these methods are **card sorting**, **journey mapping**, and **empathy maps**. The second group of methods visible in Table 1 are relevant, but they are effective with modification; these methods are: **user interview**, **contextual inquiry**, **focus groups**, **observation**, and **domain knowledge transfer**. These methods are widely recommended in UX research for their ability to produce rich, actionable insights [11]. Reasoning, why they are most effective, and how they were tailored to our domain experts' needs, is described by the strengths and limitations

Table 1. Selected research methods categorised according to relevance and the need for adjustment in the medical research and education field.

Research Method	Relevance	Adapted
Contextual Inquiry	relevant	yes
Domain Knowledge Transfer	relevant	yes
Focus Groups	relevant	yes
Observation	relevant	yes
User Interview	relevant	yes
Card sorting	relevant	no
Empathy Maps	relevant	no
Journey Mapping	relevant	no
Diary Studies	less relevant	no
Survey	less relevant	no

matrix, adaptation description and empirical examples from the case study in the following subsections. The remaining two methods have limited effectiveness and become less relevant than others - the methods are **diary studies** and **surveys**. Diary studies are time-consuming and not suitable for everyday practice. Considering the limited capacity and the optimisation of medical domain expert resources, we conclude that the diary studies method requires extra work, which is unsuitable in the medical domain. We support our conclusion with statements provided by domain experts. Surveys are less effective because, even though they can be designed effectively, this selected method fails to capture all the experiences and constraints of domain experts. After all, closed questions fail to provide the necessary depth, whereas domain experts tend to engage less with open questions, preferring to convey information through oral communication.

4.2 Research Method Selection Rationale

Research in the user experience field recognises the compromises between different selected research methods: for example, **focus groups** help to collect feedback but do not allow for the in-depth individual insights that **interviews** provide, which are more time-consuming but yield a large amount of data [25]. It also shows that **survey** methods are effective, but often fail to uncover many of the usability issues that interviews or user testing can uncover [22]. **Diary studies** are considered useful for capturing real-world contexts, but require participant engagement to avoid bias [10]. This demonstrates that choosing the most appropriate user research methods in a medical research and education field is about finding a balance between feasibility, depth of knowledge, and the ability to effectively engage experts in the cooperation. Therefore, we selected a set of methods with the following trade-off: maximize contextual richness and credibility while minimizing the time and workload for medical experts. **Contextual inquiry**,

observation and **domain knowledge transfer** were prioritised because they provide rich, contextual insights in specialised environments such as the medical domain. Contextual inquiry is uncovering the real needs of clinicians and supporting design decisions in medical contexts [4,7]. **Observation** has a place in qualitative research to understand real-world practices beyond working with existing materials and self-reporting [5,24]. **Domain knowledge transfer** is essential in specialised fields, where researchers must first familiarise themselves with the key points related to the topic to facilitate effective communication and collaboration [8]. **Card sorting**, **journey mapping**, and **empathy maps** were included as they support structuring mental models and information architecture, which are needed for proper medical user interface design. Limitations such as limited time, ethical concerns, and low availability of domain experts are often reflected in UX studies in the field of medicine [12,24]. These findings are consistent with our decision to prioritise methods, from the wide spectrum of user research methods, that balance depth of insight, ability to capture domain expert knowledge, with feasibility in medical applications.

Table 2 provides a summary of the relevant strengths and limitations of the selected research methods. Each method is also assigned a relevance factor in the medical domain, with each relevance describing its applicability in a specific context of medical education and research. The scale is defined as follows:

- *High* - applicable and highly valuable for uncovering domain experts' needs and workflows. These methods are prioritised as core to the UCD process [2,4,23].
- *Medium* - provide supportive insights in specific phases of design, but not critical for understanding the core practices of medical experts [11].
- *Low* - less feasible or effective in the medical domain due to constraints such as workload, ethical regulations or limited insight depth [15,22].

4.3 Situational Applicability of Research Methods

During the design process in a specific domain, such as medical research and education, it is essential to adhere to established standards and tailor them to the unique needs of domain experts. These standards include design methodologies such as UCD [9], the individual phases of which we can streamline through our chosen selection of suitable research methods (listed in Table 1). UCD proceeds iteratively through four phases. Each of the ten methods we considered can be situated within this cycle. In principle, all selected research methods can be applied in various stages of the UCD process; certain phases benefit more from specific methods. This alignment reflects the strengths of each approach, which support user understanding, requirement definition, solution creation, or evaluation, while ignoring their limitations, which can limit the progress of the design iteration. The mapping of methods to individual UCD phases is based on prior experience with user research in medical education and research and findings reported in literature [7,11,24]. This combination of practical insight

Table 2. Strengths and limitations of selected research methods, which support the selection choice in the medical domain.

Method	Relevance in Medical Domain	Strengths	Limitations
Contextual Inquiry	High	Uncovering hidden constraints and the real-world practices.	Ethical or logistical constraints.
Domain Knowledge Transfer	High	Reducing misinterpretation and accelerating the cooperation across domains.	Additional effort and risk of partial understanding.
Focus Group	High	Generating shared insights and exploring consensus across domains.	Risk of suppressing the individual disagreement or opinion.
Observation	High	Revealing workflows, environment constraints and domain culture.	Ethical or logistical constraints and missing internal reasoning.
User Interview	High	Uncovering deep insights, nuanced challenges and fosters engagement.	Time-intensity.
Card Sorting	Medium	Helping in the organisation of the interface content.	Domain specificities stay uncovered.
Empathy Maps	Medium	Aligning understanding between designers and domain experts.	Focusing on feelings rather than precise complex workflows.
Journey Mapping	Medium	Visualising the domain experts' processes and capturing interactions.	Oversimplify the complex workflow and too abstract for medical domain experts.
Diary Studies	Low	Giving insights into patterns and changes over time.	High participant burden and inconsistent reporting.
Survey	Low	Capturing views from multiple experts and validating hypotheses.	Limited depth and risk of missing tacit knowledge.

and evidence helped the distribution of each selected method to all phases of the iterative design process. Although we emphasize distribution across all phases, the first two phases of the process focus more strongly on the data collection part of the design process and are therefore more suitable for the application of multiple methods. The subsequent phases typically concentrate on evaluation and engage with the data and information collection only partially.

Understand and specify the context of use

The first phase of UCD is the phase whose goal is to understand and specify the context of use, which can be done only by suitable user research methods through which we learn about the user, their environment, limitations, needs, and mental models. The first step is **domain knowledge transfer**, which ensures facilitators understand the medical context and terminology before engaging deeply with experts. The domain knowledge also helps with continuity. The following step is **empathy maps** creation, which captures the emotional or contextual factors of our domain experts and future users. These methods are followed by on-site research methods such as **observation** and **contextual inquiry**, where the UX researcher can collect data about actual and real-world practices and gather relevant findings in the real practice setting without bias.

Specify the user requirements

After the first phase, where all the necessary information about the context was collected, in the second phase, the requirements and the real needs are specified. **User interviews** uncover detailed needs, challenges, and expectations from individual experts [23]. Not only the individual opinions and needs are important, and for this reason, the **focus group** application helps collect comprehensive needs and points of view. The limitations and pain points across the whole defined processes are visualised by **journey mapping**, which will support the next steps of the design process and create a clear overview.

Produce design solutions

The phase that concentrates on the design solution creation also needs suitable research methods, which are refining design concepts, structures, and prototypes. The method which helps these processes is **card sorting**, even if the domain specificities are not uncovered by this method.

Evaluate the design against requirements

The last phase in the iteration is the evaluation phase, where we compare if the solution meets user needs and refine it based on feedback. To validate findings with a broader audience at scale, the **surveys** are suitable, while long-term studies can also be supplemented with a research method as **diary study**, which provides longitudinal feedback.

4.4 Research Method Adaptations

Correctly applied methodology of a certain user research method, used in a suitable situation or design process phase and over a representative sample of end users, provides a fundamental source of valuable information for the design process. However, when applying them in specific fields such as medical research and education, it is necessary to take into account a number of aspects that significantly limit their standard use. These aspects have been identified both through existing literature [12,24] and through our own case study observations. The medical education and research are specific in facts as:

- Medical domain experts have limited time
- Medical activities are highly specialised and regulated

– Medical domain experts share their expertise only after gaining trust among researchers

For these reasons, our case study showed that some research methods needed to be adapted. Adaptation meant that the basic form of the research method was preserved, but the way it was implemented was adjusted to respect the specifics of the medical environment and at the same time, yield relevant and meaningful results. Adaptation of methods is necessary in different situations, with motivation based on mutual understanding between domains, respect and the goal of obtaining as much relevant information as possible.

Adaptation of individual user research methods is necessary in situations where their standard form fails to reflect the specifics of the environment in which they are applied. In the medical context, this is especially the case:

– When the researcher prevents domain experts from feeling overburdened and builds trust (Related to "Medical domain experts share their expertise only after gaining trust among researchers" and "Medical domain experts have limited time").
– When specialised language or knowledge is required (Related to "Medical activities are highly specialised and regulated").
– When domain experts have very limited time (Related to "Medical domain experts have limited time").
– When the research takes place in regulated fields where interruptions could harm the workflow (Related to "Medical activities are highly specialised and regulated").
– When the researcher wants to reduce the extra workload on domain experts (Related to "Medical domain experts have limited time").

The adapted research methods listed in Table 1 were modified based on above mentioned facts and situations. The following paragraphs describe how each method was specifically adapted to address these contextual challenges while maintaining its core methodological principles. The **user interview** contains predefined but flexible questions; unlike a regular interview, the application of the method is shorter and respects the limited availability of domain experts, and the facilitator has domain-specific preparation. The **focus group** was adapted to include a smaller, carefully selected group of medical domain experts, with a structured discussion guide, unlike regular application of focus groups, which is typical for large and diverse groups. **Contextual inquiry** also requires domain-specific preparation, building trust first, so that domain experts are open to sharing more context-specific information. Unlike regular contextual inquiry, the number of questions was reduced to avoid possible sensitive medical process interruption. Research in the role of observer is unobtrusive, and **observation** is conducted strictly in the home environment of medical domain experts, unlike regular observation, which often assumes tasks should be performed, not naturally practised. Typically, domain experts are expected to explain and provide basically everything from scratch, unlike in adapted user research methods in the medical field, where the researchers use **domain knowledge transfer** for prior preparation.

4.5 Real-Word Use Cases Reflecting Practical Experiences

This section presents user research methods shown in Table 1 and Table 2 tailored to the specific characteristics of medical collaboration. Their application is substantiated through empirical insights from long-term case studies, in which we describe the observed changes in interaction before and after application and outcomes resulting from each method's application, followed by a recommendation.This case study was situated in a specialised medical education and research domain specifically in histopathology by highly regulated clinical workflows, strict data-handling requirements, and limited availability of medical experts. The main objective was a exploration of suitability of user research method in data and information collection phase of design process. The selected case focuses on the development of an AI-assisted educational annotation tool. Participants included domain experts with high level of expertise in pathology, medical educators, and UX researchers collaborating over a three-year period.

Domain Knowledge Transfer

Effective user research with meaningful results begins with domain knowledge transfer. Facilitators should approach every meeting, especially the initial one, with at least a basic understanding of the domain experts' field. In highly specialised domains like medicine, familiarity with key concepts supports communication flow and reduces the burden on experts to adjust their terminology or mental models. While knowledge is essential, it does not replace the necessity of asking questions about specific details that emerge during discussions.

Before domain knowledge transfer we focused on discussing goals and defining the domain experts' needs during a case study in a medical context. Early on, we discovered that explaining fundamental nuances to laypersons clearly and translating them into language suitable for the design process posed a significant challenge for the medical domain expert.

After domain knowledge transfer, we engaged with experts after familiarising ourselves with the key points, terminology, and processes related to the topic, and the communication process became more efficient. This efficiency was assessed based on the amount of domain-specific information conveyed during meetings of identical duration; on average, the number of addressed and resolved research questions increased from two to at least six.

Recommendation: When a facilitator with domain knowledge participated in meetings, the medical experts were more open and willing to share their subjective findings and needs. After exploring this phenomenon, we wanted to find out why domain experts were able to provide more information. The response indicated hesitation in sharing all details at once, as they were concerned it might be overwhelming for those outside their domain. They also expressed uncertainty about whether all the problems they identified within the collaboration were solvable from our side. To conclude, we recommend avoiding unnecessary obstacles in collaboration by ensuring adequate preparation beforehand and fostering natural communication tailored to the needs of domain experts.

Observation

This method is used in both qualitative and quantitative research [5], particularly valuable in collaboration with medical experts [15]. Due to disciplinary differences, observation helps uncover actual needs, constraints, and workflows as experts perform routine tasks. To minimise pressure, the chosen method should feel natural to the expert, ideally conducted within their regular environment.

Before observation in the case study, we designed an interactive educational tool that includes the functionality of annotating images to create educational materials. We focused on annotating the exact shape of the area of interest. We conclude the need for this functionality from the already collected information from other user research methods. Our goal was to design a tool that allows for the creation of annotations while also improving it with the help of an AI model capable of generating precise annotations and offering them as suggestions.

After observation, where we observed the teaching process at a medical faculty. We chose to focus on the histopathology course practical laboratory seminar. Practical seminars on the specialized topic related to the target domain of the designed annotation tool proved to be an effective form of observation, as our presence did not disrupt the usual flow of education. During observation, we found that precise annotation of the exact shape of the area of interest is not essential for the tool's practical use and is unfamiliar to medical professionals. Instead, for educational purposes, annotations are required in the form of marking broader areas with a defined shape, such as a square, with an annotation description in the form of a comment. This approach is faster and more intuitive for medical professionals, especially since some areas of interest lack specific boundaries for precise annotation.

Recommendation: During the observation, we found out that the discussed functionality had different interpretations in the two domains. The perspective needed to be adjusted to meet the needs of end users, who plan to use the annotation tool to mark broader areas with additional comments. We also discovered that the ability to add textual notes to individual annotations is essential for creating educational materials. Without observation, the functionality would likely have been designed in a way that was unsuitable for this specific domain. To conclude, we recommend performing early-stage observation to uncover the diverse needs of domain experts, especially in specialised environments like medicine, where context strongly influences design decisions.

Exploratory Discussions

During the design of applications based on UCD methodologies, maintaining direct contact and open communication with users is essential. This interaction enables the collection of valuable qualitative data. However, the communication must be structured and guided to obtain such data effectively, following a clear framework to ensure the desired insights are uncovered. The methods we utilized included **interviews** and **focus groups**. The key difference between one-to-one interviews and focus-group discussions is that the latter is far more appropriate for the creative phases of the design process, typically generating new ideas. In contrast, one-to-one interviews should probe individual experiences, encouraging self-reflection on issues that could be distorted if social pressure were placed on the individual [2]. In our collaboration, we communicated with domain experts individually through interviews and conducted focus groups, where the UX expert took the role of the facilitator. Group interviews were less time-efficient, so we applied the focus group method. In this form of communication. These methods for gathering valuable information were applied regularly, with appropriate preparation, including predefined questions and an outline for the focus group.

Before Exploratory Discussions we attempted to design a more effective questionnaire-based alternative with open-ended questions based on the specifics identified during initial meetings. However, observations revealed that this method of gathering information was unsuitable, as it failed to capture all the experiences and constraints that needed to be reflected during the UCD processes.

After Exploratory Discussions, in the form of regular meetings for interviews or focus groups, we got deeper mutual understanding and clear goal definition with domain experts involved. Medical domain experts communicated most naturally through focus groups, where the facilitator posed questions and guided the group along a planned path, but also encouraged open conversation and allowed relevant digressions. In this format, the domain experts shared valuable insights, and throughout the discussions, they either built upon the ideas of others or, conversely, defined processes differently. Without adopting this research approach, there was a risk of failing to uncover the full scope of needs and constraints, while domain experts might have been left unsure whether their concerns could be effectively reflected in the design.

Recommendation: Moderated focus group discussions helped refine the design and information architecture while allowing conversational flexibility that revealed new perspectives on the issue discussed. Trust within the group grew as participants recognised shared goals, leading to more open dialogue, active engagement, and willingness to express uncertainty or ask further questions—key factors in sustaining successful collaboration. In conclusion, we recommend using exploratory discussions to uncover deeper insights, foster domain expert engagement, and ultimately gather richer qualitative data.

Contextual Inquiry (CI)

CI uncovers users' real needs through observation and interviews in their work context, enabling the design of interfaces tailored to domain experts. CI involves visiting users' work environments, observing and interviewing them as they conduct the tasks you aim to improve. It is built around three fundamental concepts: context, partnership, and focus [4].CI in medical education is about the partnership between the facilitator and the domain expert. Building trust beforehand encourages openness, increases the quality of information shared, and helps the facilitator know when and how to inquire without disrupting workflow.

Before the Contextual Inquiry in the case study, we designed the annotation flow of digitised medical tissues, where the labels were connected with a grading system used to assess the severity or grade of breast cancer, resulting in data suitable for education and also for diagnostic purposes, collected in a medical dataset. Building on prior research, expert input, and preparation, we designed the classification flow and enriched it with specific signs to support accurate grading by domain experts. We aimed to generalise the information from domain experts, who had to provide additional specifics for each grade. Based on this, we aimed to propose a novel dataset for future AI applications.

After the Contextual Inquiry, during which we observed part of the real classification process, the uniqueness of tissue specifics led us to redesign the generalisation concept behind the annotation flow rules for domain experts. Moreover, the classification is time-consuming, even without the extra specifics being noted down for our purposes.Based on CI findings, we re-evaluated the annotation methodology for future domain-specific datasets by incorporating the real classification process into the design without requiring additional effort from domain experts.

Recommendation: We defined the information flow and also designed the annotation flow, ensuring it aligns with the current workflow and mental model of domain experts. Based on collected data from CI, we reduced the unnecessary burden on domain experts, making their tasks efficient and manageable with an appropriate design proposal. In conclusion, we recommend using CI, which results in domain experts working more efficiently and increasing their trust in the system, as their expertise is respected and effectively integrated.

5 Challenges

We encountered numerous special characteristics based on the specificity of the target application domain for the UCD process. While the application of modern digital technologies plays a significant role in current modernisation and digitisation, integrating them with medicine poses challenges. This work focuses on the specific challenges connected with research during the design of applications for the domain of medicine and medical education. To get relevant and valuable results, qualified professionals who can answer medicine-related questions are needed to conduct user research on the UCD process applied to the medical education and research domain. **Recruitment of participants** with this level of domain expertise poses significant challenges. It is essential to use the resources provided by the domain experts effectively, as their involvement is crucial. It is also possible to collaborate with participants who do not have domain knowledge, though it is necessary to adapt the evaluated design and transfer it to another domain [8]. Effective **communication** with medical domain experts requires establishing natural channels, selected based on their preferences. Appointing a dedicated contact person helps build trust and facilitates communication. Given the **digital affinity** level in medical practice, it is essential to choose familiar technologies. When new tools are needed, support should include tailored manuals (textual, visual, or video), a support contact, and hands-on demonstrations. When collaborating with medical domain experts, some procedures in their routine **environment** cannot be observed or performed due to strict regulations.

If essential, alternative research methods that avoid physical presence should be used. Handling patient data requires respecting **privacy** and complying with region-specific regulations (e.g., GDPR in Europe [1]). Only archived, public, or data approved by ethical committees may be used to ensure privacy and ethical compliance. As summarised in Sect. 4.1, selected user research methods with domain experts in the field of medical education are based on open communication, observation, and asking open-ended questions. The outputs of all these methods are mainly **qualitative**. These qualitative data can also be influenced by subjectivity, which can be minimised through recordings and transcriptions of individual sessions, which multiple UX experts later review. The lack of quantitative data limits the generalisation of findings to a larger sample size.

6 Conclusion

Through a long-term case study with medical education experts, we discuss the most effective and suitable user research methods for designing user-focused systems in medical education and research. These methods balance minimal expert involvement with high-quality, relevant insights that support the design process. Key methods - such as observations, interviews, focus groups, and contextual inquiries are a strong foundation for achieving optimal outcomes of user research in the medical domain. Using these techniques, the approach to the method application plays a vital role in ensuring effective communication and the amount and quality of information and outcomes valuable for the design process. Based on insights from a case study, we emphasise that suitable user research methods in specialised fields such as medical education must be chosen carefully and adapted to the unique needs of domain experts. These adaptations are provided as recommendations and illustrated with examples from the long-term case study, and are concluded for special situations, taking into account the specificities and needs of medical domain experts. Our exploration of appropriate user research methods also reflects the challenges commonly recognized in adapting HCI methods to medical contexts, where limited availability of experts, workflow constraints, and ethical considerations require methodological adjustments.

Acknowledgments and Disclosure of Funding. The authors would like to acknowledge the funding for the financial support of the grant APVV SK-IL-RD-23-0004. Moreover, we would like to thank for the support from the Recovery and Resilience Plan of the Slovak Republic under the call 'Transformation and Innovation Consortia' (project code: 09I02-03-V01-00012). The author contributes to this research as part of a consortium coordinated by InterWay, a.s.

References

1. Regulation - 2016/679 - EN - gdpr - EUR-Lex — eur-lex.europa.eu. https://eur-lex.europa.eu/eli/reg/2016/679/oj. Accessed 20 Dec 2024
2. Breen, R.L.: A practical guide to focus-group research. J. Geogr. High. Educ. **30**(3), 463–475 (2006)
3. Chen, H., Gomez, C., Huang, C.M., Unberath, M.: Explainable medical imaging ai needs human-centered design: guidelines and evidence from a systematic review. NPJ Digital Med. **5**(1), 156 (2022)
4. Coble, J., Maffitt, J., Orland, M., Kahn, M.: Contextual inquiry: discovering physicians' true needs. In: Proceedings of the Annual Symposium on Computer Application in Medical Care, p. 469. American Medical Informatics Association (1995)
5. Ellis, P.: Understanding research: research methods, observation. Wounds UK **19**(4) (2023)
6. Gu, H., et al.: Augmenting pathologists with navipath: design and evaluation of a human-ai collaborative navigation system. In: Proceedings of the 2023 CHI Conference on Human Factors in Computing Systems, pp. 1–19 (2023)
7. Healion, D., O'Dowd, E., Russell, S.: The development of a methodology for contextual user research in healthcare design projects. In: Transforming our World Through Design, Diversity and Education, pp. 239–249. IOS Press (2018)
8. Islind, A.S., Lundin, J., Cerna, K., Lindroth, T., Åkeflo, L., Steineck, G.: Proxy design: a method for involving proxy users to speak on behalf of vulnerable or unreachable users in co-design. Information Technology & People (2023)
9. ISO, B., STANDARD, B.: Ergonomics of human-system interaction. British Standards Institution (2010)
10. Janssens, K.A., Bos, E.H., Rosmalen, J.G., Wichers, M.C., Riese, H.: A qualitative approach to guide choices for designing a diary study. BMC Med. Res. Methodol. **18**(1), 140 (2018)
11. Lazar, J., Feng, J.H., Hochheiser, H.: Research methods in human-computer interaction. Morgan Kaufmann (2017)
12. Marcilly, R., van den Berg, L., Dusseljee-Peute, L.: Usability and UX in healthcare: exploring current practices and future directions. Intelligent Health Systems–From Technology to Data and Knowledge, pp. 323–327 (2025)
13. Martin, J.L., Barnett, J.: Integrating the results of user research into medical device development: insights from a case study. BMC Med. Inform. Decis. Mak. **12**, 1–10 (2012)
14. Molin, J., Woźniak, P.W., Lundström, C., Treanor, D., Fjeld, M.: Understanding design for automated image analysis in digital pathology. In: Proceedings of the 9th Nordic Conference on Human-Computer Interaction, pp. 1–10 (2016)
15. Pope, C., Mays, N.: Qualitative research in health care. Wiley Library (2020)
16. Rakha, E.A., et al.: Prognostic significance of Nottingham histologic grade in invasive breast carcinoma. J. Clin. Oncol. **26**(19), 3153–3158 (2008)
17. Razzouk, R., Shute, V.: What is design thinking and why is it important? Rev. Educ. Res. **82**(3), 330–348 (2012)
18. Shah, A., Alshawi, S.: The role of user requirements research in medical device development (2010)
19. Sorg, H., Ehlers, J.P., Sorg, C.G.: Digitalization in medicine: are German medical students well prepared for the future? Int. J. Environ. Res. Public Health **19**(14), 8308 (2022)

20. Sudin, E., et al.: Digital pathology: the effect of experience on visual search behavior. J. Med. Imaging **9**(3), 035501–035501 (2022)
21. Váczlavová, E., Laco, M.: Medical-domain-expert-centered ai-assisted digitized histopathology education tool. In: International Conference on Human-Centred Software Engineering, pp. 281–290. Springer (2024)
22. Walji, M.F., et al.: Are three methods better than one? a comparative assessment of usability evaluation methods in an EHR. Int. J. Med. Inform. **83**(5), 361–367 (2014)
23. Wolcott, M.D., McLaughlin, J.E.: Exploring user experience (ux) research methods in health professions education. Currents in Pharmacy Teaching and Learning (2023)
24. Wolcott, M.D., McLaughlin, J.E.: Exploring user experience (UX) research methods in health professions education. Curr. Pharm. Teach. Learn. **16**(2), 144–149 (2024)
25. Woudstra, K., et al.: Participatory methods used in the evaluation of medical devices: a comparison of focus groups, interviews, and a survey. BMC Health Serv. Res. **24**(1), 462 (2024)
26. Zarella, M.D., et al.: A practical guide to whole slide imaging: a white paper from the digital pathology association. Arch. Pathol. Lab. Med. **143**(2), 222–234 (2019)

From Data to Dialogue: Towards Bidirectional Feedback of Human Digital Twins in Preventive Health Context

Yinchu Li[1,2(✉)], Regina Bernhaupt[1,3], and Carine Lallemand[1]

[1] Eindhoven University of Technology,
P.O. Box 513, 5600 MB Eindhoven, Netherlands
y.li1@tue.nl
[2] RMIT University, 124 La Trobe St, Melbourne 3000, Australia
[3] ruwido Austria GmbH, Köstendor fer straße, 85202 Neumarkt, Austria

Abstract. Human Digital Twins (HDTs) are seen as promising technologies to support health-related decision-making, provide real-time support, and simulate future scenarios, which are beneficial for both clinical settings and preventive healthcare. While HDTs are increasingly discussed for supporting individuals' health management, current work still approaches the feedback between HDTs and individuals at a surface level, overlooking how feedback can evolve into an ongoing, bidirectional dialogue. This paper reflects the design of bidirectional feedback from two design explorations: a physicalization workshop that allows users to map predictions with sensory materials and a speculative study proposing a set of relational roles of HDTs (e.g., being a coach, a forecaster, acting as a shadow). We reported several design principles for enabling bidirectional feedback between HDTs and users, highlighting aspects such as customization, adaptive feedback, and temporal aspects, and discussed their implications for building HDTs that could have such dialogue and evolve with users.

Keywords: Human Digital Twin · Preventive Health · Feedback Delivery · User Expectation

1 Introduction

A Digital Twin (DT) is a virtual replica of a physical entity, ranging from an object, a machine, to a process [2]. It typically consists of three components: the physical entity, the digital counterpart, and the bidirectional flow of data between them [2]. Initially envisioned by Michael Grieves in 2003 to enhance product life-cycle management [15], DTs have since been widely adopted across domains such as manufacturing [15] and aerospace [2], where they predict the performance of systems and machines and optimize efficiency. When applied to the healthcare domain, DTs have been studied to support early disease risk

Published by Springer Nature Switzerland AG 2026
C. Maciel et al. (Eds.): INTERACT 2025 Workshops, LNCS 16478, pp. 183–201, 2026.
https://doi.org/10.1007/978-3-032-22934-2_16

assessment, treatment planning, and clinical decision-making [10,45]. Most studies are conducted in controlled clinical environments, given the complexity and cost of building such systems. At the same time, others advocate for developing "life-course" DTs that enable dynamic and tailored interventions throughout different stages of a person's life [34,37]. It introduces new challenges to development because the data exchange between the digital and physical sides no longer operates in a technical loop as it does in the machine and its twin. Additionally, the behavioral, psychological, and cognitive dimensions of humans have made the feedback process less deterministic and more dependent on users' interpretations and responses.

These challenges have given rise to the distinct research area of **Human Digital Twin** (HDT), which is broadly defined as "a replica of a physical-world human in the digital world" [32]. Research in this area has extensively explored the technical aspects of the HDT, such as constructing a digital model of the human body [16] or specific organ [10], creating a digital representation in the simulated environment [18,32], and replicating a group of humans sharing common attributes [33]. Although these are important technical groundwork, the focus has remained largely on representation and replication, with limited attention to how the digital and physical counterparts interact during continuous data exchange. Feedback between humans and HDTs has often been presented in the paper as a one-way arrow, implying that the HDT acts and the human reacts [33,47]. What is missing is the other way around: how humans' interpretation, behavior or emotional response might in turn shape the HDTs' feedback over time. This bidirectionality may appear conceptually straightforward for the design between HDTs and users; however, few studies have investigated it and demonstrated how it should be implemented. Such framing limits HDTs' potential to support understanding, reflection, and trust from users, all of which are crucial in healthcare contexts where data must be interpreted, not merely executed.

In addition, the term *feedback* itself carries different interpretations across disciplines [42]. In most technical and engineering studies, feedback is described as a mechanism for closing the loop between the digital and the physical through real-time data updates and analytical outputs [28,33,47]. It possibly can explain why feedback design has not been studied in depth, as much of the existing work on HDTs remains rooted in technical domains. In this technical view, bidirectional feedback typically refers to continuous data exchange for synchronization, performance optimization, or task automation. In contrast, from the human–computer interaction (HCI) perspective, feedback extends beyond data output to include layers of communication, interpretation, and reflection [42]. These fundamental differences among disciplines suggest that bidirectional feedback in HDTs should be understood not just as continuous data exchange, but as an adaptive interaction loop where both the system and the user adjust their responses based on prior actions and contextual cues.

In response, this paper revisits the notion of bidirectionality in HDTs, focusing on feedback as an interactive dialogue. Based on two design explorations, including a sensory physicalization workshop and a speculative study on HDTs' roles, this paper makes three contributions: (1) It provides cross-study insights on how feedback design can move beyond linear, one-way data delivery to support more dynamic, bidirectional exchanges. (2) It proposes a set of design principles towards bidirectional feedback between HDTs and individuals in preventive-health contexts. (3) This paper also discusses the possible implications for practitioners and system developers in HDTs' development process.

2 Related Work

In this section, we review related work on current applications of (Human) Digital Twins in healthcare, bidirectionality in Digital Twins, and feedback and engagement strategies in interactive systems.

2.1 (Human) Digital Twins in Preventive Healthcare

Digital Twins are increasingly regarded as promising tools for preventive healthcare, offering the ability to create a comprehensive, continuously updated representation of a hospital, a medical device [10] and an individual's health status [33,47]. By integrating physiological signals, lifestyle data, environmental factors, and genetic information, an HDT can support early detection of potential risks and enable personalized interventions before symptoms occur [10,23]. Through simulation and prediction, HDTs have been envisioned to provide possible impacts of behavioral changes, providing a foundation for personalized risk communication and proactive personal health management [3].

Most current implementations, however, remain situated within precision-medicine and clinical environments, where the digital twin is primarily used by healthcare professionals to assist in diagnosis, treatment planning, or rehabilitation [4,29]. While these applications have shown the value of precise human body modeling and predictive analytics, they rarely address how individuals themselves interact with or interpret the information generated by their HDTs. Yet, Shengli et al. [47] pointed out that modeling humans is far more complex than modeling machines, with challenges stemming from continuous data fusion, contextual and social influences on users' behavior, and ethical problems regarding data privacy.

Recent work has begun to suggest extending HDTs beyond the clinic into everyday preventive contexts, supporting health-risk awareness and behavior change [7,10,28]. Lauer-Schmaltz et al. [28] proposed four key considerations for the design of HDTs, including regulatory and ethical considerations, transparency and trust, dynamism and flexibility, and behavioral and cognitive mechanisms. However, they noted that feedback and engagement between users and their HDTs remain under exploration. Similarly, the reviews of current research methods on (Human) Digital Twins [4,51] also indicate that limited attention has been given to interaction design and human-centered considerations, with only a few studies reporting the involvement of users in the evaluation phase.

These gaps emphasize the need to understand the feedback design between HDTs and humans, which is the focus of this paper.

2.2 Bidirectionality in Digital Twins

Bidirectionality has been highlighted as a key distinguishing feature between Digital Twins (DTs) and other digital representations, such as Digital Models and Digital Shadows [12,45]. It refers to the two-way automatic exchange of data between physical and virtual entities. Unlike a Digital Shadow, which merely mirrors physical data in one direction, or a Digital Model, which does not have automatic synchronization between the Digital and the physical, a Digital Twin enables both synchronization and active influence on the physical entity or process [12]. This capacity lays the foundation for automation control and real-time simulation across various domains, including manufacturing, aerospace, and energy systems [2,12]. For example, in cyber-physical manufacturing systems, the twin could continuously receive sensor data from machines and, in turn, send control signals to adjust operational parameters or predict maintenance needs [15]. Similarly, in aerospace, bidirectionality enables the simulation of aircraft performance under varying conditions using real-time data from the physical aircraft [2], thereby maintaining efficiency and safety for each specific aircraft.

However, when moving to the domains where humans become (part of) the physical object/system, such as in the healthcare area, bidirectionality can no longer work in the same manner. Human behavior, interpretation, and psychological factors can introduce uncertainty that cannot be managed through automatic synchronizations [28]. In such settings, the exchange between the digital and the human is rarely about transmitting control commands or enforcing real-time corrections. Rather, it involves how feedback is delivered to communicate insights, support reflection, or facilitate decision-making. Despite growing interest in applying Digital Twins to human-centered contexts [3,29], these forms of bidirectional feedback and their implications for design and interaction have received limited attention to date.

2.3 Feedback and Engagement Strategies in Interactive Systems

Feedback is critical to user engagement and understanding in interactive systems. Strategy [48], modality [11], and timing of feedback could influence how users trust and act upon system output. Studies have shown that personalized feedback could foster sustained engagement, while affective or reflective feedback can promote long-term motivation and continued use [17,22,48].

In conversational agents and adaptive systems, feedback has further evolved from a unidirectional response to multiple-turn interactions. Recent studies have explored how feedback mechanisms can support reciprocity and learning between users and chatbots. For example, Pan and Graaf [38] highlighted the co-adaptive dynamics where chatbots learn from users' responses and contexts, while users actively guide and refine the chatbots' learning path. Ait et al. [1] emphasized the need for feedback that adapts to changing user preferences. Designing an agent's personality and tone has been another approach to sustaining engagement [24], revealing that users often respond more positively to systems that display relational or empathic qualities.

These explorations resonate with HCI perspectives that treat feedback as communicative rather than purely functional. Renaud and Cooper [42] proposed that effective feedback should be conversational, context-sensitive, and continuous, distinguishing between immediate and archival forms that inform and influence users over time. Drawing on Suchman's notion of situated interaction [49], they argued that feedback sustains understanding through ongoing dialogue, a view that anticipates many principles now seen in adaptive and relational technologies [24, 39]. Building on this, our research reframes feedback in HDTs from a one-way system response toward a continuous, dialogic exchange between individuals and their digital counterparts.

3 Problem Statement

3.1 Umbrella Project

This paper is situated within a broader research program that investigates how HDTs can be designed to engage with individuals in preventive health contexts. The overall aim is to offer design insights that move HDTs beyond the technical replication of the human body toward forms that are more relational and interactive.

The specific research gap addressed in this paper concerns the lack of exploration of bidirectional feedback between humans and HDTs. While HDTs are often described as systems enabling "bidirectional data exchange" [2], this exchange described in the existing HDTs operates at the data or control level, neglecting how human emotions, behaviors, and cognitive factors influence the process of receiving and responding to data. Prior studies often treat designing feedback as designing an interface feature [2, 33] or visualization output [30] rather than an evolving process of mutual understanding and adaptation. Consequently, little is known about how feedback is experienced, contextualized, and interpreted by individuals in everyday preventive health contexts.

3.2 Approaches

Approach for Cross Study Analysis. Following the reflection-on-action approach [44], we revisited two previous design explorations to elicit insights on how feedback could be manifested in a richer sense than data transmission. Reflection-on-action refers to a structured process of critically reviewing past experiences, in this case, our previous design studies, to derive new understanding and inform future practice. To structure the reflective process, we adopted the four-stage model of user engagement, originally proposed for self-tracking applications, which includes *review, react, reflect,* and *respond* [6]. Although the model was not developed for HDTs, it describes a linear process that individuals engage with feedback through sequential stages. Given that our research also concerns preventive health, which is closely related to self-tracking practices, adopting this model could provide relevant insights into how individuals may process and respond to feedback. At the same time, it also allows us to find the aspects that fall outside the model, which are more linked to "bidirectional" feedback, gradually moving from the model's linear process into an evolving dialogue between the HDTs and humans. In the end, this revisiting informs the subsequent design principles and discussions on what it would mean to "build" an HDT that supports such evolving exchanges.

Design Exploration 1: Physicalizing Health Predictions. The first exploration has been published as a short paper [31]. We adopted a constructive data physicalization workshop approach [19], in which participants used data physicalization to represent weekly health predictions derived from a hypothetical Human Digital Twin. Constructive physicalization is a design approach that invites people to transform abstract data into tangible and materialized representations, facilitating reflection, sense-making, and personal connection to abstract information [19]. Our workshop design was inspired by previous data physicalization workshops [19,27], which show that engaging participants in sensory-rich and hands-on data exploration can effectively uncover their perspectives and mental models.

We recruited 18 participants between 21 and 32 years old (M=26.67, SD=3.01; 7 self-identified as men, 6 as women, and 1 as self-described). During the workshop, we provided scenario cards and fictional datasets simulating two weekly respiratory allergy risk predictions (examples shown in Fig. 1), indicating the continuous health data that HDTs might produce in daily life. To support creative exploration, participants were given access to a variety of materials covering multiple sensory modalities, such as textured foam balls for touch, colorful playdough for visual representation, scented oils for smell, sound-making objects, and edible items for taste. The workshop included two activities. In the first activity, participants selected specific elements from the first fictional datasets that they found meaningful, and then crafted these into physical representations using the available materials. In the second activity, we presented participants with updated datasets featuring new values. Participants were invited either to build upon their original creations or to create new representations reflecting the evolving predictions.

After conducting the workshops, we first mapped the sensory materials and modalities, along with their physicalization with the data. Then we conducted a thematic analysis of their strategies for interpreting, contextualizing, and interacting with predictive health data. This exploration provided qualitative insight into how people translate abstract data into experiential and metaphorical forms, revealing how feedback can be embodied and contextualized beyond visual interfaces.

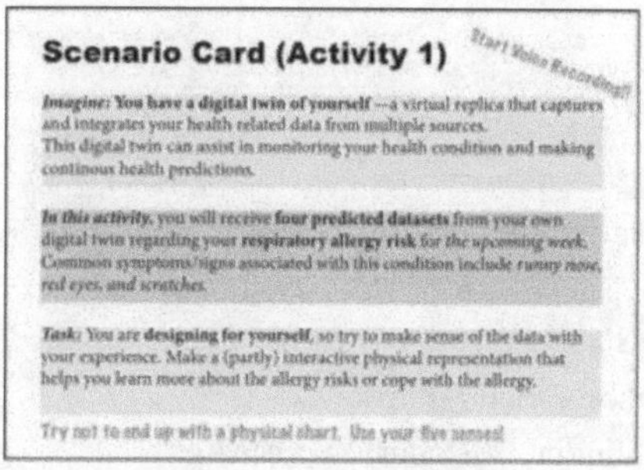

(a) Scenario in Activity 1

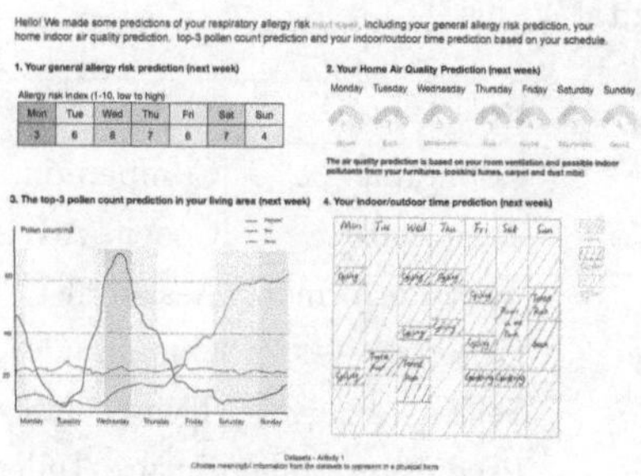

(b) Datasets in Activity 1

Fig. 1. Example scenario card and datasets from the first design exploration [31].

Design Exploration 2: Speculating Relational Roles of HDTs. The second exploration, currently under review, employed a speculative design [9] and research-through-design (RtD) [56] approach to explore the relationship between individuals and their Human Digital Twins in preventive health contexts. Our design research process (summarized in Fig. 2) drew upon diverse sources of inspiration, including science-fiction narratives, linguistic interpretations of "twinhood", and role archetypes from AI and robotics field. Through iterative ideation and scenario-building with ChatGPT (gpt-4o), we developed 20 conceptual roles grouped into seven categories (Table 1), each depicting a distinct way in which an HDT could engage with its human counterpart. The detailed descriptions and evaluations of these roles are reported in a separate publication. Rather than prescribing fixed functions, the intention of naming and grouping these roles was to broaden the design space and reflect on alternative relational possibilities for HDTs in everyday preventive-health contexts. Following reflection in-action and on-action [44] approaches, these roles are compared with each other and clustered beyond the seven role types to extract interaction dimensions behind the roles.

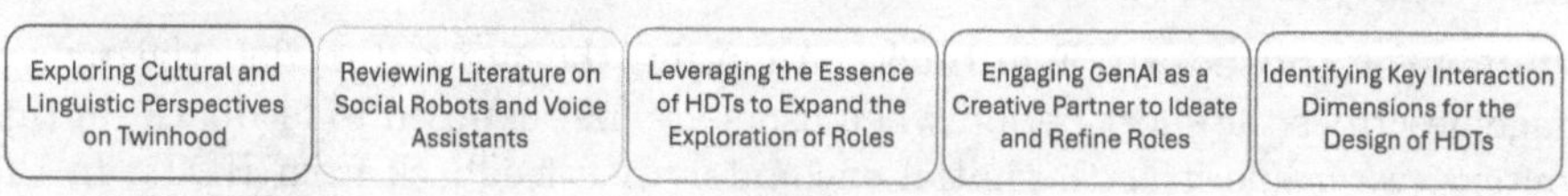

Fig. 2. The Research Process of the second design exploration (under review).

4 Cross-Study Analysis

To structure our cross-study analysis, we reinterpreted each stage of the **user engagement process model** [6] in the context of HDTs to understand how

Table 1. Description of the seven role types explored for the interaction with Human Digital Twins

Role type	Roles
Confidant	Companion, Pet
Teammate	Coach, Advisor, Teammate
Task Performer	Assistant
Expert	Commander, Guardian
Self	Twin, Shadow, Persona, Self Sculptor
Prediction Maker	Future Teller, Pathfinder, Visionary, Forecaster
Data Explorer	Time Machine, Living Memory, Librarian, Tester

individuals may encounter, experience, and act upon feedback generated by their digital counterparts. This adoption provides a structure for comparing insights across our design explorations while also allowing us to identify aspects of HDT feedback that extend beyond the model's original goal-oriented framing.

4.1 Brief Summary of the Outcomes of Two Design Explorations

The first design exploration [31] engaged participants in creating data physicalizations that translated weekly health predictions into sensory and material forms. Twelve data physicalizations were produced and analyzed, offering insights into sensory and material mapping strategies, as well as insights for designing interactions around predictions. The second exploration (currently under review) introduced a set of speculative roles and scenarios for HDTs in preventive health contexts, opening space for designers to consider how these digital counterparts might form relationships with individuals. Although feedback was not the primary focus of either exploration, the insights from both studies form the foundation for the following reflections on bidirectional feedback.

4.2 Analysis Based on the Process Model

Review: Exposed to Feedback. Adopting the process model, the review stage describes the short period when users are first exposed to feedback. In this context, we frame it as the initial encounter with feedback from HDTs. In the physicalization workshops, participants often considered how and when people will notice feedback. They used sensory cues such as color changes, scent diffusion, or shifts in material texture to communicate changes in predictions or to highlight important information from HDTs. Scents were also designed as invitations to recheck or explore feedback details, drawing users' attention naturally. Rather than providing precise analytical results, these designs focus on raising awareness and creating gentle invitations for engagement. Participants also specified when these encounters might happen, for example, during a morning tea routine, through a surprise candy box, or a scent bottle. Such designs show that feedback can be integrated into everyday flows, allowing people to encounter information in a way that fits their daily routine.

From the speculative role exploration, the moment of encounter was closely related to the HDT's specific role. Roles such as the Companion and Shadow imply a continuous and ambient presence in daily life, where feedback would be noticed gradually. In contrast, the Forecaster and Self-Sculptor may appear only at specific times, such as after progress has been made or when users need self-reflection. This difference suggests that the review stage concerns the design of presence, considering when and how the HDT should make itself noticeable to the user.

React: Emotional Response. The react stage in the original model refers to users' immediate affective responses upon receiving feedback [6]. However, our design explorations did not capture the lived emotional reactions of participants. Instead, the results reveal how participants imagine or design the emotional qualities of feedback in preventive health contexts. Thus, we adopt the react stage here to understand how emotional meanings become embedded in the ways feedback is communicated and experienced.

In the first design exploration, participants' material choices revealed how they associated sensory qualities with emotional states. For instance, several participants selected soft or fuzzy textures, associated smells, and sweet tastes to communicate safety and calmness when the health prediction results are positive. For instance, some participants used lavender scent to express calmness and reassurance when predicted risks were low or stable, while others used eucalyptus or citrus smells to signal the freshness of the predicted air quality. Participants have also used rough surfaces, tight threads, or abrupt changes in form to express a sense of alertness or rising risk. These examples show that feedback is not only about conveying the information accurately, but could also embed contextual and sensory cues that create a comprehensible and emotionally resonant experience, helping users intuitively understand and relate to the information in personally meaningful ways.

In the speculative role exploration, the imagined emotional tones of feedback are shaped by how participants understand their relationship with the HDTs. Each role carried a distinct emotional framing, for instance, the Self-Sculptor or Twin could bring up self-recognition and reflection on their own behavior and growth, while the Pathfinder or Time Machine could elicit users' curiosity and anticipation about possible futures. It indicates that when designing feedback, we can intentionally use different roles, each representing a different emotional tone, to create responses that align with users' states.

Reflect: Interpreting and Contextualizing Feedback. The *Reflect* stage indicates the cognitive engagement with the feedback, which is about how they interpret and evaluate the results in regard to their goals [6]. We adopt cognitive engagement as a perspective to understand how feedback could be contextualized, explained, and made meaningful within participants' designs and speculated roles.

In the physicalization study, feedback information was mostly conveyed and interpreted through material and sensory mappings, with very few examples showing explicit numerical data. Participants encoded health predictions metaphorically, connecting meaning to textures, tensions, smells, and tastes. For example, a group of participants designed squeezable water balls that invited users to pause, touch, and reflect, which changes the act of interaction into a moment of winding down to understand air quality and related health risks. Additionally, several physicalizations explored how time could be experienced through form, by utilizing spatial structures, modular elements, sequential transitions, or sliding mechanisms to represent changes across days or weeks. These designs encouraged users to interpret information through active engagement and contextual association, suggesting that user reflection could be supported by bodily or sensorial engagement.

In the speculative role exploration, this reflective engagement depends on how each role guides users' interpretation and sense-making. Roles such as the Librarian or Living Memory support retrospective reflection by connecting current feedback to past records or experiences, while Future Teller or Pathfinder encourage forward-looking reflection that helps users anticipate outcomes and weigh potential actions. Across both explorations, the reflect stage shows that designing for reflective engagement requires HDTs not to simply deliver definitive answers or analytical results, but to facilitate user understanding of the feedback through contextual associations, temporal framing, and metaphorical cues, inviting reflection and engagement.

Respond: Acting and Adapting. The *Respond* stage is when the behavior engagements are involved. The original model added four response tactics when users are not satisfied with the results: dismissal, procrastination, selective attention, and intentional neglect [6]. In our explorations, we did not explicitly ask participants to be aware of possible behavioral responses, but we found some small glimpses into how feedback from HDTs could guide, influence, or support users' actions.

In the physicalization workshop, several designs connected feedback to specific activities or their consequences. Some participants physicalized potential negative outcomes of the predictions to prompt preventive reflection or immediate action, while others used recurring elements, such as weekly updates or morning tea rituals, to raise awareness without demanding a response. These approaches suggest that responding can also emerge from raising awareness and regular engagement rather than from direct control to force changes in behavior.

In the speculative role exploration, roles such as the Tester allow users to explore and learn through experimentation and error, while the Time Machine and Librarian can support the comparison and curation of feedback information over time, leaving space for users to take actions based on their own reflections.

4.3 Aspects Beyond the Process Model

Although the four-stage model provides a useful framework for tracing how users engage with feedback, our reflections reveal several aspects that extend beyond its linear structure. First, feedback in both explorations often carried **ritual and temporal qualities**. Participants embedded feedback moments within recurring routines, such as morning tea, weekly updates, or small sensory events—indicating that engagement was cyclical rather than one-off. This ongoing recurrence turns feedback into a familiar presence that gradually shapes users' awareness and habits, showing the continuous and adaptive nature of bidirectional exchanges. Second, some feedback forms were designed to be **perceived collectively rather than privately**. By making the feedback sharable or ambiently perceivable by others, participants opened space for social awareness and shared interpretation, suggesting that engagement with HDTs might involve not only the individual but also those around them. Third, several artefacts and roles deliberately **introduced ambiguity** to sustain curiosity and reflection, rather than providing closure once a response had been made. Ambiguity, in this context, became a way to prolong interpretation and maintain dialogue between the individual and their HDT over time. In summary, these observations indicate that in preventive health contexts, feedback should be understood as a multisensory, relational, and ongoing process that evolves with users' routines, social settings, and interpretations, rather than as a sequential cognitive process. Recognizing these temporal, social, and interpretive dimensions could help future HDTs support more meaningful and bidirectional forms of feedback that encourage continuity, reflection, and shared understanding.

5 Design Principles

Our revisit of previous explorations highlights several design principles that are useful for enabling bidirectional feedback in future HDTs. These principles emphasize mutual adaptation, contextual sensitivity, and the temporal aspects that move beyond unidirectional data delivery toward continuous, dialogic interaction. These principles are identified by synthesizing the recurring patterns and limitations of the four-stage model.

Enable Customization in Receiving Feedback. Bidirectional feedback requires systems that allow users to determine *when* and *how* feedback is delivered. HDTs should provide mechanisms for postponing, prioritizing, or filtering feedback to match users' routines and readiness. Configurable timing and conditional triggers can help feedback integrate seamlessly into everyday life, preventing information overload and fatigue.

Design Adaptive Feedback Based on User Interaction. To support bidirectional feedback over time, HDTs should adapt the content, tone, and timing of the feedback based on users' behavior and the context they are in. In terms of system design, the architecture of the system needs to be able to incorporate feedback loops that monitor engagement patterns (e.g., frequency of response, hesitations, dismissals) and modify tone, detail level, or frequency accordingly. A system's ability to ensure adaptive responses will allow the HDT to remain aligned with changing user needs over time. Previous concepts, such as user interface plasticity [5] and context-aware adaptation [36], can serve as a good starting point for analyzing how to enable the adoption of feedback to support different roles and flexible role changes over time. Studies on conversational agents offer valuable insights into how systems can sustain long-term engagement through multi-turn interactions and continuous adaptation [20,46]. These systems learn from users' behaviors and adjust their feedback tone, timing, and content accordingly, demonstrating how iterative adaptation supports ongoing, bidirectional feedback rather than one-way information delivery [20,46].

Consider Temporal Aspect in Feedback Design. Bidirectional feedback operates over extended periods of time. HDTs should link past data, current states, and future predictions to create temporal coherence. Interfaces that present progress, reflect on historical data, and anticipate possible trajectories can help users understand change as an ongoing process rather than a discrete moment of interaction. Addressing how to design for interactions with a temporal dimension in Digital Twin is currently an active field of research [55]. Existing studies show that linear presentation, activity-based presentation, and spiral forms can affect the depth of user insights [55]. When feedback concerns personal health, these temporal representations become particularly important for communicating gradual changes, such as different stages of disease progression or variations in health conditions over time [52,53].

Represent and Communicate Uncertainty Explicitly. Feedback should clearly indicate uncertainty and the limits of predictive information. HDTs should incorporate representations such as confidence intervals, qualitative cues, or graded visualizations that express the degree of reliability in data or predictions [8,13]. Uncertainty can be designed to become part of the user experience. Making uncertainty explicit supports informed decision-making and strengthens user trust in the system [40].

Employ Multimodal Feedback to Support Interpretation and Engagement. To foster bidirectional feedback, HDTs should consider communicating through multi-sensory modalities where appropriate, integrating visual, auditory, or tactile cues to enhance comprehension and accessibility [25,35]. It enables users to interpret and respond through different sensory modalities, pushing towards a continuous exchange rather than passively receiving one-directional updates from HDTs. Designing for such multi-modal reciprocity enables HDTs to tailor feedback delivery to individual preferences and situational contexts, thereby fostering engagement and sustained interaction over time.

6 Discussion

6.1 Implications for Practitioners and HDT System Developers

Integrating bidirectional feedback into HDTs requires rethinking not only the overall system architecture but especially the early stages of requirement analysis. Recent reviews of HDT development highlight challenges in reliability, explainability, and user engagement [29], yet feedback design is often treated as an interface concern [4] in the deployment phase. Through our reflections, we suggest it should be embedded throughout the entire HDT design pipeline, from defining requirements to designing components for the architecture, to the final deployment and testing. Following the five-phase design process for HDTs outlined by Lauer-schmaltz et al. [29]: Requirement Analysis, Architecture Design, Model Development, System Integration, Deployment, Testing, and Continuous Refinement, we discuss how the design of bidirectional feedback should be integrated.

At the requirement analysis stage, bidirectional feedback should be specified as a core functional objective rather than a supplementary interface feature. From our reflections, participants imagined feedback that appeared in meaningful moments and was embedded in daily routines, for example, during morning routines or weekly rituals. These findings (from the review stage) highlight that timing and context are central to bidirectional feedback, where the individual is not a passive receiver but an active participant deciding when to engage. During requirement analysis, designers and developers should therefore define feedback as a mutual communication process, specifying when feedback should invite user action and when it should adapt based on user control signals. Specifically, requirements should document user needs for feedback timing [54], customization choices, mechanisms for user-initiated dialogue, transparency in feedback [23,29] (addressing issues of system opacity), and context-specific needs [4,51]. These detailed requirements could inform later architectural and ethical design choices.

During the architecture design phase, bidirectional feedback requires a dedicated feedback management layer that manages how information flows in both directions: from user to system (through contextual data, user manual input, etc.) and from system to user (through adaptive multi-modal representations [21], varied communication styles [17], etc.). It should operate independently of the prediction and simulation components, coordinating modality selection, feedback timing control, and data analysis of interaction, allowing for independent iterations of interacting with users without affecting other system components.

For the model development phase, identifying response patterns is essential to adjust feedback strategies accordingly and maintain long-term interactions with HDTs. To achieve this, models should learn from behavioral traces, such as recognizing hesitation, repeated postponement, or prompt engagement, and adjust their feedback strategies accordingly. This requires integrating related behavioral parameters into model training, which aligns with current co-adaptive system design [14]. Over time, the HDT can thus refine how it communicates, not just what it predicts, making feedback co-adapted to the user.

In the system integration phase, feedback needs to be connected to interfaces in ways that are both technically accurate and contextually appropriate [36]. The system integration requires synchronizing results with appropriate multi-modal channels (such as visual, auditory, or tactile) based on the user's context, helping to reduce visual complexity [25] or provide seamless assistance during high-focus work. Prior work in autonomous driving, for example, has used a fluid-concept interface to integrate Digital Twin models of the driver, vehicle, and environment, adapting feedback across three display types [41]. Another study implemented a multimodal adaptive user interface for manufacturing assistance systems and found that it supported workers in shifting tasks and acquiring new skills [21]. Realizing such integration requires context-aware feedback-scheduling mechanisms that determine when [54] and how information is delivered, taking into account factors such as social context and user fatigue. Furthermore, interfaces should support embedding feedback into users' daily routines, minimizing interruption costs and ensuring that assistance is experienced as less intrusive [7].

During the deployment and refinement phase, HDTs will move from controlled development settings into real-world contexts, so the bidirectional feedback systems should remain transparent and traceable. To sustain long-term engagement, HDTs should not only deliver accurate predictions but also communicate why and how particular feedback is generated. For example, implementing traceable and explainable mechanisms, such as contextual annotations, confidence indicators of predictions, and visualizations showing the data analysis process, as they have been employed in existing work on explainable AI [13,50]. Continuous monitoring and user testing are necessary to evaluate how individuals interpret, trust, and act upon the feedback over time. Insights from these interactions should inform iterative updates, ensuring that both data models and feedback strategies evolve together. Beyond technical refinement, this phase should also address ethical dimensions, including preserving data privacy [23], respecting user agency [43], and maintaining a sense of co-adaptation [38].

6.2 Reflecting on Design Approaches

Our explorations offer initial insights into how bidirectional feedback might be designed. We use the roles of HDTs as design material to work with, which creates a structure to explore multiple relationships between humans and HDTs. It resonates with research on role and personality design in conversational agents, which demonstrates how framing an agent's identity shapes user trust, engagement, and adaptability [24,26,43]. Designing roles also opens space for contextual adjustment and encourages reflection on how feedback is perceived and interpreted.

As described in the design principles, bidirectional feedback can also be approached as a multi-round and iterative process rather than a single act of information delivery. In this view, HDTs and users continually adapt and learn from each other, forming an evolving feedback loop over time [38,46]. Designing for such dynamics calls for HCI methods that account for the situated and changing nature of interaction, such as co-design workshops, participatory design, speculative design [9], and long-term field studies. These methods allow feedback mechanisms to emerge through ongoing negotiation with users rather than being predetermined by the system. Given that current research on HDTs rarely involves participants in the early design stages [4], adopting these approaches would help integrate user perspectives and reveal how people's perceptions of their HDTs adapt over time.

7 Conclusion and Future Work

This paper revisits the concept of bidirectionality in Human Digital Twins, focusing on feedback as an evolving dialogue between individuals and their digital counterparts. Through reflections across two design explorations, we discussed how feedback could shift from one-way data transmission to interactive and interpretive dialogue. We contribute several design principles and system implications for how bidirectional feedback can be embedded throughout HDTs' development process.

We encourage other researchers and practitioners to further explore how bidirectional feedback can be designed, tested, and sustained through participatory and contextual methods, as feedback between HDTs and users has not been explored in depth. Future research should employ contextual and participatory methods to understand how feedback flows are co-constructed between users and their digital counterparts, and how these exchanges evolve across different situations and time periods. We approach the continuous bidirectional interaction through the roles HDTs can play. Under this broader research program, our future work will focus on exploring role acceptance within specific preventive health contexts. Also, we aim to study how long-term interactions, where habits, expectations, and potential conflicts emerge, may influence the roles of HDTs over time.

References

1. Ait Baha, T., El Hajji, M., Es-Saady, Y., Fadili, H.: The power of personalization: a systematic review of personality-adaptive chatbots. SN Comput. Sci. **4**(5), 661 (2023)
2. Barricelli, B.R., Casiraghi, E., Fogli, D.: A survey on digital twin: definitions, characteristics, applications, and design implications. IEEE Access **7**, 167653–167671 (2019)
3. Barricelli, B.R., Casiraghi, E., Gliozzo, J., Petrini, A., Valtolina, S.: Human digital twin for fitness management. IEEE Access **8**, 26637–26664 (2020). https://doi.org/10.1109/ACCESS.2020.2971576, https://ieeexplore.ieee.org/document/8981975/
4. Barricelli, B.R., Fogli, D.: Digital twins in human-computer interaction: a systematic review. Int. J. Human–Comput. Interact. **40**(2), 79–97 (Jan 2024). https://doi.org/10.1080/10447318.2022.2118189, https://www.tandfonline.com/doi/full/10.1080/10447318.2022.2118189
5. Calvary, G., et al.: Plasticity of user interfaces: a revised reference framework. framework **3**, 4

6. Constantiou, I., Mukkamala, A., Sjöklint, M., Trier, M.: Engaging with self-tracking applications: how do users respond to their performance data? Eur. J. Inf. Syst. **32**(6), 941–961 (2023)
7. De Maeyer, C., Markopoulos, P.: Are digital twins becoming our personal (predictive) advisors? In: Gao, Q., Zhou, J. (eds.) Human Aspects of IT for the Aged Population. Healthy and Active Aging, pp. 250–268. Springer International Publishing, Cham (2020). https://doi.org/10.1007/978-3-030-50249-2_19
8. Dolan, J.G., Iadarola, S.: Risk communication formats for low probability events: an exploratory study of patient preferences. BMC Med. Inform. Decision Making **8**(1), 14 (Apr 2008). https://doi.org/10.1186/1472-6947-8-14
9. Dunne, A., Raby, F.: Speculative everything: Design, fiction, and social dreaming (2013)
10. Erol, T., Mendi, A.F., Doğan, D.: The digital twin revolution in healthcare. In: 2020 4th International Symposium on Multidisciplinary Studies and Innovative Technologies (ISMSIT), pp. 1–7. IEEE (2020)
11. Freeman, E., Wilson, G., Vo, D.B., Ng, A., Politis, I., Brewster, S.: Multimodal feedback in HCI: haptics, non-speech audio, and their applications. In: The Handbook of Multimodal-Multisensor Interfaces: Foundations, User Modeling, and Common Modality Combinations-Volume 1, pp. 277–317 (2017)
12. Fuller, A., Fan, Z., Day, C., Barlow, C.: Digital twin: enabling technologies, challenges and open research. IEEE Access **8**, 108952–108971 (2020)
13. Garcia-Retamero, R., Okan, Y., Cokely, E.T.: Using visual aids to improve communication of risks about health: a review. Sci. World J. **2012**(1), 562637 (2012). https://doi.org/10.1100/2012/562637
14. Gebreegziabher, S.A., Yang, Y., Glassman, E.L., Li, T.J.J.: Supporting co-adaptive machine teaching through human concept learning and cognitive theories. In: Proceedings of the 2025 CHI Conference on Human Factors in Computing Systems, pp. 1–18 (2025)
15. Grieves, M.: Digital twin: manufacturing excellence through virtual factory replication. White Paper **1**(2014), 1–7 (2014)
16. Hanson, L., Högberg, D., Lundström, D., Wårell, M.: Application of human modelling in health care industry. In: Duffy, V.G. (ed.) Digital Human Modeling, pp. 521–530. Springer, Berlin, Heidelberg (2009). https://doi.org/10.1007/978-3-642-02809-0_55
17. Hassan, L., Dias, A., Hamari, J.: How motivational feedback increases user's benefits and continued use: A study on gamification, quantified-self and social networking. Int. J. Inf. Manage. **46**, 151–162 (2019)
18. He, Q., et al.: From digital human modeling to human digital twin: Framework and perspectives in human factors. Chinese J. Mech. Eng. **37**(1), 9 (2024)
19. Huron, S., Gourlet, P., Hinrichs, U., Hogan, T., Jansen, Y.: Let's get physical: promoting data physicalization in workshop formats. In: Proceedings of the 2017 Conference on Designing Interactive Systems, pp. 1409–1422 (2017)
20. Jiang, Y., Guo, L., Wu, Y., Caliskan, A., Mitra, T., Shen, H.: Beyond one-way influence: Bidirectional opinion dynamics in multi-turn human-llm interactions. arXiv preprint arXiv:2510.20039 (2025)
21. Josifovska, K., Yigitbas, E., Engels, G.: A digital twin-based multi-modal UI adaptation framework for assistance systems in industry 4.0. In: Kurosu, M. (ed.) Human-Computer Interaction. Design Practice in Contemporary Societie, pp. 398–409. Springer International Publishing, Cham (2019). https://doi.org/10.1007/978-3-030-22636-7_30

22. Karolus, J., Feger, S.S., Schmidt, A., Woźniak, P.W.: Your text is hard to read: facilitating readability awareness to support writing proficiency in text production. In: Proceedings of the 2023 ACM Designing Interactive Systems Conference, pp. 147–160 (2023)
23. de Kerckhove, D.: The personal digital twin, ethical considerations. Phil. Trans. R. Soc. A **379**(2207), 20200367 (2021)
24. Kim, H., Koh, D.Y., Lee, G., Park, J.M., Lim, Y.k.: Designing personalities of conversational agents. In: Extended Abstracts of the 2019 CHI Conference on Human Factors in Computing Systems, pp. 1–6. ACM, Glasgow Scotland UK (May 2019). https://doi.org/10.1145/3290607.3312887, https://dl.acm.org/doi/10.1145/3290607.3312887
25. König, W.A., Rädle, R., Reiterer, H.: Interactive design of multimodal user interfaces: reducing technical and visual complexity. J. Multimodal User Interfaces **3**(3), 197–213 (2010)
26. Krapp, E., Neuhaus, R., Hassenzahl, M., Laschke, M.: In a quasi-social relationship with ChatGPT. an autoethnography on engaging with prompt-engineered LLM personas. In: Nordic Conference on Human-Computer Interaction, pp. 1–16. ACM, Uppsala Sweden (Oct 2024). https://doi.org/10.1145/3679318.3685501, https://dl.acm.org/doi/10.1145/3679318.3685501
27. Lallemand, C., Oomen, M.: The candy workshop: supporting rich sensory modalities in constructive data physicalization. In: CHI Conference on Human Factors in Computing Systems Extended Abstracts, pp. 1–7 (2022)
28. Lauer-Schmaltz, M.W., Cash, P., Hansen, J.P., Maier, A.: Designing human digital twins for behaviour-changing therapy and rehabilitation: a systematic review. Proc. Design Society **2**, 1303–1312 (2022)
29. Lauer-Schmaltz, M.W., Cash, P., Rivera, D.G.T.: ETHICA: designing human digital twins—a systematic review and proposed methodology. IEEE Access 12, 86947–86973 (2024). https://doi.org/10.1109/ACCESS.2024.3416517, https://ieeexplore.ieee.org/document/10562275
30. Lauer-Schmaltz, M.W., Kerim, I., Hansen, J.P., Gulyás, G.M., Andersen, H.B.: Human digital twin-based interactive dashboards for informal caregivers of stroke patients. In: Proceedings of the 16th International Conference on PErvasive Technologies Related to Assistive Environments, pp. 215–221 (2023)
31. Li, Y., Lallemand, C., Bernhaupt, R.: Making predictions tangible: using data physicalization to explore expectations around health predictions. In: Ardito, C., Diniz Junqueira Barbosa, S., Conte, T., Freire, A., Gasparini, I., Palanque, P., Prates, R. (eds.) Human-Computer Interaction – INTERACT 2025, pp. 521–539. Springer Nature Switzerland, Cham (2026). https://doi.org/10.1007/978-3-032-05002-1_28
32. Lin, Y., et al.: Human digital twin: a survey. J. Cloud Comput. Adv. Syst. Appl. **13**(1) (Aug 2024)
33. Miller, M.E., Spatz, E.: A unified view of a human digital twin. Human-Intell. Syst. Integr. **4**(1), 23–33 (2022)
34. Milne-Ives, M., et al.: Life course digital twins-intelligent monitoring for early and continuous intervention and prevention (lifetime): Proposal for a retrospective cohort study. JMIR Res. Protocols **11**(5), e35738 (2022)
35. Moran, D.B., Cheyer, A.J., Julia, L.E., Martin, D.L., Park, S.: Multimodal user interfaces in the open agent architecture. In: Proceedings of the 2nd International Conference on Intelligent User Interfaces, pp. 61–68 (1997)

36. Motti, V.G., Vanderdonckt, J.: A computational framework for context-aware adaptation of user interfaces. In: IEEE 7th International Conference on Research Challenges in Information Science (RCIS), pp. 1–12. IEEE (2013)
37. Mulder, S.T., et al.: Dynamic digital twin: diagnosis, treatment, prediction, and prevention of disease during the life course. J. Med. Internet Res. **24**(9), e35675 (2022)
38. Pan, S., de Graaf, M.M.: Developing a social support framework: understanding the reciprocity in human-chatbot Relationship. In: Proceedings of the 2025 CHI Conference on Human Factors in Computing Systems, pp. 1–13. CHI '25, Association for Computing Machinery, New York, NY, USA (Apr 2025). https://doi.org/10.1145/3706598.3713503, https://dl.acm.org/doi/10.1145/3706598.3713503
39. Pentina, I., Hancock, T., Xie, T.: Exploring relationship development with social chatbots: a mixed-method study of replika. Comput. Human Behav. **140**, 107600 (Mar 2023). https://doi.org/10.1016/j.chb.2022.107600, https://www.sciencedirect.com/science/article/pii/S0747563222004204
40. Pichon, A., Blumberg, J.R., Mamykina, L., Elhadad, N.: The voice of endo: leveraging speech for an intelligent system that can forecast illness Flare-ups. In: Proceedings of the 2025 CHI Conference on Human Factors in Computing Systems, pp. 1–15. CHI '25, Association for Computing Machinery, New York, NY, USA (Apr 2025). https://doi.org/10.1145/3706598.3714040, https://dl.acm.org/doi/10.1145/3706598.3714040
41. Pretto, P., Mörtl, P., Neuhuber, N.: Fluid interface concept for automated driving. In: International Conference on Human-Computer Interaction, pp. 114–130. Springer (2020)
42. Renaud, K., Cooper, R.: Feedback in human-computer interaction-characteristics and recommendations. South African Comput. J. **2000**(26), 105–114 (2000)
43. Ringfort-Felner, R., Laschke, M., Neuhaus, R., Theofanou-Fülbier, D., Hassenzahl, M.: It can be more than just a subservient assistant. distinct roles for the design of intelligent personal assistants. In: Nordic Human-Computer Interaction Conference, pp. 1–17 (2022)
44. Schön, D.: The Reflective Practitioner: How Professionals Think in Action. Taylor & Francis (2017). https://books.google.com/books?id=OT9BDgAAQBAJ
45. Semeraro, C., Lezoche, M., Panetto, H., Dassisti, M.: Digital twin paradigm: a systematic literature review. Comput. Ind. **130**, 103469 (2021)
46. Shen, H., et al.: Towards bidirectional human-ai alignment: A systematic review for clarifications, framework, and future directions **2406**, 1–56 (2024). arXiv preprint arxiv:4060.9264
47. Shengli, W.: Is human digital twin possible? Comput. Methods Programs Biomed. Update **1**(100014), 100014 (2021)
48. Shin, H., Park, J., Yu, J., Kim, J., Kim, H.Y., Oh, C.: Looping in: Exploring feedback strategies to motivate human engagement in interactive machine learning. Int. J. Human–Comput. Interact. **41**(14), 8666–8683 (2025)
49. Suchman, L.A.: Plans and situated actions: The problem of human-machine communication. Cambridge university press (1987)
50. Szymanski, M., Vanden Abeele, V., Verbert, K.: Designing and Evaluating Explanations for a Predictive Health Dashboard: A User-Centred Case Study. In: Extended Abstracts of the CHI Conference on Human Factors in Computing Systems, pp. 1–8. CHI EA '24, Association for Computing Machinery, New York, NY, USA (May 2024). https://doi.org/10.1145/3613905.3637140, https://dl.acm.org/doi/10.1145/3613905.3637140

51. Vainionpää, F., Kinnula, M., Kinnula, A., Kuutti, K., Hosio, S.: HCI and Digital Twins – A Critical Look: A Literature Review. In: Proceedings of the 25th International Academic Mindtrek Conference, pp. 75–88. ACM, Tampere Finland (Nov 2022). https://doi.org/10.1145/3569219.3569376, https://dl.acm.org/doi/10.1145/3569219.3569376
52. Wiberg, M., Stolterman, E.: Time and temporality in HCL research. Interact. Comput. **33**(3), 250–270 (2021)
53. Xu, K., Baseman, C.M., Swinger, N., Ryu, M., Arriaga, R.I.: Understanding the temporality of informal caregivers' sense-making on conflicts and life-changing events through online health communities. Proc. ACM Human-Comput. Interact. **9**(7), 1–36 (2025)
54. Yen, Y.C.G., et al.: When to give feedback: Exploring tradeoffs in the timing of design feedback (2024)
55. Zheng, Y., van Essen, H., Mitchell, S., Fennessy, L., Vaughan, L., Bernhaupt, R.: Design of temporal interfaces of digital twins in domestic energy consumption. In: Ardito, C., Diniz Junqueira Barbosa, S., Conte, T., Freire, A., Gasparini, I., Palanque, P., Prates, R. (eds.) Human-Computer Interaction – INTERACT 2025, pp. 477–498. Springer Nature Switzerland, Cham (2026)
56. Zimmerman, J., Forlizzi, J., Evenson, S.: Research through design as a method for interaction design research in HCI. In: Proceedings of the SIGCHI Conference on Human Factors in Computing Systems, pp. 493–502. ACM, San Jose California USA (Apr 2007). https://doi.org/10.1145/1240624.1240704, https://dl.acm.org/doi/10.1145/1240624.1240704

Enabling Cybersecurity Education Through Digital Twins and Generative AI

Vita Santa Barletta[1], Vito Bavaro[1], Miriana Calvano[1], Antonio Curci[1,2], Antonio Piccinno[1(✉)], and Davide Pio Posa[1]

[1] University of Bari Aldo Moro, Via E. Orabona 4, 70125 Bari, Italy
{vita.barletta,miriana.calvano,antonio.curci,antonio.piccinno}@uniba.it, {v.bavaro4,d.posa3}@studenti.uniba.it

[2] University of Pisa, Largo B. Pontecorvo 3, 56127 Pisa, Italy

Abstract. In recent years, Artificial Intelligence (AI) is taking over many fields, changing the way activities and tasks are being carried out. Among the most recent AI-based technologies, Large Language Models (LLMs) and Digital Twins (DTs) are rapidly spreading, bringing advantages and innovation from multiple point of views. This research focuses on the employment of LLMs and DTs in cybersecurity, exploiting their ability to replicate infrastructures, allowing for real-time monitoring, threat analysis, and system simulation. Specifically, we investigate how integrating DTs and LLMs in penetration testing tools can enhance cybersecurity education and the effectiveness of interventions to face threats. With this perspective, we introduce a framework, called *Cyber Red Team Knife (CRTK)* for enhancing cybersecurity education with respect to vulnerabilities for both defensive and offensive strategies. The framework is based on DTs and Generative AI in order to support the penetration testing activities thanks to the Cyber Kill Chain model in order to automate penetration testing activities thanks to Red Team Knife (RTK) that integrates it. RTK is a custom penetration testing toolkit to guide learners through key phases of cyber-attacks within a DT-powered ecosystem.

Keywords: Cyber Social Security · Penetration Testing · Cybersecurity Education · Human-AI Collaboration

1 Introduction

Cybersecurity traditionally focused on the mere protection of technical infrastructures, systems, and computer networks. Nevertheless, the evolution of the cybersecurity landscape identifies humans as the weakest link of the chain since attackers exploit their weaknesses and lack of knowledge to perform malicious activities that can harm them [18,35]. In this context, Cyber Social Security (CSS) plays an important role, emerging as a discipline that studies the intersection between social factors, human behaviors, and information security, recognizing that many of the most sophisticated attacks exploit psychological and

Published by Springer Nature Switzerland AG 2026
C. Maciel et al. (Eds.): INTERACT 2025 Workshops, LNCS 16478, pp. 202–216, 2026.
https://doi.org/10.1007/978-3-032-22934-2_17

social vulnerabilities rather than exclusively the technical ones [4,11,12]. The advent of Generative Artificial Intelligence (GenAI)—e.g., Large Language Models (LLMs)—has revolutionized this scenario, significantly amplifying attackers' capabilities to conduct large-scale social engineering operations which can damage individuals. Empirical results indicate that LLMs can achieve accuracy rates exceeding 95% in threat detection, while substantially reducing false positives compared to traditional rule-based systems [10]. LLMs can support automated interpretation of system behaviors by analyzing logs, data streams, and event sequences to identify anomalous patterns that may indicate early-stage intrusions [2,38]. In addition, LLMs are increasingly employed in real-time threat analysis, where they assist Security Operations Center (SOC) teams by summarizing alerts, correlating events, and prioritizing high-risk scenarios [41]. For example, systems supported by LLMs can turn detailed technical alerts into easy-to-understand descriptions that explain how an attack was conducted, which parts of the system were affected, and how it could spread [21]. This capability has been demonstrated in industrial control systems, where LLM-based models generate natural-language explanations to foster understanding of cyber-attacks on grid automation components, which are devices for automatize and monitor the power grid, increasing the operator's comprehension of the ongoing events while improving the response time [26]. The integration of LLMs can further increase these benefits, especially for enhancing security monitoring and decision-making. In the literature, six key cybersecurity domains are identified to categorize LLMs applications [3]: vulnerability detection, anomaly detection, cyber threat intelligence, blockchain security, penetration testing, and digital forensics. This work focuses mostly on penetration testing, which involves simulating cyberattacks on systems or networks to identify weaknesses before malicious actors can exploit them, supporting organizations to improve their defenses [40].

Another technology that is being increasingly adopted in modern society are Digital Twins (DTs); they are virtual counterparts of physical systems and that have found widespread applications across various domains. For example, in manufacturing, they enable real-time monitoring, predictive maintenance, and simulation-based optimization [1,19]; in healthcare, they can support personalized medicine, precise diagnostics, and advanced treatment planning [1,30]. They can also be useful in urban planning, energy systems, and smart infrastructures for efficient design, sustainability, and complex system management [25,30]. These applications are enabled by the convergence of Internet of Things (IoT), AI, eXtended Reality (XR), and cloud computing, which bridge the physical and digital realms [1,19]. DTs are increasingly being recognized as powerful assets also in cybersecurity, offering real-time monitoring, detailed system analysis, and high-fidelity emulation capabilities [32]. By creating accurate virtual replicas of hardware, software and firmware components, DTs enable organizations to proactively identify vulnerabilities and mitigate cyber threats with greater precision [24,32]. As a result, DTs can improve threat prediction, streamline incident response, and improve system's resilience against threats [33]. In addition, other applications of DTs in cybersecurity allow the automated extraction of the so-called Indicators of Compromise (IoCs) from unstructured Cyber Threat Intelligence (CTI) reports. DTs also allow the construction of knowledge graphs that make threat relationships more comprehensible to security managers [34]. These characteristics enable more adaptive and responsive cybersecurity operations, being a result of effective human-AI collaboration [8,44,48].

Building on this perspective, this research proposes the framework *Cyber Red Team Knife (CRTK)* that aims at exploring how current technologies—specifically DTs, LLMs, and penetration testing tools—can improve education by increasing understanding of cyber attacks and their broader technical and operational context. In this regard, since humans represent the weakest link of the chain, attackers can take advantage of their lack of knowledge to conduct malicious activities [14]. Therefore, educating individuals about cybersecurity pillars and best practices is essential to help them recognize when they are victim of an attack and understand how to respond effectively [27,28]. Specifically, the target audience of the framework are cybersecurity experts, as well as students enrolled in cybersecurity curricula (or related) of University courses. While these technologies are increasingly employed in isolation, their combined use in a unified framework has not yet been conceptualized. To address this gap, the following research question has been posed:

RQ: How the conceptual integration of DTs, LLMs, and penetration testing tools can offer a new paradigm for analyzing the structure and progression of cyber attacks?

Based on this RQ, the following Sub-RQs (SRQs) were defined

SRQ1 What potential benefits such integration may bring in terms of reasoning, interpretation, and explainability of adversarial activities?

SRQ2 To what extent the resulting architecture can serve as a theoretical model for cybersecurity education, combining technical modeling with cognitive support?

The manuscript is organized as follows: Sect. 2 describes the topics that lay the ground of this work; Sect. 3 presents the framework that can be employed in the cybersecurity education field leveraging DTs, LLMs, and penetration testing tools; Sect. 4 presents an example of how CRTK can be used in a real-world scenario in the domain of smart cities; Sect. 5 draw conclusions and present potential future developments of this research.

2 Related Work

This section aims at presenting the pillars that lay the ground of this research concerning LLMs, penetration testing tools, and DTs, as well as their application in cybersecurity education.

2.1 The Impact of LLMs and DTs in Cybersecurity

DTs enhance cybersecurity by providing dynamic virtual replicas of Information Technology (IT), Operational Technology (OT), and Internet of Things (IoT) systems, enabling real-time simulation, monitoring, and analysis [7]. Through these characteristics, DTs support also key cybersecurity functions to detect attacks and show an high potential when integrated into intrusion detection systems for IoT-based smart city environments [16]. Researchers highlight the importance of addressing cybersecurity challenges in DTs deployments, where risks such as unauthorized access and data manipulation pose significant concerns. To mitigate these risks, multiple operational frameworks have been proposed in the literature, tackling multi-layered security that incorporates encryption, access control, and anomaly detection [6]. In this regard, it is possible to introduce the concept of Cyber Digital Twins (CDTs), which can mirror IT and OT environments, enabling the simulation of cyberattacks and the evaluation of defense mechanisms in risk-free and controllable settings [9,42]. For instance, Varghese et al. [45] modeled four types of cyberattacks—including command injection and false data injection—on DT-enabled systems, highlighting how such replicas can be exploited to test vulnerabilities in protocols, like ENIP. Similarly, Dietz et al. [15] used DTs to simulate man-in-the-middle attacks via poisoning in industrial control systems, while El-Hajj [16] performed network-based attacks within DT testbeds. Beyond attack simulation, DTs have proven valuable in Security Operations Center (SOC) environments. Hadar et al. [22] introduced a cyber DT capable of automatically gathering and prioritizing security control requirements. Khan et al. [29] and Sasikala et al. [37] further showed that real-time analysis within DTs enables quicker detection and response to evolving threats. To amplify these capabilities, the integration of LLMs into CDTs represents a promising frontier. In fact, recent research explores the integration in automated penetration testing, aiming to enhance efficiency and effectiveness of cyber-threat detection. Studies have demonstrated LLMs' potential in automating various aspects of penetration testing, including task planning, vulnerability hunting, and attack vector suggestion [23]. PentestGPT, an LLM-powered tool, has shown significant improvements in task completion rates compared to traditional LLM approaches [13]. Similarly, PentestAgent leverages multi-agent collaboration and techniques like Retrieval Augmented Generation (RAG) to enhance penetration testing knowledge and automate intelligence gathering, vulnerability analysis, and exploitation stages [39]. While LLMs exhibit proficiency in specific sub-tasks and thanks to their capabilities in providing outputs in natural language, challenges remain in maintaining an integrated understanding of the overall testing scenario [13]. Despite these limitations, the integration of LLMs in penetration testing shows promise in reducing time and resource requirements while maintaining high standards of accuracy and thoroughness.

Considering the many advantages brought by the integration of LLMs, DTs, and penetration testing tools, these technologies can be leveraged in cybersecurity to enhance attack detection and response activities, including threat identification, as well as the analysis of information about potential vulnerabilities and malicious actors [20]. Therefore, in the field of cybersecurity education, DTs can support multiple stages of the learning process by providing realistic, hands-on environments in which learners can observe, experiment with, and respond to cyber threats, including conducting controlled penetration tests. When DTs are combined with LLMs, they can act as mentors capable of offering guidance by clarifying concepts. Thus, making the educational experience more interactive, personalized, and effective [31].

2.2 Cybersecurity Background and Related Concepts

This section explores some key cybersecurity concepts that represent the pillars of this research work, including the *Cyber Kill Chain*, the MITRE ATT&CK, and their relation with LLMs and DTs. The Cyber Kill Chain (CKC) is a widely adopted model that describes the sequential stages an attacker follows to execute cyber-attacks, providing cybersecurity professionals with a structured framework to understand adversary tactics and develop defensive strategies [46]. The traditional CKC consists of seven stages: (1) *Reconnaissance*, the attacker gathers information about the target to plan the attack; (2) *Weaponization*, malicious payloads are created to exploit the identified vulnerabilities; (3) *Delivery*, the attacker transmit the payload to the target environment; (4) *Exploitation*, malware code is executed on the target system, exploiting vulnerabilities to gain unauthorized access; (5) *Installation*, malware or other malicious components are installed on compromised systems; (6) *Command and Control (C2)*, the attacker establishes communication channels to control compromised systems and execute their plans; (7) *Actions on Objectives*, the final phase where the attacker achieves their ultimate goal, such as data theft, system control, or disruption [43]. The CKC has been widely used to strengthen cybersecurity defenses, especially when combined with advanced analytics and predictive techniques, allowing for proactive detection and disruption of attacks [43,47]. However, its linear structure can be limiting when addressing sophisticated or persistent threats, which has led to proposals for enhanced models capable of simultaneous analysis of multiple attack stages [29].

On the other hand, the MITRE ATT&CK[1] is a framework provides a detailed and dynamic representation of adversary behavior through a matrix of Tactics, Techniques, and Procedures (TTPs). It acts as a knowledge base and, unlike the CKC, it recognizes that attackers often act unpredictably, organizing actions into tactical objectives such as initial access, execution, privilege escalation, and lateral movement. Although highly granular and comprehensive, MITRE ATT&CK is more complex to apply directly in sequential training or simulation environments.

[1] https://attack.mitre.org/.

2.3 Red Team Knife

RTK[2] is a unified penetration test prototype for a variety of widely-used red teaming tools. The main goal of RTK is to make these tools accessible to both cybersecurity professionals and less-experienced users conducting security assessments. By bringing together multiple tools, RTK simplifies the execution of penetration tests, reduces complexity, and enables more systematic analyses. This approach allows users to evaluate the robustness of systems, identify vulnerabilities before they can be exploited by real attackers, and gain hands-on experience with realistic security scenarios. In addition, RTK serves also as an educational instrument, providing an environment for learning, practicing, and teaching penetration testing techniques in a safe and ethical way without harming end user. Despite the growing availability of penetration testing tools, there remains a gap in platforms that offer structured, comprehensive support for conducting full-spectrum security analyses. Many available solutions are either not yet mature or are limited to specific domains within cybersecurity [5].

3 Cyber Red Team Knife (CRTK) Framework

This research work proposes *Cyber Red Team Knife* (CRTK), which aims to provide a structured representation concerning the way in which learners can understand, analyze, and reason about cyber attacks by integrating four key components: (M1) DTs & Asset Modeling; (M2) CKC Mapped to DTs ActivitiesM (M3) Red Team Knife for Guided Penetration Testing; (M4) LLMs for Adaptive Guidance & Explainable Reasoning (Fig. 1). Its goal is to answer the research questions by clarifying how these technologies can collectively enhance learners' understanding of the technical, procedural, and cognitive dimensions of cyber attacks. Starting from the Nice Framework presented in [36], three additional key elements that contribute to the cyber security education through RTK are identified: (i) *Competencies* that provide a mechanism to assess learners performance; (ii) *Knowledge*, a retrievable set of concepts within memory; (iii) *Skill*, the capacity to perform an observable action. Considering these concepts, we present the four components of the framework in the following paragraphs, which are also illustrated in Fig. 1.

M1: Digital Twins and Asset Modeling. The methodological foundation of this work begins with the conceptual design of Cyber Digital Twins (CDTs) that model the essential asset categories relevant to cybersecurity education. The CDT is structured as a multi-layered representation of an operational environment, including IT networks, OT and IoT devices, web applications, databases, middleware components, and communication protocols. Rather than focusing on execution fidelity, the CDT is used as a conceptual scaffold for describing how vulnerabilities, attack surfaces, and system interdependencies are represented. The assets within the CDT are selected according to their pedagogical relevance

[2] https://github.com/Red-Team-Knife/red_team_knife.

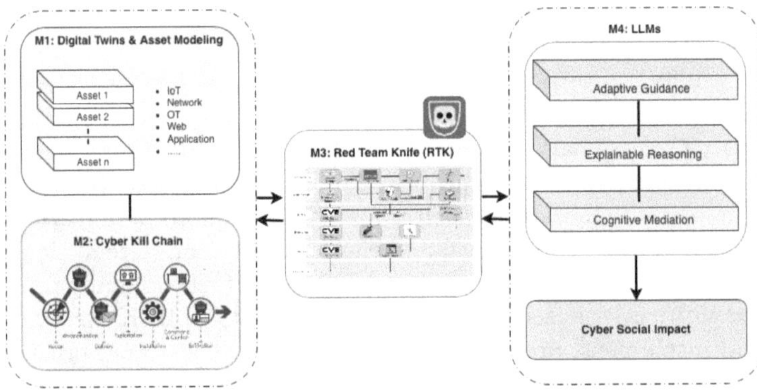

Fig. 1. CRTK Framework

for penetration testing and cyber-attack modeling. Each asset layer reflects a type of security domain, such as network, application, physical, wireless, and social engineering, which provides a comprehensive perspective on how adversarial behaviors may manifest across heterogeneous systems.

M2: Cyber Kill Chain Mapped to DTs Activities. The second component consists of aligning the CDT with the phases of the CKC. Each CKC phase, especially *Reconnaissance*, is associated with specific conceptual activities, asset interactions, and attacker intentions. This mapping provides a sequential and structured analytical framework through which cyber attacks can be described, decomposed, and reasoned about within the CDT, enabling learners to understand how an adversary progresses through the system. The DT simulates different asset classes and the CKC describes the temporal logic of attacker behavior. Therefore, the methodology supports the construction of a clear conceptual flow of an attack, while also highlighting the interdependencies between the different phases, the iterative nature of adversarial actions, and the emerging cyber-physical effects observable in the simulated environment.

M3: Red Team Knife. The third methodological component introduces RTK for guided penetration testing. It is the operational layer that structures penetration testing workflows in relation to both the DT and the CKC. RTK integrates common security tools into a unified interface capable of illustrating how different techniques correspond to different CKC stages. Within the architecture, RTK is not used for attack execution, but rather as a conceptual driver that bridges the attacker's procedural logic, the vulnerabilities modeled within the DT, and the interpretative capabilities of LLMs. The integration of RTK provides a mapping between tool outputs and the evolving attack path represented in the CDT. It also highlights the non-linear nature of penetration testing, where preliminary findings may require returning to earlier CKC phases or revisiting previously analyzed assets. In this sense, RTK supports a structured yet flexible workflow that can be explained, interpreted, and contextualized using the LLM-based reasoning layer.

M4: LLMs for Adaptive Guidance and Explainable Reasoning. This component focuses on the integration of LLMs as an intelligent, interpretive layer within the proposed architecture. LLMs serve three primary functions: *Adaptive Guidance*, providing step-by-step suggestions aligned with CKC phases, recommending tools, techniques, and reasoning paths based on RTK outputs and DT states; *Explainable Reasoning*, generating natural language interpretations of vulnerabilities, attack behaviors, anomalies, and system states, thereby making complex cyber-technical phenomena more accessible to learners; *Cognitive Mediation*, connecting technical findings with higher-level analytical constructs, such as adversarial intent, threat models, MITRE ATT&CK techniques, or socio-technical implications. By acting as a cognitive bridge between the DT simulation and the penetration testing workflow, the LLM enhances the pedagogical value of the architecture. Its contribution lies in transforming raw technical signals into articulated explanations and reasoning chains, enabling learners to understand not only what is happening in the attack, but why and how different phenomena are connected. Thus, the integration of LLMs adds an interpretive dimension that complements the technical modeling of the CDT and the operational structure of RTK, resulting in a comprehensive conceptual framework for cybersecurity education.

These four components contribute a multidimensional understanding of cyber attacks: structural (assets), procedural (kill chain progression), operational (penetration testing logic), and interpretative (LLM reasoning). This architecture provides a holistic conceptual model that can serve as the basis for educational activities, scenario analysis, and learner-driven exploration of adversarial behaviors. Table 1 shows an example of this approach and how the four components can be integrated to improve cybersecurity education: the Column "Output" reports the pieces of information revealed by the LLM that can be used in the educational context to indicate the aspects that can support practitioners in defense mechanisms.

4 CRTK in a Real-World Scenario

To validate and apply the previously discussed logical framework, the Smart City emerges as the most suitable context for exploring and outlining new multi-domain attack scenarios. This choice is consistent with ENISA's cybersecurity guidelines and with existing recommendations on DTs [17]. A Smart City encompasses four fundamental technological layers on which different assets can be replicated and cyber-attacks can be analyzed, while also considering risk assessment within the broader social context: (i) Network and infrastructure, (ii) Sensors, (iii) Service Delivery Platform, and (iv) Application and Services. The development of DT was based on Mininet[3] to create virtual networks of

[3] https://mininet.org/.

Table 1. Cyber Kill Chain Mapping (DT + RTK + LLM)

CKC Phase	Goal	Activity in DT	RTK	Output
Reconnaissance	Identify exposed assets and attack vectors.	Network analysis in the DT (web server, DB, simulated IoT device).	`nmap`, `RTK-recon`, `whois`, OSINT module	List of assets and potential vulnerabilities (RTK report).
Weaponization	Understand the exploit–payload lifecycle.	Creation of an exploit payload for a vulnerable CMS in the DT.	`msfvenom`, `RTK-payload`	Working payload (validated in a safe environment).
Delivery	Simulate the attack delivery phase.	Execution of phishing emails or exploit upload within the DT.	`sendphish.py`, `curl`, RTK-email module	Simulated email log or successfully uploaded file.
Exploitation	Execute the exploit and gain access.	Payload execution and verification of exploit success in the DT.	`RTK-exploit`, `metasploit`	Shell or active session simulated in the DT.
Installation	Implement persistence mechanisms.	Creation of a cron job, service, or (simulated) registry key.	`crontab`, `persistence.sh`	Evidence of active script (DT logging).
C2	Understand C2 traffic and detection.	Establish a simulated encrypted tunnel and detect it in the SIEM.	`RTK-C2`, `wireshark`, ELK dashboard	Alert in the DT SIEM + explanatory report.
Act on Objectives	Carry out final actions and defensive response.	Exfiltration or sabotage of dummy files.	`scp`, `zip`, `RTK-exfil`	Detection logs + drafted response plan.

critical infrastructures and on MiniCPS[4], which enables the modeling of cyber-physical processes. In addition, GRFICSv2[5] a framework designed to simulate industrial control systems (ICS)—has been integrated, with the goal of assessing the management of and response to cyber risks in critical environments. The architecture shows the topology of the network that this example is dealing with (see fig. 2). Several attacks have been identified at different levels, such as Man-in-the-Middle, Privilege Escalation, Denial of Service (DoS), unauthorized Interface, etc. For example, in a DoS attack, the Attacker node generates multiple HTTP requests to the server with the aim of saturating its resources (CPU, memory, bandwidth), thus making the service unavailable to legitimate users.

The RTK module, for example, during scanning in the reconnaissance phase and thanks to Nmap[6] (a free and open source utility for network discovery and security auditing), highlighted the presence of the SSH service open on port 22,

[4] https://github.com/scy-phy/minicps.
[5] https://github.com/Fortiphyd/GRFICSv2.
[6] https://nmap.org.

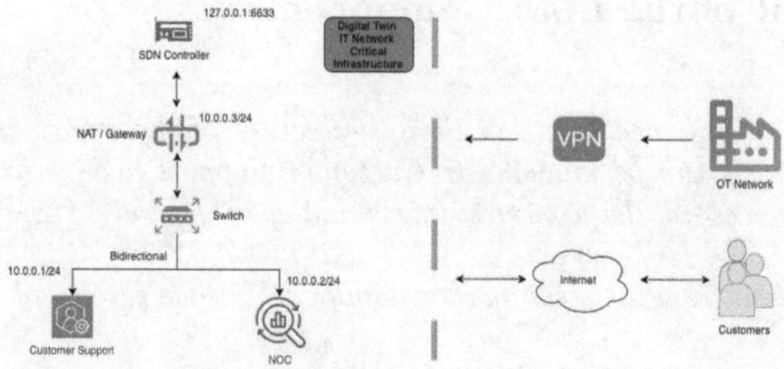

Fig. 2. Network Topology

which highlights an access point for the attacker. In addition, the LLM module enabled us not only to examine the severity score of software vulnerabilities, computed according to the Common Vulnerability Scoring System (CVSS[7]), but also to assess an additional information related to their potential social impact in the smart city. An example of the output generated by the LLM is provided in appendix A.

5 Conclusions

This paper explores the cybersecurity landscape and investigates how DTs and LLMs can enhance individuals' competencies in penetration testing. Thus, to respond to the RQ introduced at the beginning of the manuscript *How the conceptual integration of DTs, LLMs, and penetration testing tools can offer a new paradigm for analyzing the structure and progression of cyber attacks?*, we conclude that a framework that includes these technologies can represent promising groundwork for cybersecurity education: combining the conversational nature of LLMs with the advantages of DTs, learners could gain more insights concerning cybersecurity defense concepts and mechanisms. Although the framework is still in its development phase, we are currently planning user studies to assess its effectiveness and practical relevance in real-world scenarios.

Acknowledgements. This work was partially supported by the following projects: SERICS - "Security and Rights In the CyberSpace - SERICS" (PE00000014) under the MUR National Recovery and Resilience Plan funded by the European Union - NextGenerationEU. CYBER-PREDICT: Cyber vulnerability ranking prediction by prescription, Avviso "Reti—Sostegno alla ricerca collaborativa", - Codice Progetto DUQ VKW0; Patto territoriale "Sistema universitario pugliese"—CUP F61B23000 370006.

[7] https://www.first.org/cvss/.

A Output of the LLM Component

Based on the provided logs and the architecture of the smart city, the following analysis can be made: The Customer Support node, which provides critical services to the community, is under a Denial of Service (DoS) attack.
This is evident from the steadily increasing CPU usage percentage in the logs.

Main Risks and Vulnerabilities Involved:
- Denial of Service (DoS) - CAPEC-20: Amplification Reflector/Open Recursive Query (ORQ) DoS Attack.
This vulnerability allows an attacker to overwhelm a server with requests, causing a Denial of Service. Referencing CWE-400: Improper Input Validation, the attacker exploits this vulnerability by sending malformed or excessive data to the system. Base Score: 7 (high severity).
- Potential Impact: The Customer Support node becomes unresponsive or crashes, denying critical services to the community. Cross-sector effects can include disruption of other service delivery platforms and applications. - Mitigation Measures: Implement rate limiting, use defensive architectures like distributed denial of service (DDoS) protection services, and improve input validation practices.
- Resource Exhaustion - CAPEC-134: Consumption of a Critical Resource. This vulnerability arises when an attacker exhausts a critical resource, such as CPU or memory, leading to system failure.
Referencing CWE-200: Improper Resource Management, the attacker exploits this vulnerability by sending a high volume of requests that consume resources excessively. Base Score: 8 (critical severity).
- Potential Impact: The Customer Support node becomes unavailable, affecting the entire smart city environment. This can disrupt other service delivery platforms and applications, causing widespread inconvenience or even safety risks. - Mitigation Measures: Implement resource management practices, use load balancing to distribute traffic, and consider using virtualized resources to isolate and contain potential attacks.

In conclusion, the simulated cyber attack on the Customer Support node presents significant risks and vulnerabilities, including DoS and Resource Exhaustion. These issues can have severe impacts on the smart city environment and require immediate attention and mitigation measures.

References

1. A P, J., Shankar, A., J R, A.N., Koliparthy, K., Badiger, V.N., Shivakumar, V.: Exploring the applications and challenges of digital twins in various industries. In: 2024 IEEE 9th International Conference for Convergence in Technology (I2CT), pp. 1–7 (2024). https://doi.org/10.1109/I2CT61223.2024.10543818
2. Alqahtani, H., Kumar, G.: Large language models for effective detection of algorithmically generated domains: a comprehensive review. CMES - Comput. Model. Eng. Sci. **144**(2), 1439–1479 (2025). https://doi.org/10.32604/cmes.2025.067738, https://www.sciencedirect.com/science/article/pii/S1526149225002668
3. Atlam, H.F.: Llms in cyber security: bridging practice and education. Big Data Cogn. Comput. **9**(7) (2025). https://doi.org/10.3390/bdcc9070184, https://www.mdpi.com/2504-2289/9/7/184
4. Barletta, V.S., Caivano, D., Catalano, C., de Gemmis, M., Impedovo, D.: Cyber social security education. In: De Paolis, L.T., Arpaia, P., Sacco, M. (eds.) Extended Reality, pp. 240–248. Springer Nature Switzerland, Cham (2024)
5. Barletta, V.S., Caivano, D., Catalano, C., Gentile, A., Posa, D.P., Piccinno, A.: Cyber digital twin to improve security education: the redteam knife approach. In: Proceedings of the 16th Biannual Conference of the Italian SIGCHI Chapter. CHItaly '25, Association for Computing Machinery, New York, NY, USA (2025). https://doi.org/10.1145/3750069.3750102
6. Barletta, V.S., De Vincentiis, M., Buono, P., Pagano, A., Caivano, D.: Detecting attacks on in-vehicle networks through a mobile app, pp. 148–153 (2023). https://doi.org/10.1109/3ICT60104.2023.10391747, https://www.scopus.com/inward/record.uri?eid=2-s2.0-85184658966&doi=10.1109%2f3ICT60104.2023.10391747&partnerID=40&md5=1112cfc26cb9aeeb9836170d9a5bdb7d
7. Barricelli, B.R., Cotti, L., Fogli, D., Guizzardi, D., Pigoli, M.: A digital twin to enhance energy consumption awareness in a smart home (2024). https://doi.org/10.1145/3656650.3656708, https://www.scopus.com/inward/record.uri?eid=2-s2.0-85195424298&doi=10.1145%2f3656650.3656708&partnerID=40&md5=4ae35103d6e9d5cec047f1e8b2b0954c
8. Batra, L., Batra, S., Kathuria, V.: Leveraging Human-Centered AI Framework to Mitigate Security, Privacy, and Ethical Risks in AI Agents. In: Stephanidis, C., Antona, M., Ntoa, S., Salvendy, G. (eds.) HCI International 2025 Posters, vol. 2525, pp. 10–17. Springer Nature Switzerland, Cham (2025). https://doi.org/10.1007/978-3-031-94159-7_2, https://link.springer.com/10.1007/978-3-031-94159-7_2, series Title: Communications in Computer and Information Science
9. Biffl, S., Eckhart, M., Lüder, A., Weippl, E.: Introduction to Security and Quality Improvement in Complex Cyber-Physical Systems Engineering, pp. 1–29. Springer International Publishing, Cham (2019)
10. Bokkena, B.: Enhancing it security with LLM-powered predictive threat intelligence. In: 2024 5th International Conference on Smart Electronics and Communication (ICOSEC), pp. 751–756 (2024). https://doi.org/10.1109/ICOSEC61587.2024.10722712
11. Breve, B., Desolda, G., Greco, F., Deufemia, V.: Democratizing cybersecurity in smart environments: Investigating the mental models of novices and experts. LNCS (including subseries Lecture Notes in Artificial Intelligence and Lecture Notes in Bioinformatics) **13917 LNCS**, 145 – 161 (2023). https://doi.org/10.1007/978-3-031-34433-6_9

12. Carley, K.M., Cervone, G., Agarwal, N., Liu, H.: Social cyber-security. In: Thomson, R., Dancy, C., Hyder, A., Bisgin, H. (eds.) Social, Cultural, and Behavioral Modeling, pp. 389–394. Springer International Publishing, Cham (2018)
13. Deng, G., et al.: Pentestgpt: An LLM-empowered automatic penetration testing tool (2024). https://arxiv.org/abs/2308.06782
14. Desolda, G., Ferro, L.S., Marrella, A., Catarci, T., Costabile, M.F.: Human factors in phishing attacks: a systematic literature review. ACM Comput. Surv. **54**(8), 1–35 (Nov 2022). https://doi.org/10.1145/3469886
15. Dietz, M., Vielberth, M., Pernul, G.: Integrating digital twin security simulations in the security operations center. In: Proceedings of the 15th International Conference on Availability, Reliability and Security. ARES '20, Association for Computing Machinery, New York, NY, USA (2020)
16. El-Hajj, M.: Leveraging digital twins and intrusion detection systems for enhanced security in iot-based smart city infrastructures. Electronics **13**(19) (2024). https://doi.org/10.3390/electronics13193941
17. European Cyber Security Organisation (ECSO): Ecso technical paper on cybersecurity scenarios and digital twins. Tech. rep., European Cyber Security Organisation (ECSO) (May 2023). https://ecs-org.eu/ecso-uploads/2023/07/ECSO_WG6_DigitalTwin-2.1.pdf, version 1.0
18. Greco, F., Desolda, G., Buono, P., Piccinno, A.: Enhancing phishing defenses: The impact of timing and explanations in warnings for email clients. Comput. Standards Interfaces **93**, 103982 (2025). https://doi.org/10.1016/j.csi.2025.103982, https://www.sciencedirect.com/science/article/pii/S092054892500011X
19. Guo, J., Lv, Z.: Application of digital twins in multiple fields. Multimedi. Tools Appl. **81**(19), 26941–26967 (2022). https://doi.org/10.1007/s11042-022-12536-5, https://doi.org/10.1007/s11042-022-12536-5
20. Guven, M.: A comprehensive review of large language models in cyber security. Int. J. Comput. Exper. Sci. Eng. **10**(3) (Sep 2024). https://doi.org/10.22399/ijcesen.469
21. Habibzadeh, A., Feyzi, F., Atani, R.E.: Large language models for security operations centers: a comprehensive survey (2025). https://arxiv.org/abs/2509.10858
22. Hadar, E., Kravchenko, D., Basovskiy, A.: Cyber digital twin simulator for automatic gathering and prioritization of security controls' requirements. In: 2020 IEEE 28th International Requirements Engineering Conference (RE), pp. 250–259 (2020). https://doi.org/10.1109/RE48521.2020.00035
23. Hassanin, M., Moustafa, N.: A comprehensive overview of large language models (LLMs) for cyber defences: Opportunities and directions (2024). https://arxiv.org/abs/2405.14487
24. Holmes, D., Papathanasaki, M., Maglaras, L., Ferrag, M.A., Nepal, S., Janicke, H.: Digital twins and cyber security – solution or challenge? In: 2021 6th South-East Europe Design Automation, Computer Engineering, Computer Networks and Social Media Conference (SEEDA-CECNSM), pp. 1–8 (2021). https://doi.org/10.1109/SEEDA-CECNSM53056.2021.9566277
25. Joshi, R.P., Gulati, S., Kar, A.K.: Digital twin for industrial applications - a literature review. In: Sharma, S.K., Dwivedi, Y.K., Metri, B., Lal, B., Elbanna, A. (eds.) Transfer, Diffusion and Adoption of Next-Generation Digital Technologies, pp. 92–103. Springer Nature Switzerland, Cham (2024)

26. Karras, A., Theodorakopoulos, L., Karras, C., Theodoropoulou, A., Kalliampakou, I., Kalogeratos, G.: LLMs for cybersecurity in the big data era: A comprehensive review of applications, challenges, and future directions. Information **16**(11) (2025). https://doi.org/10.3390/info16110957, https://www.mdpi.com/2078-2489/16/11/957
27. Kävrestad, J., Fallatah, W., Furnell, S.: Cybersecurity training acceptance: a literature review. In: Furnell, S., Clarke, N. (eds.) Human Aspects of Information Security and Assurance, pp. 53–63. Springer Nature Switzerland, Cham (2023)
28. Kävrestad, J., Lindvall, D., Nohlberg, M.: Combating digital exclusion with cybersecurity training - an interview study with Swedish seniors. In: Furnell, S., Clarke, N. (eds.) Human Aspects of Information Security and Assurance, pp. 3–12. Springer Nature Switzerland, Cham (2023)
29. Khan, M.M.S., Giraldo, J.A., Parvania, M.: Real-time cyber-physical analysis of distribution systems using digital twins. In: 2022 IEEE International Conference on Communications, Control, and Computing Technologies for Smart Grids (SmartGridComm), pp. 34–39 (2022). https://api.semanticscholar.org/CorpusID:254153621
30. Latorre, L., Rego, E., De Leo, L., Gutierrez, M.: Tech report: Digital twins (2024). https://doi.org/10.18235/0013166
31. Lin, Y.Z., et al.: Transforming engineering education using generative ai and digital twin technologies (2024). https://arxiv.org/abs/2411.14433
32. Luzzi, J., Naha, R., Arulappan, A., Mahanti, A.: SOK: a holistic view of cyberattacks prediction with digital twins. In: 2024 Second International Conference on Emerging Trends in Information Technology and Engineering (ICETITE), pp. 1–7 (2024). https://doi.org/10.1109/ic-ETITE58242.2024.10493514
33. McLaughlin, K.L.: The power of digital twins in the cybersecurity mesh. EDPACS **68**(6), 35–39 (2023). https://doi.org/10.1080/07366981.2023.2263214
34. Meng, Y., Tang, L., Yu, F., Li, X., Yan, G., Yang, P., Xi, Z.: Benchmarking LLM-assisted blue teaming via standardized threat hunting (2025). https://arxiv.org/abs/2509.23571
35. Mulahuwaish, A., et al.: A survey of social cybersecurity: Techniques for attack detection, evaluations, challenges, and future prospects. Comput. Human Behav. Reports **18**, 100668 (2025). https://doi.org/10.1016/j.chbr.2025.100668, https://www.sciencedirect.com/science/article/pii/S2451958825000831
36. Petersen, R., Santos, D., Smith, M.C., Wetzel, K.A., Witte, G.: Workforce framework for cybersecurity (nice framework). NIST Special Publication 800-181r1, National Institute of Standards and Technology (NIST) (2020). https://doi.org/10.6028/NIST.SP.800-181r1, https://nvlpubs.nist.gov/nistpubs/SpecialPublications/NIST.SP.800-181r1.pdf
37. Sasikala, M., Mahaboob John, Y.M., Jothi, B., S, N., S, S.K.: Integrating digital twins with ai for real-time intrusion detection in smart infrastructure networks. In: 2024 International Conference on Intelligent Algorithms for Computational Intelligence Systems (IACIS), pp. 1–6 (2024). https://doi.org/10.1109/IACIS61494.2024.10721892
38. Sharshar, M., Saber, A.M., Svetinovic, D., Youssef, A.M., Kundur, D., El-Saadany, E.F.: Large language model-based framework for explainable cyberattack detection in automatic generation control systems (2025). https://arxiv.org/abs/2507.22239
39. Shen, X., et al.: Pentestagent: Incorporating LLM agents to automated penetration testing (2025). https://arxiv.org/abs/2411.05185

40. Siang, L.Y., Selvarajah, V.: Security assurance through penetration testing. In: 2022 IEEE 2nd International Conference on Mobile Networks and Wireless Communications (ICMNWC), pp. 1–5 (2022). https://doi.org/10.1109/ICMNWC56175.2022.10031663
41. Singh, R., et al.: LLMs in the soc: An empirical study of human-AI collaboration in security operations centres (2025). https://arxiv.org/abs/2508.18947
42. Somma, A., Casola, V., Cavalli, A.R., De Benedictis, A., Mallouli, W., Valdés, V.E.: A cyber digital twin framework to support cyber-physical systems security. In: 2023 IEEE Smart World Congress (SWC), pp. 1–10 (2023). https://doi.org/10.1109/SWC57546.2023.10449161
43. Tarnowski, I.: How to use cyber kill chain model to build cybersecurity? Europ. J. High. Educ. IT (2017)
44. Vajpayee, P., Raheem, T., Hossain, G.: Human centered AI and cybersecurity: an innovative approach to manage cyber risk in transportation 5.0. In: 2025 IEEE International Conference on Electro Information Technology (eIT), pp. 613–617. IEEE, Valparaiso, IN, USA (May 2025). https://doi.org/10.1109/eIT64391.2025.11103619, https://ieeexplore.ieee.org/document/11103619/
45. Varghese, S.A., Dehlaghi Ghadim, A., Balador, A., Alimadadi, Z., Papadimitratos, P.: Digital twin-based intrusion detection for industrial control systems. In: 2022 IEEE International Conference on Pervasive Computing and Communications Workshops and other Affiliated Events (PerCom Workshops), pp. 611–617. IEEE (Mar 2022). https://doi.org/10.1109/percomworkshops53856.2022.9767492
46. Yadav, T., Rao, A.M.: Technical aspects of cyber kill chain. In: Abawajy, J.H., Mukherjea, S., Thampi, S.M., Ruiz-Martínez, A. (eds.) Security in Computing and Communications, pp. 438–452. Springer International Publishing, Cham (2015)
47. Yadav, T.K., Rao, A.M.: Technical aspects of cyber kill chain. ArXiv **abs/1606.03184** (2015)
48. Zhai, J., Li, Z., Miao, H., Li, Z., Zhou, X., Yang, H.: Automatic generation of cybersecurity teaching cases using large language models. Computer Applications in Engineering Education **33**(5), e70081 (Sep 2025). https://doi.org/10.1002/cae.70081, https://onlinelibrary.wiley.com/doi/10.1002/cae.70081

Simulator-Based Distraction Analysis Procedure for User Testing of In-Vehicle Interfaces

Róbert Junas and Miroslav Laco(✉)

Faculty of Informatics and Information Technologies, Slovak University of Technology, Ilkovičova 2, 842 16 Karlova Ves, Bratislava, Slovakia
miroslav.laco@gmail.com
https://vgg.fiit.stuba.sk

Abstract. The usability of In-Vehicle Information Systems (IVIS) should be evaluated thoroughly, along with the level of distraction they cause when used while driving. User testing studies focused on evaluating these types of interfaces should include distraction analysis procedures to provide insights into the distraction patterns they elicit during interaction. Analysis and evaluation of driver distraction related to in-vehicle user interfaces without specialised equipment, laboratory design, or complex procedures is a significant challenge for simple research laboratories nowadays. We propose a lightweight eye-tracking setup and procedure to equip simple simulator-based driving environment laboratories with the capability to evaluate driver distraction caused by in-vehicle user interfaces effectively. We present a simplex setup for driving simulator laboratories, two distraction metrics for analysing attentional demand causing distraction patterns (Time Away from the Primary Task – TA-PT; Time on the Secondary Task – TO-ST), and two complementary visualisation techniques (heatmap and scanpath overlay) for interpreting distraction patterns over time and across the examined user interface. Our proposed setup was implemented in a minimalist laboratory with a simulator-based driving environment to validate the proof-of-concept and demonstrate its feasibility. We adopted the proposed distraction analysis procedure in the laboratory during a user testing case study with five participants to evaluate distraction patterns associated with three types of IVIS controls. The presented results indicate that the proposed approach may reveal meaningful distraction patterns and differentiate between various design variants in the means of distraction produced while remaining practical for laboratories with limited budgets.

Keywords: Distraction Analysis · In-Vehicle User Interfaces · Driving Simulator · User Testing · Eye-Tracking · User Experience

1 Introduction

Complex digital systems, including various *In-Vehicle Information Systems* (IVIS) user interfaces designed for drivers, are a negligible part of modern vehi-

Published by Springer Nature Switzerland AG 2026
C. Maciel et al. (Eds.): INTERACT 2025 Workshops, LNCS 16478, pp. 217–234, 2026.
https://doi.org/10.1007/978-3-032-22934-2_18

cles nowadays [31]. In-Vehicle Information Systems often allow drivers to perform tasks unrelated to driving itself. These include navigation, browsing music, or even using simplified versions of popular messaging applications [31]. While IVIS interfaces enhance the driver's experience, they may also cause distractions and pose safety risks. According to the NHTSA study conducted between 2017 and 2021, around 8% of all fatal crashes could be attributed to distracted driving (3000 in total) [26]. The most frequently observed distractors are cell phones, IVIS interfaces, and navigation systems [8]. According to the latest research on IVIS design [8], most of these systems cause significant distraction of the driver and some of their features should be completely disabled while driving. In contrast, we observe an emerging trend of expansion in IVIS features introduced with each new vehicle model [31]. Moreover, disabling such features of the IVIS could lead to even more distractive use via third-party smartphone or tablet interfaces. Hence, research in the field should focus on carefully analysing the IVIS interfaces to provide the driver with the features in a usable and safe form.

Distraction analysis is a non-negligible part of the in-vehicle interface user testing in the automotive industry [1]. Many existing research studies focus their user testing sessions on evaluating the specific distraction patterns caused by a particular in-vehicle interface proposal [5,7,11,15,16]. However, the testing environment, distraction measurement and analysis procedures, and evaluation methodology differ across workplaces, depending greatly on the workplace budget [7,17,21,23]. We aim to introduce a lightweight, generally applicable, and affordable method for analysing driver distraction arising from the use of in-vehicle user interfaces while driving. The proposed method consists of the environment setup and the procedure proposal. The proposal should serve as a plug-and-play extension of standard user testing for in-vehicle user interfaces, even in a minimalist simulator-based driving environment.

2 Related Work

Numerous state-of-the-art research presents user testing case studies of in-vehicle interfaces, focusing also on the distraction they produce while interacting with them [5,7,11,16,19–23,27]. Research in the field adapts two approaches to the evaluation of the IVIS interfaces: those presenting real-world field studies and those using simulator-based approach to induce the driving experience. Both methods have certain advantages and limitations worth mentioning.

Real-world field studies are held in a real vehicle and situated in real traffic or in a constrained real driving environment (e.g. a racing track) [7,19,23]. Many field studies use eye-tracking techniques and various measurement and evaluation procedures to examine drivers' visual behaviour while interacting with in-vehicle user interfaces. The interior of the vehicle is often modified to meet the goals of the usability study, making field studies a costly research approach. Field studies reflect real-world drivers' behaviour while performing tasks, but have certain limitations related to safety considerations for dangerous driving scenarios or for completely novel design concepts.

Simulator-based studies offer the possibility to conduct more precise behavioural analysis as part of the user testing sessions in a large scale of driving scenarios, including critical situations [5,11,20–22]. Simulator-based laboratories for user testing of the in-vehicle user interfaces vary greatly in the complexity of the simulation environment and the level of driver immersion. Nowadays, minimalist simulators feature a widescreen display that renders the entire driving environment, vehicle controls communicating with the driving simulation, and the physical elements of the cockpit, which are subject to user testing (Secondary screens, interaction devices, etc.) [21,22]. More complex driving simulators use multiple screens to render the environment for greater immersion. Participants may also be seated in a replica of the vehicle cockpit, including physical elements from the real vehicle (car seat, steering wheel, transmission controls), to make the driving experience more realistic [5,11,20]. Moreover, some driving simulator laboratories use mixed reality technologies to immerse participants in simulated driving sessions [16,27]. Such complex simulator-based studies seem to be an effective alternative to field studies for in-vehicle system user testing, as current state-of-the-art research does not indicate significant differences in the effectiveness of the obtained results from user testing sessions between the two approaches [4]. Bolder et al. [4] proposed a mixed-reality simulator-based user testing environment to compare the Time-to-completion task metric across various IVIS interaction tasks with real driving. The validation of their proposal was conducted as task-based user testing, using the same procedures in both environments. Their results show that the Time-to-completion task metric was invariant across environments, but the simulator's display quality was the main issue reported.

The approach to procedure selection for evaluating human-machine interactions (HMI) within a vehicle notably shapes the inputs for discussions of the usability of in-vehicle interfaces. Naujoks et al. [25] proposed a methodological framework for evaluating human-machine interactions (HMI) with automated driving systems (ADS). One of their methodological contributions to the state-of-the-art is the empirical evaluation of the interface with participants from diverse age groups and with comparable knowledge of ADS. The authors recommended allocating user testing sessions in a driving simulator with realistic controls to increase participants' engagement. Different approach to the HMI evaluation can be found in Crescenti et al. [7]. Authors propose using the **eye-tracking technique** to measure and evaluate visual scanning patterns related to IVIS interfaces to objectify the behavioural analysis. To showcase the proposed evaluation methodology, they proposed a field study with different vehicle types in a constrained environment of a racing track. First phase of the field study was proposed to be the training phase to ensure a comparable level of prior knowledge among participants. The second phase was proposed as the testing phase, during which participants completed 14 tasks, each repeated 3 times. The proposed evaluation method was based on different gaze and fixation metrics within the infotainment system. Authors found their approach to be effective with similar distraction patterns found for 10 different vehicle types.

Usability of IVIS interfaces was also studied by Nagy et al. [23]. The authors investigated the driver's behaviour, cognitive load, and level of distraction while using the touch-based IVIS compared to physical buttons. They used psychological tests, questionnaires, eye-tracking techniques, and pupillometry to support their evaluation. They conducted a field study with a real vehicle on a racing track. Participants were given tasks within the IVIS interface while driving at different speeds. Results showed that using a touch-based IVIS was slower and more cognitively demanding than using physical buttons. Moreover, they found that the faster the vehicle moved, the shorter the task completion time was when using touch-based IVIS controls. Similarly to the previous studies, the eye-tracking technique was used in a study by Jung S. [15]. The authors measured the effect of the button design (shape, colour) on the effectiveness of the interaction with the IVIS system. The authors proposed using eye-tracking data, complemented by cognitive load metrics, to evaluate the effect under study. The authors conclude that the button design does not significantly affect the number of glances at the infotainment system.

Informed, data-driven user interface design decisions, supported by both qualitative and quantitative data from user testing sessions, may enable advanced in-vehicle system evaluation approaches. There is a space to unlock the potential of methods such as triangulation described by Pettersson et al. [28]. The triangulation method can help discuss results from user testing studies with a stronger data-driven background. There is ongoing research to incorporate a **data-driven approach** into the evaluation of IVIS user testing studies to assess drivers' distraction patterns [9,10]. The discussed data-driven approach to usability evaluation of IVIS interfaces was proven to be useful in terms of behavioural data measurements and behavioural analysis, including glance measurements using the eye-tracking technique. Further research in the field may include proposals for advanced procedures for visual pattern analysis, in the form of distraction metrics and visualisations, to support the data-driven pillar of the usability study reports. Apart from improving the IVIS interfaces for driver interactions, there are IVIS proposals which are focused on driver-passenger collaboration, thus minimising drivers' distraction for non-critical secondary tasks while driving [2,3]. These future interfaces seem promising. However, we aim our research proposal at the current majority of driver-oriented IVIS interfaces.

To sum up the state-of-the-art in the field, we observe numerous studies and research that present ongoing efforts to evaluate the usability of IVIS interfaces and analyse drivers' distraction caused by them using data-driven methods. In parallel, we see a wide variety of proposed strategies for distraction analysis tailored for the particular workplace or designed for the specific IVIS interface evaluation. These methods for distraction analysis are not suitable for many simplistic simulator-based driving environment laboratories due to high costs or a lack of highly qualified personnel. Therefore, an effort to propose a lightweight setup and procedure for measuring and analysing driver distraction caused by in-vehicle interfaces, as an extension of standard simulator-based user testing studies, could open new possibilities for research teams operating in simpler laboratory environments. Moreover, using a straightforward, easily applicable distraction evaluation procedure across the research community could make case studies more comparable in the future.

3 Distraction Analysis Setup and Procedure

The main contribution is the proposal of a lightweight setup and procedure for distraction evaluation that extends the minimal simulator-based user testing environment of in-vehicle interfaces. Our proposed method aims to quantitatively and qualitatively evaluate the distraction patterns observed in drivers caused by in-vehicle interfaces while driving [5,11,20–22]. However, beyond the previously mentioned studies, we focus our proposal on a minimal setup for a constraint laboratory environment with limited budget, emphasising ease of adoption within existing user testing studies. For the formal distraction evaluation, we assume that driving is the driver's **primary task** and that interaction with the IVIS is a **secondary task** [1,25]. The setup and procedure proposal consists of a description of the environment setup, proposal of two distraction analysis metrics, two complementary visualisation techniques, and the corresponding procedure to evaluate the distraction impact of in-vehicle interfaces on the driver.

3.1 Methods

Our distraction evaluation procedure is built on top of the simulator-based task-oriented user testing methodology, as seen in numerous studies analysed in Sect. 2 focused on the usability evaluation of in-vehicle interfaces [4,5,11,20]. We propose adopting a task-based user testing approach with a facilitator present during the user testing session for our procedure. By the task-based user testing approach, we understand a procedure where participants are asked to complete a set of tasks while driving – often with a secondary task present (requiring interaction with the IVIS) while performing the primary task (driving). The task is considered successfully finished if the completion criteria are met, either by reaching a particular state within the system or by the participant explicitly declaring the task completed.

In addition to the task-based context, the vehicle simulator should allow the user to drive freely within the simulated environment. Participants' visual attention is proposed to be captured using a non-invasive eye-tracking approach—wearable eye-tracking glasses—with a standardised calibration procedure recommended by the eye-tracker manufacturer. It is important to allow free head movement while wearing the eye-tracking glasses to capture the gaze data with the required accuracy (see [29]). Furthermore, it is essential to define the areas of interest (AoIs) representing the driver's primary and secondary tasks within the simulator. For the distraction evaluation, we propose complementing the two metrics (Sect. 3.3) with two commonly used visualisation techniques—Heatmap and Scanpath visualisation overlays – to support qualitative understanding of the captured gaze data.

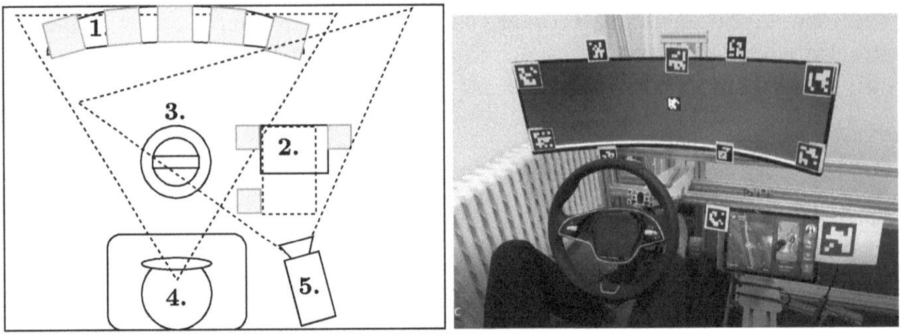

(a) Top-view schema of the setup. (b) Capture of the setup.

Fig. 1. (a) Top-view schematic representation of the proposed simulator environment setup, including the main components and marker positions to reference the data captures later on. (b) Caption of the environment setup implementation from the case study on the proof-of-concept feasibility of the proposed distraction analysis procedure.

3.2 Environment

The environment setup proposal for our distraction analysis procedure is schematically depicted in Fig. 1a. The simulator driving environment is proposed to contain the following minimal **components**:

1. Primary screen rendering the driving simulation environment (does not contain IVIS controls)
2. Secondary screen of the IVIS interface with corresponding controls
3. Vehicle controls (steering wheel, pedal controls)
4. Participant wearing eye-tracking glasses to capture the gaze
5. Static wide-angle high-resolution camera capturing the simulation environment

Dotted lines represent approximate view spans and their interlacing from both the eye-tracking and static camera video captures for the latter computational processing.

The **interaction** within the minimal setup components is designed as follows: The participant (4) interacts with the driving simulator using vehicle controls (3) involved. During the testing session, participants wear the eye-tracking glasses to collect gaze data for further evaluation of the distraction patterns. The driving environment is rendered on the Primary screen (1) and responds to participants' real-time commands via the vehicle controls. The interactive prototype of the IVIS interface is displayed on the secondary screen (2) throughout the simulation. A static wide-angle high-resolution camera captures the entire simulation environment for precise distraction analysis held after the user testing sessions. Recordings from both the screens and camera views are captured alongside the synchronisation timestamps during the testing session.

Calibration of the recording devices follows a predefined order for synchronisation purposes. Firstly, we calibrate the eye-tracking device. Afterwards, we start capturing the data from the static camera. Lastly, we start capturing the data using the eye-tracking device. We stop the capturing in the reverse order. The eye-tracker last-on and last-off rule establishes a synchronisation mechanism between devices to align recording timestamps during post-processing. However, the recordings can also be synchronised manually during post-processing for fine-tuning the capture alignment later. Before the participant performs the first task, we display a one-time calibration marker on the screen to improve synchronisation during the post-processing procedure (more on markers in the following paragraph).

Following the data collection phase, we propose the **post-processing procedure** with the captured data. We used automated video processing and computer vision methods to remap participant gaze data from the eye-tracker camera view to the static camera view, enabling more precise analysis from the static perspective rather than from the dynamic egocentric video captured by the eye-tracker device. We used the AruCo marker-based homography method as a stable, simple-to-implement solution, consistent with several state-of-the-art studies [7,23]. The AruCo markers have been shown to perform well at approximating the homography matrix between the two cameras when the reference changes over time, even when the eye-tracker camera is not sufficient to capture the entire scene [6]. The markers should be placed at the corners and on the side of the Primary and Secondary screens (Fig. 1a) in a way that is visible from the eye-tracking camera point of view while the participant is facing towards the Primary screen (driving simulation). The size of the markers may vary depending on the laboratory conditions in which the setup is used. The participant's distance from the Primary screen is an important factor to consider.

Remapping the captured gaze data into the static camera perspective allows us to remap the gaze further into the plane of the Primary screen for the analysis of visual attention over the driving simulation, or into the IVIS plane to precisely analyse distraction patterns produced by the interface (visualisation in Fig. 1a). A capture of the sample environment setup is shown in Fig. 1b.

3.3 Metrics

We propose to use two eye-tracking-based distraction metrics **Time Away from the Primary Task (TA-PT)** (Eq. 1) and **Time on the Secondary Task (TO-ST)** (Eq. 2) to analyse distraction produced by the in-vehicle interfaces on the driver. These metrics are defined as follows.

- **Time Away from the Primary Task (TA-PT)** - defined as a timespan of the participant's fixations away from the Primary screen (driving simulation) while performing the task, given by equation:

$$T_m = T - \sum_{i=0}^{n} t_i \tag{1}$$

where T is total time on the task, t_i is duration of ith fixation in array $t = (t_0, t_1, t_2, ...t_n)$ which holds durations of all fixations intersecting AOI which represents the Primary screen and $t \subseteq t_a$, where t_a represents all fixation durations while performing the task.

- **Time on the Secondary Task (TO-ST)** - defined as a timespan of the participant's fixations on the Secondary screen (IVIS) while performing the task, given by equation:

$$T_s = \sum_{i=0}^{n} t_i \tag{2}$$

where t_i is the duration of ith fixation in an array $t = (t_0, t_1, t_2, ...t_n)$ which holds durations of all fixations on Secondary screen (IVIS) and $t \subseteq t_a$, where t_a represents all fixation durations while performing the task.

We propose complementing eye-tracking-based distraction analysis metrics with a widely used task performance metric [12]—**Time on a task (TOT)**—to accurately capture the time component of task performance for further evaluation alongside distraction metrics.

- **Time on a task (TOT)** - defined as a timespan needed to complete the task, given by the difference between the task end and start timestamps.

Both the distraction metric results and the complementary task performance metric are proposed for evaluation in the post-processing phase of our distraction analysis procedure.

4 Case Study

We propose a preliminary validation of our proposed setup and procedure to examine its feasibility and ease of integration with existing user testing approaches in a case study according to the previous research and best research practice in the field [24,33]. We applied our proposed setup and procedure in a case study for simulator-based user testing of three types of IVIS interaction controls to validate the feasibility of our proposal and to present an early proof-of-concept. The case study was an extension to the standard simulator-based user testing procedure with 5 participants in a minimalist driving simulator laboratory (Fig. 1b). The core driving simulation experience of the chosen laboratory is driven by a replica of the standard driver's cockpit with a modular interior, which can integrate interchangeable physical and digital cockpit elements for research purposes.

Participants of the user testing were regular drivers aged 18–25, without any reported visual impairments. We used Tobii Pro Glasses 2 with a 1-point calibration procedure, maintaining gaze precision below 1° of visual angle, as recommended by the manufacturer [32], to capture participants' gaze.

The user testing procedure was designed as a task-based facilitated session with a total of 5 tasks to complete in a pre-defined order (Fig. 2). The tasks were designed to motivate participants to solve a secondary task while the primary task was already being performed. Standard, non-dangerous driving situations were chosen to start each task. Tasks have a correct solution path that the participant must follow to report the task as completed successfully.

The goal of the user testing scenario was to provide an insight into the level of distraction related to three various interaction methods with the IVIS interface: using touch-based control (Tasks 1, 2), hardware control knob attached vertically under the Secondary screen (Tasks 3, 4), and hardware control knob attached perpendicularly under the Secondary screen (Task 5). The IVIS prototype created for the experiment was designed to mimic the appearance of a well-known IVIS graphical user interface, CarPlay[1] [31]. At the beginning of the testing session, participants were allowed to drive freely to become accustomed to the vehicle controls and simulation behaviour, and to make themselves familiar with the IVIS user interface.

The IVIS prototype supported two common user scenarios with IVIS to showcase distraction patterns related to two common interactions of the driver with the IVIS interface:

1. User Scenario 1 (US1) Call and hang up a contact in the driver's favourite contacts (Task 1, 3, 5),
2. User Scenario 2 (US2) Switch to the next song and mark it as your favourite (Task 2, 4).

After completing the tasks, participants were asked to complete the short version of the NASA Task Load Index questionnaire [13] to obtain insight into their self-reported cognitive load associated with the IVIS interaction controls. The NASA TLX results can reveal specific distraction phenomena during the testing session, according to previous research [23,30]. We aim to discuss the drivers' distraction evidence based on self-reported methods, accompanied by the most commonly used user testing metrics (TOT, Success rate) [18], and to present the distraction evidence captured by our proposed metrics and complementary visualisation techniques.

Our goal is to discuss the added value of the distraction analysis provided by our proposed approach compared to standard user-testing methods available in simplex laboratories. Moreover, we hypothesise that objective measures based on gaze interactions and time to complete tasks might perform better at identifying task complexity and overall driver distraction than subjective self-reported measures, which might be prone to change in cognitive processes during tasks or to misremembering experiences afterwards.

[1] CarPlay Documentation. Available online on October 26, 2025, at: https://developer.apple.com/documentation/CarPlay.

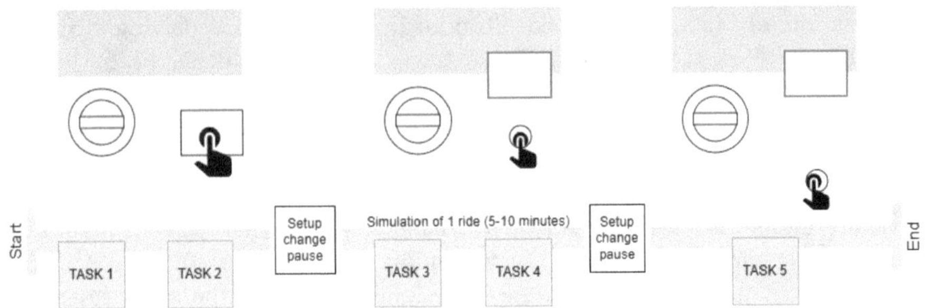

Fig. 2. Schematic view of the script for the user testing session involving three types of IVIS interaction controls in a driving simulator. The proposed setup and procedure for distraction analysis were applied during user testing as a case study to validate the feasibility and proof-of-concept of our proposal. The schema depicts the tasks for three types of IVIS controls in the following order: touch-based control, parallel hardware knob, perpendicular hardware knob.

5 Results and Discussion

We provide an overview on the **distraction metric results** captured during the proof-of-concept validation case study in Table 1. We identified certain specific findings from the distraction metric analysis worth further discussion.

5.1 Metrics

Firstly, we observed that participants focused their visual attention on the Secondary screen for more than 20% of the total Time on the Secondary Task (TO-ST). This portion of time spent focusing attention elsewhere than on the primary task itself (driving) denotes a high level of distraction produced by the IVIS controls and may be considered a distraction issue. However, we are not able to hypothesise about the cause of the distraction because the observed results may be also related to low immersion of the participants in the primary task (driving) and to low stakes associated with the simulated driving, not the disruptive IVIS interface itself. However, the identified distraction phenomenon may serve as a good starting point for further qualitative evaluation of distraction patterns and possible design improvements to the IVIS controls.

Secondly, we noticed that participants who used the parallel-oriented IVIS control knob shifted their attention towards the Secondary screen less often (18% of total attention shifts were targeting the Secondary screen) than those using the touch-based interaction (23% of total attention shifts were targeting the Secondary screen). On the other hand, they spent around the same amount of Time Away from the Primary Task (TA-PT). This observed phenomenon may be subject to the low intuitiveness of the IVIS control mechanism, which can be further improved.

By analysing distraction patterns beyond the proposed metrics, we identified that the shift of visual attention away from the primary task occurred in the

Table 1. Results of the two distraction metrics (TA-PT, TO-ST) and one commonly used user testing metric (TOT) from the proof-of-concept case study on feasibility of our proposed distraction analysis procedure across five participants of the user testing. Participants were performing 5 tasks while using three different IVIS controls (Task 1, 2 - touch-based; Task 3, 4 - vertical hardware know; Task 5 - perpendicular hardware knob). Values are reported as "Mean (Standard deviation)" in seconds; bold is best. **TA-PT** - Time Away from the Primary task, **TO-ST** - Time on the Secondary Task, **TOT** - Time on Task in total.

	Task 1	Task 2	Task 3	Task 4	Task 5
TA-PT	**5.25** (2.62)	8.61 (3.65)	7.83 (2.78)	6.02 (3.34)	9.02 (3.94)
TO-ST	4.03 (2.61)	5.62 (3.75)	4.09 (3.04)	**2.97** (2.53)	4.55 (2.81)
TOT	**16.65** (3.54)	25.10 (9.30)	23.02 (5.96)	17.84 (4.65)	23.39 (6.72)

majority within 2 s of task onset across all tasks and participants of the case study (56% of all cases). We hypothesise that the 2-second reaction time reflects an immediate response to the motivation to solve the secondary task within the IVIS interface. Assuming the participants were already familiar with the well-known copy of the IVIS user interface (CarPlay) after the free driving session, the IVIS user interface does not seem memorable or intuitive enough to start solving the task without an immediate shift of attention from the Primary screen. Moreover, the lack of haptic feedback from touch-based or knob-based IVIS controls may also be a partial cause of the distraction pattern.

5.2 Visualisation Techniques

The analysis of distraction metric results was complemented by qualitative analysis of user testing sessions using the two proposed **visualisation techniques for distraction analysis**. Figure 3 provides a visualisation using fixation Heatmap and Scanpath overlays on a representative frame captured during user testing with two participants performing Task 1. Both participants' visual focus was split between the Primary screen and the Secondary screen (IVIS), enabling the primary task (driving) while struggling to complete the given task with unchanged attention focus. A notable number of visual attention shifts (glances) towards the Secondary screen (IVIS) exhibit shorter fixation durations. This could be due to a natural tendency to return attention from the Secondary screen to the Primary screen as soon as possible. The Scanpath visualisation demonstrates that the majority of the participants' fixations were pointing at the Secondary screen while solving Task 1. The distraction patterns caused by performing the secondary task and interacting with the IVIS are visible and point towards the usefulness of the visualisation techniques for further distraction analysis. For more ambitious research goals, either a more detailed temporal analysis of the captured data using the proposed visualisation techniques or a detailed distribution of fixations over specific elements of the IVIS user interface could be performed using the captured and post-processed data from the case study.

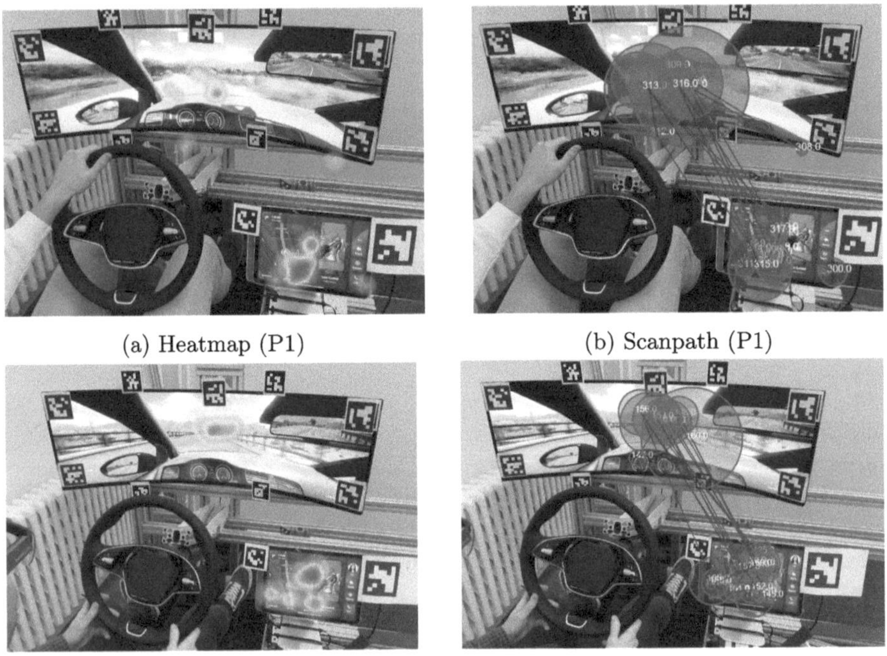

(a) Heatmap (P1) (b) Scanpath (P1)

(c) Heatmap (P2) (d) Scanpath (P2)

Fig. 3. Aggregated Heatmap (a, c) and Scanpath (b, d) overlay visualisations of the fixations of two participants (P1, P2) while performing Task 1. It is possible to observe frequent attention shifts towards the Secondary screen (IVIS) with shorter fixation durations (fixation duration mapped to the fixation point diameter) in the Scanpath visualisation overlay (b, d). We can identify the most frequently fixated areas of the IVIS interface (red, yellow, green, and blue, in order of descending visual attractivity) in the Heatmap visualisation overlay (a, c).

5.3 Traditional Approaches

Alongside the distraction analysis data captured by our proposed procedure, we analysed the commonly used Task success rate metric for each task across all participants [18], as well as the results of the widely used subjective self-assessment NASA Task Load Index questionnaire (NASA TLX; short form) [14]. Regarding the Task success rate, each participant completed all the tasks without any help from the facilitator, resulting in a 100% task success rate.

Self-reported NASA TLX results for all three tested types of IVIS controls mainly fell within the Low (1–7) to Medium (8–14) cognitive load range for each of the questionnaire categories, except for one participant who reported High

(15–21) cognitive load for most tasks (see Table 2). From the results, participants reported a wide range of different cognitive load scores for a particular task, from non-demanding to very demanding. Moreover, we encountered a limitation of the NASA-TLX self-reported evaluation: participants were often unable to recall their cognitive demands because the questionnaire is typically administered after completing the tasks, potentially leading to misremembered experiences.

Table 2. Detailed NASA TLX results reported by the participants of the case study. The rows represent each participant, while the columns represent each metric measured by the cognitive load index. The table also provides the average reported value (Mean) and the standard deviation (Std). The colours match the three cognitive load groups: Low (1–7), Medium (8–14), and High (15–21).

Part.	**Mental**	**Physical**	**Temporal**	**Perf.**	**Effort**	**Frustr.**
P1	4	5	1	4	5	7
P2	9	2	6	5	11	3
P3	4	4	12	3	14	14
P4	16	13	20	18	17	19
P5	16	11	8	11	10	5
Mean	9,8	7	9,4	8,2	11,4	9,6
STD	5,38	4,24	6,37	5,64	4,03	5,99

We assume that both the Task success rate metric and the self-reported NASA TLX scores have limited added value for evaluating and comparing the distraction patterns caused by interaction with IVIS while driving. Standard usability evaluation methods may therefore provide limited value for a thorough distraction evaluation of the IVIS interaction methods tested in similar user testing case studies. Therefore, we assume that supporting the distraction evaluation with the proposed data-driven approach [9,28] using distraction metrics and visualisation techniques could be beneficial for the user testing studies of the in-vehicle user interfaces in a simulator-based driving environment.

To conclude, we assume our proposed user testing procedure and setup to be feasible for the distraction analysis in a simple driving simulation laboratory based on the presented case study results and the corresponding discussion enabled by the outcomes of the distraction analysis procedure. Moreover, the setup adopted for the described case study points to the ease of integration as an extension of the standard simulator-based user testing procedure for future case studies.

5.4 Limitations

There are several limitations to the validation method chosen to examine the feasibility of our proposed approach in the form of a case study described in Subchapter 4 and the results reported in this Chapter.

Regarding the **methods chosen**, we acknowledge that we adopted a lightweight method validation proposal to demonstrate its feasibility and usefulness for future applications in a constrained research environment. Our proposal emphasizes its applicability in simplistic laboratories over the absolute measurement precision and the environmental fidelity offered by high-end state-of-the-art solutions. Consequently, the present case study is positioned as a proof-of-concept rather than as a summative quantitative evaluation of the proposed setup and methods.

Regarding the **internal validity**, several factors may limit the interpretation of the results provided from the validation case study. These limitations originate in the methodology of the user testing procedure, serving as a basis for our validation. The reported results may have been influenced by the fixed order of tasks during the testing session with a participant, a limited number of IVIS interaction scenarios, a small sample of participants (N=5) increasing the sensitivity to individual differences that makes the findings mostly descriptive, possibly a limited immersion of the driver during the driving simulation resulting in a lower perceived realism of the driving experience by a participant, and low stakes in the testing session originated in the simulator-based environment itself.

Regarding the **external validity**, generalizability of the results reported and the methodology for validation itself is limited in several ways. These limitations originate in the focused simulator-based user testing method where reduced traffic complexity, risk, and consequences may attenuate or reshape attention allocation relative to real driving. Moreover, the small sample of participants (N=5) involved in a case study could have been greatly influenced by demographics such as age, driving experience, and familiarity with IVIS may moderate distraction. Finally, the IVIS interface and the limited interaction methods may elicit specific behavioral patterns of the small sample of participants.

Nevertheless, the user testing procedure limitations and raised constraints should not have influenced the discussed results regarding the preliminary proof-of-concept validation of our proposal and its feasibility of integration we aimed to discuss in this Chapter. However, we acknowledge that our proposed distraction analysis procedure should be a subject to thorough validation across a broader range of case studies and a significantly larger number of participants to ensure its future validation.

6 Conclusion

We proposed a simulator-based distraction analysis setup and procedure for user testing of user interfaces in a simulator-based driving environment. Our proposed procedure extends standard user testing sessions to assess the general usability of the IVIS systems. Our setup proposal focuses on the ease of integration into a simple simulator-based driving environment in laboratories with limited budgets. The proposed distraction analysis procedure is designed to capture and process relevant data revealing distractions during the user testing session, using an eye-tracking approach to uncover distraction patterns caused by in-vehicle digital user interfaces. The proposed procedure for distraction evaluation is based on two distraction metrics (Time Away from the Primary Task – TA-PT; Time on the Secondary Task – TO-ST) and two complementary visualisation techniques (heatmap and scanpath visualisation overlay) for qualitative evaluation of the identified distraction patterns.

A proof-of-concept case study on the feasibility of our proposal was conducted during a task-based user testing session with five participants on three different IVIS interaction controls in a simple driving simulation laboratory. The ease of integration of our proposed light-weight setup in a simple laboratory environment indicates its feasibility for use in existing laboratories for simulated driving. During the case study, we successfully captured the required data for further distraction analysis using our setup. We present the results obtained and analysed using our proposed procedure, along with the metrics and visualisation techniques, and discuss them in the context of the quantitative and qualitative evaluation of the user testing session, with emphasis on the added value for the distraction analysis. Moreover, we compare our proposed distraction analysis approach with the approach based on widely used user testing metrics to showcase the depth of the discussion on the distraction patterns caused by in-vehicle IVIS interfaces in a simulated driving environment. Finally, we discuss the results of the proof-of-concept case study for our distraction analysis approach and conclude that they indicate the feasibility of the proposed setup and procedure. Hence, we believe our proposal will be adopted by more simulator-based driving laboratories with limited budgets in the future. This way, we would obtain more data on the compatibility of our proposal with various laboratory setups and be able to validate it more thoroughly across a broader range of case studies and user testing procedures.

Despite the validation of our proposal, we would like to address the limitations revealed by the case study, specifically those related to the distraction patterns associated with a single Secondary screen present. Making the proposal and technical solution more general to support multiple Secondary screens with IVIS user interfaces would open up space for more ambitious user-testing case studies in innovative design laboratories for cars of the future. Moreover, we would like to address the ease of integration of our proposal as an out-of-the-box solution, helping researchers with setup, capturing user testing sessions, and analysing distraction data through a researcher-friendly software application. This way, we would like to make a step towards thorough validation across a broader range of case studies and a significantly larger number of participants in the future.

Acknowledgments. Funded by the EU NextGenerationEU through the Recovery and Resilience Plan for Slovakia under the project No. 09I03-03-V05-00005. The authors would also like to thank the Slovak Technical University in Bratislava for the grant funding 23-07-01-B.

References

1. Becker, S., Hanna, P., Wagner, V.: Human Machine Interface Design in Modern Vehicles, pp. 1–16. John Wiley & Sons, Ltd. (2014). https://doi.org/10.1002/9781118354179.auto248
2. Berger, M., Bernhaupt, R., Pfleging, B.: A tactile interaction concept for in-car passenger infotainment systems. In: Proceedings of the 11th International Conference on Automotive User Interfaces and Interactive Vehicular Applications: Adjunct Proceedings, pp. 109–114 (2019)
3. Berger, M., Eranil, A., Bernhaupt, R., Pfleging, B.: Inshift: A shifting infotainment system to enhance co-driver experience and collaboration. In: 13th International Conference on Automotive User Interfaces and Interactive Vehicular Applications, pp. 10–15 (2021)
4. Bolder, A., Grünvogel, S.M., Angelescu, E.: Comparison of the usability of a car infotainment system in a mixed reality environment and in a real car. In: Proceedings of the 24th ACM Symposium on Virtual Reality Software and Technology. VRST '18, Association for Computing Machinery, New York, NY, USA (2018). https://doi.org/10.1145/3281505.3281512
5. Boyd, W.K.: An analysis of user experience and distraction in automative an analysis of user experience and distraction in automative infotainment units infotainment units. No. 73 (2020)
6. Bykowski, A., Kupiński, S.: Feature matching and aruco markers application in mobile eye tracking studies. In: 2018 Signal Processing: Algorithms, Architectures, Arrangements, and Applications (SPA), pp. 255–260 (2018). https://doi.org/10.23919/SPA.2018.8563387
7. Crescenti, R., Dondi, P., Porta, M., Resta, C., Rotondo, G.: An eye tracking based evaluation protocol and method for in-vehicle infotainment systems. In: 2023 IEEE 28th International Conference on Emerging Technologies and Factory Automation (ETFA), pp. 1–4 (2023). https://doi.org/10.1109/ETFA54631.2023.10275542
8. Cvahte Ojstersek, T., Topolsek, D.: Eye tracking use in researching driver distraction: a scientometric and qualitative literature review approach. J. Eye Mov. Res. **12**(3) (2019)
9. Ebel, P.: Data-Driven Evaluation of In-Vehicle Information Systems. Ph.D. thesis, Universität zu Köln (2023)
10. Ebel, P., Lingenfelder, C., Vogelsang, A.: On the forces of driver distraction: explainable predictions for the visual demand of in-vehicle touchscreen interactions. Accident Anal. Prev. **183**, 106956 (2023)
11. Fred Feng, Y.L., Chen, Y.: Effects of quantity and size of buttons of in-vehicle touch screen on drivers' eye glance behavior. Int. J. Human-Comput. Inter. **34**(12), 1105–1118 (2018). https://doi.org/10.1080/10447318.2017.1415688
12. Frøkjær, E., Hertzum, M., Hornbæk, K.: Measuring usability: are effectiveness, efficiency, and satisfaction really correlated? In: Proceedings of the SIGCHI conference on Human Factors in Computing Systems, pp. 345–352 (2000)
13. Hart, S.G.: Nasa task load index (tlx). volume 1.0; paper and pencil package (1986). https://api.semanticscholar.org/CorpusID:60009015
14. Hart, S.G.: Nasa-task load index (nasa-tlx); 20 years later. In: Proceedings of the human factors and ergonomics society annual meeting. vol. 50, pp. 904–908. Sage publications Sage CA: Los Angeles, CA (2006)
15. Jung, S., et al.: Effect of touch button interface on in-vehicle information systems usability. Int. J. Human–Comput. Inter. **37**(15), 1404–1422 (2021). https://doi.org/10.1080/10447318.2021.1886484

16. Jung, T., Kaß, C., Zapf, D., Hecht, H.: Effectiveness and user acceptance of infotainment-lockouts: a driving simulator study. Transport. Res. F: Traffic Psychol. Behav. **60**, 643–656 (2019). https://doi.org/10.1016/j.trf.2018.12.001
17. Kircher, K., Ahlstrom, C.: Evaluation of methods for the assessment of attention while driving. Accident Anal. Prev. **114**, 40–47 (2018). https://doi.org/10.1016/j.aap.2017.03.013, road Safety on Five Continents 2016 - Conference in Rio de Janeiro, Brazil
18. Kortum, P., Peres, S.C.: The relationship between system effectiveness and subjective usability scores using the system usability scale. Int. J. Human-Comput. Inter. **30**(7), 575–584 (2014)
19. Larsen, H.H., Scheel, A.N., Bogers, T., Lar-sen, B.: Hands-free but not eyes-free: a usability evaluation of siri while driving. In: Proceedings of the 2020 Conference on Human Information Interaction and Retrieval, pp. 63–72. CHIIR '20, Association for Computing Machinery, New York, NY, USA (2020). https://doi.org/10.1145/3343413.3377962
20. Liang, N., et al.: Using eye-tracking to investigate the effects of pre-takeover visual engagement on situation awareness during automated driving. Accident Anal. Prev. **157**, 106143 (2021). https://doi.org/10.1016/j.aap.2021.106143
21. Lux, B., Schmidl, D., Eibl, M., Hinterleitner, B., Böhm, P., Isemann, D.: Efficiency and user experience of gaze interaction in an automotive environment. In: Harris, D. (ed.) Engineering Psychology and Cognitive Ergonomics, pp. 429–444. Springer International Publishing, Cham (2018)
22. Mickaël J. R. Perrier, T.L.L., Carsten, O.M.J.: Usability testing of three visual hmis for assisted driving: How design impacts driver distraction and mental models. Ergonomics **66**(8), 1142–1163 (2023). https://doi.org/10.1080/00140139.2022.2136766, pMID: 36259259
23. Nagy, V., Kovács, G., Földesi, P., Kurhan, D., Sysyn, M., Szalai, S., Fischer, S.: Testing road vehicle user interfaces concerning the driver's cognitive load. Infrastructures **8**(3) (2023). https://doi.org/10.3390/infrastructures8030049
24. Nagy, V., Kovács, G., Földesi, P., Kurhan, D., Sysyn, M., Szalai, S., Fischer, S.: Testing road vehicle user interfaces concerning the driver's cognitive load. Infrastructures **8**(3) (2023).https://doi.org/10.3390/infrastructures8030049, https://www.mdpi.com/2412-3811/8/3/49
25. Naujoks, F., Hergeth, S., Wiedemann, K., S-choemig, N., Forster, Y., Keinath, A.: Test procedure for evaluating the human-machine interface of vehicles with automated driving systems. Traffic Inj. Prev. **20**, S146–S151 (2019). https://doi.org/10.1080/15389588.2019.1603374
26. NHTSA: Distracted driving in 2021. TRAFFIC SAFETY FACTS: Research Note (2023)
27. Palinko, O., Kun, A.L., Shyrokov, A., Heeman, P.: Estimating cognitive load using remote eye tracking in a driving simulator. In: Proceedings of the 2010 Symposium on Eye-Tracking Research & Applications, pp. 141–144. ETRA '10, Association for Computing Machinery, New York, NY, USA (2010). https://doi.org/10.1145/1743666.1743701
28. Pettersson, I., Lachner, F., Frison, A.K., Riener, A., Butz, A.: A bermuda triangle? a review of method application and triangulation in user experience evaluation. In: Proceedings of the 2018 CHI Conference on Human Factors in Computing Systems, pp. 1–16 (2018)
29. Pijpaert, A.R., Goossens, H., van Dijk, B.W., Roetman, L., van Nispen, R.M., van Rijn, L.J.: A validation study on the accuracy and precision of gaze and vergence using stereoscopic eye-tracking technology. Behav. Res. Methods **57**(8), 214 (2025)

30. Rubio, S., Díaz, E., Martín, J., Puente, J.M.: Evaluation of subjective mental workload: a comparison of swat, nasa-tlx, and workload profile methods. Appl. Psychol. **53**(1), 61–86 (2004)
31. Strayer, D.L., et al.: Visual and cognitive demands of carplay, android auto, and five native infotainment systems. Hum. Factors **61**(8), 1371–1386 (2019). https://doi.org/10.1177/0018720819836575, pMID: 30950645
32. Tobii, A.B.: Tobii Pro Glasses 2 User Manual. Danderyd, Stockholm (July (2023)
33. Virzi, R.A.: Refining the test phase of usability evaluation: How many subjects is enough? Hum. Factors **34**(4), 457–468 (1992). https://doi.org/10.1177/001872089203400407

SensingChair: Capturing Group Mood Dynamics Through Sensing with Objects in Physical Spaces

Tzu-Hui Wu(✉), Sebastian Cmentowski, Jun Hu, and Regina Bernhaupt

Eindhoven University of Technology, Eindhoven, The Netherlands
{t.wu2,s.cmentowski,j.hu,r.bernhaupt}@tue.nl

Abstract. Creating and preserving positive group moods is highly beneficial for well-being, collaboration, and productivity in teams. While smart technologies offer the promise of optimizing workplaces to users' individual needs, privacy-preserving methods for sensing and adapting to group mood dynamics remain limited. This paper introduces the concept of sensing-through-objects, exploring how everyday furniture can unobtrusively capture affective cues. We present the SensingChair, a prototype that uses four under-chair pressure sensors to detect sitting postures and derive indicators of group mood. A preliminary study with three participants demonstrated that distinct postures produce consistent pressure distribution patterns. The findings highlight the potential of minimal sensing for inferring affective states without relying on visual or physiological data. Building on these results, we outline implications for interpreting postures as behavioral indicators of mood, suggest directions for enhancing sensing resolution and analytical methods, and propose design opportunities for future mood-aware workspaces. This work represents an early step toward human-centered sensing for office well-being.

Keywords: Chair-based Sensor · Group dynamics · Group mood · Small groups · Posture Recognition

1 Introduction

Much of our worktime is spent in meetings, discussing and brainstorming with colleagues. A meeting room is thus not a simple functional space, but a social ecosystem where group moods and interactions emerge and influence well-being, collaboration, and productivity. As digital technology becomes increasingly common in physical workplace, understanding how these shared spaces can sense and support group emotional dynamics has become an important challenge for design research.

Group mood describes the global affective atmosphere experienced by group members at a certain point in time during a group activity [41]. It is a key factor

Published by Springer Nature Switzerland AG 2026
C. Maciel et al. (Eds.): INTERACT 2025 Workshops, LNCS 16478, pp. 235–252, 2026.
https://doi.org/10.1007/978-3-032-22934-2_19

in group dynamics, shaping how group members work together and experience their collaboration. For example, prior studies have demonstrated that group-level affective experiences influence group effectiveness in decision-making, the attitudes and behaviors of group members, team performance, and creativity [8]. As a result, fostering "positive workplace vibes" plays an increasingly important role in organizational management. Previous work on this topic has used intelligent measurements and interventions to mediate mood experiences and support positive ways of working in office environments.

Some tools visualize users' arousal levels to support a productive vibe [39]. Other researchers developed systems that transform individual physiological data into collective visualizations to enhance group stress awareness and understanding [46,47]. However, such work has so far relied on collecting personal physiological data, raising concerns around privacy and surveillance. While such data can yield valuable insights for optimizing office well-being, these systems frequently lack clarity and transparency regarding what data is collected and how it is used [6]. To address this challenge, we see the need for unobtrusive, privacy-preserving instrumentation in everyday environments.

The physical workspace, a complex system encompassing not only the objective physical stimuli within the workplace but also the ways in which these stimuli are subjectively perceived by the people [35], has been recognized as a catalyst for social interaction [3]. The integration of digital technologies into physical workspaces opens new opportunities for transforming traditional spaces to foster group connections. Such smart environments can support users by offering not only convenient functions, like room adaption, but also by acting on the user's behalf [5]. Similar digital systems have been proposed to monitor the well-being of inhabitants [22]. Spaces in which we work shape social behaviors, whether through the arrangement of objects or the spatial layout of a room. These physical "props" act as social interfaces that can unobtrusively record, mediate, and respond to human interactions [23].

While intelligent and adaptive workspaces bear great potential for improving how we work and interact together, their design and development remains highly challenging. Above all, the use of digital technologies in workspaces raises concerns regarding accuracy, privacy, and ethical deployment. Misinterpretation of group states may lead to inappropriate interventions or unintended consequences. Collecting and processing highly personal information on mood and productivity is ethically questionable and restricted by privacy regulations. Also, feeling monitored or observed not only undermines trust in the system, but is also likely to deteriorate group efficiency. To avoid these risks, we want to explore a data-sparse approach towards a *Mood-Aware Workplace Environment*, where this socio-technical system only collects the necessary data without compromising individual rights.

Creating mood-aware workplace environments involves designing digital and physical systems that continuously sense, interpret, and respond adaptively to group dynamics. We want to leverage monitoring with unobtrusive sensors to assess or understand the relationship between group behaviors and mood. To achieve a seamless solution while avoiding privacy concerns, we aim to integrate the system into the existing physical workplace, using people's interaction with the existing objects and furniture to derive information about the group well-being rather than introducing additional cameras or interfaces.

Prior research has characterized group mood along three key dimensions (type, intensity, and uniformity) [41], which provide a foundational basis for our present work. Behaviors, such as sitting postures and mimicry behavior, can be indicative of group states. Using these indications, our core idea centers around pressure-transmitting furniture to provide insights into group states, which builds on the concept of sensing through an object. Such prototypes could use subtle, unobtrusive behavioral indicators, such as sitting posture, physical activity levels, and behavioral convergence among group members to infer group mood—creating a digital twin of the intra-group dynamics. By continuously adapting environmental factors, including lighting, room temperature, seating arrangements, acoustic environments, or even ambient cues like scents and sounds, mood-aware workplace environments could use the derived information to enhance the group mood, maintain or boost group energy when disengagement is detected, or foster emotional alignment through facilitating interpersonal synchronization and mimicry behaviors. Such adaptive responsiveness addresses users' wishes for supportive workspaces, contributing to improved group cohesion, enhanced communication effectiveness and reduced conflict.

In this paper, we present an initial exploration towards designing mood-aware workplace that unobtrusively sense and respond to group affective dynamics. Building on the concept of sensing through objects, we speculate how behavioral indicators, particularly sitting postures patterns, could be used to infer group mood without relying on intrusive physiological or visual data. We describe the development and the preliminary test of a pressure-sensing chair prototype that classifies sitting postures. Through this prototype, we aim to explore how the physical workplace itself can act as a social interface for shaping collaboration and supporting group well-being in everyday work settings.

2 Related Work

2.1 Group Mood

Group mood can be defined as a pervasive affective atmosphere experienced by group members during a group activity, which emerges within a group, shaped by the interaction between individuals [8,41]. While group emotion refers to direct responses to specific stimuli [17], group mood encompasses all consistent or uniform emotional responses, representing the general emotional tone [2,28]. Recently, group mood has been explored within the fields of organizational management and human psychology. Studies have shown that group mood experiences influence decision-making quality, team performance, and creativity [9]. Therefore, organizations are seeking ways to stimulate "positive office vibes". However, this first requires an understanding of how to measure group states in collaborative settings.

Currently, HCI research primarily uses physiological, behavioral indicators or self tracking approaches to detect moods. Physiological signals commonly capture data such as respiratory rate, skin conductance, or heart activity [25,40] as proxies for mood. While effective for capturing the arousal of affect, these methods cannot reliably distinguish the valence dimension [44]. Behavioral measures such as facial expression and body language have been widely explored [12,30]. These methods benefit from not requiring physical contact [16]. However, they can be intrusive and sensitive, as users often feel overly monitored, raising concerns about ecological validity [34] in everyday settings. Self-tracking approaches, whether verbal or pictorial, remain another major category.

Mood self-tracking methods are inherently subjective [13], and users may misrepresent their experiences [19]. Research has shown that sitting posture could convey a specific meaning about the actions of a user sitting in an office [21], which can be reflective of people's mental processes [18]. Subconscious movements such as sitting postures carry information about distinctive emotions and attitudes [7,38], therefore playing an important role in emotion-relevant activity recognition. For example, forward leaning with a stretched upper body is indicating interest [14]. In contrast, bowed upper body and many shifts in body position seem to indicate boredom [4,14,24]. Accordingly, we focus on sitting behavioral indicators for group interaction, since their measurement is less invasive and more stable across different conditions. Ultimately, we aim to advance toward the automatic detection of the complex construct of group mood through minimalistic behavioral tracking.

2.2 Sensing Through Objects

The concept of sensing through objects has been researched in the form of integrating computation and sensing capabilities into the environment [5]. Researchers have instrumented the environment itself, e.g., by using light-based sensing to identify skeletal posture [27] or pressure information for recognizing activities [1]. Such a "digitalized" environment can track users and try to automatically recognize their activities. A series of research and products has used pressure-sensitive objects and furniture to monitor health or behaviors, for instance, detecting sedentary patterns [37] or sensing educational engagement through pressure sensors in shoes [36]. Drawing inspiration from these approaches, we believe that passive sensing could be well-suited for tracking mood in semi-public work environments where cameras and microphones are not appropriate. However, unlike prior research, we focus on group mood and group dynamics, using pressure-based sensing not just to monitor physical behaviors, but to infer shared mood states and synchronization in collaborative settings. Moreover, while previous work often relies on dense sensor arrays, we aim to explore a minimal sensing setup that uses only a few placed sensors to capture group-level patterns.

2.3 Digital Technology in the Workplace

In recent years, many academic disciplines have taken advantage of technologies to promote office well-being. Building management systems adjust lighting and temperature based on occupancy patterns [26,32]. Wearable devices track posture and stress levels [38,47]. Digital platforms provide real-time feedback on air quality, productivity, and energy efficiency [20,26]. Enhancing physical activity and reducing mental health problems has become a top priority in the workplace [3,10]. Ambient intelligence extends these capabilities by embedding technologies into the environment, allowing workplaces to sense and respond to users through data collected from internet of things (IoT) devices. While digital technologies offer the promise of optimized workplaces, they often compromise factors such as autonomy, transparency, and meaningful engagement [6]. Many tend to function as "black boxes", where data is collected, processed, and acted upon without offering workers clear insight into the process [29]. Therefore, our research proposes embedding privacy-preserving sensors into everyday furniture to infer mood dynamics through observable behaviors rather than personal physiological data.

3 Problem Statement and Method

A recent study by Wu et al. [45] explored how workspace features shape group dynamics through a qualitative user study using the Experience Curve method and semi-structured interviews. Their findings suggest that capturing group dynamics in physical workspaces requires integrating multimodal data sources, including physiological signals, behavioral patterns, spatial positioning, audio cues, and user self-reports. While such multimodal integration enhances the reliability of detecting subtle shifts in group mood, it also raises important privacy concerns. Participants emphasized the need for privacy issues, such as anonymous physiological data collection and the use of indirect, ambient indicators of mood. Furthermore, mood alignment emerged as a key factor in enhancing group experience. Participants also highlighted the value of shared and adaptive control over the physical environment to ensure group consent while minimizing workflow disruptions.

Building on these insights, our long-term goal is to develop and evaluate mood-aware workspace technology that can (1) infer group mood from behavioral cues, and (2) adapt environmental features (e.g., light, space, furniture) to support collective well-being and collaboration. This goal can be divided into two primary research questions:

RQ How can behavioral cues, such as sitting posture and activity, measured through sensor-enriched furniture, be used to detect and predict changes in group mood?

RQ How can adaptive interventions (e.g., lighting, sound, spatial configuration) be designed to improve group well-being by using the mood-detecting furniture?

As first step towards answering these research questions, the presented works focuses on the design of a posture-detecting chair prototype as necessary requirement for understanding and predicting how behavioral cues relate to mood and well-being. Therefore, we follow a Research-through-Design (RtD) approach [48], combining empirical studies and iterative prototyping to both explore design opportunities and generate knowledge about mood-aware workspace. The RtD process involves cycles of exploration, prototyping, testing, and reflection. In this work, the concept of "sensing-through-objects" serves as an integrative concept that bridges between the empirical study and the design work.

Specifically, we report on the development and evaluation of our chair-based sensing prototype that measures body pressure and posture as indicators of engagement and group mood. The prototype uses four load cells connected through HX711 modules and an ESP32 board, which transmits real-time pressure data to database. To investigate the usability of our design prototype and its adaptability to different context, we conducted a pilot study where we tested a set of predefined postures with 3 participants. Each participant performed a series of predefined sitting postures (e.g., upright, leaning, rotating) while the system recorded the pressure data. This pilot study aimed to validate the accuracy and feasibility of the sensing setup, and identify design requirements for future study.

4 Design Concept and Prototype

Pressure sensing on the human body can serve as a measure for recognizing activities and postures [1]. Inspired by the concept of "sensing-through-objects", we focused on unobtrusive tools to examine postures in naturalistic environment without disrupting ongoing tasks (see Fig. 1). For our concept, we build on the assumption that users' sitting postures are observable by measuring pressure

Fig. 1. Left: An illustration of our proposed concept where people collaborate in a meeting room while sitting on pressure-sensing chairs to capture sitting posture. Right: The diagram shows a top-down view of the seating arrangement. (https://storytribeapp.com/).

distributions through the use of sensors under the chairs' legs. In turn, monitoring these postures could contribute to mood recognition in environments where cameras and microphones are not appropriate [43].

4.1 Ideation: Sensing with Chair

Some prior posture recognition research already used chairs equipped with pressure sensors as a control interface [11]. Such systems typically employed on-chair sensor layouts for real-time posture tracking. For example, Tan et al. [42] used over 4000 force sensors on the seat and back surfaces of the chair. However, such systems were not suitable for practical applications because of the high implementation cost. Recent studies managed to reduce sensor number through optimization of sensor placement [31]. To improve on this, we developed a chair prototype that was equipped with only four pressure sensors, positioned at the bottom of the chair legs. Apart from the reduced costs, this layout—sensing the center of pressure—also reduces other constraints towards the chair design and seating surface materials.

4.2 Technical Design

We implemented a first version of the sensor-equipped chair prototype (see Fig. 2), integrating pressure sensors to continuously and unobtrusively capture data on individual posture, body movements, and shifts in seating position throughout group interactions. The sensing chair system is composed of a normal office chair equipped with 4 pressure sensors located under the legs. Therefore, we house a commercially available 50kg Load cell (mP0236-I42) in a 3D-printed plastic container to fit it under the chair's leg. Each sensor is connected in series to a resistor, and senses the load at a sampling rate of 2 Hz. This data is transmitted via internet to a database hosted on on-premise servers[1] to comply with GDPR regulations. This setup is affordable, modular, and extensible—we initially built six prototypes to fully equip a regular meeting room for testing. The system provides two types of information: (1) the center of the pressure applied to the chair; (2) the distribution of the weight applied to the four legs. Different body postures lead to different weight distributions (upright posture or leaning aside).

5 Preliminary Test

Ultimately, we are interested in exploring the relationship between different pressure distribution patterns and corresponding sitting postures. This is the foundation for investigating how sitting postures can serve as an indicator of individual and group mood states. To explore the feasibility and usability of our chosen approach, we conducted a preliminary test with three participants trying different

[1] https://data.id.tue.nl.

Fig. 2. An illustration of a participant sitting on the sensor-equipped chair prototype for posture sensing: the technical setup includes load cells (pressure sensors) under the chair's base and an HX711 amplifier for signal processing.

sitting postures. The goal of this pilot test was to validate the sensing accuracy of our chair prototype and to establish a basis for interpreting posture-based behavioral cues.

To test whether we could use the chair's pressure data to confidently detect postures and explore the approach's limitations, we first decided on 8 predefined sitting postures that typically occur during meetings. The postures (Fig. 3) included (a) upright sitting with backrest; (b) upright sitting without backrest; (c) leaning on the backrest; (d) front sitting without backrest; (e) leaning on the left; (f) leaning on the right; (g) rotating the trunk about 20° (left); (h) rotating the trunk about 20° (right).

During the study, participants sat on the chair in front of a desk and were asked to perform each of the postures 30 times. Meanwhile, the prototype continuously recorded pressure data from the four load cells. One camera was placed in the side of the subject to confirm that the sitting posture was correct. For this initial proof-of-concept, 3 healthy participants (2 female, 1 male, aged 25–31) participated in the preliminary testing.

5.1 Data Analysis

To characterize how different postural configurations produce unique spatial pressure distribution, we transformed the raw data from the load cells as follows:

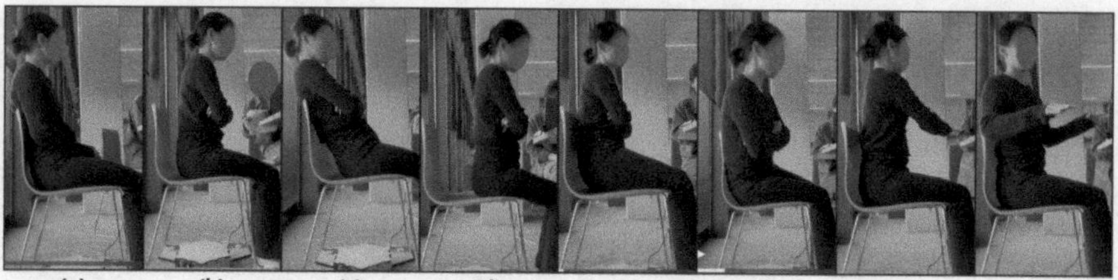

Fig. 3. Types of sitting postures adopted for the experiment: (a) upright sitting with backrest; (b) upright sitting without backrest; (c) leaning on the backrest; (d) front sitting without backrest; (e) leaning on the left; (f) leaning on the right; (g) rotating the trunk about 20°(left); (h) rotating the trunk about 20° (right).

- **Mean, root mean square, standard deviation of 4 combined sensors:** Median, root mean square, standard deviation of the sum of absolute values of 4 sensors after removing DC using a high-pass filter.
- **Center of pressure (CoP) in two directions:** calculated as the differences between sensors on the left and right side of the chair, and between the sensors on the front and backside of the chair, both divided by the sum of all 4 sensors. The CoP is a parameter, weighted by the pressure of each sensor, for measuring the center point. It is defined as the point location of the vertical seat reaction force vector. The central point is assumed as the origin of our coordinate system $O(0, 0)$, and each load cell has its location as shown in Table 1. The CoP can be easily identified by its coordinates with Formula (2)

$$CoP_x = \frac{\sum f_i * x_i}{\sum f_i} \tag{1}$$

and Formula (2)

$$CoP_y = \frac{\sum f_i * y_i}{\sum f_i} \tag{2}$$

where f_i is the pressure value of each load cell sensor, and $(x_i,\ y_i)$ represents the location, $i \in \{1, 2, 3, 4\}$.

Table 1. Location of the pressure sensors.

Sensor	Location (x,y)
S1	(–1,1)
S2	(1,1)
S3	(–1,–1)
S4	(1,–1)

Si - Load cell i.

The small sample size of $N = 3$ allowed us to deeply compare different behaviors across participants on a qualitative level, seeing how collected data varies between different people. Therefore, we plotted heatmaps, illustrating how each participants distributed and moved their body weight across the 30 trials for each tested sitting posture (SP). Each heatmap was computed from the normalized readings of four load cells. For each trial, we first calculated the total load as the sum of all sensor readings and then derived the relative pressure values for each sensor by dividing individual readings by the total load. Then, the CoP coordinates of all samples for each subject were aggregated and averaged. The resulting heatmaps visualize the spatial distribution and variability of CoP across different postures, with warmer colors indicating regions of higher load concentration. In the following figures, each subplot represents the CoP along the X–Y axes for the three participants (rows) across all posture types (columns). Different clusters in the heatmaps indicate how posture alters the pressure distribution pattern.

Figure 4 presents the CoP distribution of two similar sitting postures, upright sitting with backrest and leaning on the backrest. In the upright sitting with backrest condition (top row), all participants show CoP clusters located slightly toward the upper-middle region of the seat (higher CoP_y values), indicating that most of the body weight is supported by the central to rear area of the seat while maintaining a balanced position. This pattern reflects a stable but engaged posture, where participants sit upright and make only light contact with the backrest. In contrast, during the leaning on the backrest condition (bottom row), the CoP shifts slightly further backward, as seen at higher CoP_y positions. This shift shows that a larger portion of the weight is transferred to the backrest, reflecting a more relaxed and passive posture. While these postures are easily distinguishable from others due to their focused area and uniform observations across participants, they largely overlap with each other, making differentiation between these two postures difficult.

Next, we compared two more attentive sitting postures: upright sitting without backrest and front sitting without backrest (see Fig. 5), showing how posture changes affect the CoP distribution captured by the chair's pressure sensors. In the upright sitting without backrest condition (top row), the CoP heatmaps for all three participants are located in the middle-to-rear region of the seat (moderate CoP_y values). The CoP clusters suggest a stable and attentive posture, often associated with focus or active listening. The front sitting without backrest condition (bottom row) shows the CoP shifting further forward (lower CoP_y values). This shift indicates that participants lean toward the front edge of the seat, increasing pressure near the thighs. This posture reflects higher engagement or alertness, often observed when people lean in to participate or concentrate intensely. This picture illustrates how removing back support and moving the body forward produce measurable changes in weight distribution. The forward shift of the CoP corresponds to physical activation and engagement, distinguishing passive upright sitting from active forward leaning participation among indi-

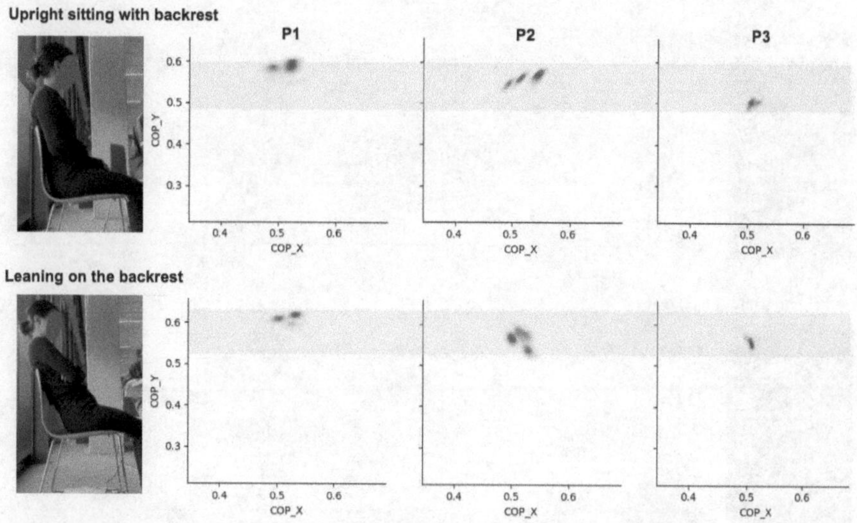

Fig. 4. The pressure distribution heatmaps of the upright sitting with backrest (top row) and leaning on the backrest (bottom row) conditions for 3 participants. Warmer colors indicate areas with higher CoP concentration.

viduals. Both postures are distinguishable from each other but also clearly from the more relaxed postures discussed earlier.

Figure 6 illustrates the pressure distribution patterns of two left-oriented sitting postures: leaning left (top row) and rotating the trunk 20° to the left (bottom row). Across participants, both postures show a leftward shift in CoP ($CoP_x > 0.5$), showing consistent lateral weight transfer. However, subtle differences can be distinguished. In the leaning posture, the pressure distribution tends to cluster toward the rear-left region (higher CoP_y), indicating more backrest engagement and a relaxed body posture. In contrast, during trunk rotation, pressure is more central or slightly forward, suggesting active engagement and less reliance on the backrest. While both postures can be clearly distinguished from neutral sitting by their leftward pressure displacement, differentiating between leaning and rotating requires examining CoP_y changes and pressure distribution spread rather than just lateral shift, indicating that multi-dimensional pressure features (both X and Y axes) are essential for accurate posture classification.

Figure 7 shows the pressure distribution of right-oriented postures: leaning right and rotating the trunk 20° to the right. In the leaning on the right posture, the CoP distributions for all three participants shift clearly toward the back-right region of the seat (lower CoP_x values), indicating that the majority of body weight is placed on the right hip or thigh. Conversely, the pressure cluster of trunk rotation moves forward and slightly inward. Individual variations are visible, for example, P2 shows broader pressure dispersion compared to P1 and P3, indicating that personal sitting habits influence the CoP range. The vertical

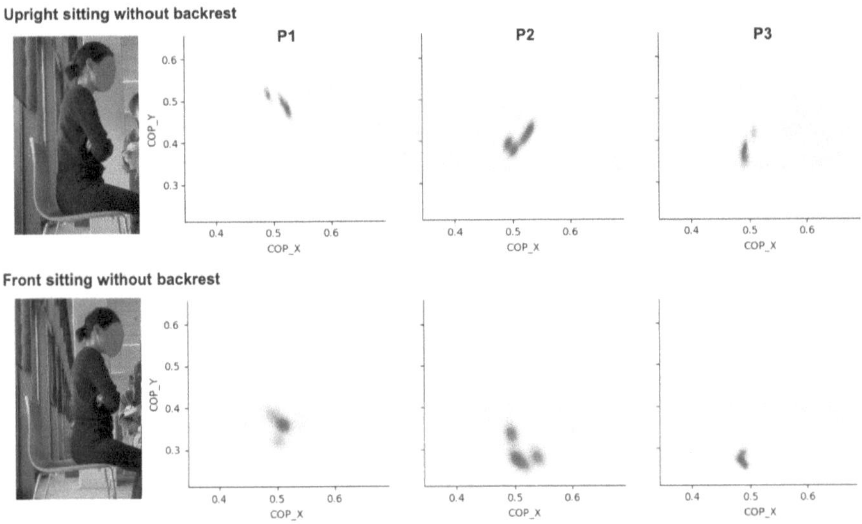

Fig. 5. The pressure distribution heatmaps of the upright sitting without backrest (top row) and front sitting without backrest (bottom row) conditions for 3 participants. Warmer colors indicate areas with higher CoP concentration.

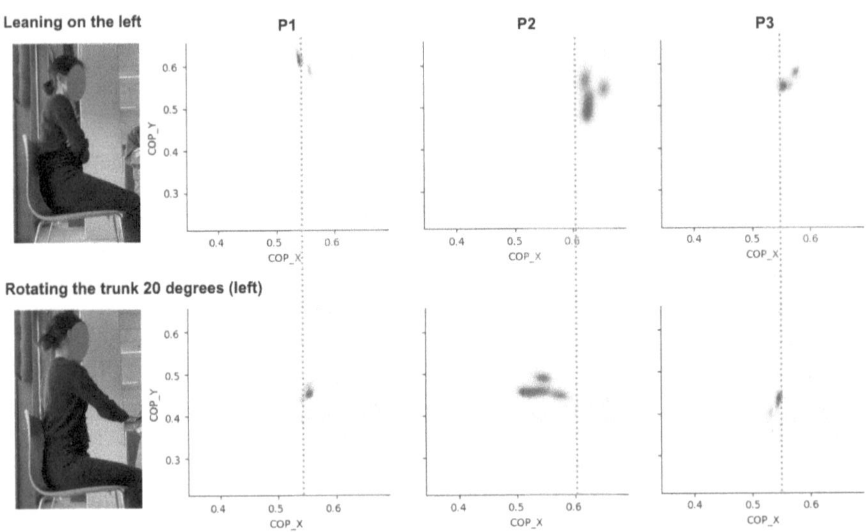

Fig. 6. The pressure distribution heatmaps of leaning left (top row) and rotating the trunk 20° to the left (bottom row) conditions for 3 participants. Warmer colors indicate areas with higher CoP concentration. The red dashed line compares the CoP_x distribution across all participants.

displacement (CoP_y) and pressure spread pattern offer better cues than lateral shifts alone. Thus, distinguishing these two postures requires multi-dimensional CoP analysis, combining both horizontal and vertical distribution features.

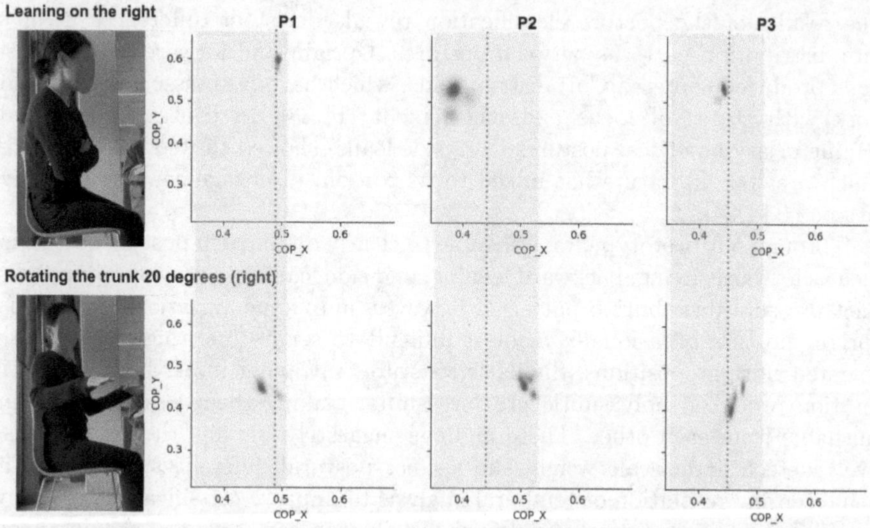

Fig. 7. The pressure distribution heatmaps of leaning right (top row) and rotating the trunk 20° to the right (bottom row) conditions for 3 participants. Warmer colors indicate areas with higher CoP concentration. The blue dashed line compares the CoP_x distribution across all participants.

6 Discussion

6.1 Sensing with Chairs

This pilot study highlights the potential of integrating pressure sensing within chairs to recognize sitting postures. Previous studies have explored chairs equipped with large arrays of pressure sensors; however, such systems are often impractical for real-world deployment due to their complexity and cost. Our findings demonstrate that sitting postures can be effectively detected using a minimal setup consisting of a few easily retrofitted sensors integrated under the chair legs. This configuration enables the unobtrusive collection of posture data during everyday office activities. A further advantage of this approach is that visual and audio information is not required, allowing for anonymous implementation. However, posture detection with limited sensor information also creates additional challenges since not every posture was easily distinguishable in our trial. Moreover, the study identifies several technical considerations for future data collection: (1) calibration differences between participants should be addressed to ensure cross-subject comparability, and (2) combining Center of Pressure (CoP) features with temporal movement dynamics could reveal emotional shifts.

6.2 Posture as an Affective Indicator

The results of the posture classification reveal consistent differences in pressure distribution patterns between postures. Upright and forward-leaning positions produced centered CoP distributions, which have been associated in prior work with states of focus and engagement [14,38]. In contrast, backward-leaning or asymmetrical postures (e.g., side leans) showed shifted CoP patterns, which previous literature has linked to relaxation, disengagement, or cognitive fatigue [4,14,24].

Through our prototype, we were able to clearly distinguish posture categories such as forward sitting, backward leaning, and side leaning, as each produced distinct pressure distribution patterns. However, individual variations in habitual upright posture occasionally made it difficult to separate sitting from slightly deviated upright positions. Similarly, postures involving upper-body or trunk rotation produced only subtle pressure shifts, making them less easily distinguishable from each other. These findings suggest that while the system effectively detects large-scale weight shifts, finer postural differences, require additional sensing resolution or temporal analysis to improve classification accuracy.

While body orientation and weight distribution can serve as behavioral correlates of affective states, they are influenced by other situational and ergonomic factors, such as comfort or chair design. Additionally, individual and neurodivergent differences may influence sitting behaviors, posing challenges for fair interpretation, as such variability could affect both the technical accuracy and social inclusivity of mood sensing systems. Therefore, the patterns detected here should be interpreted as indirect markers of affective engagement rather than direct evidence of mood. By quantifying these postural dynamics, our sensing setup offers a non-intrusive means of identifying sitting patterns that may accompany affective or attentional changes during group collaboration.

6.3 Synchrony and Group Mood Recognition

It is difficult to estimate mood using only static sitting data because sitting behavior includes physiological reactions and expressions of mood. In our future research, we will focus on group reactions; the reaction occurring simultaneously among multiple users. Prior research hypothesized that group reaction, which is a part of synchrony, would indicate shared emotional responses [43]. Synchrony is defined as the dynamic and reciprocal adaptation of the temporal structure of behaviors between group members [15]. Synchrony does not indicate physiological reactions but emotional reactions. Our goal is therefore to recognize group mood states by sensing and analyzing synchronous sitting behaviors that emerge during collaborative interactions.

6.4 Design Implications for Mood-Aware Workspaces

Overall, we believe that the fact that such results can be achieved using signals from just four simple pressure sensors mounted under the chairs legs is promising and relevant for a wide range of applications. In particular, the ability to easily retrofit large rooms (e.g. a meeting room) opens up interesting research opportunities in the area of social interaction. Beyond chairs, the sensing approach could be extended to other types of furniture (e.g., tables, couches) to enable more complex activity and interaction recognition in public spaces.

From a design perspective, our goal is to explore how everyday objects can function as unobtrusive interfaces for sensing and interpreting group behavior. Postural cues can inform adaptive responses, such as lighting adjustments during fatigue, spatial reconfiguration to encourage movement, or ambient cues that promote emotional alignment. The ability to detect convergence or divergence in postural patterns across group members could enable environments to respond collectively rather than individually. Future prototypes may extend this concept toward multimodal furniture systems or adaptive spatial configurations, contributing to mood-aware workspace design.

7 Conclusion and Future Work

In this study, we developed a sensing chair prototype to detect sitting postures from pressure distribution patterns obtained from four load cells mounted under the chair. A preliminary test showed promising results. However, we did not apply our system in real-context. Future studies should apply our method to analyze sitting postures in real-world settings. Therefore, we will proceed with exploring how the obtained data relates to changes in group mood dynamics. We will start with rationalizing each group mood dimension by mapping them into observable behavioral indicators based on prior empirical literature, using the sitting posture to represent mood type, the frequency and amplitude of posture adjustments to identify mood intensity, and measures of behavioral convergence or mimicry to quantify mood uniformity within the group. Next, we will use our prototype, integrating pressure sensors under chairs to continuously capture data on individual posture, body movements, and shifts in seating position throughout group interactions. This chair prototype will be deployed in a series of real-life group meetings. Throughout these sessions, the system will record posture data in real time, which we will synchronize with video recordings that are retrospectively annotated by participants (similar to the work by Potts et al. [33]). The resulting dataset enables us to connect the perceived mood with sensor tracking data, ultimately developing a machine-learning algorithm capable of inferring changes in group mood states from physical interaction patterns. Assessing the feasibility and validity of using embodied behavioral signals as proxies for group mood ultimately informs the design of adaptive, mood-aware workspaces.

As workplaces continue to evolve, shaped by smart technologies, and shifting organizational priorities, the need for thoughtful, human-centered approaches to office well-being becomes increasingly urgent. This work aims to advance the design of mood-aware workspaces that respond to group office well-being. We provide a lightweight solution for studying group mood through sensing objects, offering HCI researchers a novel approach to bridging interaction and affective computing. Designing for office well-being is not solely a question of technological sophistication but of aligning systems with the human experience of work. By foregrounding transparency and adaptability, designers can contribute to workplaces that are not only efficient but also genuinely supportive of the people within them.

References

1. Arnrich, B., Setz, C., La Marca, R., Tröster, G., Ehlert, U.: What does your chair know about your stress level? IEEE Trans. Inf Technol. Biomed. **14**(2), 207–214 (2009)
2. Barsade, S.G., Knight, A.P.: Group affect. Annu. Rev. Organ. Psychol. Organ. Behav. **2**(1), 21–46 (2015)
3. Bergefurt, L., Weijs-Perrée, M., Appel-Meulenbroek, R., Arentze, T.: The physical office workplace as a resource for mental health-a systematic scoping review. Build. Environ. **207**, 108505 (2022)
4. Bianchi-Berthouze, N., Kim, W.W., Patel, D.: Does Body Movement Engage You More in Digital Game Play? and Why? In: Paiva, A.C.R., Prada, R., Picard, R.W. (eds.) ACII 2007. LNCS, vol. 4738, pp. 102–113. Springer, Heidelberg (2007). https://doi.org/10.1007/978-3-540-74889-2_10
5. Bränzel, A., et al.: Gravityspace: tracking users and their poses in a smart room using a pressure-sensing floor. In: Proceedings of the SIGCHI Conference on Human Factors in Computing Systems, pp. 725–734 (2013)
6. Brombacher, H., Houben, S., Vos, S.: Sensorbadge: an exploratory study of an egocentric wearable sensor system for healthy office environments. In: Proceedings of the 2022 ACM Designing Interactive Systems Conference, pp. 1863–1877 (2022)
7. Bull, P.: Body Movement and Interpersonal Communication (1983)
8. Cernea, D., Ebert, A., Kerren, A.: Visualizing group affective tone in collaborative scenarios. In: Poster Abstracts of the Eurographics Conference on Visualization (Eurovis' 14), p. 3 (2014)
9. Cernea, D., Ebert, A., Kerren, A.: Visualizing group affective tone in collaborative scenarios. In: Poster Abstracts of the Eurographics Conference on Visualization (Eurovis' 14), p. 3 (2014)
10. Chau, J.Y., et al.: Are workplace interventions to reduce sitting effective? a systematic review. Prev. Med. **51**(5), 352–356 (2010)
11. Cheng, J., Zhou, B., Sundholm, M., Lukowicz, P.: Smart chair: What can simple pressure sensors under the chairs legs tell us about user activity. In: UBICOMM13: The Seventh International Conference on Mobile Ubiquitous Computing, Systems, Services and Technologies, pp. 81–84 (2013)
12. Dang, C.T., Aslan, I., Lingenfelser, F., Baur, T., André, E.: Towards somaesthetic smarthome designs: exploring potentials and limitations of an affective mirror. In: Proceedings of the 9th International Conference on the Internet of Things, pp. 1–8 (2019)

13. Lera, E.: Emotion-Centered-Design (ECD) New Approach for Designing Interactions that Matter. In: Marcus, A. (ed.) DUXU 2015. LNCS, vol. 9186, pp. 406–416. Springer, Cham (2015). https://doi.org/10.1007/978-3-319-20886-2_38
14. De Meijer, M.: The contribution of general features of body movement to the attribution of emotions. J. Nonverbal Behav. **13**(4), 247–268 (1989)
15. Delaherche, E., Chetouani, M., Mahdhaoui, A., Saint-Georges, C., Viaux, S., Cohen, D.: Interpersonal synchrony: a survey of evaluation methods across disciplines. IEEE Trans. Affect. Comput. **3**(3), 349–365 (2012)
16. Desmet, P.M., Vastenburg, M.H., Romero, N.: Mood measurement with pick-a-mood: review of current methods and design of a pictorial self-report scale. J. Des. Res. **14**(3), 241–279 (2016)
17. George, J.M.: Personality, affect, and behavior in groups. J. Appl. Psychol. **75**(2), 107 (1990)
18. Gravina, R., Li, Q.: Emotion-relevant activity recognition based on smart cushion using multi-sensor fusion. Inf. Fusion **48**, 1–10 (2019)
19. Guribye, F., Gjøsæter, T., Bjartli, C.: Designing for tangible affective interaction. In: Proceedings of the 9th Nordic Conference on Human-Computer Interaction, pp. 1–10 (2016)
20. Jayathissa, P., Quintana, M., Abdelrahman, M., Miller, C.: Humans-as-a-sensor for buildings–intensive longitudinal indoor comfort models. Buildings **10**(10), 174 (2020)
21. Kapoor, A., Mota, S., Picard, R.W., et al.: Towards a learning companion that recognizes affect. In: AAAI Fall Symposium, vol. 543, pp. 2–4 (2001)
22. Kientz, J.A., Patel, S.N., Jones, B., Price, E., Mynatt, E.D., Abowd, G.D.: The georgia tech aware home. In: CHI'08 Extended Abstracts on Human Factors in Computing Systems, pp. 3675–3680 (2008)
23. Kirsh, D.: Do architects and designers think about interactivity differently? ACM Trans. Comput.-Hum. Inter. (TOCHI) **26**(2), 1–43 (2019)
24. Kleinsmith, A., De Silva, P.R., Bianchi-Berthouze, N.: Cross-cultural differences in recognizing affect from body posture. Interact. Comput. **18**(6), 1371–1389 (2006)
25. Koelstra, S., et al.: Deap: a database for emotion analysis; using physiological signals. IEEE Trans. Affect. Comput. **3**(1), 18–31 (2011)
26. Lee, K.S., Shah, I., Lee, J.J., Ghahramani, A.: Built environment digital twin as mediator of shared space: Balancing personal preferences and group decision making. Build. Environ. 113935 (2025)
27. Li, T., Liu, Q., Zhou, X.: Practical human sensing in the light. In: Proceedings of the 14th Annual International Conference on Mobile Systems, Applications, and Services, pp. 71–84 (2016)
28. Menges, J.I., Kilduff, M.: Group emotions: cutting the gordian knots concerning terms, levels of analysis, and processes. Acad. Manag. Ann. **9**(1), 845–928 (2015)
29. Mortier, R., Haddadi, H., Henderson, T., McAuley, D., Crowcroft, J.: Human-data interaction: The human face of the data-driven society. arXiv preprint arXiv:1412.6159 (2014)
30. Müller, P.M., Amin, S., Verma, P., Andriluka, M., Bulling, A.: Emotion recognition from embedded bodily expressions and speech during dyadic interactions. In: 2015 International Conference on Affective Computing and Intelligent Interaction (ACII), pp. 663–669. IEEE (2015)
31. Mutlu, B., Krause, A., Forlizzi, J., Guestrin, C., Hodgins, J.: Robust, low-cost, non-intrusive sensing and recognition of seated postures. In: Proceedings of the 20th Annual ACM Symposium on User Interface Software and Technology, pp. 149–158 (2007)

32. Pereira, E., et al.: Stars: enlightenment in the office space for behavioral change. In: Proceedings of the 2016 ACM International Joint Conference on Pervasive and Ubiquitous Computing: Adjunct, pp. 1640–1645 (2016)
33. Potts, D., et al.: Retrosketch: A retrospective method for measuring emotions and presence in virtual reality. In: Proceedings of the 2025 CHI Conference on Human Factors in Computing Systems, pp. 1–25 (2025)
34. Reader, A.T., Holmes, N.P.: Examining ecological validity in social interaction: problems of visual fidelity, gaze, and social potential. Cult. brain **4**(2), 134–146 (2016)
35. Sander, E.L.J., Caza, A., Jordan, P.J.: Psychological perceptions matter: developing the reactions to the physical work environment scale. Build. Environ. **148**, 338–347 (2019)
36. Saquib, N., Bose, A., George, D., Kamvar, S.: Sensei: Sensing educational interaction. Proc. ACM Inter. Mob. Wearable Ubiquitous Technol. **1**(4), 1–27 (2018)
37. Schwartz, B., Schrempf, A., Probst, K., Haller, M., Glöckl, J.: Recognizing static and dynamic sitting behavior by means of instrumented office chairs. In: Proceedings of Biomedical Engineering (BioMed), pp. 67–74. ACTAPRESS, Calgary, AB, Canada (2013)
38. Shibata, T., Kijima, Y.: Emotion recognition modeling of sitting postures by using pressure sensors and accelerometers. In: Proceedings of the 21st International Conference on Pattern Recognition (ICPR2012), pp. 1124–1127. IEEE (2012)
39. Snyder, J., et al.: Moodlight: Exploring personal and social implications of ambient display of biosensor data. In: Proceedings of the 18th ACM Conference on Computer Supported Cooperative Work & Social Computing, pp. 143–153 (2015)
40. Soleymani, M., Lichtenauer, J., Pun, T., Pantic, M.: A multimodal database for affect recognition and implicit tagging. IEEE Trans. Affect. Comput. **3**(1), 42–55 (2011)
41. Sönmez, A., Desmet, P.M., Herrera, N.R.: Chill, fiery, slack, and five other vibes: a phenomenological inquiry into group mood. She Ji J. Des. Econ. Innov. **8**(1), 93–117 (2022)
42. Tan, H.Z., Slivovsky, L.A., Pentland, A.: A sensing chair using pressure distribution sensors. IEEE/ASME Trans. Mechatron. **6**(3), 261–268 (2001)
43. Wataya, R., Iwai, D., Sato, K.: Ambient sensing chairs for audience emotion recognition by finding synchrony of body sway. In: The 1st IEEE Global Conference on Consumer Electronics 2012, pp. 29–33. IEEE (2012)
44. Watson, D., Tellegen, A.: Toward a consensual structure of mood. Psychol. Bull. **98**(2), 219 (1985)
45. Wu, T.H., Cmentowski, S., Luo, Y., Hu, J., Bernhaupt, R.: Towards smart workplaces: understanding mood-influencing factors of the physical workspace in collaborative group settings. In: 20th IFIP TC13 International Conference on Human-Computer Interaction (2025)
46. Xue, M., Liang, J., Hu, J., Feijs, L.: Clockviz: designing public visualization for coping with collective stress in teamwork. In: 10th International Conference on Design and Semantics of Form and Movement (DeSForM 2017): Sense and Sensivity, pp. 67–78 (2017)
47. Xue, M., Liang, R.H., Yu, B., Funk, M., Hu, J., Feijs, L.: Affectivewall: designing collective stress-related physiological data visualization for reflection. IEEE Access **7**, 131289–131303 (2019)
48. Zimmerman, J., Forlizzi, J., Evenson, S.: Research through design as a method for interaction design research in HCI. In: Proceedings of the SIGCHI Conference on Human Factors in Computing Systems, pp. 493–502 (2007)

Perspectives on Privacy and Security in Collaborative AR - Insights from a Scoping Review and an Expert Interview Study

Sarah Claudia Krings(✉), Enes Yigitbas, and Stefan Sauer

Paderborn University, Zukunftsmeile 2, 33102 Paderborn, Germany
{sarah.krings,enes.yigitbas,sauer}@uni-paderborn.de

Abstract. With a range of consumer devices available, augmented reality (AR) continues to make its way into everyday life and is also increasingly used in professional and sensitive contexts. Especially collaborative use cases, such as remote meetings or maintenance, offer potential, but also move issues in the area of privacy and security into focus. We conducted a scoping review to gain an overview of the current situation and found a lack of clear standards, with most approaches focusing on single protection features. Using the knowledge from the scoping review, we set up and conducted expert interviews. They revealed that end-users are almost completely dependent on developers or device manufacturers regarding their options for protection. The interviews also showed that most developers put little focus on privacy and security, often due to external constraints, such as employers treating the topic as an "afterthought" and not budgeting enough time for it. The experts suggested offering better software support to developers to enable the inclusion of privacy and security with less overhead as a solution. It was also suggested that a general rise in privacy and security awareness could improve the overall situation.

Keywords: Augmented Reality · Privacy · Security

1 Introduction

Although Augmented Reality (AR) as a concept has existed for a long time [62], it only became more popular due to technological advances in recent years. Originally defined as an interactive combination of real and virtual contents in real-time and with registration in 3D by Azuma et al. [3], it has come to the public eye in the form of applications such as Niantic's AR game Pokémon GO[1]. These applications have hundreds of thousands of downloads, showing that AR is making its entry into everyday technology.

[1] https://play.google.com/store/apps/details?id=com.nianticlabs.pokemongo.

Published by Springer Nature Switzerland AG 2026
C. Maciel et al. (Eds.): INTERACT 2025 Workshops, LNCS 16478, pp. 253–276, 2026.
https://doi.org/10.1007/978-3-032-22934-2_20

Additionally, AR is also increasingly used in professional settings. One important factor is the use of AR in collaborative settings, such as the collaboration software Spatial[2], where users can meet in AR with users from AR, VR, or desktop applications in a shared virtual space and work together on virtual items. Especially during the COVID-19 pandemic, these types of virtual collaboration applications gained increased attention and usage. The general benefits of AR, such as seeing virtual objects in 3D in the real world, are extended to the possibility of collaboratively working on those objects with others, whether they are physically present or not. With AR collaboration, it can, for example, become easier to work on mechanical prototypes, since a real prototype is not necessary, and all users can access the virtual 3D model of the prototype.

However, the wide and diverse usage of AR collaboration introduces some risks. As collaboration inherently shares data between devices, security and privacy topics become relevant. In the context of collaborative AR, security could, for example, concern the data handled in the collaboration, but also the general functionality of the collaboration system, while the privacy of the users as well as bystanders is at risk due to the range of information AR devices collect using their sensors. The relation between privacy and security is complex since they can have synergies (e.g., when personal data is kept confidential from non-authorized AR users), but also contradictory goals (for example, security profits from traceability, e.g., by logging information on users and their actions, which contradicts user privacy).

This leads us to our problem: The issues of privacy and security are complicated even further by the nature of (collaborative) AR. As mentioned, AR devices capture the user's environment with cameras and sensors, which is necessary to ensure functionality, but records significant amounts of potentially private or even security-critical data. The data that is actively used in AR collaborative applications (e.g., the prototype model from the above example) must also be protected. All of these factors have been relevant in other technologies before, but they appear in a new combination in collaborative AR. Additionally, since AR is still a relatively young field, there are no clear official guidelines or universally agreed-upon resources yet.

This leads us to our research question: How can privacy and security for collaborative AR be improved? To solve our question, we conducted a scoping review with the goal of creating an initial overview of the state of research. We then used the information gained from the reviews to conduct expert interviews to gain deeper insights.

2 Scoping Review

To determine the state of the art, we conducted a scoping review of existing literature in privacy and security for collaborative AR. In the following, we will start by presenting our methodology, followed by the results of the research, as well as the taxonomy we derived for categorizing approaches for privacy and/or

[2] www.spatial.io.

security in collaborative AR. We discuss the current distribution of approaches in the taxonomy and derive implications for our research.

2.1 Methodology

For our survey, we searched the ACM and IEEE libraries with search terms generated from the key categories "AR", "Collaboration" and "Privacy"/"Security". We used wildcards and included alternative terms, such as "MR" and "XR", as well as different variations of the words, such as "secure" for the term "security". Our cut-off date was 2010 to focus on modern AR approaches.

To be eligible, the work's title or abstract had to contain at least one term from the key categories, those terms had to be related to each other (some works, for example, only mentioned AR as an example for high-speed network usage), and the work had to present an approach, so title pages and tables of content were excluded. We also excluded works where terms were used with different meanings (e.g., "AR" for "Action Research").

2.2 Results

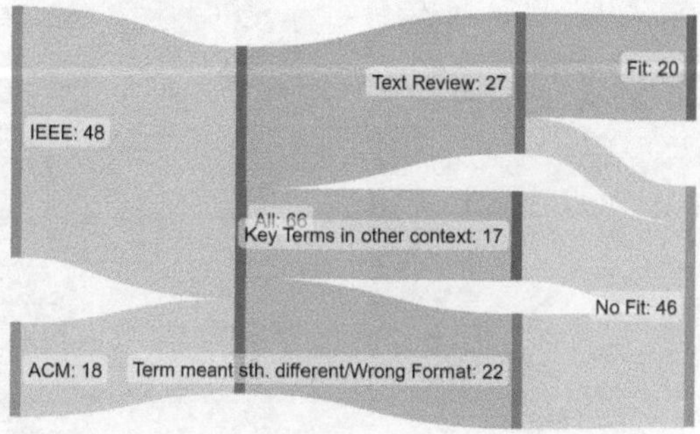

Fig. 1. The distribution of papers throughout the selection process.

Our search with the given parameters, which is also illustrated in Fig. 1, returned in 66 results, 48 from IEEE [1, 2, 6, 8, 9, 12–23, 25, 27, 29, 31–34, 38–44, 50–54, 57–60, 64–69, 69, 70] and 18 from ACM [4, 5, 7, 10, 26, 28, 30, 35, 37, 46–49, 55, 56, 61, 63, 71]. From the 66 found papers, 22 results [7, 16, 18, 23, 30, 32–34, 39–45, 47–49, 53, 60, 66, 67] were eliminated for having one of the key terms with a different meaning or for not having actual content (e.g. conference title pages). Further 17 papers [6, 10, 14, 15, 17, 25, 35, 38, 50–52, 57, 64, 68–71] were removed due to clear lack of relation between the key terms, which left 27 candidates for further investigation. This includes papers where it was not possible to clearly tell from the abstract whether they would contain an approach for security and privacy in AR collaboration. For 7 [2, 9, 12, 26, 46, 58, 59] out of these 27 results, reviewing the full text showed that their focus was on topics outside of security and privacy in AR collaboration and that at least one of the key terms was only mentioned as a side remark or was not included into the main research. For example, [26] mentioned camera sensor networks being used for AR, but then focused purely on said networks and did not mention AR or draw connections to it again.

The resulting approaches ([1,4,5,8,13,19–22,27–29,31,37,54–56,61,63,65] contain 12 results from IEEE and 8 results from ACM published in years ranging from 2010 to 2022. Even though there is some variation, possibly due to the small overall number of papers, the number of results per year is increasing, indicating an increasing interest in the topic.

2.3 Taxonomy

To develop a taxonomy for categorizing approaches to privacy and security in collaborative AR, we first reviewed a third of the above-presented eligible papers in addition to [11] and created a first taxonomy version from this. We then sorted the remaining papers into the taxonomy, adding new categories when necessary. In the finalized result, we re-evaluated our categories, especially the categories describing the approach details, combining similar ones for clearer results. This finalized taxonomy is visible in Fig. 2 and will be discussed in the following.

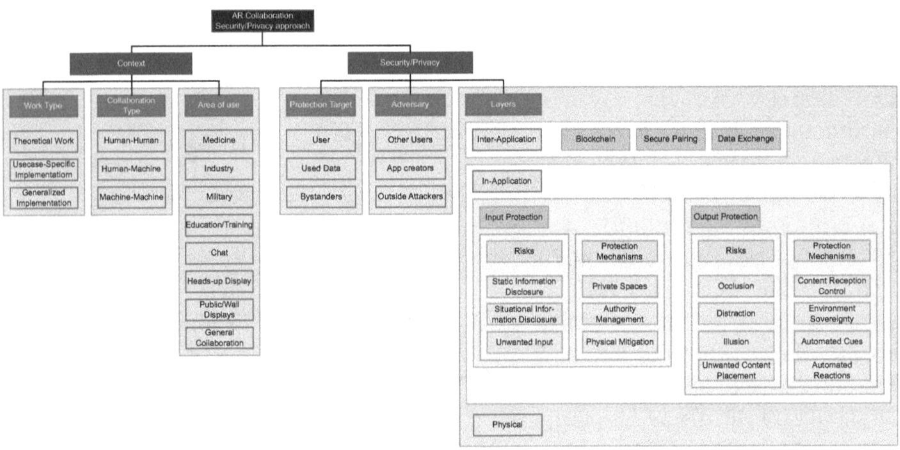

Fig. 2. The taxonomy developed in our literature survey.

Since the focus was on privacy and security in the context of AR collaboration, our taxonomy is split into two parts: one characterizing the approaches' context and one focusing on their security and privacy features. The context for the approaches is split up into the type of work, type of collaboration, and area of use. The type of work can be theoretical, where problems are identified and solutions are proposed without explicit implementation of the solutions. It can also be a work with a use case-specific implementation, where an approach was implemented for a specific use case, or a generalized implementation, where a solution is implemented in a way that makes it possible to apply it to different contexts. These categories are not mutually exclusive; for example, [55] implements a generalized solution and a concrete use case for it.

The type of collaboration is split into human-human, human-machine, and mach-ine-machine collaboration. In human-human collaboration, two human users work together using AR. In human-machine collaborations, humans use AR to interact with a machine or system. Machine-machine collaborations usually do not utilize AR, since AR is more of a display technology, which machines do not need. Some approaches, however, described machine-machine interactions in addition to one of the other types, for example, in larger networks.

The areas of use are derived from the different papers, with new ones added when grouping was not possible. The "General Collaboration" category summarizes the approaches that did not indicate a certain area of use. The specified areas are Medicine, Industry, Military, Education and Training, Chat, Heads-up Displays, and Public Displays.

Since, as mentioned previously, security and privacy are sometimes synergetic and sometimes contradictory, we decided against splitting features strictly into a security or a privacy category and created a "Security/Privacy" part (as in security and/or privacy). It is subdivided into a category for the target of protection, the adversary, and the layers of security and privacy that were taken into consideration. The target of protection can be either the application user, the data used in the application, or bystanders. When the application user is protected, this could also include protection of the data used in the application. However, this is not always the case. The protected data could be important, but not user-related (e.g., a machine prototype), meaning the used data is protected, but the user is not necessarily protected too. The adversaries from whom the protection targets have to be protected can be other users of an application, the creators of the application, or outside attackers without the previously mentioned roles.

The security/privacy layers category is subdivided into the inter-application aspects, in-application aspects, and physical aspects. Inter-application aspects treat everything that happens during the exchange of data between different instances of an application, for example, some network security techniques. In-application aspects treat the protection mechanisms taking place in a single instance of the application. This does not mean that the mechanism cannot influence other instances (e.g., by changing an object's authority settings), but the initiation of the action will come from one application. Physical aspects concern risks in or from the real environment that users might be exposed to due to an AR app (e.g., walking into a pole occluded by AR objects).

In the inter-application section, there are the subcategories of blockchain use, secure device pairing protocols, and the exchange of data between application instances for intrusion detection and therefore risk reduction.

The in-application section is subdivided into input- and output-protection (the terms and concepts are oriented on [11]), with each of the categories containing risks and protection mechanisms. These categories are defined in relation to the AR device: Input protection concerns anything that goes into inputs to the AR device (and application), such as user controls, data, and sensor readings. Output protection concerns anything the AR device outputs to the user, for example, different aspects of the AR view, such as occlusions through virtual content or content distracting the user.

As input protection risks, we found three categories: disclosure of static information, disclosure of situational information, and unwanted inputs. Static information disclosure concerns the "typical" kind of information in information security: information that is either already present in the application, gets loaded into it (e.g., a student's test results in [63]), or gets created in the application (e.g., a prototypical engine that is created in collaborative AR). This information might not be planned to be available to anyone in the application and must therefore be protected. The name does not mean that the so-called "static" information can never change, but it refers to the fact that the information will be there independent of the current situation, such as place of usage or bystanders. Situational information disclosure, on the other hand, describes information that is not actively used in or inserted into the application, but that exists in the current situation. For example, this could be the user's surroundings, which they do not want to accidentally share via the camera. It could also be the user's exact actions if they do not want others to see what exactly they are doing, or it could be the user speaking to someone (another user or a bystander) about things they do not want to share publicly. At this point, we want to mention that these risks of information disclosure are not equal to the earlier-mentioned targets of protection, which also contain mentions of data, but that they are instead two perspectives of an approach. The protection targets do not necessarily refer to input security risks. For example, a user could also be protected from output security risks, instead of from information disclosure. Approaches that protect used data will, however, also prevent static information disclosure since used data falls under our definition of static information. This relationship is, however, not bidirectional, since the protection from static information disclosure could also refer to other data, such as user data. Lastly, unwanted inputs describe interactions that happen against the user's will, for example, an adversary could shout voice commands to "hijack" the user's AR device, or someone could manipulate the user's AR objects (even as simple as another user taking them away, as in [29]).

To mitigate these risks to inputs, we found categories of protection mechanisms in the survey: private spaces, authority management, and physical mitigations. Private spaces describe the provision of a space where users can use objects or perform actions without other users being able to see them. This could be a marked area in the 3D space (e.g., in [28]), but it could also be a device, such as the mobile AR devices in [4], which were private spaces in contrast to a public screen. Authority management describes the possibility for users to control content access and authority. This can be done in different ways, for example, traditionally using a menu, as in [63], but also using physical objects to represent virtual ones, giving the users the possibility to use control authority by simply keeping them for themselves (see [56]). This also leads us to the third input protection mechanism: enabling physical mitigation behaviours. Physical mitigation describes some of the strategies of how people mitigate privacy and security risks when working with physical media: when hiding the content of a sheet of paper, they might hold it close to themselves or put it face down. The approaches in this category include the possibility for users to apply these techniques to AR, for example, [56] has cards with markers on them which represent virtual objects. Covered markers are not tracked, making it possible to hide the virtual objects.

We classified output protection into occlusion, distraction, illusion, and unwanted content placement. Occlusion can happen when a virtual object covers another object, real or virtual. [65] presents an example where a user is driving a car while using AR, and an advertisement pops up, partly blocking the view of the road. Distraction falls into a different direction: since AR content is displayed in the real world, it can easily be distracting [29] and even cause sensory overload (e.g. [8]). Additionally, especially when AR technology develops further towards realistic displays, illusions could be created, for example, making virtual objects seem real (e.g., see [54]). Lastly, there is also the risk of content being placed where it is not wanted, for example, attached to people, invading their personal space, or causing social discomfort (see [29]).

To prevent this, there are also protection mechanisms for output protection, such as content reception control, environment sovereignty, automated cues, and automated reactions. Content reception control describes the possibility for users to choose whether they want to see content, for example, when another user tries to upload it or send it to them (see [63]). Additionally, environment sovereignty enables users to control the environment that is already displayed to them to adjust it to their needs (e.g., in [8], animation speed can be controlled). Next, automated cues describe any alerts or information to the user that help them understand what is currently happening in the application. This could be a halo indicating an object as virtual [54] or dummy chat models helping users see if other users are currently busy [63]. Lastly, there are also automated reactions, where the application itself takes action to mitigate a risk. For example, [65] automatically moves virtual content to prevent occlusions. Technically, one could argue that automatic cues fall under automatic actions. However, we decided to separate the categories based on their intent: cues are there to inform the user and give them the agency to take action if they deem it necessary, but automatic reactions have the purpose of solving issues without the user being involved. Additionally, while cues in our classification would always stay on a relatively low level of intervention, reactions could theoretically go as far as blocking users out or shutting down the application (e.g., if an attack is detected).

As a last category of the security layers, there is also physical protection. This covers any approaches with the goal of protecting the physical well-being of application users. For example, [13] mentions specifically using HMDs to keep the user's hands free while handling heavy parts to protect them from accidents.

Taxonomy Distribution. Looking at the distribution of approaches into the categories of our created taxonomy, we see most (13) papers presented implemented solutions targeted towards one specific use case, but only 3 offered generalized implemented solutions that could be reused in different settings. Six works did not include an implementation but focused on theoretical foundations. Additionally, almost all (17) approaches focused on collaboration between humans, 6 included human-machine collaboration, and 3 papers additionally covered machine-machine collaboration (which, however, did not directly include AR in the collaboration).

The mentioned areas of use were diverse, with the most common area being education or training settings and industrial applications (used in 4 approaches). The next most common areas were the use of AR collaboration in industrial settings and in connection with video walls, with three approaches each. Other areas of use included chat applications, medical or military use, and heads-up displays. Six approaches were implemented in a general manner that was not focused on a specific area of use.

Regarding the specifics of security and privacy offered, most (18) of the approaches provided features to protect their users. Nearly half of them (8) covered protecting the data handled in the application, but only two approaches considered the protection of bystanders. Other users of the same application were the most mentioned adversaries (14), while 6 approaches offered protection against outside attackers, and only two approaches considered the app creators as adversaries. These two factors show that a lot of security and privacy efforts take place on the user level, with the main focus on the users, while considerations on a wider scale are less common.

Regarding the different layers of security and privacy, the inter-application layer was not focused on very often. Only three of the evaluated approaches proposed solutions, such as blockchain usage [19], a protocol for secure pairing [61], and the exchange of data between application instances to better detect issues like intrusions [65].

Nearly all approaches (19) discussed content on the in-application level, presenting risks, protection mechanisms, or both. This was the case for both input and output protection. Overall, there were 17 works that discussed a form of input protection risks, 12 approaches that discussed input protection mechanisms, 8 approaches that discussed output protection risks, and 8 works that included output protection mechanisms. It should be noted that, while most approaches discussed risks and then presented protection mechanisms to mitigate these risks, not every approach that discussed a risk also provided a protection measure for it, and vice versa. We only included clearly described risks and protection measures.

Looking closer at input security, the risks showed a clear main focus on static information disclosure with 13 approaches, while situational information disclosure was discussed in 8 approaches, and unwanted inputs were only discussed in 4 works. Regarding protection mechanisms, there were two top options: both offering users private spaces where their objects could not be seen by others and offering to control the authority on their objects were proposed by 7 works each. Three works proposed approaches to enable users to mitigate security and privacy concerns through their physical behaviour.

In output protection, occlusion was the most mentioned risk with 5 works, illusion was discussed 4 times, distraction was mentioned 3 times, and two works mentioned unwanted content placements as a risk. Concerning output protection mechanisms, the situation was balanced: 3 approaches discussed controlling content reception, automated cues, and automated application reactions each. Only one work discussed environment sovereignty. The main feature presented for output protection was preventing the creation of illusions or distracting elements that might also occlude real or virtual objects. These could be summed up as preventing interferences with users' perception, and different approaches for this were presented in 6 works. There were several different approaches that, however, each only came up once: giving users the option to reject or accept content, to adjust their (virtual) environment, and to detect attacks themselves.

Lastly, [13] included the factor of supporting the physical safety of users by keeping their hands free to prevent accidents.

2.4 Summary and Implications

Overall, some trends become clear from the survey. In-application protection, especially input protection, is the most common research topic. The most common risk that protection was offered against was the disclosure of static information, but situational information was also discussed regularly. Approaches often focused on private spaces and authority management for input protection. When output protection was discussed, occlusions and illusions were the most-referenced risks, and protection features were mostly reception control, automated cues, and automated reactions.

On the other hand, several facets, such as physical safety, inter-application protection, or the security and privacy of bystanders, that were focused on in only a few works, might offer further research potential.

Overall, the actual features, even in single categories, show high variation in the way they were implemented and executed, so there currently is no apparent reference approach or standard. Many works even discussed theoretical ideas without providing implementations. Additionally, the works that did implement solutions mostly focus on use-case-specific approaches, which are most likely not reusable in other contexts. The rare approaches that did offer re-usability only present single technologies, for example, a secure connection establishment.

While the existing work is very important and necessary to advance research, most of it will not find its way into daily practical use. Developers most likely do not have the time or motivation to read through several research papers and then try to combine the different approaches (that are most likely also using different technologies) into one project. This leads to a gap between research and practice. We decided to focus on this aspect in our further work and formulated the hypothesis that a toolbox approach offering a range of protection features could help to enhance privacy and security in AR by design. In the next sections, we will discuss how we tested this hypothesis by conducting expert interviews.

3 Interview Methodology

Using the results from the literature review, we conducted semi-structured expert interviews. In this section, we describe the methodology of deriving interview questions, participant selection, and interview execution.

The interview questions were oriented on [36] and included questions about demographics, the general situation in privacy and security in collaborative AR, as well as the users' and developers' specific situations in the area, and an outlook into the future. Regarding the general situation, we asked the participants about the current state of research and practice, as well as for potential risk factors in collaborative AR. We also asked which aspects the participants found particularly relevant. To learn more about the end-users' situation, we first asked about the users' current options to protect themselves, followed by inquiring about the users' degree of awareness regarding their privacy and security situation. Regarding the developers' perspective, we also started by asking about their privacy and security awareness and the degree to which developers include this into applications. We also had questions regarding areas and types of support that could be relevant to developers, and asked the participants which options they saw the most potential in. Lastly, we asked about future outlooks, such as the development of the significance of privacy and security in the future, and feasible or likely improvements for both end-users and developers.

We selected our participants based on relevant research work (e.g., found in the literature review). We also contacted other relevant institutions, but did not receive answers. Invitations were sent via e-mail and conducted via Zoom. When participants gave informed consent, the interviews were recorded, otherwise, notes were taken during the interview.

During the interviews, we used the predefined questions as a structural guideline while keeping the conversation as free as possible. We did, however, ensure that all participants were asked all the questions for comparability.

The next section will cover the results that we received in our interviews.

4 Results

In this section, we will present the interview results, with the themes and topics structured by the question groups presented in the methodology: we will first give a short overview of the participants' demographics and then discuss the results for the general situation, followed by the user side, the developer side, and, finally, the experts' outlook for the future.

4.1 Demographics

Table 1 gives an overview of the experts who participated in the interviews. We tried to find experts with different perspectives on the topic of privacy and security in collaborative AR, which reflects in the different fields of expertise the participants stated. Two experts (3 and 5) moved on to a slightly different focus since they published the works on the basis of which they were contacted; however, their new domains also had contact points with privacy and security for collaborative AR. For example, P3 still works on security, but in a web context, and P5 no longer works with AR, but is in the healthcare domain, where privacy and security play a big role. While most of the participants are male, the other categories, professional role and country of work, show a lot of variation, with participants coming from all over the globe and nearly all career levels of research.

Table 1. The demographic information of the participants

Participant	Professional Role	Gender	Country	Field
1	Professor	Male	New Zealand	Virtual/Augmented Reality
2	Associate Professor	Male	Canada	Spatial Cognition Ubiquitous Mobile AR/VR Sys.
3	Assistant Professor	Male	Phillipines	Usable Web Security Wireless Sensor Network (Formerly) Security & Privacy in MR Systems
4	PhD Student	Female	USA	Computer Interaction Security and Privacy in AR
5	Research Associate	Male	Germany	Healthcare Software Architecture (Formerly) Augmented Reality

4.2 General Situation

Regarding the general situation of privacy and security in collaborative AR, most participants agreed that there is a general lack of options. One (P3) was of the opinion that recently, more focus was put on privacy and security concerns, causing some releases, for example, of the current generation of Meta devices to be postponed. Related to this, P1 mentioned that it was not necessarily clear whether companies were actually invested into including privacy and security, rather than using it as a marketing effort. The other participants mentioned that most possibilities do not give much control to the users. For example, P5 mentioned that many applications do have a "Terms and Conditions" information, but users do not have the option to disagree and still use the application. P2 mentioned the app "Pokémon GO" as an example. They explained it contains issues with location privacy, as well as having more unique issues related to the game principle: the application also contained game contents positioned in private spaces or graveyards, which promoted inappropriate behaviour.

In relation to research, most participants knew of at least some efforts, but their opinions about the importance given to privacy and security approaches differed. For example, one participant described it as a "huge topic" (P2) and mentioned an ongoing project about helping collaborative AR users manage collaboration with different permissions, using, amongst other things, a heads-up display reminding users which information was secret and which could be shared to prevent slip-ups. They also mentioned that especially military research attaches a big value to security. Another participant (P4) was of the opinion that there is a variety of research on security and privacy for collaborative AR, which did, however, not reach the commercial sector yet. P1 said that the topic was under-researched, and was often a part, but not the focus of research works. They also expressed that the research community should try to be the drivers in bringing such topics more to the public eye and into businesses.

When speaking about privacy and security risk factors, two participants mentioned access control as an important detail. Also, some persons (P1, P3, P4) mentioned other "traditional" risks, such as man-in-the-middle attacks or data storage security. Bystander privacy was also mentioned twice (P3, P4), once in the context of data about bystanders being collected and once about disrupting bystanders by accidentally walking into them. Apart from that, each participant had different ideas: P1 mentioned that because every person sees only their own AR view, people could be manipulated by showing them slightly different views. Another (P2) explained that since the traces work leaves behind (e.g., in real life: writing on whiteboards) become invisible once users turn off AR, they might forget these traces exist and not remove them, leaving information unprotected. Another issue mentioned by P4 was the risk of users transmitting information about their surroundings to others, for example, by accidentally looking around while sharing a video stream and exposing private details.

When asked for the most important aspects, bystander privacy was again mentioned by multiple participants (P3, P4). Additionally, better options for informed consent were mentioned by P1, once stating that users need to learn what their device does, and once that more fine-grained options are needed instead of the current versions, where a user can either accept the conditions or not use the application. P2 mentioned the virtual traces of work again, and two P3 and P5 mentioned traditional approaches like secure data storage and authorization protocols.

4.3 User Side

When asked about current options for collaborative AR users to protect their privacy and security, most participants (P1, P3, P4, P5) did not see any powerful options. Some of them mentioned that since AR is not as commonly used yet, the pressure for such mechanisms is currently not as high (P1, P5). Some of the existing options the participants mentioned were not using AR apps at all (P1, P4), and a granularity option existed in one application where users can choose to either use their face on an avatar or use the standard version (P4). P1 brought up that the option of not using applications could be endangered if an implicit obligation to use AR appeared, for example, if a workplace required workers to use AR. P4 also mentioned that some applications give warnings that, for example, the camera is being used. Otherwise, the participants expressed several wishes or plans that were not yet available, such as p2's examples of supporting physical privacy behaviours or global permission management like in smartphones. P3 also emphasised that it is the developers' and researchers' task to come up with implemented and deployable solutions for this.

Regarding the question of how aware users currently are of their situation, all participants agreed that users were, on average, rather unaware of the privacy and security implications. Some suggested they might not care about the topic either due to a lack of security and privacy knowledge or because they only used AR in a controlled, non-private environment where there was no information that needed to be protected (e.g., in a lab or museum (P2)). Some participants mentioned single cases where users had expressed thoughts about privacy or security, such as asking about which spaces were visible to a remote collaborator or choosing a fitting environment to use AR at home (P4). P1, P3, and P4 emphasized the importance of educating the public about the privacy and security risks of AR. It was also mentioned that users should be educated about the inner workings of AR devices, for example, how devices store 3D maps of areas even if they are currently not in view, so users could understand what data they collect and give informed consent (P3).

4.4 Developer Side

The next question was to what extent developers currently include privacy and security in collaborative AR and how successful these attempts were. Most participants (P1, P2, P3, P4) answered that developers usually did not think about this a lot, especially in AR. P4 mentioned that those topics probably have not arrived in the AR domain yet. P3 said that (in general) "security and privacy is usually an afterthought. It's only when something problematic comes up, they try to address it". P1 mentioned that often, the perspectives are split into "technologists" and "non-technologists". The non-technologists do think about security and privacy topics, but can only go into things to a certain degree, while technologists who develop the actual applications do not think about the topics or let them slide because they get told what to implement by their superiors. P1 and P3 also expressed that usually, the functionalities are prioritized over security and privacy, especially in AR, and that developers often are limited in their security and privacy choices by external influences like company software. As positive points, P4 mentioned that some toolkits at least offer automatic sensor permission handling. P2 and P3 also mentioned some existing and ongoing work in research. For example, P2 spoke about an inferencing engine that could be used to configure different permissions. P1 emphasized education about privacy and security topics as a key feature to improve the situation.

When asked what could help developers to improve privacy and security in applications, the participants' answers were mostly in agreement. All but one participant (P5) mentioned better software support, especially libraries with pre-existing, ready-to-use solutions for developers were often mentioned. For example, P4 explained that it would be helpful if there were a library so developers would not have to go through the trouble of researching options first. The next commonly named point (P1, P3, P4) was training and education for security and privacy awareness, so security and privacy would be more in focus and not just a "nice-to-have" feature. Additionally, P2 and P3 mentioned that technical advances would be helpful or even necessary since developers are limited by the hardware they need to use.

When asked to name one area where developers would profit from support the most, most participants (P2 - P5) again mentioned supporting software, either as in a cross-platform software for AR for better code re-usability or in the form of development frameworks or guidelines with reliable support for developing good privacy and security. Many participants did not limit themselves to one answer and mentioned support in the form of more mature operating systems and cooperation from big platforms (like Apple, Windows, and Android) with research to offer better privacy and security options (P1, P3, P4). Also, it was mentioned that the only way to reach this would be by educating people on these security and privacy topics (P1).

4.5 Outlook

In the last section, we asked participants about their hopes or presumptions for the future, beginning with asking how they expected the public interest in the topic to develop. Several participants (P1, P3, P4) hoped that the interest in privacy and security for collaborative AR would rise. Also, several mentioned that if (collaborative) AR would become more common, the interest in privacy and security would necessarily rise as well (P3, P4). According to one participant, this would be elementary to achieve public acceptance and trust in AR (P1). P2 also mentioned how the more common use of AR would bring up several new issues, such as what spaces were acceptable to share and how representation of people in remote AR should be done (P2: "Representations [and] what do they tell about [me], am I in my pyjamas [in the representation if wearing them in real life]?"). Another (P4) mentioned how some of the technologies in some AR devices, such as eye-tracking, posed especially complicated challenges when commonly used. They explained that companies could theoretically track their workers' attentiveness using eye tracking and use this to control or punish them.

When asked about possible improvements from the user perspective, the opinions differed. One person (P2) worried that users have no choice and would just get used to the technology and the connected privacy and security issues, but still hoped that privacy and security would be added, building on existing practices. Another participant (P5) mentioned that users do not have a direct influence on these topics and have to rely on developers to improve the situation. In contrast, P1 explained that as much transparency as possible was necessary for users to even accept the technology and that it would be necessary to illustrate the inner workings of AR devices to users (e.g., what data is collected, how, and where does it go). Other participants (P3, P4) focused on compromises that might be possible in the future, such as giving users several options to choose from and informing them of their effects. For example, users could decide whether they want to put a picture of themselves on an avatar or not, but would be reminded that other users' experience would be less immersive without the picture (P4). It could also be that users can reject certain permissions, such as microphone access, and still use the application, just without certain features (e.g., without voice commands).

The last question asked for potential future improvements for developers. Again, several (P1, P2, P3, P4) participants expressed the hope for a pre-existing software support that could, for example, be pre-integrated into development environments (P1) and which would ease the development of privacy- and security-friendly collaborative AR applications (P4). One participant (P5) suggested that once AR, and privacy and security for collaborative AR gain more focus, the development of such options would likely happen. Some (P2, P4) also hoped for more possibilities to reuse such features, for example, through more standards. Some participants also suggested specific features, such as the possibility of exposing security and privacy decisions to users (P2). One participant (P3) also mentioned that they hoped for more research and development for algorithms that would make it possible to limit the data that has to be collected by the sensors of AR devices for them to still perform well.

5 Discussion

While in some cases answers skewed widely, some trends were recognizable. We will first discuss the trends in the participants' answers, and afterwards discuss some interesting opinions and trends that became apparent.

In the general situation, most participants were of the opinion that there is currently not much work, especially in practice. On the other hand, one participant mentioned delayed releases as an indicator of a higher privacy and security concern, though not specifically mentioning a connection to AR. Another participant also mentioned big companies speaking about privacy and security in general, but implied that this could rather be a marketing action. Combining all of these statements, it seems that privacy and security are not common yet in general or collaborative applications, but that there is at least a slight increase in public interest in security and privacy in general. That might have motivated companies to engage with the topic.

As soon as specific privacy and security risks were discussed, the expert opinions again differed too much to get clear results, but some traditional features, such as authorization, were mentioned multiple times. This implies that even though AR poses new challenges to privacy and security, traditional issues still need to be considered. Maybe, given that in later questions many participants wished for more (cross-platform) software support, an issue could lie in the fact that solutions for traditional issues do exist, but are not necessarily implemented to fit in with the software used for AR development. That could explain why these risks are still that present.

This would also fit with the next question's results, which showed that when asked for especially important aspects, participants mentioned mostly more AR-specific topics, especially bystander privacy. Noticeably, they thought of these features as the most important, but still mentioned traditional features first when asked about risk. A reason for this could be that the AR-specific categories are important in research to find out what risks they actually contain, as well as to develop good protection mechanisms for them. The traditional features, in return, do have protection mechanisms already, but it is also known how they can be abused, making them more known as a risk.

Regarding user options, the participants were again mostly in agreement that there are not many options for users yet. Several participants also mentioned that there are usually no fine-grained privacy and security controls; for example, users only have the option to not use an application to protect themselves. In combination with another statement made, saying that there is currently not much pressure for improvements since AR is not very widely spread, this could imply two outcomes: either, users will not accept AR technology, for example, because they choose the option of not using it to protect their privacy, or AR becomes more common anyways, provoking new and more privacy and security issues.

Since the participants also completely agreed that users are mostly unaware of privacy and security in collaborative AR, their opinion is likely true, and the second outcome above gains in plausibility. Whether the users did not care, did not know, or found the risk acceptable due to not using AR in a private setting, when AR becomes more common and maybe even required in some workplaces without the users putting an emphasis on privacy and security features, it might become very hard to protect one's personal privacy and security. For example, reconnecting to bystander privacy, some people's devices could become a risk to others' privacy, and when workplaces require a worker to use AR, they can hardly refuse due to privacy concerns.

When speaking of developers, most participants saw awareness issues as well, again indicating this to be a true issue through high agreement. They also mentioned issues with privacy and security being "afterthoughts" and developers having to cut them out since they are not functional features. Similar to the above-mentioned issue with jobs requiring the use of AR, this is an issue that is more complicated to solve. Public education about security and privacy matters, as one participant mentioned, could help to make sure the public demands these features, making them more relevant to development. It could also help the topic to reach committees and organisations that could create rules or standards requiring privacy and security.

Most participants also expressed that support from the software side could help developers. This would lower the barrier to including privacy and security in collaborative AR development, even if it is not required by an authority. Depending on the type of support, this could even supplement the privacy and security education, which was also mentioned, by adding suggestions and showing possible improvements to developers. They could discover new possibilities they did not think of before without explicitly researching them.

When speaking about areas where support could come from, software was again a common topic, supporting the ideas above. Software from the big vendors helping to reuse these solutions cross-platform as easily as possible was also mentioned and would be fitting.

Lastly, in the outlook, many participants hoped for a general increase in interest in privacy and security. When looking back to the beginning of this section, this increase might already have begun. It would also help if the second common theory, that interest in privacy and security in collaborative AR would rise if AR became more common, turned out to be true, since this could hopefully improve the situation before issues due to neglected privacy and security become too much. When speaking about users, there was no clear result, but the recurring idea of users just getting used to the new technology without considering security came up again. It is not too far-fetched when remembering the observations about current users' privacy and security awareness. For developers, the idea of overarching software support coming up from several participants again underlines the importance of the topic.

Even though it was rare that all five participants mentioned the same idea, there was a trend that was especially visible in the opinion about user and developer relations to privacy and security in collaborative AR. Mainly, it said that users, as well as developers, would profit from more knowledge and the active possibility to improve the current situation. A core topic fitting this category, even though brought in by a single participant, is the topic of educating the public, as well as developers, about privacy and security in collaborative AR. Another recurring topic was support for developers, in some form of software. Even though different participants formulated widely different approaches to the exact realisation, software support was a common topic. Lastly, it was interesting how traditional privacy and security features seemed still relevant, but also some AR-specific features, especially bystander privacy, were repeatedly mentioned.

5.1 Threats to Validity

The main threat to validity is that participants were biased based on the invitation email and answered in a way that doe not fully reflect their attitudes, behaviours and experiences. To balance this, we kept the mail vague, but did still mention that a development framework was planned in hopes of getting a clearer base of discussion from that. Additionally, participants will likely be biased towards the topics of their research, since that is where they have the most experience. We counteracted this by using the state of the art approach of speaking to different participants with different backgrounds. The fact that we might have gotten some information that goes more deeply into one field can also be seen as an advantage, since we were also looking for insights from different perspectives. We took into account whether statements repeated between participants or not, to separate opinions based on personal experience from opinions that seem to be more common.

6 Summary and Implications

The results of the expert interviews discussed above support the impression from the literature research that there is a gap between research and practice. Most participants mentioned that there is at least some research on privacy and security in AR, but also that the topic, though it might have gotten some more attention lately, has not found its way into the focus of society yet. It was mentioned several times that end users often have no or only very limited options to protect their privacy and security in AR collaboration. They are also often unaware that these risks even exist, according to the experts. It was also mentioned that the interest of the general public is necessary to lead to improvements in this area and that privacy and security education for everyone was an important factor. Informed users could also build up pressure so that companies start to see it as worthwhile to include privacy and security topics. This factor is also relevant to the developer side. If developers are aware of the applications' security and privacy implications, there still is the issue of privacy and security often being an "afterthought" compared to functional requirements. For this reason, developers rarely have the time to include them. If companies focused on this topic more, the developers would be more likely to get the chance to include privacy and security at all. Most participants explained that supporting software could help to lower the barrier for developers to add security and privacy aspects to their projects. They also suggested that supporting software could even help to educate developers by showing them suggestions and options without the need to research them first.

The insights we gained in the expert interviews verified our hypothesis that a toolbox approach with a set of protection features could help to enhance privacy and security in AR by design. It could also be a possibility to offer education to developers.

The matching results from the scoping review and the expert interviews substantiating our hypothesis also enable us to answer our research question ("How can privacy and security in collaborative AR be improved?"): A developer toolbox approach was determined (by a literature survey and expert interviews) likely to help enhance security and privacy by design in collaborative AR. Additionally, there are other options, such as additional work in less-researched areas (e.g., bystander privacy), as well as educating the public on privacy and security (in addition to what the development of a toolbox could offer).

We have explored the approach of implementing TARPS, a toolbox for introducing privacy and security to collaborative AR applications, in further work [24], which supports developers in integrating privacy and security features into existing projects. The developers can use a menu to select their protection goals, and the necessary protection features are automatically added and explained by the framework. This way, prior security/privacy knowledge is not needed, and the developers can learn from the toolbox. TARPS was evaluated in developer interviews, where it was well received. In an additional end-user study, it was also shown to produce results that were usable and accepted by end-users.

References

1. Al-Barhamtoshy, H.M., Al-Ghamdi, A.: Toward cloud-based mixed reality e-learning system. In: 2017 International Conference on Informatics, Health & Technology (ICIHT), pp. 1–6 (2017). https://doi.org/10.1109/ICIHT.2017.7899008
2. Avalle, G., De Pace, F., Fornaro, C., Manuri, F., Sanna, A.: An augmented reality system to support fault visualization in industrial robotic tasks. IEEE Access **7**, 132343–132359 (2019). https://doi.org/10.1109/ACCESS.2019.2940887
3. Azuma, R.T.: A survey of augmented reality. Presence: Teleoper. Virtual Environ. **6**(4), 355–385 (1997)
4. Baldauf, M., Fröhlich, P.: The augmented video wall: multi-user AR interaction with public displays. In: CHI '13 Extended Abstracts on Human Factors in Computing Systems. pp. 3015–3018. CHI EA '13, Association for Computing Machinery, New York, NY, USA (2013). https://doi.org/10.1145/2468356.2479599
5. Baldauf, M., Lasinger, K., Fröhlich, P.: Private public screens: detached multi-user interaction with large displays through mobile augmented reality. In: Proceedings of the 11th International Conference on Mobile and Ubiquitous Multimedi, pp. 1–4. MUM '12, Association for Computing Machinery, New York, NY, USA (2012). https://doi.org/10.1145/2406367.2406401
6. Balfour, R.E., Donnelly, B.P.: The what, why and how of achieving urban telepresence. In: 2013 IEEE Long Island Systems, Applications and Technology Conference (LISAT), pp. 1–6 (2013). https://doi.org/10.1109/LISAT.2013.6578234
7. Barbosa, A.F., G. Neto, G.T., Lencastre, M., Fagundes, R.A.A., Santos, W.B.: Fostering industry-academia collaboration in software engineering using action research: A Case Study. In: 19th Brazilian Symposium on Software Quality, pp. 1–9. SBQS'20, Association for Computing Machinery, New York, NY, USA (2021). https://doi.org/10.1145/3439961.3440005
8. Bauer, V., Bouchara, T., Bourdot, P.: Designing an extended reality application to expand clinic-based sensory strategies for autistic children requiring substantial support: participation of practitioners. In: 2021 IEEE International Symposium on Mixed and Augmented Reality Adjunct (ISMAR-Adjunct), pp. 254–259 (2021). https://doi.org/10.1109/ISMAR-Adjunct54149.2021.00059
9. Bhosale, K., Rohokale, V.: Computer vision for green and secure cooperative augmented reality in next generation converged wireless networks. In: 2015 International Conference on Pervasive Computing (ICPC), pp. 1–5 (2015). https://doi.org/10.1109/PERVASIVE.2015.7087189
10. Brewster, S.: eXtended reality and passengers of the future. In: Proceedings of the 2022 International Conference on Advanced Visual Interfaces, p. 1. AVI 2022, Association for Computing Machinery, New York, NY, USA (2022). https://doi.org/10.1145/3531073.3538399
11. De Guzman, J.A., Thilakarathna, K., Seneviratne, A.: Security and privacy approaches in mixed reality: a literature survey. ACM Comput. Surv. **52**(6) (2019). https://doi.org/10.1145/3359626
12. Djenouri, Y., Belhadi, A., Srivastava, G., Lin, J.C.W.: Secure collaborative augmented reality framework for biomedical informatics. IEEE J. Biomed. Health Inf. **26**(6), 2417–2424 (2022). https://doi.org/10.1109/JBHI.2021.3139575, conference Name: IEEE Journal of Biomedical and Health Informatics
13. Fangyang, S., Jun, J., Xuejun, L., Yue, Q.: 3D modeling and augmented reality. In: 2010 4th International Universal Communication Symposium, pp. 185–192 (2010). https://doi.org/10.1109/IUCS.2010.5666644

14. Fournaris, A.P., Lalos, A., Kapsalas, P., Koulamas, C.: Decentralized, secure and cognitive architecture for automotive cyber physical system of systems. In: 2020 9th Mediterranean Conference on Embedded Computing (MECO), pp. 1–5 (2020). https://doi.org/10.1109/MECO49872.2020.9134336, iSSN: 2637-9511
15. Gamal, Y.E.: Keynote speech I: use of ICT to combat COVID-19. In: 2020 30th International Conference on Computer Theory and Applications (ICCTA), pp. 1–1 (2020). https://doi.org/10.1109/ICCTA52020.2020.9477687
16. Guo, P., Wang, P., Zhou, J., Jiang, S., Patel, V.M.: Multi-institutional collaborations for improving deep learning-based magnetic resonance image reconstruction using federated learning. In: 2021 IEEE/CVF Conference on Computer Vision and Pattern Recognition (CVPR), pp. 2423–2432 (2021). https://doi.org/10.1109/CVPR46437.2021.00245, iSSN: 2575-7075
17. IEEE: Workshop: Using Mobile Computing for Learning and Sharing in the Post Web Era (2011). https://doi.org/10.1109/C5.2011.13. iSSN: 1556-0090
18. IEEE: Message from IEEE 2021 CIC General Chairs and PC Chairs (2021). https://doi.org/10.1109/CIC52973.2021.00005
19. Islam, A., Masuduzzaman, M., Akter, A., Young Shin, S.: MR-Block: A blockchain-assisted secure content sharing scheme for multi-user mixed-reality applications in internet of military things. In: 2020 International Conference on Information and Communication Technology Convergence (ICTC), pp. 407–411 (2020). https://doi.org/10.1109/ICTC49870.2020.9289327, iSSN: 2162-1233
20. Jouet, P., Alleaume, V., Laurent, A., Fradet, M., Luo, T., Baillard, C.: AR-Chat: an AR-based instant messaging system. In: 2020 IEEE International Symposium on Mixed and Augmented Reality Adjunct (ISMAR-Adjunct), pp. 153–157 (2020). https://doi.org/10.1109/ISMAR-Adjunct51615.2020.00050
21. Kamei, G., Matsuyama, T., Okada, K.: Augmentation of check in/out model for remote collaboration with Mixed Reality. In: 2010 IEEE International Symposium on Mixed and Augmented Reality. pp. 243–244 (2010). https://doi.org/10.1109/ISMAR.2010.5643588
22. Kilger, F., Kabil, A., Tippmann, V., Klinker, G., Pahl, M.O.: Detecting and preventing faked mixed reality. In: 2021 IEEE 4th International Conference on Multimedia Information Processing and Retrieval (MIPR), pp. 399–405 (2021). https://doi.org/10.1109/MIPR51284.2021.00074
23. Kong, Z., Xu, C.Z., Kwok, Y.K.: Downlink resource auction in a tree topology structured wireless mesh network. In: 2010 IEEE 16th International Conference on Parallel and Distributed Systems, pp. 578–584 (2010). https://doi.org/10.1109/ICPADS.2010.115, iSSN: 1521-9097
24. Krings, S.C., Yigitbas, E.: Tarps: A toolbox for enhancing privacy and security for collaborative AR. Proc. ACM Hum.-Comput. Interact. **8**(EICS) (2024). https://doi.org/10.1145/3660251
25. Krupke, D., Steinicke, F., Lubos, P., Jonetzko, Y., Görner, M., Zhang, J.: Comparison of multimodal heading and pointing gestures for co-located mixed reality human-robot interaction. In: 2018 IEEE/RSJ International Conference on Intelligent Robots and Systems (IROS), pp. 1–9 (2018). https://doi.org/10.1109/IROS.2018.8594043, iSSN: 2153-0866
26. Kyrkou, C., Theocharides, T., Panayiotou, C., Polycarpou, M.: Distributed adaptive task allocation for energy conservation in camera sensor networks. In: Proceedings of the 9th International Conference on Distributed Smart Cameras, pp. 92–97. ICDSC '15, Association for Computing Machinery, New York, NY, USA (2015). https://doi.org/10.1145/2789116.2789131

27. Langfinger, M., Schneider, M., Stricker, D., Schotten, H.D.: Addressing security challenges in industrial augmented reality systems. In: 2017 IEEE 15th International Conference on Industrial Informatics (INDIN), pp. 299–304 (2017). https://doi.org/10.1109/INDIN.2017.8104789, iSSN: 2378-363X
28. Lapides, P., Sultanum, N., Sharlin, E., Sousa, M.C.: Seamless mixed reality tracking in tabletop reservoir engineering interaction. In: Proceedings of the International Working Conference on Advanced Visual Interfaces, pp. 725–728. AVI '12, Association for Computing Machinery, New York, NY, USA (2012). https://doi.org/10.1145/2254556.2254694
29. Lebeck, K., Ruth, K., Kohno, T., Roesner, F.: Towards security and privacy for multi-user augmented reality: foundations with end users. In: 2018 IEEE Symposium on Security and Privacy (SP), pp. 392–408 (2018). https://doi.org/10.1109/SP.2018.00051, iSSN: 2375-1207
30. Lin, Y., et al.: Meta matrix factorization for federated rating predictions. In: Proceedings of the 43rd International ACM SIGIR Conference on Research and Development in Information Retrieval, pp. 981–990. SIGIR '20, Association for Computing Machinery, New York, NY, USA (2020). https://doi.org/10.1145/3397271.3401081
31. Liu, C.Z., Kavakli, M.: An agent-based collaborative information processing system for mixed reality applications — Part A: Agent-aware computing. In: 2018 13th IEEE Conference on Industrial Electronics and Applications (ICIEA), pp. 1273–1278 (2018). https://doi.org/10.1109/ICIEA.2018.8397905, iSSN: 2158-2297
32. Lopes, I.M., Oliveira, P.: Evaluation of the adoption of an information systems security policy. In: 2015 10th Iberian Conference on Information Systems and Technologies (CISTI), pp. 1–6 (2015). https://doi.org/10.1109/CISTI.2015.7170418, iSSN: 2166-0727
33. Ludhiyani, A., Joshi, S., Pathak, R., Parandkar, P., Katiyal, S.: Quant techniques and regime analysis for increase in trade & business between India and Israel. In: 2015 2nd International Conference on Computing for Sustainable Global Development (INDIACom), pp. 442–447 (2015)
34. Lukosch, S., Billinghurst, M., Kiyokawa, K., Feiner, S., Alem, L.: Collaboration in mediated and augmented reality (CiMAR) summary. In: 2015 IEEE International Symposium on Mixed and Augmented Reality Workshops, pp. 1–2 (2015). https://doi.org/10.1109/ISMARW.2015.26
35. Lukosch, S., Lukosch, H., Datcu, D., Cidota, M.: On the spot information in augmented reality for teams in the security domain. In: Proceedings of the 33rd Annual ACM Conference Extended Abstracts on Human Factors in Computing Systems, pp. 983–988. CHI EA '15, Association for Computing Machinery, New York, NY, USA (2015). https://doi.org/10.1145/2702613.2732879
36. Lutz, C., Schöttler, M., Hoffmann, C.P.: The privacy implications of social robots: scoping review and expert interviews. Mob. Media Commun. **7**(3), 412–434 (2019). https://doi.org/10.1177/2050157919843961
37. Machuca, M.D.B., Chinthammit, W., Yang, Y., Duh, H.: 3D mobile interactions for public displays. In: SIGGRAPH Asia 2014 Mobile Graphics and Interactive Applications, p. 1. SA '14, Association for Computing Machinery, New York, NY, USA (2014). https://doi.org/10.1145/2669062.2684184
38. Nijholt, A., et al.: Trends & Controversies. IEEE Intell. Syst. **27**(6), 60–75 (2012). https://doi.org/10.1109/MIS.2012.116
39. n.n.: 2010 IEEE International Conference on Systems, Man and Cybernetics. https://ieeexplore.ieee.org/xpl/conhome/5629466/proceeding

40. n.n.: 2011 IEEE 2nd International Conference on Software Engineering and Service Science. https://ieeexplore.ieee.org/xpl/conhome/5967841/proceeding
41. n.n.: 2011 Seventh International Conference on Signal Image Technology & Internet-Based Systems. https://ieeexplore.ieee.org/xpl/conhome/6120130/proceeding
42. n.n.: 2014 IIAI 3rd International Conference on Advanced Applied Informatics. https://ieeexplore.ieee.org/xpl/conhome/6909097/proceeding
43. n.n.: 2015 17th International Conference on Advanced Communication Technology (ICACT)
44. n.n.: 2015 IEEE International Conference on Self-Adaptive and Self-Organizing Systems Workshops. https://ieeexplore.ieee.org/xpl/conhome/7305895/proceeding
45. n.n.: 2016 6th International Conference on IT Convergence and Security (ICITCS). https://ieeexplore.ieee.org/xpl/conhome/7740253/proceeding
46. n.n.: FRAME 2022 | Proceedings of the 31st International Symposium on High-Performance Parallel and Distributed Computing. https://doi.org/10.1145/3502181.3535103
47. n.n.: IH&MMSec '15: Proceedings of the 3rd ACM Workshop on Information Hiding and Multimedia Security. https://doi.org/10.1145/2756601
48. n.n.: IH&MMSec '16: Proceedings of the 4th ACM Workshop on Information Hiding and Multimedia Security. https://doi.org/10.1145/2909827
49. n.n.: Proceedings of the 25th ACM international conference on Multimedia
50. n.n.: SITIS 2012 - Objectives. In: 2012 Eighth International Conference on Signal Image Technology and Internet Based Systems, pp. xxiii–xxiii (2012). https://doi.org/10.1109/SITIS.2012.7
51. n.n.: Next Generation Internet of Things Distributed Intelligence at the Edge and Human Machine-to-Machine Cooperation. In: Next Generation Internet of Things Distributed Intelligence at the Edge and Human Machine-to-Machine Cooperation, pp. i–xxiv. River Publishers (2018), conference Name: Next Generation Internet of Things Distributed Intelligence at the Edge and Human Machine-to-Machine Cooperation
52. Peng, Y., et al.: Securing radio resources allocation with deep reinforcement learning for ioe services in next-generation wireless networks. IEEE Trans. Netw. Sci. Eng. **9**(5), 2991–3003 (2022). https://doi.org/10.1109/TNSE.2022.3149750, conference Name: IEEE Transactions on Network Science and Engineering
53. Pérez-López, D., Contero, M., Alcañiz, M.: Collaborative development of an augmented reality application for digestive and circulatory systems teaching. In: 2010 10th IEEE International Conference on Advanced Learning Technologies, pp. 173–175 (2010). https://doi.org/10.1109/ICALT.2010.54, iSSN: 2161-377X
54. Regenbrecht, H., Zwanenburg, S., Langlotz, T.: Pervasive augmented reality-technology and ethics. IEEE Pervasive Comput. **21**(3), 84–91 (2022). https://doi.org/10.1109/MPRV.2022.3152993
55. Reilly, D., Salimian, M., MacKay, B., Mathiasen, N., Edwards, W.K., Franz, J.: SecSpace: prototyping usable privacy and security for mixed reality collaborative environments. In: Proceedings of the 2014 ACM SIGCHI symposium on Engineering interactive computing systems, pp. 273–282. EICS '14, Association for Computing Machinery, New York, NY, USA (2014). https://doi.org/10.1145/2607023.2607039
56. Salimian, M.H., Reilly, D., Brooks, S., MacKay, B.: Physical-digital privacy interfaces for mixed reality collaboration: an exploratory study. In: Proceedings of the

2016 ACM International Conference on Interactive Surfaces and Spaces, pp. 261–270. ISS '16, Association for Computing Machinery, New York, NY, USA (2016). https://doi.org/10.1145/2992154.2992167

57. Sarvesh, P., K, P., R, D.K.J., Naren, S., Ashwin, M., Kavin, T.: A systematic AR based ATM model to enhance Security and Safety. In: 2021 Second International Conference on Electronics and Sustainable Communication Systems (ICESC), pp. 879–886 (2021). https://doi.org/10.1109/ICESC51422.2021.9532897
58. Schild, J., Elsenbast, C., Carbonell, G.: ViTAWiN - developing multiprofessional medical emergency training with mixed reality. In: 2021 IEEE 9th International Conference on Serious Games and Applications for Health(SeGAH), pp. 1–9 (2021). https://doi.org/10.1109/SEGAH52098.2021.9551890, iSSN: 2573-3060
59. Sharma, S.K., Woungang, I., Anpalagan, A., Chatzinotas, S.: Toward tactile internet in beyond 5G era: recent advances, current issues, and future directions. IEEE Access **8**, 56948–56991 (2020). https://doi.org/10.1109/ACCESS.2020.2980369
60. Shim, K.A.: BASIS: a practical multi-user broadcast authentication scheme in wireless sensor networks. IEEE Trans. Inf. Forensics Secur. **12**(7), 1545–1554 (2017). https://doi.org/10.1109/TIFS.2017.2668062, conference Name: IEEE Transactions on Information Forensics and Security
61. Sluganovic, I., Serbec, M., Derek, A., Martinovic, I.: HoloPair: securing shared augmented reality using microsoft HoloLens. In: Proceedings of the 33rd Annual Computer Security Applications Conference, pp. 250–261. ACSAC '17, Association for Computing Machinery, New York, NY, USA (2017). https://doi.org/10.1145/3134600.3134625
62. Sutherland, I.E.: A head-mounted three dimensional display. In: Fall Joint Computer Conference, pp. 757–764. Association for Computing Machinery, New York, NY, USA (1968)
63. Tran, L.A., Hensen, B., Klamma, R., Chantaraskul, S.: Privacy and security in mixed reality learning environments by input and user/bot interaction protection. In: 2022 4th Asia Pacific Information Technology Conference. pp. 63–71. APIT 2022, Association for Computing Machinery, New York, NY, USA (2022). https://doi.org/10.1145/3512353.3512363
64. Vasconcelos, J.V.R., Villa, D.K.D., Caldeira, A.G., Sarcinelli-Filho, M., Brandão, A.S.: Agent fault-tolerant strategy in a heterogeneous triangular formation. In: 2020 International Conference on Unmanned Aircraft Systems (ICUAS), pp. 1040–1047 (2020). https://doi.org/10.1109/ICUAS48674.2020.9213851, iSSN: 2575-7296
65. Wang, F., Liu, Y., Liu, J., Argyriou, A., Wang, L., Xu, Z.: Output security for multi-user augmented reality using federated reinforcement learning. In: 2021 IEEE Symposium on Computers and Communications (ISCC), pp. 1–7 (2021). https://doi.org/10.1109/ISCC53001.2021.9631507, iSSN: 2642-7389
66. Wang, K., et al.: a trusted consensus scheme for collaborative learning in the edge AI computing domain. IEEE Netw. **35**(1), 204–210 (2021). https://doi.org/10.1109/MNET.011.2000249
67. Wang, Y., Su, Z., Luan, T.H., Li, R., Zhang, K.: Federated learning with fair incentives and robust aggregation for UAV-aided crowdsensing. IEEE Trans. Netw. Sci. Eng. **9**(5), 3179–3196 (2022). https://doi.org/10.1109/TNSE.2021.3138928, conference Name: IEEE Transactions on Network Science and Engineering
68. Wu, D., Han, X., Yang, Z., Wang, R.: Exploiting transfer learning for emotion recognition under cloud-edge-client collaborations. IEEE J. Sel. Areas Commun. **39**(2), 479–490 (2021). https://doi.org/10.1109/JSAC.2020.3020677

69. Yan, M., Chen, B., Feng, G., Qin, S.: Federated cooperation and augmentation for power allocation in decentralized wireless networks. IEEE Access **8**, 48088–48100 (2020). https://doi.org/10.1109/ACCESS.2020.2979323
70. Zeyu, H., Geming, X., Zhaohang, W., Sen, Y.: Survey on edge computing security. In: 2020 International Conference on Big Data, Artificial Intelligence and Internet of Things Engineering (ICBAIE), pp. 96–105 (2020). https://doi.org/10.1109/ICBAIE49996.2020.00027
71. Zodik, G.: Cognitive and contextual enterprise mobile computing: invited keynote talk. In: Proceedings of the 9th India Software Engineering Conference, pp. 11–12. ISEC '16, Association for Computing Machinery, New York, NY, USA (2016). https://doi.org/10.1145/2856636.2876471

Navigation for People with Disabilities and Older People: Current Challenges and Opportunities

Navigation for People with Disabilities and Older People: Current Challenges and Opportunities

Helen Petrie[1(✉)] and Gerhard Weber[2]

[1] University of York, York YO10 5DD, UK
helen.petrie@york.ac.uk
[2] Technische Universität Dresden, Dresden, Germany
gerhard.weber@tu-dresden.de

Abstract. This workshop brought together researchers and practitioners interested in the use of technology to support navigation and mobility for people with disabilities and older people. This includes both indoor and outdoor navigation in the real world, as well as navigation in virtual worlds. Technologies such as GPS, robotics and AI have provided many advances in independent, safe navigation for these groups, but there are new technologies emerging and many challenges still to be addressed. Participants at the workshop presented their research and interests in the area, including the technologies and methods used and the user groups of relevance. The workshop synthesized the current challenges and opportunities in the area, current areas of research and gaps in the research portfolio as well as issues for users which are not currently being addressed. Finally, a comprehensive review of recent research in this area was begun. This will serve as a useful resource for researchers and develop a roadmap for future research in the area.

Keywords: navigation · wayfinding · obstacle detection · people with disabilities · older people

1 Introduction

Navigation can be a problem for anyone from time to time. Whether it is trying to find one's way in an unfamiliar town or in the country, in a complex office building, or a hospital, airport or museum. Increasingly, we need to navigate through virtual environments as well as real ones. For people with disabilities and older people, these situations can be particularly challenging. This in turn means that disabled and older people may miss opportunities for work and leisure, are less independent and have poorer quality of life overall.

Technologies have provided exceptional advances in relation to navigation for everyone, from GPS guidance and digital maps to beacon-based audio guides in museums. These developments have also been very important to disabled people, for example providing pedestrian navigation systems for visually disabled people. Other technologies have support people with physical disabilities, for example power wheelchairs with

Published by Springer Nature Switzerland AG 2026
C. Maciel et al. (Eds.): INTERACT 2025 Workshops, LNCS 16478, pp. 279–287, 2026.
https://doi.org/10.1007/978-3-032-22934-2_21

autonomous navigation and exoskeletons for mobility. However, many gaps remain and new technologies are constantly emerging which might be put to use to help older and disabled people. This workshop will be an opportunity for researchers and practitioners to discuss recent research on technologies for navigation for disabled and older people, the gaps in research which could be addressed, as well as methodological issues and different approaches.

2 Background Literature Review

A systematic review of recent research literature (2019–2025) on these topics is being undertaken as part of the activities related to the workshop. This was begun before the workshop and will continue in the future. The databases being searched are the ACM Digital Library, the IEEE Xplore Digital Library and the Web of Science. Inclusion criteria include that the publication is in English, and there is involvement of users (or other relevant stakeholders) in the research, either in the initial understanding of the issues to be addressed by the technology, in ongoing co-design or in evaluation of a technology. We appreciate that sometimes researchers need to test out an idea or develop some kind of prototype before involving users, but to publish without involving users either in the design or evaluation phase seems very dangerous. Similarly, evaluations of technologies for users with disabilities or older users which conducted evaluations with able-bodied or young participants were not considered. There are cases for which conducting an initial evaluation with such participants, but to publish without including an evaluation with the target users of a system is in our opinion inappropriate.

Finding appropriate search terms for the review was particularly difficult. After some experimentation the following search string was used:

((mobil*) OR (navig*)) AND ((disabl*) OR ((impair*) OR (old*) OR (elderly) OR (senior))

It proved impossible to automatically filter out a number of topics not relevant to the review, for example research on navigation through information for disabled or older people, research on social mobility of disabled or older people and most importantly research in scope on technology for navigation or mobility for disabled or older people which did not include any user involvement. For example, from the ACM Digital Library, 38 papers were initially returned for 2025, but 23 did not meet our criteria, leaving a sample of 15 papers.

Conversely in analyzing the papers returned, we realize we may be missing research on navigation in AR/VR, as in that area of research, the term used is "locomotion". A further search will address that issue. There have also been issues of the exact scope of "navigation and mobility", for example should research which addresses technology to mobility rehabilitation of people with Parkinson's disease be included or research on driving and dealing with autonomous vehicles by disabled and older people. For the moment, these two topics have been included.

Thus far, only the papers from the ACM Digital Library have been analyzed in a preliminary way, yielding relevant 44 papers. Three were review papers themselves [10, 27, 35] and one short introductory piece [45]. One particularly striking result thus far is that even in the ACM Digital Library, relevant research has been published in a surprising range of journals and conferences, 19 in total. Although 50% of papers were published either in the ACM's International SIGCHI Conference on Human Factors in Computing Systems (CHI, 12 papers) or the International SIGACCESS Conference on Computers and Accessibility (ASSETS, 10 papers), there was a wide variety of other publications. In addition, researchers from a wide variety of countries have conducted relevant research. 16 countries in total are represented in the ACM papers, with the USA and China contributing the most research, but with research conducted in Europe, Asia, South America and Australasia also represented.

This body of research covers a wide range of topics in terms of the particular user groups and issues addressed, the technologies proposed and methodologies used. The research could be usefully grouped and discussed on each of these dimensions. The different user groups considered were: 12 papers addressed either more than one disability group or people with disabilities in general (sometimes including older people), older people were addressed in 11 papers, 9 addressed issues for people with physical disabilities, people with visual disabilities in 6 papers, and one paper each about people with hearing and intellectual disabilities.

Another perhaps more useful way to get an overview of the research is to consider the more popular topics which have been investigated in this period. A preliminary grouping suggests that at least six different topics have been considered (some papers were placed in more than one topic). As these categories are very preliminary, numbers of papers are not given, but the categories might be:

- new solutions for already researched issues, and solutions to issues that have not been addressed yet. In this category were proposals for new solutions for indoor navigation proposals for outdoor navigation, new methods to navigate motorized wheelchairs, and to allow wheelchair players to participate in games with non-disabled players
- the use VR and AR in a variety of ways, to directly aid people in indoor navigation in the absence of GPS-based navigation, to train people in navigational skills both for the real world and for using VR. VR is also being used to model and understand the issues of navigation for disabled and older people
- Supporting disabled or older users in route planning
- Studies of user needs and concerns in particular mobility and navigation-related areas
- Accessibility of public transport
- Relevant user skills and abilities, for example spatial skills used in navigation.

Undoubtedly as the review grows, these topics will evolve and be refined.

3 Workshop Presentations and Discussions

The workshop was hybrid and took place over two days as part of the INTERACT 2025 Conference. Some participants were on location at the conference in Belo Horizonte, Brazil and others were online. Participants were from China, Germany, Israel, Spain, the United Kingdom and the United States of America.

People with a disability experience navigation and orientation as challenging. **Gerhard Weber** presented an overview on some of the challenges to be addressed in research. These include gaining a better understanding of the needs of more and wider groups of users and their abilities, improving accessibility of maps and apps, handling management of data on accessibility issues in a more sustainable way and empowering users for participation when developing services. Modelling user needs and abilities has received considerable attention in research in the past. Accessibility of built environment impacts people in a wheelchair, but insufficient information on limitations and temporal obstacles such as a broken elevator can lead to wasting time and effort on a specific route. Blind people need also route information but follow different routes and master stairs. Obstacles can be dangerous and loosing orientation in large buildings must be avoided. Older people enjoy VR-based exploration of places around the world if setup can be mastered. Populating digital twins by means of AI tools can lower the resources for setting up VR scenes. More research on needs of autistic people and in general neurodiversity in complex environments is needed.

Research on accessibility of navigation includes also research on methodologies how to evaluate successful navigation. **Helen Petrie** gave a presentation about the different methodologies she has used in the elicitation of user requirements and the evaluation of prototype systems with disabled people, and some of the lessons learnt. In particular she discussed the problems of the ecological validity of evaluations for outdoor navigation systems which need to be conducted in real urban environments. These present many potential hazards for both evaluation participants and the researchers which need to be carefully negotiated.

One interesting method she found very useful was a variation of the well-known "Wizard of Oz" evaluation method, in which the functionality of a system is simulated by a researcher. To assess what kinds of information and message content blind pedestrians might want in an outdoor navigation system, she used an "ambulatory Wizard of Oz" method. A route in central London was carefully assessed for all the information which might be useful to a blind pedestrian – street names and numbers, pedestrian crossings, traffic lights, tactile paving and surface changes, entrances to buildings, information about the building such as businesses and shops as well as the smells that might emanate from them, street furniture such as street lights, signs, electricity boxes and rubbish bins, and many other things. A large variety of messages were prepared about all these types of information, with different message formats and levels of detail. Then a number of blind participants walked the route with two researchers (one acting as the Wizard of Oz simulation of the system by providing messages at the appropriate points and the other ensuring the safety of the participant and the researcher and making notes). This proved extremely valuable in understanding how to design the subsequent system.

Another interesting measure used during evaluations of navigational aids is the preferred walking speed (PWS) of the individual. If individuals walk more slowly or more quickly than their PWS, they become fatigued. A navigational aid for a disabled pedestrian should not alter their PWS. If an aid is taking considerable cognitive load, as many mobility and navigational aids for blind and partially sighted pedestrians do, that is likely to cause them to walk at less than their PWS, which is not ideal and likely to be tiring.

Roland Graf presented how "peripersonal circle interaction" helps to tailor gameplay interactions to individual reachable spaces. Peripersonal space (PPS) takes assistive technology and tools into account but enables individuals to take action by moving and play with a virtual ball. PPS has been implemented in the iGym system and helps to leverage personal boundaries through embodied interaction with their peripersonal sphere. The concept of perceiving and controlling PPS is possibly increasing spatial awareness by children with neurodevelopmental disorders and helps to build up social competences in team play. Intuitive feedback mechanisms such as from wearable haptic devices signal complex tactile sensations can augment or even replace the visual perception. Adaptivity can address specific user needs in new game play situations to reduce cognitive demand and increase mobility.

Craig Smith focused in his talk on people with a visual impairment (VIP) and how modern streetscapes present a range of old and new barriers. These can be categorized as infrastructural legacy, modern interventions, and technology. While lack of tactile markings can be overcome only slowly to improve infrastructure, there are many examples of how urban spaces are transformed into shared spaces and increased complexity. Sharing a bus stop with bicycles requires extreme caution when leaving a bus with a white cane, for example. Better understanding walking behaviors of VIPs can help to point out unknown information and obstacles in particular. To evaluate a better navigation system, a VR-based methodology will be adopted for a mixed-reality approach. The footage developed in these experiments can help to educate urban planners in academic and professional training.

Bela Usabaev reported on a Wizard-of-Oz study to analyse multimodal interaction with tactile graphics. The study setup consisted of two wizards. One wizard provides feedback a screen reader gives for gestural input and the second wizard responds to more general spoken input. 8 participants who are blind participated in the study. They had played TicTacToe to become familiar with spatial layout. Magnets served as tangibles to help users in identifying locations and learn how to verbalize addresses. The analysis shows gestures and voice input are performed independently but also synergistically in parallel. Future keyboard-less interactive scenarios with tactile graphics should support also co-verbal gestural input to allow bi-manual exploration of complex tactile graphics for example representing maps, spreadsheet or calendar sheet.

Yasmin Felberbaum presented her work on practicing navigation as a cognitive skill while walking. She applied a user-centered design approach to design and develop a mobile application that suggests circular accessible walking routes outdoors in the user's home environment. Navigation functioned as a cognitive task accompanied to the walking activity, providing the user a dual-tasking practice of cognitive and physical activities and, by that, create a more meaningful practice.

Francisco Garfias presented his work Human-Centered Perspectives on Indoor Navigation and Spatial Design for People with Disabilities, that is described in his contribution in this volume. Lourdes Moreno was not able to present live, but her work with Paloma Martínez, Angela Diaz-Redondo and Fernando Alonso on urban mobility for people with intellectual disabilities is also described in their contribution to this volume.

Minghui Liu was unable to present live but provided a video describing her work on navigation tools for older adults. She presented several case studies about indoor wayfinding in complex spaces, particularly wayfinding in hospitals for older adults.

In addition to the presentations and discussions, participants in the workshop took part in a group exercise of designing the navigation and support in an accessible gym for older people (who may have disabilities), drawing on their different backgrounds and approaches. This led to further interesting discussions about indoor navigation and support needed in public spaces for disabled and older people.

4 Future Work and Collaboration

In addition to the papers prepared by the organizers and the participants presented in this volume, we will continue to work on the systematic review of recent research on technology to support mobility and navigation for disabled and older people, with the aim of publishing a comprehensive survey of this research.

Acknowledgments. The organisers of this workshop are members of IFIP TC13 Working Group 13.3 on HCI, Disability and Ageing (https://wg1.ifip-tc13.org/). They thank all the participants for their participation in the workshop and their valuable contributions.

References

1. Abraham, A.: Lessons learned from designing, deploying and testing an accessible BLE Beacon-based wayfinding system in a multi-floor indoor environment. In: 24th International ACM SIGACCESS Conference on Computers and Accessibility. ACM Press (2022)
2. Abraham, A., Namboodiri, V.: Designing exploration-based indoor wayfinding systems to enhance spatial learning for the visually impaired. In: Proceedings of the 27th International ACM SIGACCESS Conference on Computers and Accessibility (2025). https://doi.org/10.1145/3663547.3759760
3. Batbold, T., Soro, A., Schroeter, R.: Driven by learning: exploring older adults' pedagogical preferences in highly automated vehicle interactions. In: Proceedings of the Extended Abstracts of the CHI Conference on Human Factors in Computing Systems (2025). https://doi.org/10.1145/3706599.3719842
4. Bennett, C.R., Fink, P.D.S., Giudice, N.A.: "X-ray vision" as a compensatory augmentation for slowing cognitive map decay in older adults. In: CHI Conference on Human Factors in Computing Systems. ACM Press (2024)
5. Bynum, L., Parker, J., Lee, K., et al.: Navigating in the dark–designing autonomous driving features to assist old adults with visual impairment. In: 15th International Conference on Automotive User Interfaces and Interactive Vehicular Applications. ACM Press (2023)
6. Cai, S., Ram, A., Gou, Z., Hsu, D., et al.: Navigating real-world challenges: a quadruped robot guiding system for visually impaired people in diverse environments. In: CHI Conference on Human Factors in Computing Systems. ACM Press (2024)
7. Cao, J., Jain, K., Zhang, J., Peng, Y., Patel, S., Mankoff, J.: "a tool for freedom": co-designing mobility aid improvements using personal fabrication and physical Interface modules with primarily young adults. In: Proceedings of the 2025 CHI Conference on Human Factors in Computing Systems (2025). https://doi.org/10.1145/3706598.3713366
8. Chen, Q., Wu, Z., Liu, Y., et al.: Silver cycling: exploring the impact of bike-based locomotion on spatial orientation for older adults in VR. ACM Interact. Mobile, Wearable Ubiquit. Technol. **8**(3), 95 (2024)
9. Cheraghi, S.A., Sharma, A., Namboodiri, V., Arsal, G.: SafeExit4All: an inclusive indoor emergency evacuation system for people with disabilities. In: 16th International Web for all Conference. ACM Press (2019)

10. Façanha, A. R., Darin, T., Viana, W., Sánchez, J.: O&M Indoor Virtual Environments for people who are blind: a systematic literature review. ACM Transactions on Access. Computing, 13(2), 9a (2020).
11. Fietkau, J., Stojko, L.: Activity Support for Seniors Using Public Displays: a Proof of Concept. ACM Press, Mensch und Computer (2021)
12. Fink, P.D., Dimitrov, V., Yasuda, H., et al.: Autonomous is not enough: designing multisensory mid-air gestures for vehicle interactions among people with visual impairments. In: CHI Conference on Human Factors in Computing Systems. ACM Press (2023)
13. Franz, R.L., Yu, J., Wobbrock, J.O.: Comparing locomotion techniques in virtual reality for people with upper-body motor impairments. In: International ACM SIGACCESS Conference on Computers and Accessibility. ACM Press (2023)
14. Garfias, F.J.R., Namboodiri, V.: MABLESim: a simulation framework for studying accessibility challenges for people with disabilities within indoor environments. In: 21st International Web for all Conference. ACM Press (2024)
15. Gerling, K., Hicks, K., Szymanezyk, O., et al.: Designing interactive manual wheelchair skills training for children. In: Designing Interactive Systems Conference. ACM Press (2019)
16. Girish, A., Selladurai, S., Murugan, V.V.S., Viboosithasri, N.S.: Carla - making transport hubs accessible. In: ACM/IEEE International Conference on Human-Robot Interaction. ACM Press (2023)
17. Giudice, N. A., Guenther, B. A., Kaplan, T. M. et al.: Use of an indoor navigation system by sighted and blind Travelers: performance similarities across visual status and age. ACM Transactions on Accessible Computing, 13(3), 11 (2020).
18. Goyena, M., et al.: A Study on Immersive Behavioral Therapy for Individuals with Intellectual Disabilities with Fear of Stairs Proceedings of the 2025 ACM International Conference on Interactive Media Experiences (2025), doi:https://doi.org/10.1145/3706370.3727851
19. Graf, R., Benawri, P., Whitesall, et al.: iGYM: an interactive floor projection system for inclusive exergame environments. In: Annual Symposium on Computer-Human Interaction in Play. ACM Press (2019)
20. Graf, R., Park, S.Y., Shpiz, E., Kim, H.S.: iGYM: a wheelchair-accessible interactive floor projection system for co-located physical play. In: Extended Abstracts of the 2019 CHI Conference on Human Factors in Computing Systems, pp. 1–6 (2019)
21. Gupta, M., Abdolrahmani, A., Edwards, E., et al.: Towards more universal wayfinding technologies: navigation preferences across disabilities. In: CHI Conference on Human Factors in Computing Systems. ACM Press (2020)
22. Han, H., Li, F.M., Martelaro, N., et al.: The Robot in our Path: Investigating the Perceptions of People with Motor Disabilities on Navigating Public Space alongside Sidewalk Robots ACM SIGACCESS Conference on Computers and Accessibility. ACM Press (2023)
23. Huang, W., Su, X., Froehlich, J.E., Zhang, Y.: Accessibility scout: personalized accessibility scans of built environments. In: Proceedings of the 38th Annual ACM Symposium on User Interface Software and Technology (2025). https://doi.org/10.1145/3746059.3747624
24. Hwang, J., Li, C., Kang, H., Hosseini, M., Froehlich, J.E.: "Where can I Park?" understanding human perspectives and Scalably detecting disability parking from aerial imagery. In: Proceedings of the 27th International ACM SIGACCESS Conference on Computers and Accessibility (2025). https://doi.org/10.1145/3663547.3746377
25. Jain, D., Desjardins, A., Findlater, L., Froehlich, J.E.: Autoethnography of a hard of hearing traveler. In: 21st International ACM SIGACCESS Conference on Computers and Accessibility. ACM Press (2019)
26. Jiang, L., Yoshihara, Y., Karatas, N., Harada, A., Kanamori, H., Tanaka, T.: Exploring a safe-driving instruction framework for older drivers based on the GDE framework and motor learning theory: a pilot study. In: Proceedings of the Extended Abstracts of the CHI Conference on Human Factors in Computing Systems (2025). https://doi.org/10.1145/3706599.3720166

27. Johnson, H.L., Mutlu, B.: Accessible Technology for Adults with down syndrome: a scoping review. ACM Trans. Accessible Comput. **18**(3), 12 (2025). https://doi.org/10.1145/3748333
28. Joseph, S., Namboodiri, V.: Auxiliary location-based Services for Persons with disabilities: what do City planners and non-profit agencies think? In: 21st International ACM SIGACCESS Conference on Computers and Accessibility. ACM Press (2019)
29. Koustriava, E., Alexiadis, M., Chronopoulou, E., Skalidis, N.: The contribution of assistive Technology in the Development of orientation and mobility skills: the case of twins with mild intellectual disability and blindness. In: Proceedings of the 11th International Conference on Software Development and Technologies for Enhancing Accessibility and Fighting Info-Exclusion (2025). https://doi.org/10.1145/3696593.3696640
30. Kubczak, A., et al.: Designing rehabilitation system for people with Parkinson's: targeting dual-task training. In: Proceedings of the 27th International ACM SIGACCESS Conference on Computers and Accessibility (2025). https://doi.org/10.1145/3663547.3759733
31. Kulkarni, M., Li, C., Ahn, J.J., et al.: BusStopCV: a real-time AI assistant for Labeling bus stop accessibility features in streetscape imagery. In: 25th International ACM SIGACCESS Conference on Computers and Accessibility. ACM Press (2023)
32. Liu, M., Su, Y.: Enhancing Airport Wayfinding for Older Adults through Gesture-Based Navigation. ACM Symposium on Spatial User Interaction, ACM Press (2024)
33. Liu, M., & Su, Y.: Mediguide: Reducing Cognitive Load and Improving Elderly Patients' Healthcare Experience Proceedings of the Extended Abstracts of the CHI Conference on Human Factors in Computing Systems (2025), doi:https://doi.org/10.1145/3706599.3706701
34. Nikanfar, S., et al.: A survey on assistive Technologies for Visually Impaired Individuals: recent innovations, limitations, and future directions. In: Proceedings of the 18th ACM International Conference on PErvasive Technologies Related to Assistive Environments (2025). https://doi.org/10.1145/3733155.3734895
35. Seo, M., Lee, H., Choi, S., et al.: Exploring experiences of virtual reality among young and older adults in a subway fire scenario: a pilot study. In: 25th ACM Symposium on Virtual Reality Software and Technology. ACM Press (2019)
36. Sharif, A., Ramesh, A., Nguyen, T.-A., et al.: UnlockedMaps: visualizing real-time accessibility of urban rail transit using a web-based map. In: 24th International ACM SIGACCESS Conference on Computers and Accessibility. ACM Press (2022)
37. Sogani, R., Giri, A., Lee, R., Berge, S., Saini, B., Roberts, J.: BARRS: a multimodal, tactile mapping system to support spatial learning and autonomy in BVI children. In: Proceedings of the 2025 ACM Symposium on Spatial User Interaction (2025). https://doi.org/10.1145/3694907.3765955
38. Takagi, H., Naito, K., Sato, D., Murata, M., Kayukawa, S., Asakawa, C.: Field trials of autonomous navigation robot for visually impaired people. In: Proceedings of the Extended Abstracts of the CHI Conference on Human Factors in Computing Systems (2025). https://doi.org/10.1145/3706599.3706663
39. Gomez Torres, I., Parmar, G., Aggarwal, S., Mansur, N., Guthrie, A.: Affordable smart wheelchair. In: Extended Abstracts of the 2019 CHI Conference on Human Factors in Computing Systems, pp. 1–6 (2019)
40. Williams, T.M.M., Cooper, E.H.S., Dew, K.: From point a to point B: identity-informed safety in navigation technology. In: CHI Conference on Human Factors in Computing Systems. ACM Press (2023)
41. Xiong, Z., Liu, B., Zhao, B., Jiang, L.: A study on the influencing factors of senior mountaineering experience based on explanatory structural modelling. In: Proceedings of the 2025 International Conference on Machine Learning and Neural Networks (2025). https://doi.org/10.1145/3747227.3747267

42. Yan, J., Ren, L., Zhang, Q., Zhang, D.: Research on interaction Design of Personalized Intelligent Exercise System for seniors in China. In: Proceedings of the 4th International Conference on Biomedical and Intelligent Systems (2025). https://doi.org/10.1145/3745034.3745077
43. Yu, J.E., Chattopadhyay, D.: "Maps are hard for me": identifying how older adults struggle with Mobile maps. In: 22nd International ACM SIGACCESS Conference on Computers and Accessibility. ACM Press (2020)
44. Zhou, J., Qiu, C., Guo, B., Yu, Z.: The challenges and future of navigation for people with disabilities. XRDS. **28**(3), 32–36 (2022)

Human-Centered Perspectives on Indoor Navigation and Spatial Design for People with Disabilities

Francisco Javier Rafful Garfias(✉)

Rogers State University, Claremore, Oklahoma, USA
fraffulgarfias@rsu.edu

Abstract. Navigating complex indoor environments requires the coor-dination of spatial, cognitive, and sensory processes that vary signifi-cantly across individuals. This paper frames indoor navigation as an interdisciplinary challenge at the intersection of human-computer interac-tion, environmental design, and predictive modeling. It reflects on how simulation-based and data-informed approaches can anticipate naviga-tional challenges and foster more intuitive spatial design. Rather than detailing a specific system, this discussion emphasizes the broader method-ological potential of virtual modeling to identify environmental barriers and improve spatial legibility before construction. By integrating compu-tational analysis with human-centered thinking, this paper argues for a proactive design philosophy that aligns technological innovation with the real-world complexities of human movement, perception, and experience.

Keywords: Indoor navigation · human-centered design · simulation-based design · ·spatial layouts · predictive modeling · cognitive load.

1 Introduction

Navigating indoor environments is a cognitively demanding process, shaped by individual abilities, spatial layouts, and environmental cues. In today's large and often crowded buildings, like university campuses, hospitals, or transit hubs, even first-time visitors can easily become lost or disoriented. These universal challenges are significantly amplified for individuals with specific needs. People with visual impairments, for instance, frequently encounter significant challenges in unfamiliar buildings, where inconsistent landmarks or sensory feedback can lead to disorientation and elevated cognitive load [7]. Similarly, older adults may face obstacles due to age-related changes in attention and spatial reasoning, which hinder mental map formation [1, 8]. Cognitive impairments, including early-stage dementia, further complicate wayfinding, as individuals often rely on predictable layouts to execute routes effectively [2, 5]. Poorly designed indoor spaces amplify these challenges, restricting independence and participation in social and professional life [3, 10].

Published by Springer Nature Switzerland AG 2026
C. Maciel et al. (Eds.): INTERACT 2025 Workshops, LNCS 16478, pp. 288–294, 2026.
https://doi.org/10.1007/978-3-032-22934-2_22

Figure 1 illustrates a common design flaw where the designated accessible route is substantially longer and less direct than the alternative, placing a disproportionate navigational burden on some users. While legislation such as the Americans with Disabilities Act (ADA) in the United States, along with international mandates like the European Accessibility Act (EAA) and the UN Convention on the Rights of Persons with Disabilities (CRPD) [16–18], establish standards for physical accessibility, they often do not fully account for the cognitive load or navigational complexity of a space. A building can therefore be technically compliant yet remain confusing and difficult to navigate, creating practical barriers to true inclusion.

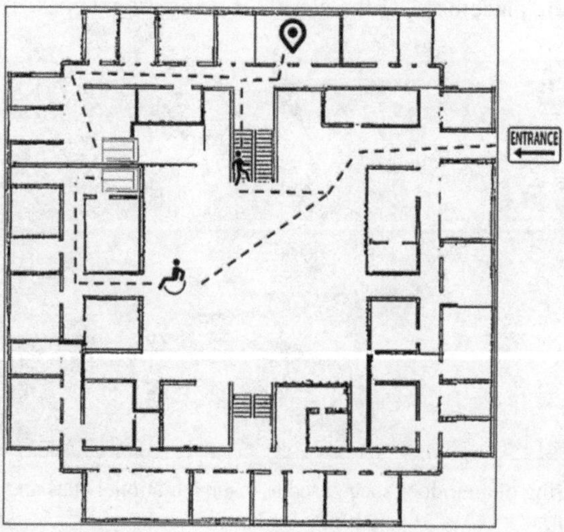

Fig. 1. A floor plan contrasting a direct path via stairs with the longer, circuitous route required for accessible elevator access.

While technological solutions like augmented reality and sensory aids have improved orientation in some contexts [2, 9], they often target specific naviga-tional aspects and may overlook the dynamic interplay between users and their environment. In contrast, human-centered and participatory approaches position users as active collaborators, uncovering needs that conventional design may miss [4, 6, 11].

Building on those approaches, this paper utilizes a framework that integrates simulation and predictive metrics. This combination enables a systematic explo-ration of how individuals with varying abilities interact with their surroundings. The following sections outline this methodological framework, explore its ap-plications, and conclude with reflections on its implications for future spatial design.

2 A Framework for Proactive Spatial Analysis

A methodological framework that integrates simulation and predictive modeling can be used to anticipate navigational barriers before they are built. This approach merges behavioral observation with computational analysis to understand how spatial features shape human perception, orientation, and comfort. The goal is not merely to measure efficiency, but to interpret how design elements can either support or hinder the process of forming spatial understanding.

Simulation-based environments allow for the rapid prototyping and testing of movement patterns under varied spatial and sensory conditions. Using 3D modeling or game-engine platforms (as shown in Fig. 2), designers can visu-alize how individuals with different abilities might interact with architectural features. This approach builds upon prior work that introduced a software tool for visualizing and analyzing pathfinding in complex floor plans [12, 13, 15]. Key parameters—such as lighting, spatial configuration, or signage—can be modified to identify potential challenges related to layout complexity, obstacle placement, or the clarity of navigational cues.

Fig. 2. A 3D rendering of an indoor space used to test navigational cues and route complexity in a virtual environment.

Predictive modeling complements these simulations by providing quantitative measures of navigational difficulty [14]. By analyzing variables like route efficiency, obstacle density, and visual complexity, models can estimate the cognitive load a layout might impose on different user profiles. This data-informed approach allows architects to compare design alternatives and mitigate navigational strain in the earliest stages of planning.

Used iteratively, simulation and predictive analysis create a powerful feedback loop (Fig. 3): visual patterns in simulations reveal behavioral tendencies, while predictive metrics quantify their implications. This interplay bridges computa-tional efficiency with human experience and fosters dialogue between architects, cognitive scientists, and engineers. It encourages a shift from reactive problem-solving to anticipatory design, reframing navigability as an essential element of spatial quality (as summarized in Table 1).

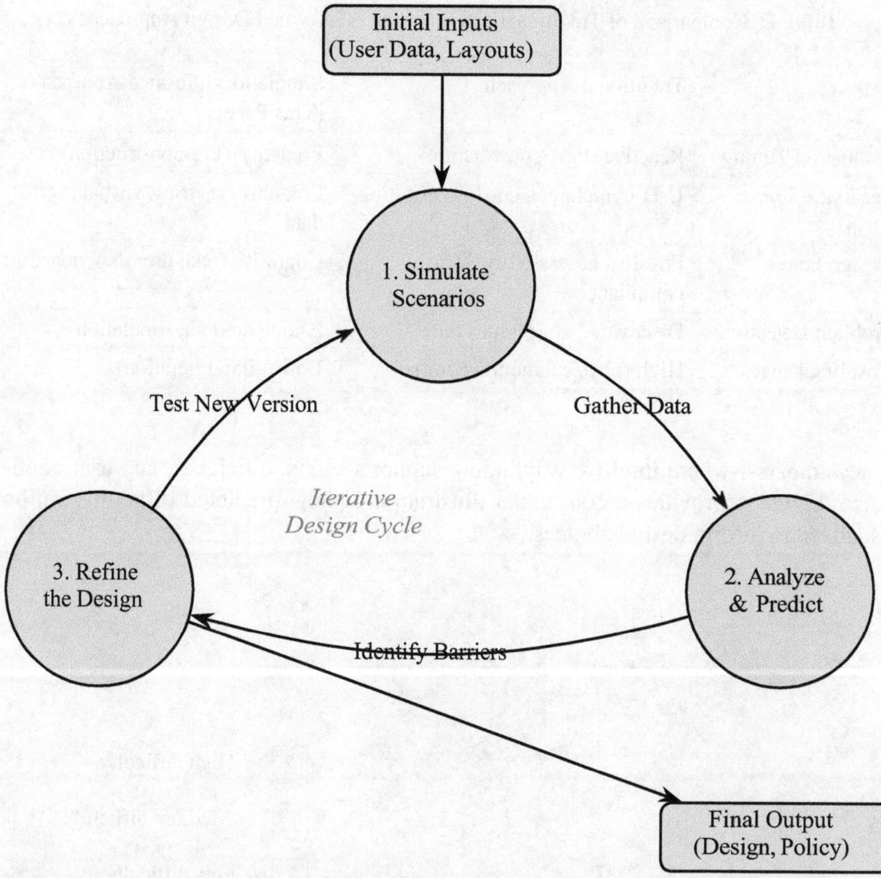

Fig. 3. An intuitive view of the framework as an iterative design cycle. Inputs are used to simulate scenarios, which are analyzed to find barriers, leading to design refinements that are then re-simulated.

3 Applications and Implications

This framework has practical applications across several domains where clear navigation is critical.

3.1 Design Evaluation and Planning

In architecture and urban planning, simulation allows designers to test how spatial configurations influence movement and orientation. By adjusting variables

Like corridor width or signage, they can evaluate design hypotheses before construction. Predictive analysis can then identify layouts that minimize complexity and enhance clarity. This is particularly valuable in large-scale public venues like hospitals, airports, and university campuses—environments that are often crowded and unfamiliar

Table 1. Comparison of Traditional and Simulation-Informed Design Approaches

Aspect	Traditional Approach	Simulation-Informed Approach (This Paper)
Evaluation Timing	Reactive (Post-construction)	Proactive (Pre-construction)
Feedback Source	User complaints; costly retrofitting	Predictive metrics; virtual user data
Design Focus	Physical accessibility; legal compliance	Cognitive load; user experience
Problem Detection	Discovered after issues arise	Anticipated via simulation
Cost of Changes	High (physical modification)	Low (digital iteration)

to newcomers—where intuitive wayfinding supports safety, efficiency, and user confidence. Figure 4 provides a conceptual illustration of how predicted difficulty can be visualized to inform design choices.

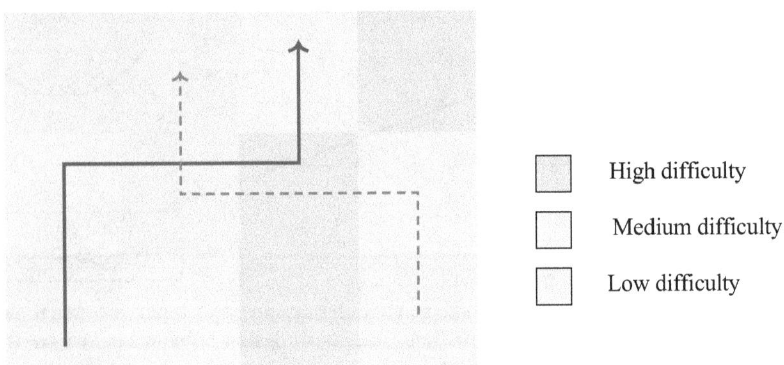

Fig. 4. Conceptual heatmap of predicted navigation difficulty. Color-coded zones indicate varying cognitive or spatial demand, guiding design refinements before construction.

3.2 Architectural Research and Education

In academia, the framework provides a structured method for studying the relationship between environmental design and human cognition. Architecture and HCI students can use simulations to visualize how spatial cues affect wayfinding, bridging design theory with behavioral science. These tools foster an evidence-based mindset and provide deeper insight into the human factors that underlie spatial perception.

3.3 Policy and Facility Management

For policy-makers and facility managers, this approach offers a way to audit public buildings and transportation hubs for accessibility and efficiency. By visualizing and quantifying navigation difficulty, these methods strengthen the case for data-informed design guidelines. They allow stakeholders to move beyond minimum legal compliance with national and international accessibility standards (e.g., ADA, EAA) [16, 18], encouraging policy frameworks that prioritize navigability and legibility as integral aspects of user well-being. As digital twins become central to urban management, simulation-based evaluation provides a vital bridge between predictive technology and lived human experience.

4 Conclusion and Future Directions

Indoor navigation is more than a technical problem; it is a deeply human experi-ence at the intersection of cognition, perception, and the built environment. This paper argues that simulation and predictive modeling are powerful tools for ex-ploring this intersection, offering a means to design spaces that anticipate—rather than react to—navigational barriers.

As this framework is a conceptual work in progress, the immediate next steps are crucial for grounding it in practice. A key priority is to move beyond simulated behaviors by validating the models with empirical, real-world data to ensure predictive accuracy. Concurrently, future iterations will expand the simulation's fidelity by incorporating multisensory feedback—such as acoustics and textural cues—to achieve greater ecological validity.

Refining these models and integrating diverse user perspectives can better inform inclusive design standards and policy. In the long term, this research could contribute to intelligent environments that adapt dynamically to human needs. Ultimately, the goal is to foster spaces that communicate clearly, function seamlessly, and empower all individuals to navigate their world with confidence and independence.

References

1. Bosch, S., Gharaveis, A.: Flying solo: A review of the literature on wayfinding for older adults experiencing visual or cognitive decline. Appl. Ergon. **58**, 327–333 (2017). https://doi.org/10.1016/j.apergo.2016.07.010
2. Chang, Y.J., Peng, S.M., Wang, F., Chen, S.F., Chen, Y.R., Chen, H.C.: Au-tonomous indoor wayfinding for individuals with cognitive impairments. J. Neuroeng. Rehabil. **7**, 45 (2010). https://doi.org/10.1186/1743-0003-7-45
3. Davis, R., Calkins, M.: Wayfinding design in long-term-care communities: evaluation of complexity. Innovation Aging. **6**(Supplement_1), 699 (2022). https://doi.org/10.1093/geroni/igac059.2560
4. Fraser-Barbour, E., et al.: Shifting power to people with disability in co-designed research. Disabil. Soc. (2023). https://doi.org/10.1080/09687599.2023.2279932

5. García-Catalá, M.T., Martín-Barroso, E., Rodríguez-Sánchez, M.C., Delgado-Álvaro, M., Novak, R.: Sensory navigation system for indoor localization and orientation of users with cognitive disabilities in daily tasks and emergency situations. Sensors. **24**(22), 7154 (2024). https://doi.org/10.3390/s24227154
6. Hattstein, J., Molthahn, J.P.: Indoor navigation for people with special require-ments: results of a user-centered design approach and possible design solutions. In: Proceedings of Mensch Und Computer: Hybrid Worlds (MuC '24), p. 4. ACM, New York, NY, USA (2024). https://doi.org/10.18420/muc2024-mci-src-233
7. Jeamwatthanachai, W., Wald, M., Wills, G.: Indoor navigation by blind people: be-haviors and challenges in unfamiliar spaces and buildings. Br. J. Vis. Impair. **37**(2), 140–153 (2019). https://doi.org/10.1177/0264619619833723. original work published 2019
8. Mishler, A.D., Neider, M.B.: Improving wayfinding for older users with selective attention deficits. Ergon. Des. **25**(1), 11–16 (2017). https://doi.org/10.1177/1064804616659992. epub 2016 Nov 15. PMID: 28286405; PMCID: PMC5343508
9. Oliveira, L.C.d., Soares, A.B., Cardoso, A., Andrade, A.d.O., Lamounier Júnior, E.A.: Mobile augmented reality enhances indoor navigation for wheelchair users. Res. Biomed. Eng. 32(2), 111–122 (2016). https://doi.org/10.1590/2446-4740.01515, Received: 23 July 2015; Accepted: 11 May 2016
10. Patil, A., Raghani, S.: Designing accessible and independent living spaces for visually impaired individuals: A barrier-free approach to interior design. Int. J. Equity Health. **24**(1), 137 (2025). https://doi.org/10.1186/s12939-025-02503-5. pMID: 40375267; PMCID: PMC12082883
11. Peyrard, E., Chamaret, C.: Designing for all but with whom? Three cases of co-design with disabled persons. Gérer et Comprendre. **141**, 57–70 (2020)
12. Rafful Garfias, F.J., Namboodiri, V.: MABLESim: A simulation framework for studying accessibility challenges for people with disabilities within indoor envi-ronments. In: Proceedings of the International Web for all Conference (W4A). Association for Computing Machinery (2024), Reused with permission). https://doi.org/10.1145/3677846.3677852
13. Rafful Garfias, F.J., Namboodiri, V.: On the use of a simulation framework for studying accessibility challenges faced by people with disabilities in indoor envi-ronments. In: Proceedings of the International Conference on Computers Helping People with Special Needs (ICCHP). Springer, Cham (2024), Reused with permission). https://doi.org/10.1007/978-3-031-62846-7_4
14. Rafful Garfias, F.J., Namboodiri, V., Joseph, S.: Quantifying navigational difficulty for visually impaired users in indoor spaces with accessquotient. In: The 27th Inter-National ACM SIGACCESS Conference on Computers and Accessibility. ASSETS '25, ACM, New York, NY, USA (2025). https://doi.org/10.1145/3663547. 3759696
15. Rafful Garfias, F.J., Namboodiri, V.: Mablesim: A tool for simulating indoor accessibility. J. Technol. Persons Disabil., 169 (2025)
16. The European Parliament and the Council of the European Union: Directive (eu) 2019/882 on the accessibility requirements for products and services (european accessibility act). Official Journal of the European Union, L 151/70 (2019)
17. United Nations General Assembly: Convention on the rights of persons with dis-abilities (crpd). United Nations, Treaty Series, vol. 2515, p. 3 (2006)
18. U.S. Congress: Americans with disabilities act of 1990. Public Law 101–336, 42 U.S.C. §12101 et seq. (1990)

Towards Inclusive Urban Mobility for People with Intellectual Disabilities

Lourdes Moreno[1(✉)], Paloma Martínez[1], Angela Diaz-Redondo[1], and Fernando Alonso[2]

[1] Computer Science and Engineering Department, Universidad Carlos III de Madrid, Madrid, Spain
{lmoreno,pmf}@inf.uc3m.es, andiazr@pa.uc3m.es

[2] The Basement LAB, Madrid, Spain
f@thebasement.io

Abstract. Urban mobility remains a significant barrier for people with intellectual disabilities, who often face challenges in route planning, digital ticketing, real-time navigation, and requesting assistance. While recent advances in mobile technologies and IoT-enabled transport systems have improved physical accessibility, cognitive accessibility is still largely overlooked. This paper presents an inclusive mobility initiative developed within the ZERO project, aimed at supporting autonomous travel through a cognitively accessible mobile application, a caregiver coordination platform, and context-aware infrastructure providing route guidance, deviation alerts, and local assistance. The system is designed through participatory methods and aligns with cognitive accessibility standards to address key gaps identified in existing navigation tools. Although deployment is forthcoming, the proposed framework contributes a scalable approach to inclusive urban mobility that integrates technology, user-centered design, and community support.

Keywords: integrates accessible technology · user-centered design · and community-based assistance

1 Introduction

Mobility is widely recognized as a fundamental right and a prerequisite for autonomy, social inclusion, and quality of life. Nevertheless, navigating urban environments continues to pose substantial challenges for people with disabilities and for older adults. In Spain, 3.85 million people have disabilities, and more than 40% report significant difficulties when using public transport independently [1]. For individuals with intellectual disabilities, these barriers are particularly acute and typically relate to route planning, digital ticketing, interpreting signage, and requesting assistance.

Although recent advances in navigation apps and IoT-enabled transport infrastructures have improved physical accessibility, cognitive accessibility remains insufficiently addressed. Mainstream mobility systems often neglect the cognitive load associated

Published by Springer Nature Switzerland AG 2026
C. Maciel et al. (Eds.): INTERACT 2025 Workshops, LNCS 16478, pp. 295–303, 2026.
https://doi.org/10.1007/978-3-032-22934-2_23

with trip planning and real-time navigation, the emotional stress triggered by unexpected changes, and the importance of community-based support networks essential for independent travel [2].

A growing body of research underscores the relevance of cognitive accessibility in mobility contexts. Studies identify sensory and cognitive barriers in digital mobility services [3] and highlight the effectiveness of simplified, age-friendly interfaces that are directly applicable to users with intellectual disabilities [4]. Participatory and co-design approaches have further demonstrated their value in fostering inclusive mobility ecosystems [5, 6], showing how co-created digital mobility services and local communities of practice can engage users and stakeholders in real contexts.

Trust and acceptance are additional critical dimensions of smart mobility. Recent studies on automated vehicles identify key determinants of user (dis)trust and highlight how interface design and information presentation can mitigate trust-threatening factors [7], while Lin and Takatori show how people with different disabilities perceive and evaluate Mobility-as-a-Service (MaaS) systems [8], reinforcing the need for cognitively tailored designs.

Large-scale European initiatives such as TRIPS [9] and DIGNITY [10] provide structured methodologies that integrate co-creation, accessibility auditing, and real-world validation.

Simultaneously, mobility innovation risks amplifying digital inequalities if structural barriers persist. Research on digital exclusion [11] and transport equity [12, 13], together with recent European data [14, 15], highlights ongoing disparities among older adults and economically disadvantaged groups. These findings reinforce the ethical imperative of mobility solutions grounded in cognitive accessibility and inclusive design.

In response to these challenges, this paper presents a community-based navigation pilot that integrates cognitive accessibility principles, participatory design methods, IoT-enabled contextual awareness, and localized real-time support to promote safer and more autonomous travel for people with intellectual disabilities.

In the following sections, we outline related work, describe the pilot design, and present the methodological approach supporting its development.

2 Related Work

This section reviews recent work on inclusive navigation technologies, co-creation approaches, and cognitive and policy frameworks that inform accessible transport systems.

2.1 Mobility and Navigation Tools for People with Intellectual Disabilities

Independent mobility research for people with intellectual disabilities has explored smartphone-based guidance and structured travel-training interventions. Early mobile navigation systems demonstrated that digital wayfinding aids could support autonomy in supervised bus travel, although scalability and long-term adherence remained limited [16]. More recent studies involving adapted mainstream apps such as the use of Google Maps with step-by-step prompts show potential for skill development but also reveal challenges related to maintaining motivation, confidence, and emotional reassurance during real journeys [17].

Across these initiatives, cognitive accessibility remains insufficiently addressed. Mainstream navigation tools often lack simplified communication channels, multimodal cues, or strategies to reduce anxiety during unexpected changes. These limitations reinforce the need for participatory, cognitively aligned design approaches, which guide the ZERO initiative.

2.2 Inclusive Design and Co-creation in Transport

Co-creation methodologies have gained traction in mobility innovation, promoting systems that are developed with, not just for, users. European projects such as TRIPS and DIGNITY have established structured processes combining co-creation, accessibility auditing, and real-world validation [9, 10]. Likewise, initiatives such as MOBI-MIX and the Inclusive Mobility Alliance advance shared mobility solutions and cognitive accessibility standards [18, 19].

Recent works contribute domain-specific frameworks for cognitive accessibility. Their studies examine user needs in inclusive UX design [20], define interaction principles tailored to individuals with mild intellectual disabilities [21], and demonstrate participatory evaluation strategies through the Eleuteria App [22]. These contributions offer methodological foundations that inform the ZERO pilot, extending inclusive design practices to IoT-enabled mobility contexts.

2.3 Cognitive and Policy Frameworks

Several policy frameworks directly influence inclusive mobility design. At the European level, the European Accessibility Act and its Spanish transposition establish mandatory accessibility requirements for digital services, including transport applications. The EU Disability Rights Strategy 2021–2030 and the EU Urban Mobility Framework emphasize smart, sustainable, and inclusive mobility, explicitly incorporating cognitive accessibility into policy objectives [23, 24].

National strategies such as Spain's Sustainable and Connected Mobility Strategy 2030 [25] and the Spanish Disability Strategy 2022–2030 reinforce this direction, integrating accessibility into mobility planning and digital transformation agendas. Internationally, the UN Convention on the Rights of Persons with Disabilities offers a global foundation for accessibility, while documents such as the UK Inclusive Transport Strategy and the US DOT Accessibility Guidelines highlight broader global commitments to inclusive, technology-supported transport [26–28].

Together, these research and policy trends underscore the importance of combining cognitive accessibility, participatory methods, and supportive regulatory frameworks principles that shape the development of the ZERO pilot.

3 ZERO Pilot: An Initiative for Inclusive Navigation

As part of the ZERO project (Integrated and Inclusive Mobility: Barrier-Free Access, Payment, and Transit), a community-based pilot is being deployed in the city of Leganés (Madrid, Spain) to support independent navigation for people with intellectual disabilities in urban public transport. The pilot focuses on strengthening autonomy, confidence, and cognitive accessibility during real bus journeys.

This initiative addresses a need repeatedly identified by local organizations: although there are programs to promote employment and social participation among people with intellectual disabilities, such as job-matching services or vocational training, daily transport to and from educational centers or workplaces continues to represent a major barrier. Many users require structured support to travel safely, especially in unfamiliar or unpredictable situations. The pilot aims to address this gap through an integrated technological and human-centered approach.

The system brings together four core components:

1. a cognitively accessible mobile application for users,
2. a web platform for caregivers enabling planning and real-time support,
3. IoT devices placed on buses and stops to trigger context-aware prompts, and
4. a "safe mode" that activates assistance from trained local actors.

These components operate collectively to enhance autonomy, safety, and emotional reassurance during public transport use (Table 1).

The pilot is being developed by a company[1] specialized in advanced technologies and is tested with individuals supported by a local organization dedicated to the education and personal development of people with intellectual disabilities. The deployment takes place at one of the organization's educational centers in Leganés. By reinforcing routine commuting as a meaningful context for autonomy, the pilot bridges the gap between inclusion initiatives and their long-term sustainability in everyday life.

Table 1. Core Components of the Inclusive Navigation Pilot System

Component	Description
Mobile application	Co-designed with users; provides simplified guidance, clear prompts, and accessible help options.
Web platform for caregivers	Co-designed with users; enables planning, real-time monitoring, and remote support.
IoT devices on buses and stops	Detect location and trigger context-aware prompts (e.g., stop reminders).
Safe mode	Let's users request immediate help from trained local actors.

[1] https://www.thebasement.io/

4 Design Methodology

The pilot system is being designed and developed through a participatory co-design methodology grounded in the lived experiences and needs of people with intellectual disabilities. Building on previous work by the co-authors on inclusive UX research and interaction design [20, 21], the approach adapts design thinking principles to ensure accessibility across all stages. The process involves not only users but also educators, caregivers, families, and local community stakeholders.

The first phase focuses on requirements elicitation through interviews and co-creation workshops with individuals supported by a local organization for people with intellectual disabilities. These sessions explore everyday mobility challenges, preferences, anxieties, and expectations related to public transport, using visual aids, storyboards, and simplified prototyping to guarantee cognitive accessibility.

Consultations with caregivers, families, and professionals complement these insights by identifying essential forms of support and monitoring required to ensure user safety and autonomy. This dual engagement guides the inclusive design of the system's core features.

From the outset, the technical design incorporates accessibility principles such as simplified navigation, iconographic language, easy-to-read text, and multimodal cues. These principles align with the Web Content Accessibility Guidelines (WCAG) [29] and the W3C Cognitive and Learning Disabilities Accessibility Task Force (COGA) recommendations [30]. A multidisciplinary team of developers, accessibility specialists, and professionals from the disability sector translate these insights into user-centered interaction flows and service components.

A key innovation of the methodology is the integration of a community-based support network involving local actors such as drivers, shopkeepers, and municipal staff. These stakeholders receive basic training to provide assistance through the app's "safe mode," reinforcing the social dimension of accessible mobility.

Prototyping and iterative validation take place in real-world settings, with users testing early versions of the application during guided simulations. Their feedback is used to refine accessibility, usability, clarity, and comfort.

Beyond improving functionality, the co-design process empowers participants, validates their experiences, and strengthens the connection between technical development and inclusive, ethical design.

5 Evaluation Framework

The pilot evaluation will adopt a mixed-methods approach, combining quantitative and qualitative methods tailored to users with cognitive accessibility needs. The goal is to assess not only accessibility and functionality, but also the system's real-world impact on autonomy, confidence, and perceived safety during public transport use.

Quantitative evaluation will include simplified instruments adapted for cognitive accessibility, measuring:

- Task success, including completion of planned routes and correct activation of the "safe mode."

- Alert analytics, monitoring the frequency and resolution of deviation alerts and assistance requests.
- Time-on-task, to evaluate navigation efficiency across design iterations.
- Usability and accessibility indicators, derived from task-based user testing sessions with people with intellectual disabilities, using predefined metrics (e.g., error rate, help requests, task completion rate).

Qualitative evaluation will involve:

- Semi-structured interviews with users, caregivers, and transport staff to gather insights on perceived usefulness, barriers, and emotional reactions.
- Ethnographic observations during real-world trials, documenting behavior, route strategies, and incidents.
- Focus groups with professionals from the disability organization to contextualize user experiences and identify systemic improvements.
- UX-focused feedback from users after completing navigation tasks, using simplified scales and facilitator-supported reflections.

All instruments will be adapted using pictograms, easy-to-read language, and facilitator support to ensure comprehension.

In parallel, accessibility expert reviews will be conducted using heuristic checklists and established cognitive accessibility guidelines, ensuring early-stage compliance and identifying potential interface barriers prior to user testing.

The evaluation will also examine the effectiveness of the community-based support network, focusing on:

- Responsiveness and availability of trained local actors.
- Coordination between users, caregivers, and support personnel.
- User trust and engagement with the assistance system.

Ethical safeguards include cognitively adapted informed consent, compliance with GDPR and national data regulations, and guaranteed withdrawal rights without impact on service access.

Findings will guide future iterations, support system scalability, and contribute to the evidence base on inclusive navigation technologies.

6 Key Challenges

The initial requirement-gathering phase has revealed several critical challenges that must be addressed to design effective mobility solutions for people with intellectual disabilities.

- Cognitive accessibility gaps. Most existing navigation tools are not cognitively accessible. They often lack simplified language, intuitive cues, and emotional support, causing overload and anxiety.
- Autonomy vs. safety. Families and caregivers express concern about disorientation, missed stops, or users' vulnerability, pointing to the need for discreet yet reliable support systems.

- Digital divide. Limited access to smartphones, internet, or digital skills among some users and caregivers may hinder adoption, highlighting the importance of low-barrier, affordable solutions.
- Community support. While local actors like drivers or shopkeepers show interest, further work is needed to define how they can provide consistent real-time assistance.

Despite these challenges, early engagement with users and stakeholders supports a participatory, user-centered approach. The next design phase will seek to turn these insights into accessible, scalable tools combining technology with community support. Tackling these issues early may boost adoption, impact, and long-term sustainability.

7 Conclusions

This paper has presented an inclusive mobility pilot aimed at improving autonomous navigation for people with intellectual disabilities in urban public transport. The initiative responds to a persistent barrier identified by supporting organizations: while programs exist to foster employment and social participation, daily travel to educational centers or workplaces remains a significant challenge. The proposed system combines an accessible mobile application, a caregiver coordination platform, and IoT-enabled infrastructure to provide contextual guidance, deviation alerts, and community-based assistance. Designed through participatory methods and aligned with cognitive accessibility standards, the pilot addresses key gaps in existing mobility tools.

Beyond offering a technical solution, the pilot outlines a replicable model of cognitively accessible mobility rooted in inclusive design, user autonomy, and community support. The co-design approach can be extended to other vulnerable groups, such as older adults or neurodivergent users, helping to foster empathy and shared responsibility among local stakeholders.

Future work will focus on prototyping, iterative testing, and real-world deployment in a Spanish mid-sized city to validate usability, safety, and user experience, and to assess the pilot's scalability across different urban contexts.

Acknowledgments. This research is supported by the project ZERO: Integrated and Inclusive Mobility: Barrier-Free Access, Payment, and Transit (CPP2023-010411) by MICIU/AEI /10.13039/501100011033; and grant PID2023-148577OB-C21 (Human-Centered AI: User-Driven Adapted Language Models-HUMAN_AI).

References

1. INE: Encuesta sobre discapacidad, autonomía personal y situaciones de dependencia (EDAD). Instituto Nacional de Estadística (2021)
2. European Disability Forum (EDF): Accessibility of Transport Services for Persons with Disabilities in the European Union. EDF (2020)
3. Ribeiro, D.M., et al.: A comparative study on accessibility for autistic individuals with urban mobility apps. In: Proceedings of the XXIII Brazilian Symposium on Human Factors in Computing Systems, pp. 1–13 (2024)

4. Chua, C.S.W., Lim, W.M., Teh, P.L.: Designing age-friendly mobile apps: insights from a mobility app study. Act. Adapt. Aging. **48**(3), 409–429 (2024)
5. Eichholz, L.: The implications of a co-created software solution for mobility in rural areas. Smart Cities. **6**(5), 2706–2721 (2023)
6. Di Ciommo, F., et al.: INDIMO communities of practice in Monghidoro, Antwerp, Galilée, Madrid, and Berlin: a common space for co-designing inclusive digital mobility solutions. In: Towards User-Centric Transport in Europe 3: Making Digital Mobility Inclusive and Accessible, pp. 127–141. Springer, Cham (2023)
7. Yun, H., Yang, J.H.: Configuring user information by considering trust-threatening factors associated with automated vehicles. Eur. Transp. Res. Rev. **14**(1), 9 (2022)
8. Lin, B., Takatori, C.: Perceptions of MaaS and its impacts on travel Behaviors among individuals with disabilities. SSRN Working Pap. No. 5006700. (2024). Available at: https://ssrn.com/abstract=5006700
9. TRIPS Project. Transforming Transport for People with Disabilities. (2023). https://trips-project.eu/
10. DIGNITY Project: Guidelines for Inclusive Digital Transport. (2023). https://www.dignity-project.eu
11. Goodman-Deane, J., Kluge, J., Bosch, E.R., Nesterova, N., Bradley, M., Clarkson, P.J.: Digital mobility services: a population perspective. In: Proceedings of the 34th British HCI Conference, pp. 144–154. BCS Learning & Development (2021)
12. Adorno, G., Fields, N., Cronley, C., Parekh, R., Magruder, K.: Ageing in a low-density Urban City: transportation mobility as a social equity issue. Ageing Soc. **38**(2), 296–320 (2018)
13. Litman, T.: Evaluating Transportation Equity. Victoria Transport Policy Institute, Victoria, BC (2017)
14. Eurostat. Individuals' Level of Digital Skills: (2024). https://ec.europa.eu/eurostat
15. Statista. Digital Literacy by Income and Age in the EU: (2024). https://www.statista.com
16. Davies, D.K., Stock, S.E., Holloway, S., Wehmeyer, M.L.: Evaluating a GPS-based transportation device to support independent bus travel by people with intellectual disability. Intellect. Dev. Disabil. **48**(6), 454–463 (2010)
17. Hester, O.R., Cooney, L.E., McMahon, D.D.: Navigation support for students with intellectual disability using Mobile devices. J. Spec. Educ. Technol. **39**(4), 557–566 (2024). https://doi.org/10.1177/01626434231210989
18. MOBI-MIX Project. Promoting Innovative Mobility Solutions for Urban Inclusion: (2023). https://www.interregnorthsea.eu/sharedimobihub/about-us
19. Inclusive Mobility Alliance. Towards Cognitive Accessibility in Public Transport: (2022). https://www.transportforall.org.uk/
20. Corsetti, B., Hervás, R., Moreno, L.: Knowing users with mild intellectual impairments in UX design processes. In: Proceedings XXIII Interacción Persona-Ordenador. ACM (2023). https://doi.org/10.1145/3612783.3612792
21. Corsetti, B., Moreno, L., Hervás, R.: Shaping interactive systems: defining features to meet the needs of individuals with mild intellectual disabilities. In: Proceedings XXIV Interacción Persona-Ordenador. ACM (2024). https://doi.org/10.1145/3657242.3658593
22. Corsetti, B., Moreno, L., Hervás, R.: Evaluating Eleuteria app: deliver stage of an inclusive double diamond process. In: Proceedings XXV Interacción Persona-Ordenador (INTERACCIÓN 2025). CEUR-WS, Vol. 4000 (2025)
23. European Commission: Union of Equality: Strategy for the Rights of Persons with Disabilities 2021–2030 (2021)
24. European Commission: The New EU Urban Mobility Framework (COM/2021/811 final) (2021)
25. Ministerio de Transportes: Movilidad y Agenda Urbana (MITMA). Estrategia de Movilidad Sostenible y Conectada (2030). (2023). https://www.mitma.gob.es

26. United Nations: Convention on the Rights of Persons with Disabilities (2006)
27. UK Department for Transport. Inclusive Transport Strategy (2018). https://www.gov.uk/government/publications/inclusive-transport-strategy
28. US Department of Transportation. DOT Accessibility Guidelines (2022). https://www.transportation.gov/accessibility
29. W3C. Web Content Accessibility Guidelines (WCAG) 2.2: (2023). https://www.w3.org/TR/WCAG22/
30. W3C: Cognitive and Learning Disabilities Accessibility Task Force (COGA). Making Content Usable for People with Cognitive and Learning Disabilities. (2021). https://www.w3.org/TR/coga-usable/

Technology Design for and with Neurodivergent Users: Considerations from Research Practices

Technology Design for and with Neurodivergent Users: Considerations from Research Practices

Vivian Genaro Motti[1(✉)], David Gollasch[2], Meinhardt Branig[2], and Bruna C. R. Cunha[3]

[1] George Mason University, Fairfax, VA 22030, USA
vmotti@gmu.edu
[2] TUD Dresden University of Technology, Dresden, Germany
{david.gollasch,meinhardt.branig}@tu-dresden.de
[3] ICMC University of São Paulo, São Carlos, Brazil
brunaru@icmc.usp.br

Abstract. This paper presents the results of the workshop 'Technology Design for and with Neurodivergent Users: Considerations from Research Practices' held during Interact 2025 on September eighth in Belo Horizonte, Brazil. The main motivation for the organizers to propose this workshop is the growing opportunity to critically reflect on the design methods, approaches employed, and artifacts created thus far for neurodivergent people. To promote the debate around neuroinclusivity, we invited experts in neuroinclusion to discuss the methodological approaches adopted for research, main limitations in recruitment, co-design practices, and design activities as well as user studies. The full-day workshop included hands-on activities (world café), four presentations, and a panel with two invited guests who are experts in neurodivergence. In the discussions, we sought to identify the approaches that facilitate the integration of lived experiences of neurodivergent users to inform the research and development of interactive systems and novel digital technologies that are neuroinclusive. We invited the community to submit and share their considerations from research and development, experience reports, as well as methodological approaches to ensure that neuroinclusive designs can effectively meet the unique needs of neurodivergent users.

Keywords: Neurodivergent people · neuroinclusion · accessibility · Inclusive HCI methods · Assistive Technology

1 Introduction and Background

Neurodivergent people (those with non-normative neurocognitive functioning, including autism, ADHD, anxiety, or sensory processing differences [6]) face systemic barriers in education, employment, and social participation due to environments tailored for neurotypical norms. Challenges faced by neurodivergent people range from sensory overload in public spaces to workplace inefficiencies in shared offices, alongside social expectations that restrict access to leisure. Human-Computer Interaction (HCI) research has

Published by Springer Nature Switzerland AG 2026
C. Maciel et al. (Eds.): INTERACT 2025 Workshops, LNCS 16478, pp. 307–314, 2026.
https://doi.org/10.1007/978-3-032-22934-2_24

long explored technological artefacts that aim to improve quality of life for neurodivergent people. For instance, prior work revealed that interaction patterns vary significantly depending on the user location, gender, and neurodivergence [10]. However, prior work tends to prioritize neurotypical frameworks, pursuing heteronormative goals, such as training social skills in children or mitigating ADHD symptoms. Still, this body of work does not promote neurodivergent users' autonomy and agency but instead try to fix them by adopting a medical model and excluding principles of disability justice. While tools such as noise-cancelling headphones address sensory needs for end users, technologies designed without end users' needs consideration risk reinforcing normative pressures by masking neurodivergent traits, thereby constraining agency and sidelining personal aspirations from each individual [17].

Critiques within the HCI community highlight these pitfalls, exemplified by satirical concepts such as FaceSavr, which humorously proposes tools for neurotypical individuals to suppress emotional mirroring [15]. Scholars further emphasize problematic trends, including solution-driven research agendas [17] and inadequate inclusion of neurodivergent voices in design processes [18]. In response, emerging projects foreground neurodivergent lived experiences—such as workplace adaptations [6] or technology-enabled leisure activities [21]—demonstrating how collaborative design can empower self-determination among neurodivergent communities and accommodations must arise from within companies' cultures.

This workshop [14], has explored in depth three key themes: (1) how neurodivergent individuals repurpose existing technologies to meet their needs, (2) principles for designing inclusive technologies aligned with end users' priorities, and (3) developing tools to educate neurotypical people about neurodivergent experiences, fostering shared responsibility for inclusion. Participants engaged in a critical discussion in order to examine wearable assistive technologies, self-determination frameworks, and the interplay between individual accommodations and societal change.

2 Topic Areas

The topics that have driven the workshop encompassed neuroinclusive design [4]. Specifically, the submissions received, the talks presented, the workshop activities and panel hosted sought to understand previous experiences designing for and with neurodivergent people; challenges and limitations in interactive technologies; description of applications created to address the users' requirements; proposals for novel methods that facilitate the integration of neuroinclusive design and research practices; as well as design considerations and critical reflections seeking to improve current approaches to enhance the recruitment of and engagement with neurodivergent communities.

2.1 Technology Design for and with Neurodivergent Users

This workshop promoted an active conversation around: (1) design considerations to elevate neurodivergent voices in research experiences, by prioritizing first-person views; (2) neuroinclusion in technology development to meet users' unique needs through approaches, requirement elicitation, and evaluation of technology; (3) addressing trade-offs of universal design versus personalization for users in a spectrum of cognitive abilities; (4) education, awareness, and advocacy to enhance standard HCI practices among practitioners and researchers to promote cognitive accessibility for neuroinclusivity.

We invited workshop attendees to actively participate and engage in a conversation about the inclusive technology design aimed at neurodivergent people taking a reflective approach centered on disability justice, ethics, fairness, and inclusion. We began the event by setting up the expectations and ground rules, ensuring that divergent perspectives were considered in a fair manner. Then, we had a hands-on activity to promote the discussion, followed by four short talks, and a panel discussion with two invited speakers: Professor Laurianne Sitbon and Professor Chorong Park. The workshop concluded with final remarks and dissemination of a brief evaluation survey.

In the context of the workshop, we opted to adopt the term neurodivergence in its broader sense. Hence, submissions that were related to various forms of cognitive abilities were accepted. Likewise, we accepted contributions that report on the technology design regardless of application domain, including inclusive workplaces, well-being and wellness, and education.

2.2 Neurodivergence in Education

Neurodivergent learners and educators face exclusion within mainstream educational systems, despite the United Nations Convention on the Rights of Persons with Disabilities guaranteeing choice in institutional enrolment. However, even when families opt for public schools, these institutions frequently remain ill-equipped to support students with diverse needs—such as those prone to sensory overwhelm, distraction, or requiring individualized crisis support.

Inclusive education research emphasizes transforming pedagogical practices and institutional structures to accommodate neurodivergent learners [22]. Initiatives like the Index for Inclusion have proven effective in identifying systemic barriers in schools [3]. While inclusive pedagogy is emerging in teacher training programs, challenges persist in preparing educators to address both sensory communication systems (e.g., for deaf/hard-of-hearing students) and neurodivergent needs. These issues intensify in higher education: large lecture halls amplify distractions, quiet spaces are scarce, and exam accommodations (e.g., remote testing) lack standardized legal frameworks in countries like Germany [8]. Institutional inertia, coupled with limited awareness among faculty and administrators, and limitations in physical spaces, further complicate reforms hindering societal and environmental changes. However, hybrid approaches combining top-down policy changes and grassroots advocacy from community members show promise. When properly designed, digital tools enable steady progress, aiding asynchronous, location-flexible learning models.

2.3 Neurodivergence at Work

Neurodivergent individuals frequently face barriers in vocational training, acquiring a job, and attaining employment [1], resulting in disproportionate unemployment and underemployment within mainstream labor markets [2]. Core challenges involve workplace communication norms, organizational demands, and sensory sensitivities.

Employers prioritize verbal fluency for roles with greater responsibility [5], yet neurodivergent employees exhibit varied verbal expression patterns—from nonverbal to inconsistent speech—including word-retrieval difficulties, fluctuating articulation, or auditory processing differences. Augmentative and Alternative Communication (AAC) systems supplement or replace speech through multimodal supports [9], while assistive technologies like speech synthesis or interactive interfaces show efficacy in bridging communication gaps [13]. For autistic individuals, tailored solutions such as structured task-management frameworks and sensory-friendly workspace, along with constructive feedback and praise in the task design are critical. Sensory hyperreactivity, common among autistic people, can lead to workplace overwhelm. Tools like noise-cancelling headphones mitigate auditory overstimulation, yet current assistive strategies remain limited. Existing research focuses predominantly on stress detection [19] or alerting colleagues to sensory triggers in meetings [16], rather than systemic environmental adaptations [20] and awareness.

2.4 Neurodivergence and Leisure

Another sector that can benefit from neuroinclusive practices is leisure. Such contexts present unique opportunities for technology design that engages with neurodivergence through two lenses. First, innovations can enhance access to traditional leisure domains—such as cultural activities, athletics, or recreational play—addressing barriers neurodivergent individuals face. Concurrently, research should study how neurodivergent communities creatively adapt existing tools to fulfill their own needs. Second, we advocate reframing neurodivergence as a design asset rather than a deficit. This involves developing technologies that center neurodivergent joy, sensory preferences, and self-expression. Such approaches prioritize amplifying strengths and fulfilling experiences over compensatory strategies, exploring how tools can empower rather than "correct" neurodivergent ways of engaging with leisure.

3 Objectives

This workshop brought together an international community of HCI researchers with interest and experience designing for and with neurodivergent people. Assistive technology and neuroinclusive applications have been created across domains, ranging from education support, to workplace inclusion, and leisure. Yet, most of the techniques and methodological approaches traditionally employed in HCI do not meet the unique needs of neurodivergent users and their cognitive abilities manifested in a spectrum. We invited the community to reflect and discuss design considerations that take a first-person view so that technology serves the needs of end users. We invited attendees to engage in a critical reflection seeking to identify and address barriers for neuroinclusivity, transforming current design practices so that we not only spark discussions around the topic but also propose and implement methods that promote the full potential of neurodivergent users to be fully integrated in society.

4 Key Organizers

This workshop has received support from the IFIP Working Group TC 13.3, which focuses on Human-Computer Interaction, Disability, and Aging. WG 13.3 aims to increase awareness of the requirements of individuals with disabilities and the elderly. It provides guidance through recommendations for designing technologies that cater to the broadest possible user base, keeps track of the latest advancements in HCI and their effects on accessibility and usability, and promotes the creation of information and communication technologies, along with complementary tools, that can be adapted to meet the diverse needs of users. Additionally, all the workshop organizers have research interests and experience working for and with neurodivergent users, including autistic people, users with ADHD, and other cognitive differences.

Vivian Genaro Motti is an Associate Professor at George Mason University investigating workplace accessibility for neurodivergent adults and assistive smartwatch applications for emotion-regulation [11, 12, 22].

David Gollasch is a PhD student at the TU Dresden, Germany with research interests in diversity-sensitive interaction design as well as structured methods and processes around software variability and AI to build adaptive user interfaces [7].

Meinhardt Branig is a PhD student at the TU Dresden, Germany with research interests in accessibility, data physicalization and tangible interaction with focus on user-group diversity [7].

Bruna Cunha is an Assistant Professor at the University of São Paulo, Brazil, with extensive experience in health interventions, older adults, and computational assistive technologies designed to address diverse users' needs.

5 Participants

We have welcomed workshop participants from academia or industry, with experience and interests in learning more and exchanging knowledge about neurodivergent design approaches. First view experiences with technology, and critical perspectives that reflect upon methods and artifacts, were also incorporated to enrich the conversation. We had participants at various academic levels (PhD students, junior and senior Professors), and registrations from diverse academic institutions around the globe, including TU Dresden in Germany, University of São Paulo in Brazil, George Mason University in the US, Ireland, Denmark, Ceara – Brazil, Queen Mary University of London in the U.K..

6 Results

We accepted four publications, and the papers were presented in short talks followed by an open discussion. First, Daniel Allan Gil, from Queen Mary University of London, presented his work on a 'Lived Experience Report: A Neurodivergent Neurodivergence Technology Researcher', opening the discussion with a first-person perspective and critical reflection about the motivations and need for societal changes to promote neuroinclusion in academic institutions and beyond it. Then, David G. and Meinhardt B., from TU Dresden in Germany, shared their work on 'Assistive Technologies to Enhance

Email Communication in Neurodiverse Work Environments', discussing the results of a multidisciplinary work in partnership with industry to promote performance in assistive technology by adapting and customizing web browsers. Afterwards, Anika Islam presented her paper on 'Supporting Workplace Productivity of Neurodivergent Individuals: Opportunities and Challenges of Smartwatch-based Off-Task Detection'. Her talk was on wearable sensors and AI models for task recognition in inclusive employment. Her talk was followed by Bruna Cunha's and Leo Ribeiro's research study on 'How Can We Help? Computational Assistive Technologies for Crises Intervention in ASD'--exploring detection of meltdown and shutdown with wearable sensors and AI models.

The authors' presentations were followed by a discussion with questions and answers' sessions and a panel. The conversations held in collaboration with attendees have enriched the contributions prior to publication. In the panel discussion, we invited two speakers to answer five questions:

1. What are the drivers and motivations that lead you to investigate neuroinclusion?
2. What do you consider to be a grand challenge in research and design considerations to actively involve neurodivergent participants?
3. Which is a best practice that you would like to recommend (in terms of methodological approach) for the community to adopt?
4. What are the main focus areas for future research and next-generation technologies for neuroinclusive design?
5. Do you have any surprising success stories you would like to share with attendees? Something that worked well in your research studies or design experience.

The panellists emphasized the importance of community involvement throughout the design and creation process of inclusive technology. Also, they highlighted the importance of breaking ground and addressing the common challenges related to neuroinclusive work in HCI to design technology across application sectors and adapt the methods to consider end users' needs. Lastly, they cited the importance of persistence when trying to pioneer a domain that has been understudied and embrace divergent perspectives.

Regarding the common *Challenges* faced in the domain the authors, attendees and panellists are in agreement that the incorporation of first-person voices is currently limited in design research for novel inclusive technologies, due to the strict practices that have been traditionally used in HCI research and methodological approaches for user studies (e.g. think aloud, interviews, usability questionnaires, etc.). Also, reliance on purely quantitative methods that are primarily focused on statistical significance fail to account for the unique differences across participants who are in a spectrum of abilities, and therefore their perspectives often do not culminate with saturation of topics (for example in a thematic analysis) and convergence in their opinions. Hence, methods as single-subject studies or case studies may prove to be more appropriate to embrace unique users' profiles.

Concerning the *Open Questions* that remain as grand challenges to be studied we remark that innovation in neuroinclusive approaches are needed to gather information from the community who are neurodivergent, taking into account diverse modalities for data collection and requirement elicitation. Likewise, the analysis of such data requires navigating inherent trade-offs between a 'universal' design that is neuroinclusive and personalized to meet individual abilities of each user. Reflective approaches that question inherent bias and shift the power dynamics to avoid heteronormative and patriarchal approaches are also necessary.

Regarding the *pathways for future research,* we highlight that the changes that impact society to enable education systems to all would allow for cognitive differences to be celebrated and integrated in the curriculum, so that the talents and strengths of all users could also contribute to create technological advancements that are well suited for community members, embracing innovation and inclusiveness.

As future work, the organizers have further plants to create additional outcomes such as a book chapter, a WAVE track reporting the event to the Interaction magazine, a discord channel to build community.

7 Acknowledgments

This material is based upon the work supported by the Federal Ministry of Labour and Social Affairs (BMAS) under the grant number FT 1–58330 and the National Science Foundation (award n. 2326270). Any opinions, findings, conclusions, or recommendations expressed in this material are those of the author(s) and don't necessarily reflect the views of the National Science Foundation.

References

1. Ara, Z., et al.: Collaborative job seeking for people with autism: challenges and design opportunities. In: Proceedings of the 2024 CHI Conference on Human Factors in Computing Systems, pp. 1–17 (2024)
2. Bader M.. Labruier M., Proft J., Vogeley K.: Menschen mit Autismus im Arbeitsleben – Informationen und Handlungsempfehlungen. (2018). Online: https://publi.lvr.de/publi/PDF/823-18_1040-Arbeitsheft-Autismus-im-Beruf-barrierefrei.pdf (Retrieval: 02.11.2021)
3. Booth, T., Ainscow, M., Black-Hawkins, K., Vaughan, M., Shaw, L.: Index for inclusion. Developing Learn. Participation Schools **2** (2002)
4. Boyd, L.: Neuro-inclusive design considerations for assistive and accessible technologies and beyond. In: The Sensory Accommodation Framework for Technology: Bridging Sensory Processing to Social Cognition, pp. 113–124. Springer (2024)
5. Bryen, D.N., Potts, B.B., Carey, A.C.: So you want to work? What employers say about job skills, recruitment and hiring employees who rely on AAC. Augment. Altern. Commun. **23**(2), 126–139 (2007). https://doi.org/10.1080/07434610600991175
6. Das, M., Tang, J., Ringland, K.E., Piper, A.M.: Towards accessible remote work: understanding work-from-home practices of Neurodivergent professionals. Proc. ACM Hum.-Comput. Interact. **5**(183), 30 (2021). https://doi.org/10.1145/3449282
7. Gollasch, D., Branig, M.: Designing technology for neurodivergent self-determination: challenges and opportunities–workshop results. In: IFIP Conference on Human-Computer Interaction, pp. 107–114, Springer (2023)
8. Hähne, C., Marquardt, G., Rudolph, E., Schmidt, H. J., Weber, G., Wegner, G.: Inklusion benötigt verschiedene Prozesse: Aktivitäten und Strategien an der TU Dresden. Zeitschrift für Hochschulentwicklung, 15(3), 363–376, (2020)
9. Happ, M.B., et al.: Effect of a multi-level intervention on nurse patient communication in the intensive care unit: results of the SPEACS trial. Heart Lung. **43**(2), 89–98 (2014)

10. Johansson, S., Gulliksen, J., Gustavsson, C.: Disability digital divide: the use of the internet, smartphones, computers and tablets among people with disabilities in Sweden. Univ. Access Inf. Soc. **20**(1), 105–120 (2021)
11. Kalantari, N., Bagale, A., Motti, V.G.: Designing assistive technologies for and with neurodivergent users: considerations from research practice. Interact. Comput. **iwaf037** (2025)
12. Kender, K., Spiel, K.: FaceSavr™: designing technologies with Allistic adults to Battle emotion echolalia. In: CHI Conference on Human Factors in Computing Systems Extended Abstracts, pp. 1–8 (2022)
13. Motti, V.G.: Designing emerging technologies for and with neurodiverse users. In: Proceedings of the 37th ACM International Conference on the Design of Communication, pp. 1–10 (2019)
14. Motti, V.G., Gollasch, D., Branig, M., Cunha, B.C.: Technology design for and with Neurodivergent users: considerations from research practices. In: IFIP Conference on Human-Computer Interaction, pp. 401–406. Springer Nature Switzerland, Cham (2025)
15. Rispoli, M., Franco, J., Van Der Meer, L., Lang, R., Camargo, S.: The use of speech generating devices in communication interventions for individuals with developmental disabilities: a review of the literature. Dev. Neurorehab. **13**, 276–293 (2010)
16. Sanfilippo, F., Raja, K.: A multi-sensor system for enhancing situational awareness and stress Management for People with ASD in the workplace and in everyday life. In: Hawaii International Conference on System Sciences (2019). https://doi.org/10.24251/HICSS.2019.494
17. Spiel, K., Gerling, K.: The purpose of play: how HCI games research fails Neurodivergent populations. ACM Trans. Comput.-Hum. Interact. 28, (2) 40 (2021). https://doi.org/10.1145/3432245
18. Stefanidi, E., Schöning, J., Feger, S.S., Marshall, P., Rogers, Y., JNiess., J.: Designing for care ecosystems: a literature review of Technologies for Children with ADHD. In: Interaction Design and Children (IDC '22), pp. 13–25. ACM, New York, NY, USA (2022)
19. Tomczak, M.T., Wójcikowski, M., Listewnik, P., Pankiewicz, B., Majchrowicz, D., Jędrzejewska-Szczerska, M.: Support for employees with ASD in the workplace using a Bluetooth skin resistance sensor–a preliminary study. Sensors. **18**(10), 3530 (2018)
20. Wali, L.J., Sanfilippo, F.: A review of the state-of-the-art of assistive Technology for People with ASD in the workplace and in everyday life. In: Pappas, I.O., Mikalef, P., Dwivedi, Y.K., Jaccheri, L., Krogstie, J., Mäntymäki, M. (eds.) Digital transformation for a sustainable society in the 21st century. I3E 2019 LNCS, vol. 11701. Springer, Cham (2019). https://doi.org/10.1007/978-3-030-29374-1_42
21. Wyeth, P., Summerville, J., Adkins, B.: Stomp: an interactive platform for people with intellectual disabilities. In: Proceedings of the 8th International Conference on Advances in Computer Entertainment Technology (ACE '11) Association for Computing Machinery, pp. 51, 1–58, New York, NY, USA (2011). https://doi.org/10.1145/2071423.2071487
22. Zheng, H., Motti, V.G.: Assisting students with intellectual and developmental disabilities in inclusive education with smartwatches. In: Proceedings of the 2018 CHI Conference on Human Factors in Computing Systems, pp. 1–12 (2018)

Lived Experience Report: A Neurodivergent Neurodivergence-Technology Researcher

Daniel Gill(✉)

Queen Mary University of London, London, UK
d.a.gill@qmul.ac.uk

Abstract. As an autistic PhD student working with neurodivergent users and research participants, I feel a deep responsibility to ensure that their voices are heard and valued in research about neurodivergent conditions. I achieve this by benefitting from my own experiences to make a safe and welcoming research environment, both in qualitative and quantitative methodologies. As I describe however, I am conscious of the possible risks that being autistic myself may impact and bias the methodologies and aims of my research, so I also reflect on how my keen use of participatory and co-design methodologies (within this accessible environment) can create truly rich research which benefits from the unique experiences of neurodivergent people.

1 Introduction

I am an autistic PhD student who is developing technology for and with neurodivergent users. At first glance, one might assume that I am well placed to take on this challenge: a computer science and engineering background and a lifetime of autism *should* make my job trivial. However, this is not always the case. While my research projects have been motivated by my own lived experience, it has been the feedback and input from neurodivergent participants which have shaped my work the most.

My goal is to conduct truly useful research which has real impacts for neurodivergent people. Traditionally, impactful and telling research might be that which includes huge numbers of participants, doing tasks which are designed around the need to quickly rattle through participants, and not necessarily focusing on individuals. In this lived experience report, I reflect on how my own experiences of being an 'insider' in a neurodivergent world enables me to conduct research that has great meaning for me and other neurodivergent people.

With integrating myself into my research too much, however, comes the challenges associated with relying too much on my own position and experiences of my small part of the *spectrum* of neurodivergent conditions and traits. To remedy this, I discuss how I have, and continue, to benefit from the perspectives of other neurodivergent people through using participatory methodologies, and

Published by Springer Nature Switzerland AG 2026
C. Maciel et al. (Eds.): INTERACT 2025 Workshops, LNCS 16478, pp. 315–319, 2026.
https://doi.org/10.1007/978-3-032-22934-2_25

how I advocate for, and work with, other neurodivergent researchers with the same passion.

2 Mutual Understanding

One of the greatest benefits of working in this area is the inherent mutual understanding that comes with being neurodivergent. In Crompton *et al.* [1], for example, autistic individuals expressed increased anxiety and difficulty in interactions with neurotypical friends and family, while conversations with autistic peers were accompanied with feelings of ease and comfort. Though there are some caveats (unpredictability of autistic strangers, for example) and individual differences, the lack of expectation to follow the unspoken rules of social interaction and decreased awkwardness of silence is a nice reminder that you're not alone. This sentiment is expressed nicely as a quote in the title of Crompton *et al.*'s paper: "I never realised everybody felt as happy as I do when I am around autistic people".

I argue that these experiences and sentiments are described by the "Double Empathy Problem" [3,4], which describes how communication breakdowns are not a deficit related to neurodivergent conditions themselves, but a *mutual* misunderstanding between neurotypes, as demonstrated effectively by Crompton *et al.* [1].

I have found that this innate understanding supports my research with other neurodivergent people. My own pursuit for order and organisation, for example, is reflected in my research methodology, and therefore improving the experience of participants. In my Master's research project, weekly emails sent to participants were delivered on time (usually by scheduling them ahead of time) while trying to keep them both clear and detailed. I was thrilled to receive this lovely unprompted message from a participant following the study: "The organisation and execution of the study were commendable, and it was evident that a lot of thought and effort went into its planning. I appreciate the time you took to explain the process and ensure ease and accessibility throughout."

This organisation has continued into my PhD research, ensuring participants feel comfortable in increasingly laboratory-like surroundings. I insisted on starting my PhD work by initially running focus groups with a number of neurodivergent collaborators to critically evaluate the overall aim of our research, and to introduce some of the technologies we would later be using in our more experimental work. Feedback we received from participants of these focus groups meant that we could ensure that our research remained relevant, and that the methodology and environment would be suitable for our participants.

Alongside talking with others in the focus groups, thinking of challenges that I would have faced in the participants' shoes was also important. When it came to run practical experiments, I prioritised creating a friendly and welcoming environment. I gave clear instructions to participants of what to expect and do, including reminders about being able to take breaks when they needed them, provided access to a wide selection of fidget/stim toys to everyone, and gave the opportunity for a debrief after the experiment to answer questions which I couldn't during the session, lest it impact the results. Given the novelty of the robotics we are using, and the environment created to support neurodivergent, it was clear to me that participants enjoyed the experience, with some even describing the task as meditative.

3 The Wrong Focus

As mentioned in the Introduction, the motivation of my projects often stemmed from my own experiences: an attempt to solve my own problems, assuming (to a certain extent) that other neurodivergent people have the same experience. It may, however, be naïve to assume this, especially given the extensive *spectrum* within which neurodivergent conditions lie. While I, of course, follow the standard research methodologies for identifying relevant literature and creating hypotheses, it is a risk that my experiences have too much of an impact the choice and direction of higher level research aims and methodologies.

For example, I have a long-held preference for identity first (autistic person) rather than person first (person with autism) language, which impacts how I write about neurodivergence. Participants in my focus groups, however, had differing preferences, and might have felt excluded or uncomfortable if we hadn't changed to using mixed language in the sessions and future research outputs.

It is for this reason that I've been drawn to more qualitative, co-produced, and participatory research methods. My master's research project–evaluating a mood tracking system based around emoji interpretations–was enhanced by the semi-structured interviews conducted after each month-long study period. In this study, we took advantage of individuals' own preferences for and interpretations of emojis to enhance emoji-based mood tracking, notably allowing participants to pick from all emojis rather than the conventional happy-to-sad-face selection. Although we did collect some quantitative data (specifically on the entries made and overall happiness throughout), only the interviews could tell us how and, importantly, why participants used the application the way they did. This allowed us to investigate the individuality inherent in neurodivergence: rather than solely relying on one interpretation of the task, participants could mould their use of the system to their own needs, reflected in very interesting results.

4 Co-design and Neurodivergence

I am not alone in extolling the virtues of using participatory research methods when working with neurodivergent people, legends of neurodiversity research highlight its inclusivity [2,5]. As a neurodivergent researcher, I feel I have an additional responsibility to bring others like me into research: to ensure their voices are heard and that they directly benefit from research about them that they might take part in.

Pellicano *et al.* [5] share striking anecdotes from autistic adults and parents of autistic children who took part in research, describing a deep "disconnect" between research being done and that which could make a difference to autistic people. Autistic research participants described how the eventual research outputs were "indigestible" as a result of being full of science jargon and "stuff that neurotypicals write about autism" which is "gobbledygook". Having taken part in research myself, and while receiving the promise of hearing of the results and being in a privileged position to be able to understand science jargon in this area, I have yet to receive many of these.

As a result of this, I always make sure to send out updates to my research participants, sending out any publications in both their original form (for those more academically inclined), but also simplified versions through mine or other organisations' blogs, and video and presentations for those who prefer a more visual summary.

It is not just my own research that I am concerned with, however. MI**ND**S, or Mutual Inclusion through Neurodiversity in Science, is a network I created for researchers, neurodivergent people, and neurodivergent researchers. The aim is bring together these groups to support research dissemination to neurodivergent people in 'Accessible Academia' posts, where summaries of recent research are written in smaller paragraphs in a simpler way, with important science jargon having drop-down explainers. We also aim to create a space for neurodivergent researchers to share their experiences, and to bring other voices into research through interactive workshops, of which we've held two very successful sessions so far.

5 Conclusion

I hope that this lived experience report has been of some use, demonstrating the dual-nature of being an 'insider' researcher. My experience of autism is not a substitute for rigorous co-design and participatory methodologies, but a tool to enhance it. I believe that reflecting on the concern of the risks of projecting my own experiences onto my research aims and methodologies has enabled me to instead benefit my experiences in setting a baseline for the participatory experiences of neurodivergent people. I work to ensure that neurodivergent participants and collaborators are in a comfortable and suitable environment to be able to share their own experiences, providing a unique opportunity to hear individual experiences which make my research far richer.

Acknowledgments. Thanks, as ever, to Ekaterina Ivanova, Rachael Bedford, Simon Lund-Lack, and Tony Stockman for their support.

Disclosure of Interests. The author has no competing interests to declare that are relevant to the content of this article.

References

1. Crompton, C.J., Hallett, S., Ropar, D., Flynn, E., Fletcher-Watson, S.: 'I never realised everybody felt as happy as I do when I am around autistic people':

A thematic analysis of autistic adults' relationships with autistic and neurotypical friends and family. Autism **24**(6), 1438–1448 (2020). https://doi.org/10.1177/1362361320908976
2. Fletcher-Watson, S., Brook, K., Hallett, S., Murray, F., Crompton, C.J.: Inclusive practices for neurodevelopmental research. Curr. Dev. Disord. Rep. **8**(2), 88–97 (2021). https://doi.org/10.1007/s40474-021-00227-z
3. Milton, D., Gurbuz, E., López, B.: The 'double empathy problem': ten years on. Autism **26**(8), 1901–1903 (2022). https://doi.org/10.1177/13623613221129123
4. Milton, D.E.: On the ontological status of autism: the 'double empathy problem'. Disabil. Soc. **27**(6), 883–887 (2012). https://doi.org/10.1080/09687599.2012.710008, http://www.tandfonline.com/doi/abs/10.1080/09687599.2012.710008
5. Pellicano, E., Dinsmore, A., Charman, T.: Views on researcher-community engagement in autism research in the United Kingdom: a mixed-methods study. PLOS ONE **9**(10), e109946 (2014). https://doi.org/10.1371/journal.pone.0109946, https://journals.plos.org/plosone/article?id=10.1371/journal.pone.0109946, publisher: Public Library of Science

Exploring Smartwatch-Based Off-Task Detection: Opportunities, Challenges and Early Design Considerations for Supporting Neurodivergent Workers

Anika Binte Islam(✉), Niloofar Kalantari, Sarah Wittman, and Vivian Genaro Motti

George Mason University, Fairfax, VA 22030, USA
{aislam22,nkalanta,swittman,vmotti}@gmu.edu

Abstract. Off-task behavior presents a significant challenge for neurodivergent workers, particularly those with Attention Deficit Hyperactivity Disorder (ADHD) and Autism Spectrum Disorder (ASD) in the workplace environment. The detection of such behavior in the moment could enable timely interventions that help maintain focus and improve workplace productivity. Prior works indicate that wearable sensing is underexplored in this context. Therefore, this paper explores the potential of smartwatches and machine learning models to detect off-task behavior in neurodivergent individuals. Drawing on a pilot study with ten young adults with ADHD and ASD, we reflect on the initial observations and challenges encountered during the user study. Moreover, the paper outlines the early design considerations for neuroinclusive smartwatch-based interventions, grounded in prior literature and practical research experience.

Keywords: Neurodivergent users · Off-task detection · Workplace productivity · Smartwatch · Intervention design

1 Introduction

The term neurodiversity refers to a concept that includes diverse cognitive profiles, such as ASD, ADHD, and Intellectual and Developmental Disabilities (IDD). Their cognitive abilities, information processing, and executive functions vary significantly, leading them to face numerous challenges in academic and professional settings. These challenges include difficulty in maintaining attention, social interaction, sensory sensitivities, organizing tasks, and managing time as well [6]. These may affect the productivity of neurodivergent employees in their jobs [15].

Off-task behavior is often referred to as a loss of attention and disengagement in learning activities in educational settings [3]. It occurs not only in the educational system but also in any environment that lacks sufficient engagement,

Published by Springer Nature Switzerland AG 2026
C. Maciel et al. (Eds.): INTERACT 2025 Workshops, LNCS 16478, pp. 320–328, 2026.
https://doi.org/10.1007/978-3-032-22934-2_26

structure, and support. In many workplace environments, engaging in task completion and maintaining attention are the keys to success at work. Behavioral intervention strategies demonstrate promising approaches to stay focused and eventually improve engagement, overall productivity, and promote the autonomy of neurodivergent employees in the workplace [4]. These strategies include positive reinforcement, creating a supportive environment, reminders, and feedback.

Wearable technologies are ubiquitous in workplace applications, used to compute worker performance, monitor, assist, augment, and track it. At the forefront of human technology integration, wearables, particularly smartwatches, have incredible potential to enhance worker productivity, especially when technology is designed to meet employees' needs [17]. Commercial smartwatches and platform development have enabled researchers to build customized applications to collect, analyze, and study intervention data [14]. Machine learning (ML) also shows promise in analyzing wearable sensor data and detecting various tasks [1]. For off-task behavior detection in educational environments, previous works utilized data collected through surveys, self-reported data, mouse tracking, eye-tracking and so on [3,7,10]. Thus, in this study, we leveraged smartwatch sensor data and ML models to detect off-task behavior of neurodivergent employees. To provide support and improve the workplace productivity of individuals with ASD and ADHD, it is also essential to understand how to design the intervention after detecting off-task moments in real time.

Our study will focus on the following research questions:

- What are the opportunities and challenges of using smartwatches to detect off-task behavior of young adults with ASD and ADHD?
- What factors should be considered when designing smartwatch-based interventions to support neurodivergent employees?

This paper reflects the authors' experience in detecting off-task behaviors of young adults with ASD and ADHD using smartwatch sensors and machine learning models. We focus on the potential of smartwatches in task design, data collection, and analysis. After that, we present some challenges we faced during the user study and data analysis. In addition, we extend our discussion by presenting some early design considerations for interventions based on our research experiences and existing literature. We conclude with some reflections regarding the overall task design, data collection, and analysis.

Positionality Statement. The authors include three human computer interaction (HCI) researchers and one organizational behavior researcher. One of them identifies as neurodivergent and draws on lived experiences, while the others have 10 years of experience in neurodiversity and accessibility research. We adopt the critical disability studies approach rather than the medical model.

2 Study Overview

Recruitment: Upon Institutional Review Board (IRB) approval of the study protocol by the university, we recruited ten neurodivergent young adults (age range from 18 to 24 years) with ASD and ADHD. We advertised the study using flyers, emails, and word-of-mouth. The recruitment took place from Fall 2024 to Spring 2025.

Data Collection: The data were collected in an in-person lab study through interviews. We first selected a workplace simulated task of putting coins into containers that requires precise hand movements and closely resembles tasks performed in various sectors, such as coffee shops, grocery stores, and many more. Prior to the data collection, we obtained consent from the participants to gather their demographic information (age, gender, race, ethnicity, and neurodiversity). Afterward, we accumulated sensor data through a Garmin Venu 3 smartwatch while participants performed the selected task in a controlled lab setting (Fig. 1). We also utilized the accelerometer data to identify tasks and off-tasks through hand movements. We recorded the overall session via Zoom. Each participant was compensated with a gift card delivered by email after participation in the study.

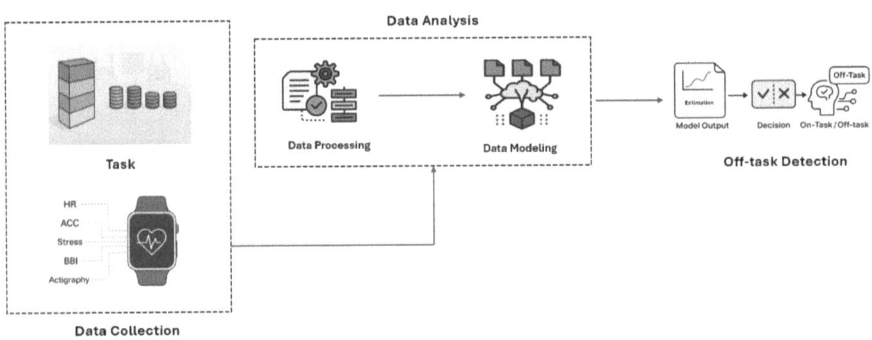

Fig. 1. Overview of the smartwatch-based off-task detection process.

Data Analysis: The sensor data were annotated manually in accordance with the Zoom video recording. After that, we employed conventional machine learning techniques to detect the off-task behavior of neurodivergent individuals. Researchers reviewed and analyzed video recordings to capture and understand participants' behavior (off-task or performing a task) throughout the sessions.

3 Detecting Off-Task Behavior with Smartwatches: Opportunities and Challenges

This section reflects on both the opportunities and challenges we experienced in detecting off-task behavior in young adults with ASD and ADHD, leveraging smartwatch sensors and ML models.

3.1 Opportunities of Smartwatch Sensors and ML Models

Task Design and Smartwatch Sensing. In our study, the tasks involved hand movement activities, including taking items, moving them, and placing them in a specific area. These are very common for individuals working in retail-trade industries or grocery stores, involving repetitive tasks such as placing items on the shelves, packing items and so on. In fact, our task included hand movements that tend to be repetitive and moderate in range of motion, with several degrees of freedom that resemble activities in various job sectors. Smartwatches have the ability to capture motion patterns in real-time through various sensors, such as an accelerometer, gyroscope, and magnetometer, providing the scope to identify different activities by applying ML models [1]. Similar to other hand-oriented task detections, we aimed to detect off-task behavior by leveraging smartwatch sensor data. Our observational study led to the definition of off-task as not performing or disengaging from the assigned work for an extended period. The indicators of disengagement include both long periods of inactivity during active tasks and sudden stops of structured movements, as well as irregular movement patterns. The smartwatch sensors can detect these patterns through passive data collection, which enables practical solutions for real-world applications and simple deployment in everyday workplaces.

Data-Driven Analysis. The task design and seamless smartwatch sensor data collection offer a strong foundation for developing data-driven models for off-task detection. Smartwatches bring practical utilities to fine-grained hand movement and gesture detection [1]. Machine learning models exhibit potential for identifying patterns in sensor data that correspond to different activities [1]. By training models on the collected data, we can automate the detection process and ultimately provide timely and individualized interventions. We used time-series accelerometer data to develop machine learning model-based frameworks for detecting off-task behavior. Based on prior research in hand activity recognition, we applied conventional supervised techniques such as Random Forest, Support Vector Machine and K-NN. These models achieved promising performance in detecting the task activities, while off-task detection showed average accuracy (around 54%). The initial results revealed that better sensing technology, combined with customized model approaches, would improve model reliability; however, additional studies are required to address off-task detection challenges.

Off-task detection using smartwatch sensors is still in development, and our findings highlight the promise of smartwatch-based systems in this regard. The ability to unobtrusively capture hand movement patterns and feed them into machine learning models creates meaningful opportunities to support neurodivergent users to improve their workplace productivity by providing interventions.

3.2 Challenges

Controlled Lab Setting. The task design simulated real workplace activities; however, the study was conducted within a controlled lab environment. A controlled lab setting where the participants performed the tasks individually might have had an impact on the way they approached the tasks. Moreover, the environment of the lab setting might not fully replicate the intricate nature of real-world operational settings in its entirety, as the external influencing factors have been minimized by the setup.

Overlapping Motion Pattern. Our initial observation after analyzing the data revealed that task and off-task motion patterns overlapped, leading to misclassifications. Moreover, the data also showed overlapping patterns among different task activities.

Individual Variability in Off-Task Behavior. The major difficulty that we observed was in terms of the differences in off-task behavior among participants. The inconsistent nature of off-task behavior across participants makes it difficult to come up with a generalized pattern, thereby affecting the model's performance.

4 From Detection to Workplace Support: Early Design Considerations for Neuroinclusive Interventions

While smartwatches show potential for detecting off-task behavior, they are also promising platforms for intervention because of their small size, long battery life, and increased processing power [4]. Interventions can include reminders, prompts, or even personalized feedback to improve productivity in workplace settings. In this section, we reflect on the existing design considerations for interventions from the literature as well as our experience working with neurodivergent individuals.

4.1 Insights from Literature

Feedback Modality. There are different feedback modalities of smartwatch interventions to accommodate the needs of neurodivergent individuals, such as haptic, visual, auditory, biofeedback, and so on [5,18]. Individuals who are sensitive to multiple sensory inputs respond better to visual prompting [12], while others benefit from subtle vibrations or real-time biofeedback to improve attention and self-regulation [11]. Thus, it is recommended to implement tailored multimodal feedback to accommodate diverse needs and preferences.

Tone and Framing. The framing of intervention feedback has a significant impact on an individual's emotional response. Encouraging phrases and positive feedback can motivate neurodivergent individuals to engage in the task and sustain attention [4,8].

Personalization. Neurodivergent individuals have unique needs; hence, a one-size-fits-all approach will not be effective when designing systems. The system should allow users to choose their preferred feedback modalities, text, time of intervention, or even their preferred intervention. Personalized intervention helps individuals address unique needs and overcome their challenges [13].

Environmental Context. The design of the intervention also requires the evaluation of the environmental context, which includes the physical, social, and sensory aspects of the workplace settings [9]. A prompt or feedback that works well in one environment could become inappropriate in other settings. For example, haptic cues like vibration might be helpful in a quiet work environment but are incoherent in a noisy or chaotic workplace. Systems need to be context-aware because they should provide users with options to choose feedback according to work environments and task complexities [2,16].

4.2 Practical Insights from Researchers' Experience

Based on our research experience working with neurodivergent individuals, we identified several recurring patterns relevant to designing supportive technologies. These are commonly observed considerations across various forms of user interaction, including interviews, surveys, and co-design sessions.

Tailored Feedback and User Control. One of the most prominent emerging themes is designing intervention feedback that is tailored to users' preferences. Neurodivergent individuals often expressed in various user studies their preferences for feedback that is individually relevant, including customized motivational quotes, visuals, or notifications. These preferences also reflect individuals' strengths and challenges. Moreover, individuals also reported having control over the timing and delivery of the intervention, such as the ability to pause the notifications or modify the feedback type. Providing individuals with autonomy and tailored feedback ensures that interventions remain supportive and user-centered.

Context-Aware and Non-Disruptive Feedback. Another frequently observed aspect of designing technology for neurodivergent workers is context awareness. The effectiveness of an intervention largely depends on the workplace surroundings and social context. Neurodivergent workers often emphasized the significance of situational awareness, highlighting that reminders should consider factors such as meeting or task timing and environmental aspects to avoid unnecessary disruptions. They often preferred gentle and adaptive nudges, including subtle vibrations, visual cues, or simple alarm sounds in workplaces. These underscore the importance of designing non-intrusive and context aware interventions.

Designing for Self-awareness and Self-regulation. We observed another recurrent pattern indicating that technologies are better fostered when they help individuals recognize their own emotions and behaviors, as well as support them in acting on that awareness. Self-regulation strategies help individuals manage their own emotions and focus, ultimately improving overall well-being.

Supportive Framing. While engaging with neurodivergent individuals in co-design and interview sessions, we noted that they exhibited preferences for interventions that adopt a positive or encouraging tone. For example, prompting motivational quotes and encouraging messages are considered effective strategies for enhancing productivity and well-being. Moreover, providing goal-setting rewards helped neurodivergent individuals increase their self-esteem and motivated them to engage in the work.

5 Reflection

Our observations while working with smartwatch sensors and ML models for detecting off-task behavior revealed key insights that go beyond just performance measures. While we observed that tasks were reliably recognized, the detection of the off-task motion patterns proved more challenging due to various factors, including contextual ambiguity, subtle variations in hand movement patterns, and individual off-task variability. Hence, we need an off-task detection model that can take these factors into consideration. The model accuracy will improve if we can come up with a framework that is more context-aware and facilitates user-driven interpretation of motion data. In this pilot study, we selected a simple task that resembles workplace activities to explore the feasibility of smartwatch-based off-task detection. Our observations suggest that the models should be tested with different workplace activity data. Additionally, both literature and our research experience with neurodivergent individuals suggest that technology designed for them should serve as a tool that promotes self-regulation and self-awareness.

6 Conclusion

This paper investigates the opportunities and challenges of leveraging smartwatch sensing to identify off-task behavior in neurodivergent individuals. While the ML models fed on the smartwatch sensors' data showed promising results for task recognition, detecting off-task behavior remained challenging. On the other hand, interventions designed for neurodivergent individuals must be personalized, context-aware and supportive. These observations emphasize the importance of moving beyond purely technical solutions to consider user agency, environmental fit, and inclusive design. This preliminary study also presents an early foundation for understanding the opportunities and challenges of smartwatch-based off-task detection. In future work, we aim to extend this pilot study by collecting data from a diverse group of neurodivergent employees and developing more robust off-task detection models. Additionally, we aim to conduct studies to examine different intervention strategies to support the workplace productivity of neurodivergent employees.

Acknowledgments. This study is based on work supported by the National Science Foundation under Grant No. 2326270.

References

1. Bhattacharya, S., Adaimi, R., Thomaz, E.: Leveraging sound and wrist motion to detect activities of daily living with commodity smartwatches. Proc. ACM Interact. Mob. Wearable Ubiquitous Technol. **6**(2), 1–28 (2022)
2. Boyd, L.E., et al.: SayWAT: augmenting face-to-face conversations for adults with autism. In: Proceedings of the 2016 CHI Conference on Human Factors in Computing Systems, pp. 4872–4883 (2016)
3. Carpenter, D., et al.: Detecting off-task behavior from student dialogue in game-based collaborative learning. In: Artificial Intelligence in Education: 21st International Conference, AIED 2020, Ifrane, Morocco, July 6–10, 2020, Proceedings, Part I 21, pp. 55–66 (2020)
4. Cibrian, F.L., Lakes, K.D., Tavakoulnia, A., Guzman, K., Schuck, S., Hayes, G.R.: Supporting self-regulation of children with ADHD using wearables: tensions and design challenges. In: Proceedings of the 2020 CHI Conference on Human Factors in Computing Systems, pp. 1–13 (2020)
5. Dibia, V.: FOQUS: a smartwatch application for individuals with ADHD and mental health challenges. In: Proceedings of the 18th International ACM SIGACCESS Conference on Computers and Accessibility, pp. 311–312 (2016)
6. Doyle, N.: Neurodiversity at work: a biopsychosocial model and the impact on working adults. Br. Med. Bull. **135**(1), 108–125 (2020)
7. Ge, Y., et al.: Towards contactless human concentration monitoring using mmWave signals. In: 2024 IEEE 10th International Conference on Collaboration and Internet Computing (CIC), pp. 19–28. IEEE (2024)
8. Hall, K., Arora, P., Lowy, R., Kim, J.G.: Designing for strengths: opportunities to support neurodiversity in the workplace. In: Proceedings of the 2024 CHI Conference on Human Factors in Computing Systems, pp. 1–14 (2024)
9. Kim, J.G., et al.: The workplace playbook VR: exploring the design space of virtual reality to foster understanding of and support for autistic people. Proc. ACM Hum.-Comput. Interact. **6**(CSCW2), 1–24 (2022)
10. Liu, Y., Deng, L., Lin, L., Gu, X.: Patterns of triggers for on-task and off-task behaviors: university students in independent study. Interact. Learn. Environ. **31**(5), 2792–2808 (2023)

11. Morris, M.R., Begel, A., Wiedermann, B.: Understanding the challenges faced by neurodiverse software engineering employees: towards a more inclusive and productive technical workforce. In: Proceedings of the 17th International ACM SIGACCESS Conference on Computers & Accessibility, pp. 173–184 (2015)
12. O'Brien, A.M., Schlosser, R.W., Yu, C., Allen, A.A., Shane, H.C.: Repurposing a smartwatch to support individuals with autism spectrum disorder: sensory and operational considerations. J. Spec. Educ. Technol. **36**(4), 215–226 (2021)
13. Sharmin, M., Hossain, M.M., Saha, A., Das, M., Maxwell, M., Ahmed, S.: From research to practice: informing the design of autism support smart technology. In: Proceedings of the 2018 CHI Conference on Human Factors in Computing Systems, pp. 1–16 (2018)
14. Silva, L.M., et al.: Unpacking the lived experiences of smartwatch mediated self and co-regulation with ADHD children. In: Proceedings of the 2023 CHI Conference on Human Factors in Computing Systems, pp. 1–19 (2023)
15. Wali, L.J., Sanfilippo, F.: A review of the state-of-the-art of assistive technology for people with ASD in the workplace and in everyday life. In: Digital Transformation for a Sustainable Society in the 21st Century: 18th IFIP WG 6.11 Conference on e-Business, e-Services, and e-Society, I3E 2019, Trondheim, Norway, September 18–20, 2019, Proceedings 18, pp. 520–532. Springer (2019)
16. Wright, R.E., McMahon, D.D., Cihak, D.F., Hirschfelder, K.: Smartwatch executive function supports for students with id and ASD. J. Spec. Educ. Technol. **37**(1), 63–73 (2022)
17. Yildirim, H., Ali-Eldin, A.M.: A model for predicting user intention to use wearable IoT devices at the workplace. J. King Saud Univ.-Comput. Inf. Sci. **31**(4), 497–505 (2019)
18. Zhou, K., Richard, C., Kim, J.: Employment-related assistive technologies for autistic individuals: a scoping review. J. Vocat. Rehabil. **62**(2), 191–206 (2025)

How Can We Help? Computational Assistive Technologies for Crises Intervention in ASD

Bruna C. Rodrigues da Cunha and Leo Sampaio Ferraz Ribeiro(✉)

Instituto de Ciências Matemáticas e de Computação, Universidade de São Paulo (ICMC-USP), São Carlos, Brazil
{brunaru,leo.ribeiro}@icmc.usp.br

Abstract. Meltdowns and shutdowns are overwhelming responses to sensory, emotional, or social demands often experienced by autistic individuals. These reactions stem from overstimulation, unexpected changes or stress and differ significantly from person to person. Many autistic people also struggle with identifying and articulating their emotions – a condition called alexithymia – which makes it harder to pinpoint potential triggers before a crisis occurs. Existing studies have used physiological data and video recordings to detect these episodes, but these methods only respond in the moment, leaving little room for proactive support. Since meltdowns and shutdowns are deeply influenced by personal circumstances – such as surroundings, individual traits, daily routines, and social dynamics – gathering and interpreting contextual data could help anticipate these reactions and create opportunities for early intervention. In this paper, we examine the current gaps in research and share our perspectives as neurodivergent researchers. We aim to collaborate with knowledge regarding opportunities of Assistive Technologies for crisis management.

Keywords: Autism · ASD · Meltdown · Shutdown · Intervention · Regulation

1 Introduction

The Diagnostic and Statistical Manual of Mental Disorders, 5th Edition (DSM-5) [3] defines Autism Spectrum Disorder (ASD) through two core diagnostic criteria: (1) persistent deficits in social communication and interaction, and (2) restricted, repetitive patterns of behavior, interests, or activities. These criteria encompass a wide range of traits, including sensory hyper- or hypo-sensitivity (e.g., to sounds, lights, textures, or smells), difficulties in emotional or sensory processing, distress caused by unexpected routine changes or unpredictable situations, and communication challenges [3]. Such individual differences can precipitate extreme anxiety, frustration, and stress, which may escalate into crisis

Published by Springer Nature Switzerland AG 2026
C. Maciel et al. (Eds.): INTERACT 2025 Workshops, LNCS 16478, pp. 329–337, 2026.
https://doi.org/10.1007/978-3-032-22934-2_27

episodes: meltdowns (outwardly directed reactions) or shutdowns (inward withdrawal) [29].

Lewis and Stevens (2023) surveyed 32 autistic adults to understand the crisis experiences. Participants described meltdowns as overwhelming sensory, social, or emotional episodes in which extreme emotions disrupt self-regulation [18]. In contrast, shutdowns involve an inward collapse and emotions remain intensely felt but unexpressed, leaving individuals feeling "frozen" and temporarily unable of performing basic tasks [26]. Recent literature also includes the "autistic burnout", which is defined as a state of severe and chronic exhaustion resulting from prolonged exposure to overwhelming stimuli and cognitively demanding activities [2,26].

Research indicates that difficulties with sensory modulation – including extreme sensitivity or insensitivity in at least one sensory domain – are common in both autistic children [5] and adults [8]. Similarly, disruptions such as routine changes, task transitions, or unexpected events frequently provoke distress, significantly impacting daily functioning [28]. Social anxiety further compounds these challenges for many autistic individuals [4]. Collectively, these factors are empirically established as precipitants of crises [18], highlighting the necessity of contextual awareness for both predicting episodes and designing effective interventions.

While recent studies emphasize context as a key crisis trigger [9], prediction models systematically neglect this critical dimension. The field has primarily focused on physiological and behavioral dimensions for crisis detection, employing measures such as heart rate variability (HRV) [7,11,17,22,27] and interbeat intervals (IBI) [27], galvanic skin response (GSR) [11,17,27], skin temperature fluctuations [17], accelerometer-derived movement patterns [1,11], and audio-visual analysis of behavioral cues [33,35]. While these approaches enable momentary detection of crisis states, their exclusive reliance on immediate physiological or behavioral signals results in fundamentally reactive systems with limited predictive windows. Most critically, failing to incorporate environmental, situational, and interpersonal contexts creates a significant barrier to developing truly preventive interventions.

Incorporating contextual information could enhance crisis prediction and intervention by identifying the root causes of sensory or emotional overload. Evidence indicates that structured, remotely delivered interventions – such as the suggestion of self-regulation tools or engagement of caregiver support systems – can effectively mitigate crises [7,15,22]. Proactive crisis detection thus creates broader opportunities for timely interventions, reducing their severity and improving quality of life for autistic individuals and their support networks.

In light of these considerations, this paper examines current research on the prediction of meltdowns, shutdowns, and burnout crises in autistic individuals, along with interventions aimed at supporting self-regulation. We then present a theoretical framework exploring how assistive technologies could contribute to a deeper understanding of crisis causation and potentially offer mitigating interventions to improve quality of life. This perspective is developed through three key considerations: the existing literature, the importance of supporting autonomy for autistic individuals, and our own viewpoints as autistic researchers.

2 Related Work

Adopting the perspective of neurodivergent researchers, we examine the literature through the lens of recent studies and potential future research directions. We also identify problematic methodological approaches that researchers should avoid. This section is organized into two parts: prediction models and self-management interventions.

2.1 Models for Crisis Prediction

Existing research on meltdown prediction in autistic individuals predominantly focuses on physiological measures. Although current predictive models demonstrate promising accuracy results, they face two fundamental limitations: (1) the narrow temporal gap between detection and a crisis escalation and (2) the absence of mechanisms to identify triggering factors. These limitations hinder the creation of individualized and preventative interventions.

Some studies focus on behaviors categorized by their authors as "aggressive" [11] or "problematic" [22]. In [11], researchers collected peripheral cardiovascular and electrodermal activity alongside accelerometer data to predict aggressive episodes in high-support autistic youth. Their findings indicate aggression toward others can be anticipated one minute in advance using three minutes of preceding biosensor data. Another model, proposed by Manu *et al.* [22], achieved 91% accuracy in predicting designated "problematic" behaviors in children using heart rate and heart rate variability data. We argue that aggressive behavior is not exclusive to autistic children, and these studies did not investigate the underlying causes of explosive actions.

The study by Al-Rammah *et al.* [1] utilized video data to detect movement changes for predicting pre-meltdown states, achieving 98% recall. The authors observed that these movement alterations correspond to increased stereotypical motor behaviors (i.e., stimming). However, recent research incorporating autistic perspectives demonstrate that stimming often serves as a self-regulation mechanism [16,24], being itself a preventive measure to counteract future crisis. Employing stimming then as a meltdown indicator requires careful consideration to avoid stigmatization of this behavior.

The study by Redd *et al.* [27] analyzed physiological measures to assess their predictive capacity for imminent emotional changes in autistic children, including meltdowns, shutdowns, frustration, fatigue, and distraction. The researchers developed a wearable physiological monitoring system that collected Blood Volume Pulse (BVP), IBI, Electrodermal Activity (EDA), peripheral skin temperature, heart rate, and accelerometer data. Their classification models attained 68% average accuracy for generalized predictions, with individualized models reaching up to 85% accuracy [27]. These results highlight the importance of developing individualized predictive models, which aligns with the inherent variability of the autism spectrum.

Research on crisis detection in adults and corresponding self-regulation interventions remains limited. The study by Coulter *et al.* [7] collected physiological data in participants' home environments while implementing relaxation interventions. Their approach demonstrated reductions in anxiety levels and significant physiological improvements. This work exemplifies how tailored, straightforward interventions can enhance self-regulation capabilities, thereby promoting autonomy and quality of life. Notably, such strategies may prove effective even for individuals that require higher levels of support.

Although physiological data provide valuable predictive indicators, meltdowns, shutdowns and burnouts frequently originate from multiple sources: sensory overload, social demands beyond comfort zones, disruptions to established routines, and emotional triggers [2,9,18,26]. Furthermore, the current literature contains a significant gap regarding the prediction and management of shutdown episodes, despite their particularly debilitating impact on autistic adults. Incorporating contextual data also offers critical potential for elucidating individual crisis etiology.

2.2 Self-regulation and Management Interventions

Emotional regulation is important for all individuals, yet neurodivergent people face greater challenges controlling emotions [34], especially during crises that involve emotional outbursts or paralysis [26]. Alexithymia further complicates self-regulation by impairing identification of dysregulating events and their impacts. When the type and causes of a crisis are known, health professionals can plan personalized regulation interventions tailored to the person's needs and level of support [15].

Digital interventions have demonstrated effectiveness in supporting regulation processes [6], showing particular benefits for neurodivergent individuals [37,38]. Wearable technologies facilitate discreet intervention delivery [15], while Just-in-Time Adaptive Interventions (JITAIs) provide tailored support at critical moments to enhance regulation [25]. However, intervention efficacy in this context depends on appropriate contextual triggers.

While typically delivered through text format, we argue that interventions can be more complex given recent technological innovations. For instance, Immersive Virtual Reality (VR) represents an emerging intervention approach for anxiety treatment in adults. Recent work shows promise with immersive relaxation environments. In [14,36], participants reported positive mental state impacts from VR "relaxation rooms", including increased body awareness, tranquility, calmness, and wellbeing. Such immersive relaxation environments could benefit emotional regulation and crisis mitigation for autistic individuals, though research is needed to evaluate their effectiveness.

Immediate interventions support emotional regulation, while long-term strategies prove essential for anxiety reduction and adverse event preparation [30]. Autistic individuals face particular challenges in anxiety-inducing social contexts [4], creating potential for serious games as intervention tools. Serious games have the potential to enable skill development through diverse simulated scenarios, including realistic situations valuable for socialization and daily living training [12]. The inherent design of digital games promotes learning via instant feedback, progressive challenges, and experiential concept application [10,21]. While systematic reviews demonstrate VR social skills interventions' effectiveness [13,20,31,32], current research remains limited by predominant focus on environment development, small sample sizes, and insufficient experimental rigor.

Based on our analysis of related work, we propose a theoretical framework outlining intervention practices specifically designed for emotion regulation in neurodivergent individuals. While our primary focus is on self-management strategies, this approach can be adapted for individuals requiring higher support levels by incorporating a caregiver as facilitator.

3 Theoretical Framework for Crisis Management

Our proposal is to combine contextual elements with physiological measurements and self-reports to analyze the causes of crises such as meltdowns, shutdowns, and burnout, and provide appropriate interventions. We emphasize that the participation of autistic individuals in the creation and validation of framework-related solutions is essential. Understanding the causes of crises, as well as intervention effectiveness, can only be properly investigated through the active involvement of the target population. Figure 1 presents a schematic of the proposed theoretical framework. Following, we explain its components in terms of context, sensors, and interventions.

Considering known crisis triggers, we identify the following key information categories:

1. Ambient audio: which may consist of volume or frequencies beyond an individual's tolerance threshold;
2. Ambient light: including its intensity, source, and variability;
3. Social interaction: which may relate to duration, participants, location, or stressful events such as presentations;
4. Routine disruption: potentially involving activities, environments, routes, meals, socialization, and other factors - the most complex component in terms of dimensions

Contextual elements can be captured by users' sensors (wearables and smartphones) and smart home devices. These can capture: audio volume and frequency; user movement (both location changes and activity-related motions like daily tasks, exercise, or stimming); ambient light (intensity, color, and variations); socialization (via audio, text, or other users' device locations); and images (either natural sources like environmental video or explicit captures like food photos). This data collection of course involves privacy concerns requiring careful handling and we refer to the specialized literature on privacy-preserving methodologies [19]?? on how to protect any data that is collected or models produced from these studies.

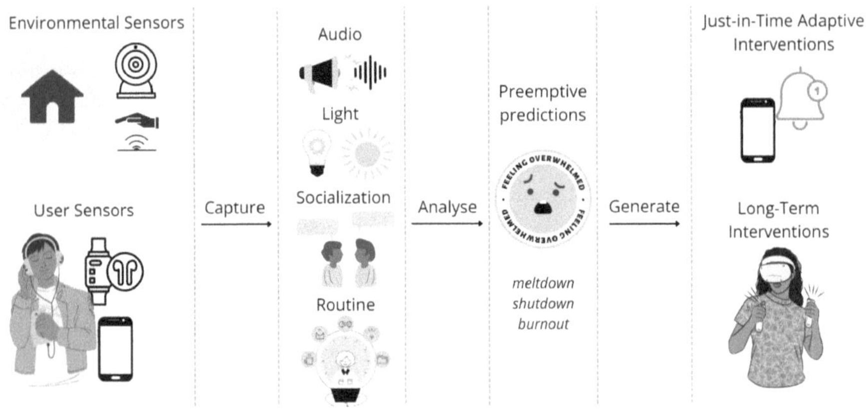

Fig. 1. Visual schematic of the proposed theoretical framework for contextualized prediction and regulation interventions for ASD-related crises.

Current literature primarily focuses on meltdowns for prediction models and interventions. However, this approach overlooks broader spectrum needs, as shutdown identification and management are equally crucial for autistic individuals. Additionally, while burnout remains poorly understood in literature, with limited scientific validation, the framework could support its understanding and validation.

4 Discussion

Through this work, we aim to foster discussions on how computational technologies can support neurodivergent individuals – particularly autistic people – to improve their mental health and quality of life. The proposed framework can be extended to include other neurodivergent conditions that also experience significant mood and emotional fluctuations stemming from environmental interactions.

We observe that current literature in computing still fails to include autistic individuals as self-aware agents of their own needs. Even individuals requiring higher support levels should have their needs actively considered, rather than being treated merely as subjects of study. In the context of User-Centered Design, this limitation is unacceptable yet it remains common for AI research to exclude the very people affected by its solutions.

This failure in current literature exposes a broader systemic issue within AI research, which, as Messeri and Crockett explain [23], risks fostering "scientific monocultures". Research is and should always be a fundamentally social endeavor but current AI practices often reinforce the idea of a singular, objective knower with an unbiased view. When AI tools are developed to support autistic people without their active involvement, there's a significant risk that these tools will embed "homogeneous standpoints" of dominant social groups [23], rather than the actual needs and experiences of users. To counter this, we advocate not just for User-Centered Design, but specifically for truly participatory design, ensuring systems are made for and, crucially, together with autistic people.

References

1. Al-Rammah, F., Masmoudi, M., Jarraya, S.K.: CNN-LSTM based approach for analyzing and detecting stereotypical motor movements of autistic children in pre-meltdown crisis. In: Proceedings of IEEE/ACS International Conference on Computer Systems and Applications, AICCSA, 2022-December (2022). https://doi.org/10.1109/AICCSA56895.2022.10017965
2. Arnold, S.R., Higgins, J.M., Weise, J., Desai, A., Pellicano, E., Trollor, J.N.: Towards the measurement of autistic burnout. Autism **27**(7), 1933–1948 (2023)
3. Association, A.P.: Manual Diagnóstico e Estatístico de Transtornos Mentais - DSM-5-TR: Texto Revisado. Artmed, 5 edn. (2023)
4. Bellini, S.: The development of social anxiety in adolescents with autism spectrum disorders. Focus Autism Other Dev. Disabil. **21**(3), 138–145 (2006)
5. Ben-Sasson, A., Hen, L., Fluss, R., Cermak, S.A., Engel-Yeger, B., Gal, E.: A meta-analysis of sensory modulation symptoms in individuals with autism spectrum disorders. J. Autism Dev. Disord. **39**, 1–11 (2009)
6. Bettis, A.H., Burke, T.A., Nesi, J., Liu, R.T.: Digital technologies for emotion-regulation assessment and intervention: a conceptual review. Clin. Psychol. Sci. **10**(1), 3–26 (2022)
7. Coulter, H., Donnelly, M., Mallett, J., Kernohan, W.G.: Heart rate variability biofeedback to treat anxiety in young people with autism spectrum disorder: findings from a home-based pilot study. JMIR Formative Res. **6** (2022). https://doi.org/10.2196/37994, https://pubmed.ncbi.nlm.nih.gov/36018712/
8. Crane, L., Goddard, L., Pring, L.: Sensory processing in adults with autism spectrum disorders. Autism **13**(3), 215–228 (2009)
9. Doherty, M., McCowan, S., Shaw, S.C.: Autistic space: a novel framework for meeting the needs of autistic people in healthcare settings. Br. J. Hosp. Med. (London, England : 2005) **84** (2023). https://doi.org/10.12968/HMED.2023.0006, https://pubmed.ncbi.nlm.nih.gov/37127416/
10. Gee, J.P.: What video games have to teach us about learning and literacy. Comput. Entertainment (CIE) **1**(1), 20–20 (2003)
11. Goodwin, M.S., Mazefsky, C.A., Ioannidis, S., Erdogmus, D., Siegel, M.: Predicting aggression to others in youth with autism using a wearable biosensor. Autism Res. Official J. Int. Soc. Autism Res. **12**, 1286–1296 (2019). https://doi.org/10.1002/AUR.2151, https://pubmed.ncbi.nlm.nih.gov/31225952/
12. Grossard, C., Grynspan, O., Serret, S., Jouen, A.L., Bailly, K., Cohen, D.: Serious games to teach social interactions and emotions to individuals with autism spectrum disorders (ASD). Comput. Educ. **113**, 195–211 (2017)

13. Idowu, O., Aderinto, N., Olatunji, G., Kokori, E.: A systematic review of virtual reality vs. standard social skills training for improving social interaction skills and reducing social anxiety in children with autism spectrum disorder (ASD). BJPsych Open **10**(S1), S46–S47 (2024)
14. Ilioudi, M., Wallström, S., Steingrimsson, S., Lindner, P., Thunström, A.O., Ali, L.: Patient experience of a virtual reality calm room in a psychiatric inpatient care setting in Sweden: a qualitative study with inpatients. BMJ Open **13**(12), e076285 (2023)
15. Kalantari, N., Zheng, H., Graff, H.J., Evmenova, A.S., Motti, V.G.: Emotion regulation for neurodiversity through wearable technology. In: 2021 9th International Conference on Affective Computing and Intelligent Interaction, ACII 2021 (2021). https://doi.org/10.1109/ACII52823.2021.9597458
16. Kapp, S.K., et al.: 'people should be allowed to do what they like': Autistic adults' views and experiences of stimming. Autism **23**(7), 1782–1792 (2019)
17. Khullar, V., Singh, H.P., Bala, M.: Meltdown/tantrum detection system for individuals with autism spectrum disorder. Appl. Artif. Intell. **35**, 1708–1732 (2021). https://doi.org/10.1080/08839514.2021.1991115, https://www.tandfonline.com/doi/abs/10.1080/08839514.2021.1991115
18. Lewis, L.F., Stevens, K.: The lived experience of meltdowns for autistic adults. Autism: Int. J. Res. Pract. **27**, 1817–1825 (2023). https://doi.org/10.1177/13623613221145783, https://pubmed.ncbi.nlm.nih.gov/36632658/
19. Liu, B., et al.: DP-Image: Differential Privacy for Image Data in Feature Space (2021). https://doi.org/10.48550/arXiv.2103.07073
20. Mak, G., Zhao, L.: A systematic review: the application of virtual reality on the skill-specific performance in people with ASD. Interact. Learn. Environ. **31**(2), 804–817 (2020)
21. Malpartida, K.F.C., da Hora Rodrigues, K.R.: Building serious games to exercise computational thinking: initial evaluation with teachers of children on the autism spectrum. J. Interact. Syst. **16**(1), 148–162 (2025)
22. Manu, M., et al.: Heart rate predictive value using wearable sensors in social robotics conversations to help children with autism. In: 2024 4th International Conference on Advance Computing and Innovative Technologies in Engineering, ICACITE 2024, pp. 729–732 (2024). https://doi.org/10.1109/ICACITE60783.2024.10616482
23. Messeri, L., Crockett, M.J.: Artificial intelligence and illusions of understanding in scientific research. Nature **627**(8002), 49–58 (2024). https://doi.org/10.1038/s41586-024-07146-0
24. Morris, I.F., et al.: Beyond self-regulation: autistic experiences and perceptions of stimming. Neurodiversity **3**, 27546330241311096 (2025)
25. Nahum-Shani, I., et al.: Just-in-time adaptive interventions (JITAIs) in mobile health: key components and design principles for ongoing health behavior support. Ann. Behav. Med. 1–17 (2018)
26. Phung, J., Penner, M., Pirlot, C., Welch, C.: What i wish you knew: insights on burnout, inertia, meltdown, and shutdown from autistic youth. Front. Psychol. **12** (2021). https://doi.org/10.3389/FPSYG.2021.741421, https://pubmed.ncbi.nlm.nih.gov/34803822/
27. Redd, C.B., et al.: Physiological signal monitoring for identification of emotional dysregulation in children. In: Proceedings of the Annual International Conference of the IEEE Engineering in Medicine and Biology Society, EMBS, 2020-July, pp. 4273–4277 (2020). https://doi.org/10.1109/EMBC44109.2020.9176506

28. Rydzewska, E.: Unexpected changes of itinerary-adaptive functioning difficulties in daily transitions for adults with autism spectrum disorder. Eur. J. Spec. Needs Educ. **31**(3), 330–343 (2016)
29. S, M., RM, F., A, S.: Autism spectrum disorder. StatPearls (2018). http://europepmc.org/books/NBK525976, https://europepmc.org/article/nbk/nbk525976
30. Sánchez, M., Lavigne, R., Romero, J.F., Elósegui, E.: Emotion regulation in participants diagnosed with attention deficit hyperactivity disorder, before and after an emotion regulation intervention. Front. Psychol. **10**, 1092 (2019)
31. Satu, P., Minna, L., Satu, S.: Immersive VR assessment and intervention research of individuals with neurodevelopmental disorders is dominated by ASD and ADHD: a scoping review. Rev. J. Autism Dev. Disorders **12**(1), 50–68 (2023)
32. Sideraki, A., Drigas, A.: Development of social skills for people with ASD through intervention with digital technologies and virtual reality (VR) tools. Res. Soc. Dev. **12**(5), e11512541407 (2023)
33. Silva, J.L., Oliveira, I., Topolniak, Z., Alvarez, A.B.: A CNN approach implemented to emotional facial expression recognition for the prevention of autistic meltdowns. In: 2021 2nd Sustainable Cities Latin America Conference, SCLA 2021 (2021). https://doi.org/10.1109/SCLA53004.2021.9540183
34. Tonello, L., et al.: Crisis behavior in autism spectrum disorders: a self-organized criticality approach. Complexity **2018**(1), 5128157 (2018)
35. Villanueva, A., et al.: Design of a behavior classification system for monitoring autism spectrum disorder using deep learning. In: 3rd International Informatics and Software Engineering Conference, IISEC 2022 (2022). https://doi.org/10.1109/IISEC56263.2022.9998273
36. Wang, Z., et al.: Effects of restorative environment and presence on anxiety and depression based on interactive virtual reality scenarios. Int. J. Environ. Res. Public Health **19**(13), 7878 (2022)
37. Zheng, H., Genaro Motti, V.: Assisting students with intellectual and developmental disabilities in inclusive education with smartwatches. In: Proceedings of the 2018 CHI Conference on Human Factors in Computing Systems, pp. 1–12 (2018)
38. Zheng, H., Motti, V.G., Giwa-Lawal, K., Evmenova, A., Graff, H.: Evaluating WELI: a wrist-worn application to assist young adults with neurodevelopmental disorders in inclusive classes. In: Human-Computer Interaction–INTERACT 2019: 17th IFIP TC 13 International Conference, Paphos, Cyprus, September 2–6, 2019, Proceedings, Part II 17, pp. 114–134. Springer (2019)

Author Index

Published by Springer Nature Switzerland AG 2026
C. Maciel et al. (Eds.): INTERACT 2025 Workshops, LNCS 16478, pp. 339–340, 2026.
https://doi.org/10.1007/978-3-032-22934-2

FSC
www.fsc.org
MIX
Papier | Fördert
gute Waldnutzung
FSC® C083411

Zeitfracht Medien GmbH
Ferdinand-Jühlke-Straße 7
99095 Erfurt, Deutschland
produktsicherheit@kolibri360.de